A History of Everyday Twentieth-Century Scotland

A History of Everyday Life in Scotland

SERIES EDITORS: CHRISTOPHER A. WHATLEY AND ELIZABETH FOYSTER

A History of Everyday Life in Twentieth-Century Scotland

Edited by Lynn Abrams and Callum G. Brown

Edinburgh University Press

Edinburgh University Press Ltd
22 George Square, Edinburgh
www.euppublishing.com

Typeset in 10/12pt Goudy Old Style by
Servis Filmsetting Ltd, Stockport, Cheshire, and
printed and bound in Great Britain by
CPI Antony Rowe, Chippenham and Eastbourne

A CIP record for this book is available from the British Library

ISBN 978 0 7486 2430 0 (hardback)
ISBN 978 0 7486 2431 7 (paperback)

Published with the support of the Edinburgh University
Scholarly Publishing Initiatives Fund.

Contents

Contents

Tables

Figures

Series Editors' Foreword

Christopher A. Whatley and Elizabeth Foyster

The four books in this series examine the ordinary, routine, daily behaviour, experiences and beliefs of Scottish people from medieval times until the present day. Their focus is on the 'common people', that is, most of the population, the ordinary folk below the ranks of the aristocracy, substantial landowners, opulent merchants, major industrialists, bankers and financiers, even if it is true that people from relatively humble beginnings have managed periodically to haul themselves into the ranks of the nation's social elite. Contributors in each volume describe the landscapes and living spaces that formed the familiar contexts for daily life. The events and activities that determined how individuals spent their time are explored, including the experiences of work and leisure, and ranging in duration from those that affected the passage of a single day, through to those that impinged on peoples' lives according to the calendar or the seasons and weather, to those that were commonly experienced over the course of the life-cycle. Scottish people made sense of their everyday lives, it is argued, through ritual and belief, by their interactions with others and by self-reflection.

As a whole, the series aims to provide a richer and more closely observed history of the social, economic and cultural lives of ordinary Scots than has been published previously. This is not to suggest that accounts and analyses of the everyday in Scotland have not been written. They have.[1] And this present series of four volumes overlaps with the publication of the fourteen volumes of the *Scottish Life and Society* series, sponsored by the European Ethnological Research Centre in Edinburgh, led by Alexander Fenton. The first volume in this series was published in 2000, with others following at intervals through to 2008. Unlike the series of which this volume is part, which is structured by chronological periods in which selected broad themes are studied, each of the books in the *Scottish Life and Society* series has been organised around a particular topic, including: farming and rural life; domestic life; boats, fishing and the sea; and religion.[2] They are substantial, multi-authored volumes and eclectic in the range of subjects and sub-topics covered, entirely befitting the series sub-title, *A Compendium of Scottish Ethnology*. It represents a monumental resource for future researchers.[3] Where appropriate, contributors to this series *A History of Everyday Life in Scotland* have drawn upon the *Scottish Life and Society* team's findings. Rather than clashing, however, or overlapping to the point of repetition, the two series complement each other, with ours concentrating more on continuities and change, and historical explanations for this, and written, mainly but not entirely, by professional historians. Together, both series offer readers a heady mix of historical information, and an array of approaches, analytical styles and depths and insights.

The everyday had a context, or contexts. At the individual level what was everyday altered across time and often differed according to class, gender, age, religion and ethnic group. It was also shaped by national and regional surroundings, and could vary between urban and rural environments, highland and lowland, inland and coastal settings, the northern and western islands.[4] Contributors pay attention to regional and local variations and peculiarities, especially with regard to language, dialect, practices and customs. The series reveals aspects of the everyday that were distinctively Scottish, but it also shows how the everyday lives of Scots were influenced by other cultures and nations. This resulted from travel, trading relations, or migration by Scots who lived and worked abroad, both temporarily and permanently. Indirectly, Scots read and learned of the shared or conflicting ideas and practices of everyday life in near and distant lands. Contributors to the series can point to inter-national differences and similarities because of the pioneering work on the everyday that has been conducted by historians on other countries across a range of periods. While relatively little has been published specifically on the everyday in Scotland or even Britain, we are fortunate to be able to draw upon an extensive body of historical research for Europe and the Americas.[5]

The roots of this historical endeavour, and the approaches that this series takes, lie in a range of developments within the discipline. In Britain, the interest of social historians – often with a Marxist perspective – in writing 'history from below', has brought the lives of working-class people to centre stage.[6] In Scotland the study of 'new' social history was pioneered by T. C. Smout, with his seminal *History of the Scottish People, 1560–1830* (1969), although Smout's approach was liberal rather than leftist.[7] This was followed in subsequent decades by a surge of research on a range of topics, and a plethora of publications written by a small army of historians examining different historical periods, including the same author's *Century of the Scottish People, 1830–1950* (1986).[8] Furth of Scotland, *Annaliste* historians, such as Fernand Braudel, focused attention on the material culture of daily life, and a later generation of French and then Italian historians narrowed the scale of study to produce 'microhistories'. These examined in detail the history of one individual, village or incident in order to understand the wider *mentalité* of the societies of which they were a part.[9] Historians in Germany have addressed the issue of the everyday most directly, where the concept of *Alltagsgeschichte* ('the history of everyday life') was conceived, and continues to be the source of lively debate.[10] Preceding, running alongside and occasionally influencing historical work has been the study of everyday life by academics in other disciplines, including ethnology, sociology, social anthropology, geography, psychology and cultural theory.[11] Academics from these disciplines contribute to some of the volumes of this series.

What can the reader expect from this series, and how does the content of the books that comprise it differ from other social histories of Scotland?

First, by uncovering the everyday, we provide fresh insights into a diverse range of historical topics. Whereas much social history can focus on the structures, ideals or prescriptions that were intended to govern daily living, this series examines the practices and realities of life experience. Although not the primary purpose of the series, people's experiences of major change, like wars, famine and environmental disaster, are incorporated. The result is to demonstrate how the extraordinary affected the ordinary. But as Alexander Fenton correctly observed of Scottish rural society some years ago, broad trends, big ideas and eye-catching technologies can explain only so much; how they impacted on the everyday depended on local conditions and responses. As important for understanding the everyday lives of ordinary people, and the pace and nature of change, were, for example, how small-scale pieces of equipment were adopted and used, and how things were done in the home or barn or yard far from power centres that passed legislation, or from which sprang – as in the case of Edinburgh and east-central Scotland in the early eighteenth century – models for and aids to agrarian improvement. But on Orkney even in the later eighteenth century weighing machines – the pundlar and the pindlar – weights and measures, and the commonly used one-stilt plough, had been in use since Viking times.[12] Change on the ground was invariably slow, piecemeal and indigenous rather than spectacular.[13]

Examples and case studies of aspects of everyday life in these volumes also enhance our understanding of some long-standing subjects of debate within Scottish history. Hence, readers will gain new insights about the role of the kirk in social and moral discipline, the impact of enclosure and the Clearances in the Lowlands as well as the Highlands, the struggles between popular and elite forms of culture, standards of living and the significance of 'public' and 'private' spaces in daily life. In addition, the exploration of the everyday has allowed our contributors to cover less familiar historical territory – some of which has posed considerable challenges. We discover how Scottish people's fears, anxieties and perceptions of danger changed over time, we learn about the importance of gestures as well as forms of verbal and written communication and we begin to recover how ordinary Scots experienced their sensory worlds of taste, sound, sight and touch. The everyday enables historians to engage with important emerging topics within the discipline of history, for example, the history of the Scottish landscape and the environment. Chapters in the books in the series explore the changing relationship with and impact of Scots upon their natural environment.[14] The series also demonstrates how women, whose lives were once considered too everyday and mundane to merit serious academic study, played a central part particularly in the negotiation and management of home and family daily life.[15] In addition, women could play an active role in everyday life beyond the domestic scene, as recent research has begun to reveal.[16] Scottish men's gendered identities were also constructed and experienced in the context of the everyday.

The contributors to this series have been able to write these histories not, on the whole, because they have discovered vast quantities of new evidence in the archives, although much original material has been uncovered. Rather, a new history has emerged because they have asked novel questions of material with which they were familiar, and have pieced together a wide range of what was often unused information from both primary and secondary sources. Undoubtedly, writing the history of the everyday presents unique problems of evidence for the historian. These problems can vary with historical period; those researching the everyday in medieval times can face a dearth of written sources, while it is easy to be overwhelmed by the mass of information available for the twentieth century. However, there are also more fundamental issues of evidence at stake that have to be faced by all historians of the everyday. As Braudel recognised, 'everyday life consists of the little things one hardly notices in time and space'.[17] Everyday life could be so banal, repetitive, tedious, boring, easily forgotten or taken for granted that our predecessors rarely bothered to record it. Sometimes this means we have to read 'against the grain' of the sources that do survive. In other words, examining the exceptional incident or object to deduce its opposite. For the most part, however, writing about the everyday necessitates the laborious sorting through and amalgamation of fragments of the past: written, visual and material. Contributors to this series have found evidence of the everyday in artefacts, archaeological sites, buildings, diaries, letters, autobiographies, polite and popular literature, trial records of church, burgh and state courts, estate papers, directories, prints, maps, photographs and oral testimony. It is the incidental comment, remark or observation, chance survival, brief glimpse or snapshot that often contains a clue to and even the core of the everyday. The historian's task is to put these details together, 'as in a jigsaw puzzle', so that we can present to readers a picture of the everyday.[18]

What the reader will not get from the series is a complete or comprehensive compendium of everyday life. This, as indicated earlier, is to be found elsewhere. It has not been our intention to list or describe all everyday objects and occurrences, even if this were practicably possible. Rather, our purpose is to explain and analyse the everyday as well as record it. The methodological tools used by contributors are diverse, and reflect their differing disciplinary backgrounds. This is especially the case in the twentieth century volume, where interdisciplinary approaches are most widely employed.

The second distinctive contribution of this series to our understanding of the Scottish past is concerned with what it reveals about historical change.

Across the series the reader can expect to find enduring continuities within everyday life, but also transformations, some rapid, but most long and drawn out. These can be observed by the historian; how far and in what ways they were experienced by ordinary people is harder to know. Yet it is clear that, over time, changes did occur in everyday life, as new ways of working, forms of social organisation, products, sights and sounds expanded the experiences of ordinary Scots. Even the fundamentals that comprise everyday life – what people ate and drank, where they slept, what they wore, where they worked and how they travelled from A to B – were indisputably transformed. Even so, these volumes also present evidence of elements of everyday life stubbornly resistant to change. The consecutive volumes in this series do not signify a set of breaks with the last, or a turning point in all aspects of the everyday. Hence, to take some examples: Scots continued to trust self-administered and home-made cures for illness even as medicine became professionalised and institutionalised; oral culture continued to thrive long after literacy had become the norm; and families and their communities continued to mark birth, marriage and death as significant rites of passage. Ale is still widely drunk at the start of the twenty-first century; and walking and other earlier forms of transport, the use of the bicycle for example, are growing in popularity. The enduring qualities of everyday life have attracted comment. For the Marxist cultural theorist, Henri Lefebvre, the everyday in more recent times offered a glimmer of hope in capitalist societies, because it revealed 'a corrective to the spectacularizing discourse of modernity'. Despite industrial and technological change, the humdrum and main concerns of everyday life for many people remained little altered.[19] Historians have noted people's determination to maintain the routines of daily life in the face of dramatic change, such as during periods of crisis and conflict.[20] Our predecessors shared our need for food, drink and shelter, and our yearning for love and affection, but when other parts of their lives faced serious disruption, the relative importance of fulfilling these needs had to be adjusted. Scots could be proud of 'making do' in times of hardship, and of the fact that daily life 'went on' despite the havoc and destruction around them. This series looks more closely at why particular aspects of the everyday were so hard to disrupt.

By so doing, revealing perspective is provided upon the meaning for ordinary Scots of 'great events', such as wars, which traditionally have been seen as the key moments of change in Scottish – and other nations' – history. Arguably, it was in the context of the 'non-event-ness' of the everyday that the vast majority of Scots spent their lives.[21] Indeed, as Dorothee Wierling has observed, 'most persons have *nothing but* . . . ordinary everyday life'.[22] Studying the history of everyday life is about retrieving the history of what most people did most of the time.

The series demonstrates that the speed of change in everyday life could vary between that experienced within the space of a generation, to barely perceptible shifts across centuries. However, the series also offers some explanations for what brought about change when it occurred. More important is how change was accommodated within the everyday; this was a social process. The seeds for change in Scottish society were frequently contained within the everyday. The everyday was often 'political'. Studying the everyday allows us to see how ordinary people could exercise power over their lives to resist, counter, accommodate or adapt to the changes they encountered. As Ben Highmore has observed, everyday life often serves in helping people to cope with 'the shock of the new'. The everyday becomes the setting:

> for making the unfamiliar familiar; for getting accustomed to the disruption of custom; for struggling to incorporate the new; for adjusting to different ways of living. The everyday marks the success and failure of this process. It witnesses the absorption of the most revolutionary of inventions into the landscape of the mundane. Radical transformations in all walks of life become 'second nature'.[23]

In short, it is by examining the minutiae of people's daily lives that we can uncover the significance of historical change as this affected ordinary people.

Above all – and this is our third aim – the series aims to provide an accessible history that will interest, excite and engage with the reader. This should not be difficult to achieve given the degree of public interest in the everyday. From the popularity of 'reality' TV shows, where individuals are exposed to reconstructed life as their Iron Age ancestors might have lived it, for instance, to the fact that it is often the kitchens and servants' living quarters of stately homes which attract the most visitors and curiosity, it is clear that there is an appetite to find out more about the everyday. This is because the history of the everyday is one to which most people can relate, or at least with which we can empathise. It is the bread and butter of life in the past. This is not to suggest that the reader will find any straightforward or single narrative of everyday life in these volumes. The history of the everyday is complex in the extreme: the range of experience is immense, what evidence we do have is often contradictory and there are enormous black holes in our knowledge and understanding. The books in the series reflect all of this, but they have also identified patterns and processes that make some sense of the everyday life of the Scots over the centuries in all its diversity.

Notes

1. A classic in its time was H. G. Graham, *The Social Life of Scotland in the Eighteenth Century* (London, 1899), while Marjory Plant's *Domestic Life of Scotland in the Eighteenth Century* (Edinburgh, 1948) and Marion Lochhead's *The Scots Household in the Eighteenth Century* (Edinburgh, 1948) broke new ground in revealing much

about everyday life in and around the home. It was Alexander (Sandy) Fenton, however, who led the way in Scotland in modern exploration of the everyday, particularly that of rural society: see, for example, A. Fenton, *Scottish Country Life* (Edinburgh, 1976, 1977; East Linton, 1999) and *The Northern Isles: Orkney and Shetland* (Edinburgh, 1978; East Linton, 1997).

2. *Scottish Life and Society: A Compendium of Scottish Ethnology* (fourteen volumes, John Donald, in association with the European Ethnological Research Centre and the National Museums of Scotland).

3. Perhaps the most enduring research tool deriving from the project will be H. Holmes and F. Macdonald (eds), *Scottish Life and Society: Bibliography for Scottish Ethnology* (Vol. 14, Edinburgh, 2003).

4. For a fine study of the impact of environmental factors and changing international conditions upon a locality, and aspects of everyday life in the northern isles, see H. D. Smith, *Shetland Life and Trade, 1550–1914* (Edinburgh, 1984).

5. See, for example, C. Dyer, *Everyday Life in Medieval England* (London, 1994); S. Wilson, *The Magical Universe: Everyday Ritual and Magic in Pre-Modern Europe* (London, 2000); R. Sarti, *Europe at Home: Family and Material Culture 1500–1800* (New Haven, 2002); R. Braun, *Industrialisation and Everyday Life*, trans. S. H. Tenison (Cambridge, 1990); S. Fitzpatrick, *Everyday Stalinism. Ordinary Life in Extraordinary Times: Soviet Russia in the 1930s* (Oxford, 1999); 'The Everyday Life in America series' edited by Richard Balkin; and M. Wasserman, *Everyday Life and Politics in Nineteenth-Century Mexico: Men, Women and War* (Albuquerque, 2000).

6. The work of E. P. Thompson was especially important in this regard, notably his seminal *The Making of the English Working Class* (London, 1965). See also the collection of his essays in *Customs in Common* (London, 1991). Thompson pays little attention to Scotland; more inclusive – and comparative – is Keith Wrightson's *Earthly Necessities: Economic Lives in Early Modern Britain* (New Haven, 2000), which contains much on everyday lives and how these were affected by the emergence of the market economy.

7. Marxist analyses of Scottish society appeared later, for example T. Dickson (ed.), *Scottish Capitalism: Class, State and Nation from before the Union to the Present* (London, 1980); Dickson also edited *Capital and Class in Scotland* (Edinburgh, 1982).

8. Some sense of what has been achieved over the past half century or so can be seen in the bibliographies that accompany each of the chapters in R. A. Houston and W. W. Knox's *New Penguin History of Scotland from the Earliest Times to the Present Day* (London, 2001).

9. See, for example, F. Braudel, *Civilization and Capitalism 15th–18th Century Vol. I: The Structures of Everyday Life: The Limits of the Possible*, trans. S. Reynolds (London, 1981); E. Le Roy Ladurie, *Montaillou: Cathars and Catholics in a French Village 1294–1324*, trans. Barbara Bray (Harmondsworth, 1980); and C. Ginzburg, *The Cheese and the Worms: The Cosmos of a Sixteenth-Century Miller*, trans. J. and A. Tedeschi (Baltimore, 1980).

10. See, for example, A. Lüdtke (ed.), *The History of Everyday Life: Reconstructing Historical Experiences and Ways of Life*, trans. W. Templer (Princeton, 1995).
11. See, for example, A. J. Weigert, *Sociology of Everyday Life* (London: Longman, 1981); J. M. White, *Everyday Life of the North American Indian* (New York, 2003); T. Friberg, *Everyday Life: Women's Adaptive Strategies in Time and Space*, trans. M. Gray (Stockholm, 1993); G. M. Davies and R. H. Logie (eds), *Memory in Everyday Life* (Amsterdam, 1993); H. Lefebvre, *Critique of Everyday Life*, 2 vols (London, 1991 and 2002); Michel de Certeau, *The Practice of Everyday Life*, trans. S. Rendall (Berkeley, 1984); and M. Certeau, L. Giard and P. Mayol, *The Practice of Everyday Life Volume 2: Living and Cooking*, trans. T. J. Tomasik (Minneapolis, 1998).
12. W. S. Hewison (ed.), *The Diary of Patrick Fea of Stove, Orkney, 1766–96* (East Linton, 1997), pp. 21, 24.
13. Fenton, *Scottish Country Life*, p. v.
14. See T. C. Smout, *Nature Contested: Environmental History in Scotland and Northern England Since 1600* (Edinburgh, 2000); and for a study which looks more closely at the relationship between one element of the environment, trees, and aspects of everyday life, T. C. Smout (ed.), *People and Woods in Scotland: A History* (Edinburgh, 2003).
15. For discussion of the links between women and the everyday, see D. Wierling, 'The history of everyday life and gender relations: on historical and historiographical relationships', in Lüdtke, *History of Everyday Life*, pp. 149–68.
16. See, for example, E. Ewan and M. M. Meikle (eds), *Women in Scotland, c.1100–c.1750* (East Linton, 1999); L. Abrams, E. Gordon, D. Simonton and E. J. Yeo (eds), *Gender in Scottish History since 1700* (Edinburgh, 2006); W. W. Knox, *Lives of Scottish Women: Women and Scottish Society, 1800–1980* (Edinburgh, 2006). A pioneering if eccentric account of women's role in popular protest was J. D. Young's *Women and Popular Struggles: A History of Scottish and English Working-Class Women, 1500–1984* (Edinburgh, 1985).
17. Braudel, *Civilization and Capitalism*, p. 29.
18. Sarti, *Europe at Home*, p. 1.
19. J. Moran, 'History, memory and the everyday', *Rethinking History*, 8, 1 (2004), pp. 54–7.
20. See, for example, N. Longmate, *How We Lived Then: A History of Everyday Life During the Second World War* (London, 1971).
21. The concept of 'non-event-ness' is taken from B. Highmore, *Everyday Life and Cultural Theory* (London, 2002), p. 34.
22. Wierling, 'The history of everyday life', p. 151; the emphasis is in the original.
23. Highmore, *Everyday Life*, p. 2.

Introduction

Conceiving the Everyday in the Twentieth Century

Lynn Abrams and Callum G. Brown

INTRODUCTION

At the root of everyday theory is the notion that in the smallest aspect of daily life, in the smallest ritual or rite, is to be found an imprint of the whole of culture. Nothing too commonplace, nor too trivial, escapes from having the distinctive mark of the times, from the food we consume to the way we spend our spare time. Through the everyday is refracted the spectrum of society's structures and values, as well as the individual's responses. To track the changes to a society, the theory goes, the historian should track the changes to the everyday.

The aim of this book is to ruminate upon what the everyday life of twentieth-century Scotland unveils about the country as a whole. By consideration of the small, we hope to illuminate the large. The volume sets about this task in diverse ways, employing no single method of envisaging what constitutes the nature of the everyday, but rather cultivating the authors' varied perceptions of the customary, and how it changed between 1900 and 2000, in the creation of a *bricolage*.[1] And like a *bricolage* composed of available *matériel* and tools, borrowed and pressed to new use, the production of a book such as this uses ideas and approaches from across disciplines to create a way of seeing its subject, the Scotland of the last century. Each approach to the Scotland of the twentieth century presented here is analytically sharp. The point is not to encyclopaedically record and tour the highways and byways of Scottish life, to archive the mundane for posterity, nor to engross the whole through cataloguing as many minutiae as is possible to compress between two boards. To compose an archaeology of the everyday is a forlorn ambition, certainly for the twentieth century; and from our early twenty-first-century vantage point, it is a much less interesting undertaking than the production of an interpretive work. Thus we have selective, but distinctive, approaches, undertaken by scholars of varying backgrounds and interests. The history here does not offer mere opinion, reflection and synopsis – the last a flourishing format in Scotland. Each essay here is rooted in original research and it is this that propels the contributors, via acute angles of approach, to a better appreciation of the Scotland of the last century.

The task is made more complex by our proximity to the subject. Each of the contributors was born and raised in the twentieth century, and, being Scots by birth or residence, we are each up close and personal with our topic. Our canvases are not blank, our minds not neutral, and we are each rich and ripe with back-stories to our engagement in the country and its modern development. We have each negotiated, too, our way through the mythology of the country from our various intellectual, political and personal standpoints. Twentieth-century Scotland produced an astonishing ensemble of contradictory narratives about itself – idyllic Highlands but slum cities, a poor people but rich elites, an oppressed nation but empire builders, radical workers but Tory lairds, drunken pastimes but puritan culture, hard men but battered wives, the educated 'lad o'pairts' but zealous bigots. In the land of whisky and golf, asbestosis and Europe's murder capital, there is no singular story accepted by all Scots or its visitors. In politics, too, the twentieth century comprises a narrative of conflict: devolution and the reclamation of 'national destiny' sit astride a heritage of socialism, empire and fierce unionism. The historians cannot agree on a single story. On top of this, historians may be outshone in the work of understanding the twentieth century by geographers, sociologists, anthropologists and literary specialists. Understandings of the modern are fractured, denying the historian's impulse to compress and homogenise in order to tell a coherent story. To be a *bricoleur* has an honesty where to be an historian in pursuit of a singular narrative may not.[2] This is made the more necessitous in the century of multiple understandings still alive and disputed in our present – Marxism, Freudianism, feminism, Darwinism and nationalism among them. So, the task is the more complex for the proximity of the century and the profusion of its self-understandings. To proximity and profusion is added pace of change. As the twentieth century progressed beyond mid-century, older certainties that were once held to have been born with time fell by the wayside with disconcerting speed: the certainties of faith, family, morality, empire, culture and economics. In their place came adaptation to religious diversity, secularisation, multi-culturalism, economic change (and change in economic theory), new chains of migration, new family structures, and what theologians of the late 1950s and early 1960s called 'the new morality'. To these changes were added others, shared in the modern world – the changes of health, habits, labour, the role of the state, and the changes of technology, prosperity, communication and consumption. The lives of Scottish people changed more quickly, in more profound ways, and with greater cultural significance than in any previous century. Some of these changes were generic and common to Britons and western Europeans, but others were distinctive in consequence or in severity to Scots. Indeed, in the twentieth century and certainly since the Second World War there is probably less that is distinctive about the everyday in Scotland than in earlier times. The things that made Scotland different – at least from the rest of the United Kingdom, like religion, poverty, overcrowding, rural isolation – have to a great extent been ameliorated.

To reflect and draw upon this diversity, this volume will be spun around a number of themes (gender, class, religiosity, materiality, ritual and identity), using a variety of methods (statistical, popular survey, documentary, biographical and oral-historical). In order that this volume does not merely become a catalogue of social change in modern Scotland, or a compendium of lists and things and activities, it is necessary to identify a number of frames of analysis within and around which contributors orientate their research and writing. We start by reflecting on theories of the everyday, and proceed to the methodology of experience, and thence to introduce our contributions.

THE THEORY OF THE EVERYDAY

The everyday appears as something it is not. It seems through its banality to be uninteresting and uncontested, something so ordinary it is hardly worth commenting upon. But this is not so. Lives are shaped in the main by everyday practices rather than exceptional events. The rituals of social experience provide not just the backdrop to social lives but the main event. They define the boundaries and shape of our lives. The everyday is constituted by the daily patterns of activity with which we fill time and space; it is the minutiae of repetitive experience, not the occasional punctuations. It has been said that the history of everyday life 'concentrates on the plane of microstructures' rather than on the large processes or structures that traditionally are seen as history's motors of change.[3] Thus the everyday cuts across and through apparently life-changing and traumatic events, whether they be on a global scale like the two world wars or a family or personal level like death. And indeed people's memories of the past are sharply defined by their experience of the everyday, since it is the repetitive actions and daily routines that act as templates for experience in other planes.[4] Memories of past events are invariably narrated by recollecting the rituals, routines and commonplaces through which such events were experienced. But narration is also an active process of creation of meaning and thus an expression of culture.[5]

It was only in the twentieth century that everydayness began to be theorised. The notion that the smallest facet of daily life, from the most whimsical ritual to the major *rites de passage*, reflects the whole of a culture developed in diverse disciplines throughout the twentieth century, but with very different perspectives. As the century delivered its distinctive problems for society and for the individual, so everyday life theory evolved to assist in encapsulating and evaluating these years. Freud saw the everyday as the zone of repressed thoughts and emotions, while for many the everyday is tedium, boredom, repetition containing experiences largely devoid of emotion, passion or even conscious thought. But for most scholars invoking the concept, the everyday was a deliberate shift in the perception of social interest and historical change from the elites and the state to the lives of the people. In the interwar years, the everyday became a legitimate zone for research. Sociologists and anthropologists got into the everyday via the Lynds' 1929 study of *Middletown* in the United States, which focused attention upon 'the small duties and responses to the custom of the daily round of living which imperceptibly but surely mitigates the tragedies and disappointments of existence'.[6] This was followed from 1936 in Great Britain by the Mass-Observation projects in which everyday life was transformed from merely a recording machine into a social movement; its leader, anthropologist Tom Harrisson, wrote that: 'Not all the dramas and dunghills on earth can affect the fact: that real life is not what these boys [poets] mean these days and that dramatic incident . . . is an isolate from its social contacts of mass continuity.'[7]

The perspectives developed by twentieth-century theorists such as Simmel and Lefebvre were grounded in the societies in which they lived – societies characterised by urbanisation, modernisation and capitalism – and thus their ideas were informed by the confrontation with wider social realities. Georg Simmel wrote at the start of the century: 'To involve ourselves deeply and lovingly with the even most common product, which would be banal and repulsive in its isolated appearance, enables us to conceive of it, too, as an image of the final unity of all things from which beauty and meaning flow.'[8] And for Henri Lefebvre, the everyday likewise signified something bigger, exposing the rhythms of capital, the relentless move of capitalism to control lives through the interstices of daily culture, ritual and rites, by invading citizens' space and activities on a microscopic, not a large scale. This adaptability of capitalism to the everyday was, he sensed, the means of its growing victory in modernity, and for him the people's resistance was mostly at the same level of the everyday. That theme of resistance was taken up many commentators, notably the church historian Michel de Certeau, and by the subaltern studies historians James C. Scott and Ranajit Guha.[9] They it was who pointed the historian and anthropologist to the way in which the great universal themes of revolt and revolution were not only to be detected in the *great* revolts and revolutions, but in the daily lives of the oppressed. It was in the small resistances – the cocking a snook at authority, the pulled face, the slow working of the labourer, the deliberate obstruction of the lowly official, and the failure to obey the smallest commands – this was how peoples as a whole took control of their lives in the face of state authority, homogenising forces and the fatalism of class or imperial struggle. For gender historians, too, there was significance in this theoretical position. If one accepted that a woman's experience is dominated more by the mundane-ness of everyday life than a man's, there might be the accompanying liberating notion that for women to reform their lives and alleviate their subordination, they must

revolt against the everyday that confines them to home, children, housework
and poorly paid labour.

How is the resistance, the revolt to the everyday, conceived and manifested? A recurrent theme in the treatment of left-leaning radical and Marxist
scholars is that of the carnival, of 'the world turned upside down', for
making the special day of Mardi Gras or carnival the contrast to the everyday. The occasion of the fête is the spectacle, the moment when revolutionary possibilities arise, an idea that brought Lefebvre into harmony with the
Situationists in the late 1950s and early 1960s for whom 'the Happening' was
a moment of revolutionary possibility to be fostered by artistic manoeuvre.
Though situationism failed to ignite Scots intellectuals, happenings became
important features (as Angela Bartie recounts in Chapter 8) that defined
the *avant garde* of that Scottish phenomenon of the post-1950 period, the
arts festival. Lefebvre was interested in these 'moments' that could create
revolutionary possibilities in the same way that the situationists were interested in situations that could do the same.[10] For de Certeau, too, as with the
subaltern studies specialists, the fête was part of the everyday, and thus part-
and-parcel of the daily resistance that the people undertook – in the way they
walked and talked around cities, their movements into and out of buildings,
in the very unseenness of their daily lives. He sees the everyday as impossible
for complete colonisation, as Lefebvre did, because resistance is built into
the way individuals negotiate the banal and the repetitious. Resistance in the
everyday is as much about inertia for de Certeau as for Lefebvre it was about
action; it was about walking against the arrows in public queues, or exiting
via the entrance to buildings, of climbing 'down'-stairs and descending 'up'-
stairs.[11] In this way, the everyday was a source of self and of identity – a
subject upon which there is now a vast and sophisticated literature.

Lefebvre was less sanguine about the ability of the people to resist the capitalist everyday. He noted the importance of 'la fête' in medieval culture as a
day when capitalist activity was suppressed by the people's celebration of the
other.[12] But though the modern people's festivals could allow the venting of
pent-up furies, they tended, as he put it, to 'tighten social links' and were thus
not as fully subverting, as fully capable of inverting the established order, as
the medieval and early-modern fête. For him, carnival is a moment when
everyday life is reconfigured, but – and this is crucial – this different order
of things is present in everyday life itself: 'Festival differs from everyday life
only in the explosion of forces which have been slowly accumulated in and
via everyday life itself.'[13] But Lefebvre's big point is that the transformative
power of the fête has to transform everyday – it should not be allowed to be
purely momentary, and about this he seemed pessimistic.

His pessimism came from looking at the late-medieval and early-modern
world which had a distinctive capacity for the fête to absorb the everyday
and to overturn the established order, to signal revolt or merely the breakdown in social order.[14] Even into the nineteenth century in Scotland, festival

on the King's Birthday had the capacity for anarchic breakdown; though the inversions at Scottish Yule and New Year became, as in the guisers of Lerwick's Up-helly-aa and Comrie's flambeaux, eventually more peaceable and unthreatening of the world order, the subversion of the everyday survived in ritualised, contained and ultimately safe satire.[15] But Yuletide aside, Britain, including Scotland, became to a degree distinctive in Christendom for the weakness of the traditions of resistance at the Carnival at Lent. While many twentieth-century Europeans revived, modernised and reinvested carnival with new meanings and traditions, as Lefebvre experienced himself in rural France, there was little equivalent development in Scotland. Scholars of more centrist political sympathies have been interested in everyday theory too. Three decades ago, the American sociologists Berger and Luckmann coined the notion of everyday life as underpinned by what they termed 'paramount reality'.[16] Paramount reality was the dense and intense necessity of daily life – the pressing needs of work, human exchange, the handling of life's complexity. In this conception, paramount reality envelops the individual; identity is stuff that we push into the interstices to carve out an identity for ourselves that is not competing, crushed and obliterated by the overpowering force of paramount reality. So, in this sense, there was a struggle in everyday life for the individual to battle against the depersonalising forces of the day. This was in part seen as the struggle between the structure of the paramount and the post (or non) structure of the identity work which, in turn, raises the possibility of there being a tension between self and society, between what Erving Goffman described as role identity and the resistance to it, the little everyday resistances, deviances and personal enthusiasms that define our identity as something not overpowered by the everyday.[17] The structures of life – the very houses and gardens we create, the routines and rituals we perform between work and home – are mediated by the ways in which we personalise those places and rituals. In another way of looking at this, Stanley Cohen and Laurie Taylor used the total institution of Durham Gaol, a place where everyday life becomes itself oppressively routinised and reproduced. In this context they speak of individuals 'distancing' themselves from their everyday roles, to avoid what they call 'the nightmare of repetition'.[18]

The everyday thus has a number of possible emotional consequences: reassuring, oppressive or exciting in its revolutionary possibilities. The sociologist Georg Simmel saw in the fragments of daily life a key to the larger questions about the meaning of life and society. 'Every philosophical system, every religion, every moment of our heightened emotional experience searches for symbols which are appropriate to their expression. . . . To the adequately trained eye the totality of beauty, the complete meaning of the world as a whole, radiates from every single point.'[19] For Simmel, it was urban society, the metropolis, that was the seat of the everyday – a sensory phantasm that bombarded the individual. Henri Lefebvre's everyday is the one dominated by the rhythm of capital. In his *Critique of Everyday Life*, Lefebvre proposes that everyday life facilitates the study of alienation under modernity. He also hints at the gendering of the everyday – that women have the bulk of the burden of the everyday. He saw in the commodification of life in France in the post-war years, notably the Americanisation of culture, the spectre of a specific temptation to women that might break down female everyday duties. As a Marxist he saw the everyday as exploitative. He recoiled at the extent of Christianity penetrating the everyday life of the village people he lived with in childhood. He recoiled too at capitalist commodification: the fashion system he labelled as 'the terrorism of everyday life'. He saw capitalism as colonising the everyday; modernity was the continuation of colonialism as a reordering of the world, promulgating the dialectics of modern everyday life – the struggle, the resistance, the temptations. As the century progressed, he argued that the urban became more sophisticated and tuned to the needs of each group, and adapted to their everyday needs, thus intensifying the colonisation. Lefebvre's everyday life (*la vie quotidienne*) is that of recurrence and repetition, of the banal and the ordinary, the oppressive. Daily chores are crucial in his understanding of the everyday; the weekend trip, the annual holiday, are also part of the everyday for him, because they are parts of the cycle of the everyday. For him, leisure is a continuation of the dialectic of the everyday. He sees this especially in the camping holiday in which work and leisure, he says, become indistinguishable. For him, leisure in the modern world is a routinised instance of a capitalist everyday life. It is at the same time the presence of festival; both recur together. So, a critique of everyday life is also a critique of political life, since the everyday also contains the political. The alienation of the individual is embedded in the everyday. The failure of Marxist revolution was the failure to transform the everyday and that alienation. He said: 'It was only after the Second World War that capitalism succeeded in thoroughly penetrating the details of everyday life. We need new concepts of Marxism if it is to retain its capacity to help us both understand and transform this radically commodified contemporary world.'[20]

Theory of the everyday is thus at the very centre of many conceptions of historical change. In the century of greatest theorising on the everyday, it is important for the historian of the everyday to grasp the nettle of the theory produced.

DOCUMENTING THE EVERYDAY IN THE TWENTIETH CENTURY

Although the social survey was born in the nineteenth century, it was in the twentieth that the documentation of the everyday became itself almost a part of everyday life. Following the pioneering poverty surveys conducted by Joseph and Seebohm Rowntree and Charles Booth, the social survey tradition developed further in the twentieth century using the sampling method pioneered by statistician Arthur Bowley in 1912. The decennial census of course collected huge datasets of information on every household in the United Kingdom but it could not get at the interstices of people's lives, the routines and the rituals, the likes and dislikes, the things that could not be counted. So while the census can tell us a huge amount about where Scots lived, with whom and in what conditions, their occupations, their mobility, their stated beliefs and so on, it cannot give us much insight into how they lived their day-to-day lives.

It was not until the creation of Mass-Observation in 1937 that the everyday lives of the British people began to be documented in all their detail, variety and quirkiness. Mass-Observation set out to study every aspect of life in Britain from the 1937 Coronation to the Lambeth Walk dance craze. The founders of the movement, Charles Madge, Tom Harrisson and Humphrey Jennings, aimed to produce an 'anthropology of ourselves', or in other words, to 'collect a mass of data based upon practical observation, on the everyday life of all types of people'.[21] Its qualitative research methods – notably the collection of surveys and observations from an army of volunteer diary writers and social observers distributed across the UK – were based on the assumption that the techniques deployed by anthropologists to study alien or 'uncivilised' cultures could equally be applied to a 'civilised' culture like Britain but, at the same time, it suggested a rough equivalence between the contexts, that is ritualistic behaviour was ritualistic behaviour wherever it was performed, be it in the rain forests of Papua New Guinea or the streets of Bolton or 'Worktown' as it was dubbed by Mass-Observation. However, there was a radicalism inherent in the ethnographic methods pioneered by Mass-Observation – in allowing their informants to become ethnographers Mass-Observation challenged the interpretive power of the 'expert' anthropologist or ethnologist.

Mass-Observation certainly pre-empted the social history of the 1960s and 1970s and created a huge database on almost every aspect of daily life from popular culture to national political events.[22] In 1937, apart from their study of mass reactions to the abdication crisis and the Coronation, the project identified a number of elements of British everyday life to be recorded by an army of fifty observers: 'Behaviour of people at war memorials; shouts and gestures of motorists; the aspidistra cult; anthropology of football pools; bathroom behaviour; beards, armpits, eyebrows; anti-semitism; distribution, diffusion and significance of the dirty joke; funerals and undertakers; female taboos about eating; the private lives of midwives.'[23] Subjects like these had never been documented before; indeed, no one had believed them worthy of serious attention. Not only did the diarists record information on a huge range of topics from cinema and music, fashion, the family, sex and marriage, they also recorded the details of a single day (12 May 1937, the Coronation of George VI) and from 1939 writers responded to 'directives' from Mass-Observation to write on specific topics of contemporary significance such as religion, race, jazz and, during the Second World War, attitudes to propaganda and air raids. When the first reports arrived from ordinary diarists the everydayness of British people's worlds began to emerge as they described their journeys to work, their working routines, the food they ate, the clothes they wore and their leisure activities. One of the early reports 'on a normal day' from a 'housewife' included the details of the food the family ate that day, '1.45: having fried chips we all sit down to meal Rhubarb from garden for pudding with vanilla sauce.'[24] Never before had the minutiae of the everyday been recorded and, more importantly, deemed significant, presaging by some decades the rising interest among historians in social life.

Mass-Observation has achieved what few scholars have managed to do – to 'get at the everyday'. As Cohen and Taylor observe, everyday life rarely appears in scholarly studies purporting to be about just that: 'there are few accounts of boredom, elation, despair, happiness or disappointment, no sense of the one obsessive problem which we always knew was ours: . . . how to get through the day.'[25] Yet some scholars like Lüdtke do focus on the repetitiveness of everyday routine, in his case in the workplace.[26] And out of such a focus, for some, the everyday is the very centre of historical change. This is especially the case in how historians of second-wave feminism approach the 1960s and 1970s; feminists had to deal with the 'unproblematic' and invisible everyday – such as the banality of wash day considered in Chapter 2 of this volume – and raise consciousness of it as a sphere of women's oppression.[27] The monotony of daily housework and childcare, for instance, became the focus of resistance for some. Scottish historians are starting to look at the everyday of sexuality, notably in work on feminism and gay liberation, with the massive changes wrought in the 1960s and 1970s.[28] Furthering this work, Lynn Jamieson in Chapter 3 brings the whole arena of everyday sexual and social intimacy in Scotland within the domain of inquiry. But so much of the Scottish everyday already recorded in places such as the Mass-Observation archive remains for the historian to exploit.

THE EVERYDAY IN WRITING ON TWENTIETH-CENTURY SCOTLAND

It is of course on account of the everyday's sheer banality and apparent unchanging nature that historians have veered away, preferring instead to document change. Despite the rise of the history of everyday life (*Alltagsgeschichte*) as a sub-discipline of social and cultural history in the 1970s and 1980s, it had little impact on historical writing in Scotland. When historians do invoke the everyday in Scotland there is a tendency to refer to a limited number of (stereotypical) 'myths' as a way of conjuring up a past that all Scots can recognise. Such myths include tenement overcrowding and poor housing conditions, the wash-day routine of women at the steamie, the Presbyterian Sabbath, football. These myths are not untruths but they do little to reveal a complex everyday life and furthermore they perpetuate the notion of Scotland's difference. It is rare to find an invocation of the everyday in the Scottish context that acknowledges commonality with the everyday in the rest of the United Kingdom or that acknowledges plurality within Scotland.

The exceptions to the historiographical trend were T. C. Smout's pioneering social histories of the Scottish people, histories from below which dealt with the elements of the everyday: food, housing, sex, work and so on. *Scottish Voices 1745–1960* purports to tell 'the real history of ordinary people doing everyday things'[29] – here we have the writer Edwin Muir describing the working-class predilection for getting drunk noisily and publicly, Molly Weir's invocation of Halloween and Bob Crampsey's vivid description of the rituals of the football spectator.[30] Beyond Smout's beginnings in this style of inquiry, though, modern Scottish history has a tendency to be driven by the political or national(ist) narrative peppered with references to Scottish culture and distinctiveness.[31]

Ethnographers have, in the Scottish context at least, made greater steps than the conventional historian towards cataloguing the everyday, albeit in a relatively untheorised fashion. As mentioned in the series Foreword, the work of the School of Scottish Studies at the University of Edinburgh from the 1950s to the present has focused on recording song and story as it is embedded in Scottish life and culture. The European Ethnological Research Centre also at Edinburgh has contributed to our knowledge of Scottish life broadly conceived, publishing a series of oral history collections and a multi-volume series, *Scottish Life and Society*, dealing with themes from religion and education to domestic and community life. The ethnographic approach has tended to be more descriptive than analytical, utilising a largely unproblematic definition of the everyday. The problem with encyclopaedic recording of the banal is the choice of what is actually 'banal'; the traditional archive is barren on so much of twentieth-century urban life and work, leisure and recreation, that even in an archaeological mode, everyday life studies can fail to link to either theoretical or historical analysis.

Everyday life in twentieth-century Scotland, especially since the Second World War, has been extensively documented by official and government bodies, by journalists, filmmakers and writers. Accessing one version of the everyday can be accomplished by statistics, collected by Registrars General for Scotland, by decennial census enumerators, by official opinion pollsters, by government agencies and public bodies like the Forestry Commission, and by Britain's original and still reliably unchanging statistical unit, the Board of Trade; data from each of these have been collected, collated and displayed for Chapter 1 of this volume in the specific exercise in 'charting' the everyday. But this can only be a limited approach. From 1965 the Central

Statistical Office produced statistics on selected aspects of demographic, economic and consumer behaviour to make some general statements about family size, income and expenditure. But while we may know how many television sets were owned by Scots, we don't know much about their viewing routines; we know Scots consumed more fizzy drinks than the UK average, but we don't know who consumed them and in what circumstances.

The sheer quantity and sophistication of data (compared with previous eras) and the mass media's relentless recording of every aspect of daily life makes us prone to the assumption that it is relatively easy to reconstruct everyday life and that everyday life in this century was more complex, more materialistic and more subject to change than in earlier times. Indeed, one of the difficulties which might flummox the historian is the apparent rapidity and complexity of twentieth-century change. Smout describes the twentieth century as mixed and perplexing in contrast with the much less complicated everyday world of the late eighteenth century; he contrasts a 'traditional' poor world with a rapidly changing present where prosperity and abundance are, relatively, more diffuse. Yet, the historian can make some sense of this complex world. The expansion of statistical collection in annual tabulations (not just by the state, but also by organisations such as the churches) allows the historian to construct time-series in a way the historian of previous centuries can only dream of. Yet, with some notable exceptions, little has been done by Scottish historians in this regard. One fears that the very profusion of data after 1900, and the constant changes of definitions as methods of collection and interrogation improved, puts the scholar off. Chapter 1 seeks to begin to remedy this want. There, data for many aspects of life are gathered and displayed to a degree of detail, and in its own statistical *bricolage*, not seen before. The chapter paints a picture of continuities and changes as background to the analytical accounts that follow.

Statistics are only as good as the categories chosen, the questions posed and 'the countability' of the everyday habit. Not everything can be counted. This is why media productions and publications, particularly of personal testimony, provide us with greater complexity and personalised experiences. This is especially the case in autobiographical writing. From the nostalgic memories of Molly Weir from Springburn and Finlay Macdonald from Harris, to the darker memories of Ralph Glasser from the Gorbals and the warts-and-all reminiscences of John Burnside from Dunfermline, the historian can find the richness and banality of everyday life in most parts of twentieth-century Scotland.[32] This was joined from the 1970s and 1980s by oral history testimonies which provided even more extensive reach into the everyday lives and identities of the 'ordinary people'; some oral projects were specifically geared to working-class history and women's history.[33] In this, the archive of the everyday became ever more a political project.

The growing archive has not been matched by the work of Scottish academic history in analysing the twentieth-century everyday. In part historians are interested in change, and the everyday is mistakenly assessed as banal and unchanging. The historian's disinterest in the everyday has also been fuelled by recoiling from the anthropologists' interest in 'non-eventness', in what are seen as banalities. Data has often been collected in snapshot form, and more used by anthropologists and sociologists; one thinks of Littlejohn's 1960s work on Eskdalemuir, Cohen's 1970s work on the islanders of Whalsay in Shetland, Parman's work on crofting or Macdonald's work on Skye.[34] For the historian, the concern for Scottish society in rural, island and marginal communities seems to reflect a concern for the minorities, not for the flourishing majorities.[35] The historical anthropology of Glasgow's Calton or Edinburgh's Morningside still seems a long way off.

Thus, even more for Scotland, the *bricolage* approach seems justified. Until the Scottish historian becomes interested and gifted enough to apply those techniques of anthropological micro-history now so well practised elsewhere in Europe, the everyday must use the smaller and diverse studies of the kind in this book.

THIS VOLUME: *LE BRICOLAGE*

The dominant frame of analysis in everyday life studies is experience, and this book reflects this. The contributors have thought about their subjects experientially, reflected in the widespread use of oral testimony and biographical or life writing. Oral history has become an invaluable methodology for those wishing to chart everyday experience in the recent past, since it allows us to hear Scots' own perceptions and interpretations of the everyday and often privileges the banal over the spectacular. Most people narrate and interpret their lives via the routines of everyday life, albeit often against a backdrop of national, political and economic change. The majority of the authors here utilise oral history to greater or lesser extent, not merely as colourful illustration but as new and revealing evidence and as a means of gaining insight into meaning. Whether respondents are recalling childhood reading habits, early intimate relationships, domestic living arrangements or working lives, they do so with an openness and degree of reflection which oral history alone can facilitate. But equally, there is an interest among many of the contributors in representation – in seeking to understand changing practices, values, discourses and mentalities, whether contested or shared, through the texts, images and objects that have represented and expressed the Scottish everyday during the twentieth century. Representations of idealised behaviour and identities – of masculinity, for instance, as Hilary Young explores in Chapter 5, or of the Scots Presbyterian as Steven Sutcliffe addresses in Chapter 7 – were important for Scots in negotiating their way through modern culture.

The nature of the everyday in the twentieth century is very different in kind from the everyday of previous centuries, and this is detectable in comparing this with the earlier volumes in the series. The treatments are different for a number of reasons: firstly, because of the proximity of the twentieth century and the currency of many of the issues in contemporary experience; secondly, because of the overlap and availability of several academic disciplines – including anthropology and sociology – which have as much if not more experience and contribution to offer to our volume and the task at hand than does social and cultural history in Scotland; thirdly, the dramatic nature of the changes of the century in most respects dwarf those of earlier centuries, even those promulgated by Reformation or industrialisation; fourthly, theory and method of academic study of society changed during the century we are studying, affecting what we perceive in a unique way in the meeting of method, theory and content; fifthly, the century developed a diversity, fragmentation and multiplication of cultural experiences and identities in Scotland unheard of before; and sixthly, in methodological terms, the contributors here have access to first-hand testimony, collected by themselves or by others, in which the investigators' questions have been directly put.

To introduce the contributions here, it may be helpful, first, to visualise the everyday as a series of scripts or 'mini-dramas'. Every action or process which we undertake, from dressing for work to cooking and eating the evening meal, is shaped by a script, a way of doing things that is widely accepted and recognised, whether or not everyone conforms to that script.[36] This analytical model not only helps one to identify norms or commonalities but also illustrates change over time. For example, Lynn Abrams and Linda Fleming explore in Chapter 2 the many changes to the nature and structure of the Scottish home between 1900 and 2000, noting that despite radical changes to housing stock, the scripts by which people lived their domestic lives altered little, in part because of long-standing conceptions among housing designers and planners about how people should live. Even the arrival of New Towns and then high rises after the Second World War failed to impinge drastically upon the rituals and routines conducted by people in their homes, and newcomers to Scotland throughout the century found themselves castigated if they failed to conform to the script of a Scottish way of life. Callum Brown discusses in Chapter 6 the family Sunday which in 1900 conformed to a pretty universal script that included church attendance (sometimes repeatedly), the Sunday lunch (with its prescribed ideal diet) and no games, but which by 2000 had been transformed for most families into a leisure script (of what one scholar has described as 'the secularized Sabbath') that included shopping, sports spectating, games, DIY, as well as pleasures of all sorts (such as cinema, pub-drinking, rail travel) previously proscribed or limited by law and custom. Lynn Jamieson shows in Chapter 3 how patterns of intimacy, from friendship to marriage, have been structured by a perceived script which might have been read differently by men and women but which nevertheless contained certain rules of engagement (such as marriage being an automatic response to pregnancy). Other changes to scripts are reviewed in relation to masculinity, work, to the conceptions of religion and culture. The script examined in each chapter expresses particular beliefs, ideologies, conformities and emotions. This can be seen in Elaine McFarland's chapter in which she describes changes in death and mourning rituals. But not everything is scripted. In opposition to such rituals and routines are what Cohen and Taylor describe as 'free areas'; places and activities where we are less in thrall to commonly recognised behavioural rituals and can express ourselves more freely and safely. Hobbies, holidays, sex, travel and the internet might offer individuals an escape from the routine of the everyday in modern life; but as such activities become more organised, frequent and regarded as necessary they are more likely to be routinised and scripted and thus reincorporated into the everyday. This may be especially noticeable in the role of arts festivals, explored by Angela Bartie in Chapter 8; these were at one time small and exceptional in the midst of post-war gloom and reconstruction, but as the decades wore on 'doing the festival' became mundane, widespread and part of mainstream Scottish experience.

One particular type of script remains central to everyday life – that of morbidity and mortality. John Stewart provides a detailed view of how the life of the Scot was transformed by the arrival in 1948 of the National Health Service. Many diseases, notably those of childhood, were conquered after a fifty-year heroic struggle by doctors and medical services in schools and local authorities; Chapter 1 provides additional data illustrating some of the changes. The NHS completed the victory by 1960, but then new illnesses dominated the medical and political agenda – notably heart disease and cancer. With among the highest death rates in the world, Stewart reflects how Scots hold health issues as a major element in their everyday lives while showing how the experience and management of sickness has perceptively altered. This 'script' is approached from a different angle by Elaine McFarland who, in exploring the management of death in Scotland, shows how the rituals changed, especially late in the century, surrounding this *rite de passage*. Even death – both the experience and its management – was not immune to the dramatic changes in everyday life.

A second approach is to look at the theme of resistance. The essays examine how it was precisely within the routines of everyday life that twentieth-century Scots resisted power and authority and challenged hegemonic ideologies and ways of being. We look through Arthur McIvor's essay at how work practices changed during the century, driven by technological modernisation and the rise of new work methods, driven seemingly inexorably by the demands of capitalism in its compulsion to compete overseas and reduce costs in production. Yet at the same time, these changes instigated resistance and revolt, the everyday conditions of work providing the basis for trade-union affiliation and action, and indeed providing the basis for a wider sense of collective solidarity. Behind work practices and changes to these lay the very basis of class unity and expression. In many places in this book, the reader will come upon resistance to the everyday conformities, and the tension between conformity and nonconformity. In the rise of arts festivals, Angela Bartie examines the reverential elitism of the Edinburgh Arts Festival and how it was challenged immediately by a more democratic conception of art and culture, with the rise of the Festival Fringe and the challenges to order, control, public decency and politics that artists from home and abroad brought to church halls all round the capital. In the campaigns over the control of the Sabbath, Callum Brown shows how the absence of definitive national law in this area resulted in spectacular local contests in peace and war, and how the Sabbath sits in some awkwardness amid the theories of the everyday outlined here.

The theme of revolt and resistance is brought down to the level of the individual in Steven Sutcliffe's innovative study of three exemplary figures who experienced the overthrow of traditional Presbyterianism. His study of Dugald Semple, Sheena Govan and R. D. Laing explores the ways in which the everyday culture of Presbyterianism was challenged at the level of the individual, and the disturbing effects this had. It also shows how, in the case of Govan, Scottish society reacted (in the form of press demonisation) and, in the case of Laing, how professional peers reacted to the apparent maverick and free thinker. The breakdown in Scottish Presbyterian polity is shown in its intimate and disquieting agonies upon the individual. After seeming to be a fixity of Scottish character and everyday law, Scotland shed its Presbyterian culture after 1960 faster than snow off a dyke. As free and easy as this process seemed for commerce and pleasures, Sutcliffe illustrates just how damaging it could be for the individual Scot. The negotiation away from the everyday identity Scots (presbyterians) carried around in their heads until mid-century could be complex and tortuous. Meanwhile, in the other chapters, oral testimony is called upon freely to provide a sense of the forces behind changes to everyday life and rituals, and to the reactions to those changes. In his study of work, Arthur McIvor deploys evidence from different industries in various parts of Scotland to show how the meanings of labour changed between 1900 and 2000, and how, though trade unions might rise and fall in popularity, the workplace remained a site of contest and alienation.

In 1990 Scottish historians Whatley and Brown challenged the myth of 'the uninflammability' of the Lowland Scot of the eighteenth century; in 1973, Eric Richards had done the same for the Highlander of the same period.[37] In the twentieth century, historians have debated how close Scotland came to workers' revolution in the Red Clydeside of the 1910s and 1920s.[38] The evidence we present in this book is that, notwithstanding the paucity of carnival, the scripts of everyday life were constantly being challenged by twentieth-century Scots. True, it was often hard to rebel, especially in the small ways, when the shops and cinemas and football grounds were so resolutely closed on Sundays, reinforcing the sense of obedience and submission instilled in school with the aid of 'the Lochgelly' (tawse). But this world of controlled behaviour and emotions slid pretty comprehensively from view in the 1960s, and did so remarkably elegantly, and without much rancour or effective challenge from the churches, the schools or anybody else. Only in the Hebrides by 2000, as Brown in Chapter 6 recounts, did there remain a shadow of the seventeenth-century Covenanter polity of the Lowlands.

The diverse specialists here set up different lenses through which to view the experiences that so many readers will themselves recall. There will be much that will be familiar in this volume to those who lived the twentieth century, or part of it. But at the same time we aim to provoke new and fresh ways of thinking about everyday experience, the things taken for granted and unremarked upon. We expect there to be disagreement, and call upon it.

Notes

1. The term, applied to social science by Levi-Strauss in 1962, is influential in cultural studies, arts and philosophy. Derrida said of it: 'The *bricoleur*, says Levi-Strauss, is someone who uses "the means at hand," that is, the instruments he finds at his disposition around him, those which are already there, which had not been especially conceived with an eye to the operation for which they are to be used and to which one tries by trial and error to adapt them, not hesitating to change them whenever it appears necessary, or to try several of them at once, even if their form and their origin are heterogenous. . . .' J. Derrida, *Writing and Difference* (London, orig. 1967, 2003 ed.), p. 360.
2. Derrida denies the possibility of constructing an original 'totality': 'The notion of the engineer who supposedly breaks with all forms of *bricolage* is therefore a theological idea; and . . . the odds are that the engineer is a myth produced by the *bricoleur*.' Ibid.
3. H. Dehne, 'Have we come any closer to *Alltag*? Everyday reality and workers' lives as an object of historical research in the German Democratic Republic', in A. Lüdtke (ed.), *The History of Everyday Life: Reconstructing Historical Experiences and Ways of Life* (Princeton, 1995), p. 121.
4. L. Passerini, *Fascism in Popular Memory: the Cultural Experience of the Turin Working Class* (Cambridge, 1987).
5. A. Portelli, 'What makes oral history different?', in Portelli, *The Death of Luigi Trastulli and Other Strories* (Albany, 1991), p. 37.
6. N. Hubble, *Mass-Observation and Everyday Life: Culture, History, Theory* (Basingstoke, 2006), p. 37.
7. Hubble, *Mass-Observation*, p. 143.
8. Quoted in Ben Highmore, *Everyday Life and Cultural Theory: an Introduction* (London, 2002), p. 39.

9. M. de Certeau, *The Practice of Everyday Life* (Berkeley, 1984), pp. xiv–xv, 200–3; J. C. Scott, *Domination and the Arts of Resistance: Hidden Transcripts* (London, 1990); R. Guha, 'The prose of counter-insurgency', in N. B. Dirks, G. Eley and S. B. Ortner (eds), *Culture/Power/History: A Reader in Contemporary Social Theory* (Princeton, 1994), pp. 335–6, 358, 360, 365.

10. See the 1983 interview with Lefebvre at http://www.notbored.org/lefebvre-interview.html

11. Highmore, *Everyday Life*, p. 148.

12. H. Lefebvre, *Critique of Everyday Life*, vol. 1 (London, 2002) p. 202.

13. Quoted in A. Merryfield, 'Guest editorial', in *Environment and Planning: Society and Space* vol. 20 (2002), p. 130.

14. E. Le Roy Ladurie, *Carnival in Romans: A People's Uprising at Romans 1579–1580* (London, 1980); C. Humphries, *The Politics of Carnival: Festive Misrule in Medieval England* (Manchester, 2001).

15. C. A. Whatley, '"The privilege which the rabble have to be riotous": carnivalesque and the monarch's birthday in Scotland, c.1700–1860', in J. Blanchard (ed.), *Labour and Leisure in Historical Perspective* (Stuttgart, 1994); C. G. Brown, *Up-helly-aa: Custom, Culture and Community in Shetland* (Manchester, 1998).

16. P. L. Berger and T. Luckmann, *The Social Construction of Reality* (Harmondsworth, 1969), especially pp. 21–5.

17. E. Goffman, *The Presentation of Self in Everyday Life* (orig. 1959, London, 1990).

18. S. Cohen and L. Taylor, *Escape Attempts: the Theory and Practice of Resistance to Everyday Life* (London, 1992), p. 66 *et seq.*

19. G. Simmel, *The Conflict in Modern Culture and Other Essays* (New York, 1968), p. 68, quoted in Highmore, *Everyday Life*, p. 39.

20. Highmore, *Everyday Life*, p. 131. Highmore suggests Lefebvre was thinking of the hypermodern rather than the postmodern in his work.

21. Quoted in Highmore, *Everyday Life*, p. 145.

22. www.massobs.org.uk

23. Quoted in Highmore, *Everyday Life* , p. 147.

24. Quoted in Highmore, *Everyday Life*, p. 151.

25. Cohen and Taylor, *Escape Attempts*, p. 30.

26. For Lüdtke the everyday is repetitiveness and routine; the everyday is contrasted to non-everyday eventfulness and historical change seen as the outcome of action by real groups and individuals, *History of Everyday Life*, p. 6.

27. Highmore, *Everyday Life*, p. 2.

28. See R. Davidson, '"The Sexual State": sexuality and Scottish governance 1950–1980', *Journal of the History of Sexuality* vol. 13 (2004), pp. 500–21; idem, 'The cautionary tale of Tom: the male homosexual experience of Scottish medicine in the 1970s and early 1980s, *Journal of Scottish Historical Studies* vol. 8 (2008), pp. 122–38; Sarah Browne is currently completing doctoral research into the women's liberation movement in Scotland at the University of Dundee.

29. T. C. Smout and S. Wood, *Scottish Voices 1745–1960* (London, 1991), p. 1.

30. Smout and Wood, *Scottish Voices*, pp. 153–4, 170–3, 194–6.

31. See M. Pittock, *A New History of Scotland* (Stroud, 2003), Chapter 7 'Modern

Scotland'. An exception is C. Harvie, *No Gods and Precious Few Heroes: Twentieth Century Scotland* (Edinburgh, 1998).

32. M. Weir, *Shoes were for Sunday* (London, 1973): F. Macdonald, *Crowdie and Cream* (London, 1982); R. Glasser, *Growing Up in the Gorbals* (London, 1986); J. Burnside, *A Lie About my Father* (London, 2006).

33. Such as J. D. Stephenson and C. G. Brown, 'The view from the workplace: women and work in Stirling 1900–1950', in E. Gordon and E. Breitenbach (eds), *The World Is Ill Divided: Women's Work in Scotland in the Nineteenth and Twentieth Centuries* (Edinburgh, 1990), pp. 7–28.

34. J. Littlejohn, *Westrigg: The Sociology of a Cheviot Parish* (London, 1963); A. P. Cohen, *Whalsay: Symbol, Segment and Boundary in a Shetland Island Community* (Manchester, 1987); S. Parman, *Scottish Crofters: an Historical Ethnography of a Celtic Village* (Fort Worth, 1990); S. Macdonald, *Reimagining Culture: Histories, Identities and the Gaelic Renaissance* (Oxford, 1997).

35. This is even true of the authors' two books on Shetland; L. Abrams, *Myth and Materiality in a Woman's World: Shetland 1800–2000* (Manchester, 2005); C. G. Brown, *Up-helly-aa: Custom, Culture and Community in Shetland* (Manchester, 1998).

36. Cohen and Taylor, *Escape Attempts*, p. 71.

37. C. A. Whatley, 'How tame were the Scottish Lowlanders during the eighteenth century?', and C. G. Brown, 'Protest in the pews: interpreting presbyterianism and society in fracture during the Scottish economic revolution', both in T. M. Devine (ed.), *Conflict and Stability in Scottish Society 1700–1850* (Edinburgh, 1990); E. Richards, 'How tame were the Highlanders during the clearances?', *Scottish Studies* xvii (1973), pp. 35–50.

38. For a recent review, see W. Kenefick, *Red Scotland: The Rise and Fall of the Radical Left in Scotland 1870 to 1932* (Edinburgh, 2007).

Chapter 1

Charting Everyday Experience

Callum G. Brown

INTRODUCTION

The historian of the twentieth century has a great opportunity to chart everyday life through statistics. This is the more useful for the unprecedented transformations that were experienced. Scotland was no exception to this, and in some respects distinctive. This chapter will survey some of the key elements of change in everyday experience in twentieth-century Scotland by pulling together a range of quantitative materials on life which, for the most part, have not been collated over the whole century, nor in the detailed, usually year-by-year, format in which they are displayed here. Intended as a reference guide to the timing, magnitude and form of change in Scottish everyday life, this chapter also acts as a quantitative prelude to the more qualitative exploration of the everyday experience explored in the chapters that follow.

POPULATION

Underlying everyday life are demographics. Scotland's population, shown in Table 1.1, rose during the century from 4,479,000 in 1900 to 5,062,940 in 2000, an increase of 13 per cent. The scale of this rise is quite modest compared to most western and developing nations; the population of England and Wales grew 60 per cent (of Wales alone 69 per cent), that of France 45 per cent, Ireland 73 per cent, Norway 96 per cent. Though a high point of population size at 5,240,800 was reached in 1974, it means that in relative terms Scotland has not become an appreciably more crowded place. Indeed, some of the most crowded places became less populous. Table 1.2 shows the populations of selected towns, showing how the peak population of many was reached in mid-century, to be followed by depopulation resulting from slum clearance, overspill policies (moving families to suburbs, new towns or distant towns) and urban regeneration. Glasgow's population fell between 1951 and 2001 from over a million to 629,000. Rural areas in general became less populous – notably the Highlands and Hebrides (though the Northern Isles ended population decline with the discovery of oil in the early 1970s). The relative overall stasis in Scottish demographic change is also evident

Table 1.1 *Scottish population, 1900–2000.*

1900	4,437,000
1910	4,739,000
1920	4,866,866
1930	4,828,004
1940	4,841,241
1950	5,114,513
1960	5,177,658
1970	5,213,700
1980	5,193,900
1990	5,081,270
2000	5,062,940

Source: Mid-year population estimates, from B. R. Mitchell and P. Deane (eds), *Abstract of British Historical Statistics* (Cambridge, 1962), pp. 9–10; and http://www.gro-scotland. gov.uk/statistics/publications-and-data/population-estimates/population-estimates-time-series-data.html

Table 1.2 *Urban populations, 1901–2001.*

	1901	1951	2001
Glasgow	918,000	1,090,000	577,869**
Edinburgh	395,000	467,000	448,624**
Aberdeen	154,000	183,000	212,727**
Dundee	161,000	177,000	145,663**
Paisley	79,000	94,000	73,190
Perth	32,872*	40,487	43,680
Greenock	68,000	76,000	43,820
Dumfries	17,081†	26,322	31,146
Inverness	21,193*	28,107	42,400

* Parliamentary and municipal burgh ** Council area † Royal burgh
Sources: B. R. Mitchell and P. Deane (eds), *Abstract of British Historical Statistics* (Cambridge, 1962), pp. 24–7; *Census* 1901, 1951, 2001 (Population Report, Table 2, www.gro-scotland.gov.uk).

from the number of births and deaths, shown in Figure 1.1. Between 1900 and 2000, births fell from 131,401 to 53,076, and deaths fell from 82,296 to 57,799. In general, the number of births showed a much greater tendency to violent change; after both world wars there was a great surge in births, followed by sharp decline which, in the case of the inter-war period, continued for two decades but which, in the case of 1952–64, turned into a sustained vigorous growth – the 'baby boom' – which then gave way to a sharp fall. The numbers of deaths, on the other hand, were less susceptible to wide

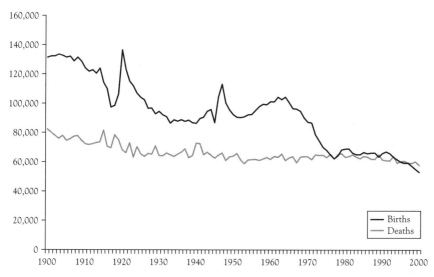

Source: *Registrar General (Scotland), Annual Report* 1900–2000.

Figure 1.1 *Births and deaths in Scotland, 1900–2000.*

variation, but were prone to a cyclical change over periods of 2–4 years. Yet in comparison to births, deaths declined by a modest number across the century. Despite increasing life expectancy, the greater fall in births over deaths, coupled with periods of net outmigration, held in check the growth of Scotland's total population.

In these ways, the Scots demonstrated some degrees of change in under-lying behaviour surrounding the rituals of life. The violent changes in numbers of births, shown in the graph, demonstrate the impact of changing sexual habits. Between 1964 and 1978, births fell from 104,355 to 64,295, caused in large measure by the advent of the oral contraceptive pill and aided by the wider availability of condoms, contraceptive advice and knowledge. It did not mean that sex was going out fashion.[1] Indeed, the evidence of Figure 1.2 is that the proportion of births taking place outwith marriage showed that pre-marital sex was on the increase, and continued to be from the mid-1970s despite contraceptives. This followed a distinctive period in the late 1940s and 1950s when the illegitimacy rate in Scotland was declining markedly, from 8.6 per cent in 1945 to 4.1 per cent in 1957 and 1958, before starting to rise continuously and sharply in the ten years before the pill became available to single women (under new BMA regulations introduced in 1968). Indeed, it is remarkable that the illegitimacy rate in Scotland was at its century's lowest in the 1950s, marking something of the moral climate of that decade.

All of this points to fundamental changes to the nature of the Scottish

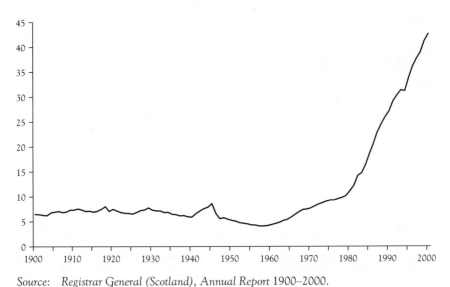

Source: *Registrar General (Scotland), Annual Report 1900–2000.*

Figure 1.2   *Illegitimacy rate in Scotland 1900–2000: percentage of births outwith marriage.*

household taking place from around 1970. There was a distinct decline in the number of first marriages, a rise in divorce and remarriage, and a move towards cohabitation. Remarriages were kept high by rising divorce; in 1963 there were 5,000 remarriages, representing only around 12 per cent of marriages, but this rose by the late 1990s to more than 15,000, representing more than 50 per cent.[2] We can follow the general parameters of marriage and divorce in Figure 1.3. The number of marriages showed a general upward trend, accelerated temporarily by two world wars, to a high plateau between 1948 and 1975, followed by a general decline. In the period 1931–40, only 0.7 per cent of both Scottish grooms and brides were divorcees, but these figures rose sharply in 1971–80 to 10.6 per cent of grooms and 10.3 per cent of brides, and in 1991–2000 to 25.2 percent of grooms and 24.4 per cent of brides.[3] The popularity of first marriage was waning very sharply, and even more sharply than the crude statistics show. This is because late in the century there was a rising trend of marriages in Scotland by non-residents; by 2005, 30 per cent of marriages registered in Scotland involved couples with neither partner resident in Scotland.[4] The greatest single cause of this was the blossoming of Gretna Green as a location of romantic marriage for visitors to the country. In 1975 there were 74 marriages at Gretna; by 2000 there were 5,278 (representing 17.4 per cent of all Scottish marriages), of which 2,966 were by religious rites, the bulk of them Church of Scotland.[5] One feature late in the century was that changes to the nature of the family meant shifting experiences for children. As Table 1.3 shows, the surge in divorce and cohabitation in the last decade of the century led to a rise from

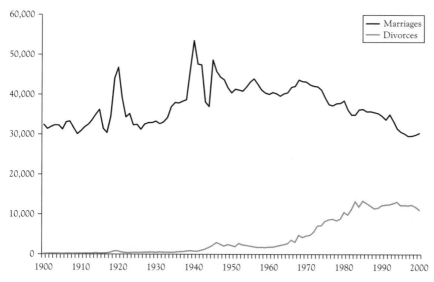

Source: Registrar General (Scotland), *Annual Report*, 1900–2000.

Figure 1.3 *Marriages and divorces in Scotland, 1900–2000.*

Table 1.3 *Children by family type, Scotland, 1991–2001.*

	1991	2001
Married couple	76%	64%
Cohabiting couple	4%	10%
Lone parent	19%	25%
Not in a family	0%	1%

Source: Data from 'Family formation and dissolution: trends and attitudes among the Scottish population', Anita Morrison, Debbie Headrick, Legal Studies Research Team, Scottish Executive; Fran Wasoff, Sarah Morton, Centre for Research on Families and Relationships, University of Edinburgh, online at http://www.scotland.gov.uk/Publications/2004/03/19144/35014 accessed 9 June 2008

23 per cent to 36 per cent in the proportion of children being raised outwith married-couple families.

ETHNICITY AND RELIGION

Until the later twentieth century, Scotland was comparatively undifferentiated in religions and ethnicity. In 1900, the vast bulk of people were Christians (though divided into many denominations), with only about ten thousand Jews and small numbers of other religions.[6] All but a tiny number

Callum G. Brown

Table 1.4   *Religious affiliation of Scots, 2001.*

	Percentage of all respondents
Church of Scotland	42.40
None	27.55
Roman Catholic	15.88
Other Christian	6.81
Muslim	0.84
Buddhist	0.13
Jewish	0.13
Sikh	0.13
Hindu	0.11
Another religion	0.53
Question not answered	5.49

Source: 2001 census given at http://www.scrol.gov.uk/scrol/warehouse/NewWards_
ER_N.jsp, Table KS07, accessed 28 January 2009.

were white. Although there were significant numbers of immigrants (from Ireland, England and eastern Europe especially), what we now understand as 'ethnic composition' was fairly uniform.

The ethnic composition of Scotland, like the rest of western Europe, changed dramatically in the last four decades of the century, resulting mainly from large-scale immigration from former British colonies. Yet, Scotland remained more uniformly white than most other European countries. By 2001, the Scottish population regarded itself as 97.9 per cent white, with only 15,037 Indian, 39,970 Pakistani and other south Asians, 16,310 Chinese, and 30,360 others.[7] But the religious diversity of Scotland was much greater than its ethnic diversity. Table 1.4 demonstrates how Christians still made up 65.09 per cent of respondents, but those claiming 'None' for their religious affiliation was greater than any category other than the Church of Scotland (and significantly greater than the proportion answering the equivalent question in England, Wales and Northern Ireland). Those with a religion tended to be strongly female. In 2001, women made up 51.9 per cent of the population but 54.1 per cent of Church of Scotland, 53.71 per cent of Roman Catholic and 56.12 per cent of other Christians; conversely, they made up only 47.55 per cent of those declaring no religion, and significantly smaller proportions of all non-Christian religions.[8]

The pattern of change to religious adherence during the century was strongly influenced by the case of the largest denomination, the Church of Scotland (and including the United Free Church until 1929). Figure 1.4 shows that there was a steady proportion of the people in adherence with these kirks until the late 1950s, when a sharp and unremitting downward trend started, coinciding with other changes affecting the place of religion

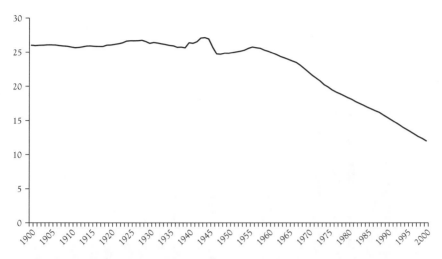

Note: The shape of this graph differs slightly in certain periods (notably 1939–45) from previous versions I have published; this is because I have reconfigured the data from a base using decennial census figures for population to one using Registrar General (Scotland) annual mid-year estimates (which decreases the estimate of wartime home population at a period when the kirk kept those serving overseas on the communicants' roll, thus inflating the wartime proportion). Interestingly, no similar effect is evident in 1914–18. Graph includes United Free Church communicants, 1900–29.

Sources: R. Currie, A. Gilbert and L. Horsley, *Churches and churchgoers: patterns of churchgoing in the British Isles since 1700* (Oxford, 1977), pp. 133–5; *Church of Scotland Yearbook, 1971–2000; Registrar General (Scotland), Annual Reports, 1900–2000.*

Figure 1.4   *Church of Scotland communicants as a proportion of Scottish population, 1900–2000.*

in Scottish civil society. The changes that affected some other Christian churches (notably the Roman Catholic Church) are less easy to follow because of the absence of a membership category. However, it seems that the decline in the Roman Catholic Church started a little later than in the Church of Scotland, in the late 1970s, but by the 1990s was in many respects steeper; for example, between 1994 and 2002, mass attendance fell 18 per cent and numbers of marriages 33 per cent.[9]

WORK

Scotland's workers experienced significant shifts in their working environments during the century. Scotland's staple industries declined overall (though in complex patterns), employment grew in service and professional occupations, and women's contribution to the labour market rose very significantly. In addition, late in the century, there was a revolution in higher education.

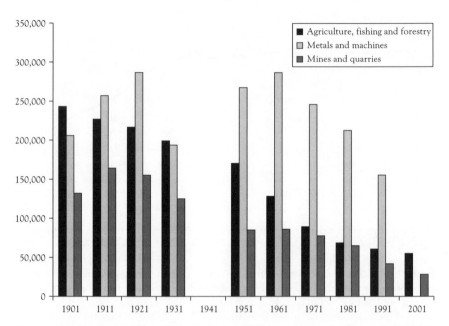

Note: The data for metals and machines for 2001 is currently not listed on SCROL online census data.
Source: Census, occupational volumes, 1901–31, 1951–2001 (the last online).

Figure 1.5   *Workers in selected industries, Scotland, 1901–2001.*

Figure 1.5 shows the fortunes of three staple sectors of the economy – agriculture, fishing and forestry, metal and machine making, and mining and quarrying. The first of these showed a steady decline through the century, with the greatest decline in the fishing industry. Metal-manufacturing industries, notably shipbuilding and engineering, grew during the first half of the century with a downturn in the early 1930s caused by the depression. The 1950s witnessed a significant growth from 267,406 to 286,540 workers, equalling the 1921 figure, after which this sector entered a slide to 155,350 workers in 1991. Mining and quarrying, made up overwhelmingly of coal miners, reached a peak of production in 1913, illustrated by the highpoint of census occupations in 1911, after which an extended decline was sustained until the demise of virtually the entire deep-mining coal industry in the 1980s and 1990s.

Four contrasting patterns of employment are shown in Table 1.5. In food, drink and tobacco, there was a very marked decline until 1951 followed by a sharp rise in the 1950s (that was to be sustained over successive decades) indicative of the growing leisure market. Construction showed a very volatile pattern of employment, following the economic cycle very closely, with lows in 1921 and 1931, and peaks in 1901 and 1961. Domestic and personal services experienced stability to the 1920s, followed by a cyclical pattern

Table 1.5 *Employment by selected sector in Scotland, 1901–61.*

	1901	1911	1921	1931	1951	1961
Food, drink and tobacco	152,119	158,746	56,459	45,688	39,151	82,980
Construction	136,639	106,539	65,336	64,712	102,117	174,050
Domestic and personal services	201,230	201,066	199,887	238,629	192,121	204,870
Transport and communications	163,202	177,731	180,959	195,486	184,175	176,010

Source: Decennial censuses, occupational volumes, 1901–31, 1951 and 1961.

Table 1.6 *Paid women workers as a proportion of the workforce in Scotland, 1901–2001.*

	1901	1911	1921	1931	1951	1961	1971	1981	1991	2001
Occupied population*	29.8	28.7	29.2	29.9	30.3	32.0	37.7	40.9	43.4	46.5

* The definition changed in 1961 to 'economically active', in 1971 and 1981 to 'in employment', and in 1991 and 2001 back to 'economically active'.
Sources: Figures calculated from data in decennial censuses, occupational volumes, 1901–91; and www.scrol.gov.uk, Table CAS028.

as the sector shifted away from female-dominated domestic service. Lastly, transport and communications shows a remarkable stability of employment despite changes in the means of transport and the growing diversification in telecommunications.

One of the most important changes of the century was the growing significance of women to the labour market. This involved a series of processes. First, women workers shifted from being predominantly single at the start of the century to being a majority married from the 1970s to the 1990s. Second, there was a very marked increase in the proportion of women who worked. And third, the wage and salary differentials between men and women narrowed.[10] The result was a trend towards equalisation of opportunity for men and for women, but one that was highly differentiated between occupations. Table 1.6 shows the percentage of the workforce that was female, which indicates that the proportion was virtually constant from 1901 to 1951, rising marginally to 1961, but then rising steeply in the 1960s and by significant amounts in successive decades.

A broadly similar picture of the timing of gender change comes from data on female access to higher education. Figure 1.6 shows the growth in the numbers of male and female students at universities from 1919,

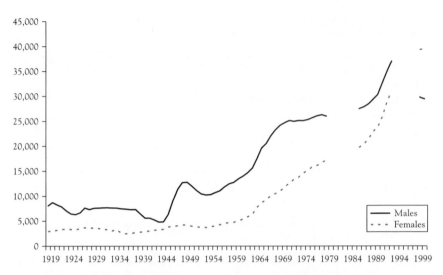

Note: The two graph lines cross at some point in the mid-1990s, so that in 1999–2000 females exceed males.
Sources: University Grants Commission, *Returns from Universities and University Colleges in Receipt of Treasury Grant,* 1919–65; *Statistics of Education,* 1965–97; *University Statistics,* 1987–96; *Higher Education Statistics for the UK,* 2000–1.

Figure 1.6   *Full-time students at Scottish universities by sex, 1919–2000.*

demonstrating the impact of the Second World War and the growth from the 1960s. It shows that the real boom in the university student population came after 1963 when the growth accelerated, but then for male students experienced a spectacular downturn in growth from 1971 to 1990. In those two decades, the growth in female student numbers was much larger, a growth which continued in the 1990s until, by 1999 and 2000, the numbers of women students exceeded male students for the first time. But perhaps interestingly, these data show that the proportion of women among students was never below a quarter for the whole century, and often much higher – 34.5 per cent in 1925, and 40.9 per cent in 1944.[11]

Unemployment levels changed significantly across the twentieth century. Measuring this change with time-series data is more fraught with difficulty than almost any other statistical series. Until the early 1920s there was no comprehensive system of recording and calculating unemployment. From that date, the *Labour Gazette* published detailed figures of those out of work, but annual average totals for Scotland were not published in general statistical series. Later in the century, new problems arose. There were repeated changes in the definition of unemployment published by government, and the retrospective application of changes to the data for years immediately preceding. Between 1976 and 2000, there were five changes in definition

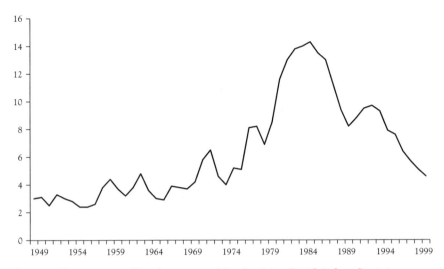

Sources: Department of Employment and Productivity, *British Labour Statistics: Historical Abstract 1886–1968* (London, 1971), p. 328; *Annual Abstract of Statistics* vols 109 (1972), 111 (1974), 116 (1990), 136 (2000); *Abstract of Regional Statistics* no. 1 (1965).

Figure 1.7   *Unemployment rate for Scotland, 1949–2000 (%).*

observable from the government data; the most significant were in 1982 when it was defined as the Claimant Unemployment Rate (when the unemployed were defined as those claiming unemployment benefit at a benefit office on the day of the monthly count, and who satisfied the conditions for benefit), and in 1996 when it changed to Claimant Count Rate (those claiming Jobseeker's Allowance which lasted six months before becoming means tested). Every change reduced the unemployment rate.

Despite these shortcomings, the data charted in Figure 1.7 provide a reasonable outline of the changing incidence of unemployment in the second half of the century. The years from 1952 to 1979 illustrate the impact of 'stop-go' economic policies – 'boom and bust' as they latterly became known – but set against a steady secular rise in unemployment. From 1979 to 1985 there was a dramatic rise, followed by an equally sharp fall to 1990, a rise again to 1993, and then a fall to the end of the century. While the graph line after 1981 may underscore unemployment compared to the definition used in the 1950s, the overall trends (if not the gradients) of change are probably fairly shown.

HEALTH

Among the most profound of the changes for the Scottish people in the twentieth century has been their experience of sickness and health.

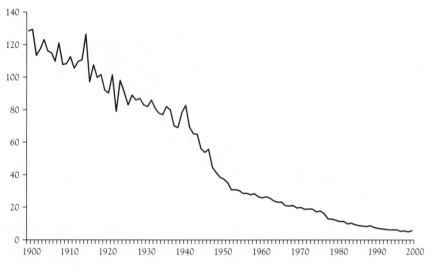

Source: Registrar General (Scotland), Annual Report, 1900–2000.

Figure 1.8   *Infant mortality rate, Scotland, 1900–2000; deaths in first year of life per 1,000 live births.*

In 1900 almost 13 per cent of babies died in the first year of life; by the end of the century this figure had fallen to under 0.6 per cent. The infant mortality rate (IMR) is the figure for deaths in the first year of life as a proportion of 1,000 live births. Figure 1.8 shows that the course of decline in IMR had three characteristic features: a steady but sharply cyclical decline from 1900 to 1941, a steep and less cyclical pattern from 1941 to 1952, and then a slower and much smoother gradient from 1952 until 2000. By 1970, Scotland stood with the USA with an IMR of 20 deaths per 1,000 live births at midway point in the league of infant mortality rates among western nations; Portugal (59) was highest followed by Italy (29), West Germany (24) and Northern Ireland (23), but at the other end of the scale the lowest figures were for the Netherlands and Finland (both 13), France (15) and England & Wales (18).[12]

The cause of the fluctuations in IMR in the first four decades of the century was the sweeping incidence of various childhood diseases which ravaged the child population every few years: notably, measles, whooping cough and scarlet fever. Figure 1.9 shows the number of deaths each year from these three major childhood diseases. It demonstrates very clearly the highly erratic nature of the incidence of each, and the tendency in many periods (though not all) for two diseases to take it in turns to strike severely. The highpoint of each disease occurred for measles in 1922 (2,695 deaths), for scarlet fever in 1915 (950 deaths) and for whooping cough also in 1915 (2,820 deaths). Even more striking is the way in which the severe oscillations in incidence gradually diminished between 1925 and 1944, and were

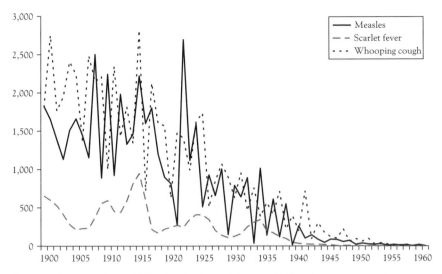

Source: *Registrar General (Scotland), Annual Report, 1900–60.*

Figure 1.9 *Deaths from major childhood diseases in Scotland, 1900–60.*

then suppressed entirely between 1950 and 1960. The impact of medical services was clearly becoming more effective; the importance of health advances before the NHS arrived comes across very strongly, continuing in the Second World War when there was a dramatic fall in IMR, followed in the late 1940s and 1950s by the impact of the National Health Service, from when the causes of infant death became increasingly narrowed to non-disease causes. The decline in IMR and the childhood diseases was one of the major success stories of health provision between the 1920s and 1960s.

The story of decline was also dramatic for adult diseases, though tempered by the rise of new causes of death. One of the major adult diseases to decline, tuberculosis, is shown in Figure 1.10 along with one of the major new causes of death, cancer. The decline in the incidence of TB, which carried off 10,336 dead in 1900, was well underway in the early twentieth century, showing particularly sharp falls between 1907 and 1910 and at the end of the First World War. In marked contrast to the experience with childhood diseases, the Second World War brought a halt to progress with TB, with a sharp and sustained rise in 1939–40. This only started to be tackled in the late 1940s, and then through the 1950s with a massive NHS campaign of screening and treatment which reduced the incidence very sharply to only 509 cases in 1960. But the decline of TB left the growth of two major causes of death: heart disease and cancer. As Figure 1.10 demonstrates, cancer deaths rose in an almost precise mirror image of the decline of mortality from TB. In 1900, there were 3,503 cancer deaths, rising to 11,033 in 1960. From then,

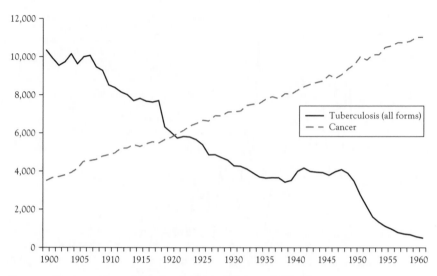

Source: Registrar General (Scotland), Annual Report, 1900–60.

Figure 1.10   *Deaths from tuberculosis and cancer in Scotland, 1900–60.*

Table 1.7   *Death rates from malignant neoplasms (all sites) in Scotland, 1950–2000 (per 100,000 population).*

	Males	Females
1950–2	206	185
1960–2	241	195
1970–2	272	218
1980–2	291	247
1990–2	310	278
2000	306	291

Source: Registrar General (Scotland), Annual Report, 2000, p. 119.

cancer death rates, indicated in Table 1.7, rose steadily; by the 1990s, the growth had been reversed for men, but was sustained for women. This trend towards gender convergence was partly accounted for by declining smoking among men but its continued strength among women. In later twentieth-century Scotland, cancer and heart disease became the two principal concerns of the health services. In 1970, 33.8 per cent of deaths were caused by heart disease, 19.8 per cent by malignant neoplasm (broadly cancer), 15.6 per cent by cerebrovascular disease (brain dysfunctions), 4.8 per cent by pneumonia, 4.6 per cent by violence and 4.6 per cent by bronchitis.[13]

One rising cause of death in the later twentieth century was suicide. As

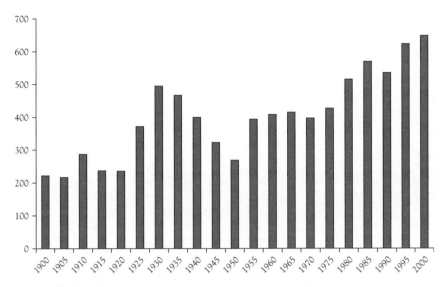

Note: The bar chart displays suicides at five-yearly intervals.
Source: *Registrar General (Scotland), Annual Report, 1900–2000.*

Figure 1.11 *Suicides in Scotland, 1900–2000.*

Figure 1.11 indicates, there had been an increasing incidence between 1900 and 1930, when suicides more than doubled from 222 to 495, before falling back to 269 at 1950, and then rising from 1960 (with a downturn in 1970) to 648 in 2000. The manner of suicide varied; in 1980 515 took their own lives, of which 184 were by poison, 118 by hanging, 69 by drowning, 51 by gas or vapours, 37 by jumping from high places, and 27 by firearms or explosives, and the remainder by other means. Men have outnumbered women in suicide in Scotland, but to varying proportions, with a marked increase in the proportion of men towards the end of the century: in 1900 161 men to 61 women, in 1950 170 men to 99 women, and in 2000 512 men to 136 women.[14]

The decline in death rates overall brought increased life expectancy and an aging population. This brought new burdens for families and the NHS in caring for the surviving elderly. The implications of ill-health, disability and aging have impacted most often upon relatives. In 1999–2000, 12.3 per cent of Scottish households included someone requiring regular help or care; often, this was where a pensioner lived alone (which applied in 22 per cent of those types of household).[15]

Though Scotland was widely regarded as 'the sick man of Europe' for its poor health record late in the century, Scots were by no means the most given to reporting high rates of sickness. In the General Household Survey of 1976, Scots had significantly lower rates of reporting long-standing (or chronic) illness than people in England and Wales. Among men, 20.4 per cent of those in Scotland reported long-standing illness, compared to 25.1 per cent in England and Wales; similarly, 22.2 per cent of women in Scotland reported this compared to 27.0 per cent in the other two countries. Unlike men south of the border, these figures showed Scottish males as being less likely to report chronic illness than women.[16]

THE HOME

The Scottish home has, if anything, undergone greater change in the twentieth century than any other category of everyday experience. In 1901, 26 per cent of Glasgow families lived in one-roomed houses and a further 44 per cent lived in two-roomed houses. With similar figures for smaller industrial towns like Falkirk, Greenock and Port Glasgow, and only mildly better figures for Dundee (where the two-roomed house was the norm) and Edinburgh, the Scottish experience of the everyday life of the home was a distinctively cramped one.[17] It had all sorts of consequences, including poor health and rickets, but also including poor experience of domestic leisure. Even the middle classes in the early twentieth century were, unlike most of their equivalents elsewhere in Europe, living in cramped quarters.

Scotland had by far the most overcrowded housing in Britain, the product of three main causes: the distinctive tenement housing in towns and cities; croft houses in Highland and Island areas; and pit-village houses on a par with the worst in the northern English coalfields. Improvement was slow and patchy. In 1901, there were four counties with domestic overcrowding at averages in a house of over 1.75 persons per room (including kitchens and bathrooms, if any): Lanarkshire (including Glasgow), Renfrewshire, West Lothian, and Orkney & Shetland. In the second rank of overcrowding at 1.5 to 1.74 persons per room came Ayrshire, Dunbartonshire and Stirlingshire. And in the third rank at 1.25 to 1.49 persons per room came Angus (including Dundee), Fife, Ross & Cromarty, Caithness, Midlothian (including Edinburgh) and Peeblesshire. Improvement came quickest to crofting areas, ironically because of out-migration in the inter-war years, while cities and mining villages benefited from the advance of subsidised council housing. By 1951, only Lanarkshire retained an average of more than 1.25 persons per room, but most Scottish counties had overcrowding worse than all of England and Wales bar its most northern coalfields.[18]

Comparatively better provision existed in Scotland for certain domestic appliances. In 1951, 5 per cent of Scottish homes lacked piped internal water supply, compared to 6 per cent in England and Wales. The Scottish figure rose to 14 per cent in rural areas, but did not match England's 21 per cent for rural districts; the figures rose to over 20 per cent in Wigtonshire and Inverness-shire, and to over 35 per cent in Ross & Cromarty, Sutherland

and Orkney & Shetland. Scotland was also better provided with domestic water closets by 1951; only 6 per lacked this amenity, compared to 8 per cent in England and Wales. Again it was rural areas that were the worst: 18 per cent in Scotland, but a huge 35 per cent in England and Wales; the worst Scottish counties were again the crofting areas of Ross & Cromarty, Caithness, Sutherland and Orkney & Shetland, each with over 35 per cent of homes without WCs. But Scotland was poorly off for internal cooking stoves and fixed baths. In 1951, 9 per cent of rural homes, and 5 per cent of all Scottish homes, lacked stoves, while 43 per cent lacked fixed baths (47 per cent in cities), compared to 37 per cent in England and Wales.[19]

This made housing construction one of the most important indicators of change to the lives of the Scottish people. In this regard, housing was widely regarded as the greatest priority for social action in Scotland; it was seen as the key to social change without which low wages, poor health, adverse family conditions, drunkenness and other social problems would not be conducive to significant improvement. The result of this was the strength of state-subsidised house building in Scotland. In 1911, 98.2 per cent of Glasgow homes were rented, the vast majority from private land-lords, and, with perhaps a slightly lower figure for other major towns and cities, this was probably reflective of the general state of home tenures in Scotland.[20] In England and Wales, the rental culture in housing was trans-formed almost equally by state-subsidised and private-sector housing, but in Scotland it was the former which bore the brunt of change from the early 1920s to the early 1970s. By 1975–6, local authorities and new-town cor-porations (but excluding the Scottish Special Housing Association (SSHA)) accounted for 59 per of Scottish households (compared to 34 per cent of Britain as a whole, and a low of 26 per cent in the south-east of England outside of London); home ownership was low – 29 per cent in Scotland, compared with 50 per cent in Britain as a whole, and 53 per cent in the south-east. One stark division at that time was in the take-up of mortgages: only 13 per cent of households in Scotland compared to 28 per cent in the whole of Britain. But things changed again with the home-ownership revolution instigated by the 'right-to-buy' policy from 1979 by Margaret Thatcher's Conservative government. By 1999/2000, home ownership had risen in Scotland to 62 per cent (of which 38 per cent of households were buying with a mortgage or similar), while rental from the local authority or Scottish Homes (the successor to the SSHA) had fallen to 26 per cent. In both the 1970s and 2000, one sector to have contracted markedly since the start of the century was that of the private landlord, accounting for 7 per cent of households in 1975–6 and 5 per cent of households in 1999/2000.[21] With new homes came improved conditions. Whether council houses or privately bought, the new houses erected from the 1920s were characteristi-cally three- or four-bedroomed, with internal kitchens, dining rooms and bathroom/WCs.

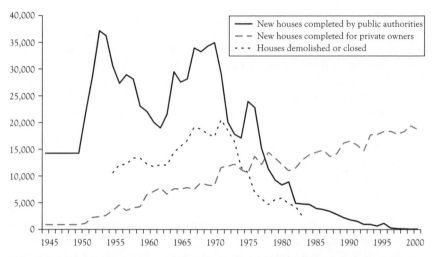

Figure 1.12 Housing construction and slum clearance in Scotland, 1945–2000.

Notes: (a) The construction figures refer to permanent homes completed in a given year. The figures include SSHA and Scottish Homes, but exclude housing association and co-operative homes (which numbered 2,264 in 1991, and 4,894 in 2000). (b) The number for each year of 1945–50 expresses the average for that period. (c) The number of housing completions for a given year could be subject to repeated correction in the years following publication of the first figure. The last (that is, final corrected) figure has been used.
Sources: *Housing Statistics* n. 1 (1966), pp. 1, 29; n. 17 (1970), p. 46; 4th quarter, 1972, p. 22; 4th quarter 1979, pp. 23, 42; 1st quarter, 1975, p. 41; March 1984, p. 4; *Housing and Construction Statistics*, March 1982, p. 5; March 1988, p. 4; March 1991, p. 4; *Scottish Housing Statistics* 1983, p. 10; *Statistical Bulletin Housing Series*, January 2000, p. 4; March 2002, p. 4.

The brunt of housing improvement for working-class Scots, and also for many middle-class Scots, came from council houses. Figure 1.12 shows the change in the housing industry in Scotland in the second half of the century. Between 1945 and 2000, 1.43 million new homes were completed in Scotland, of which 61 per cent (874,069 houses) were built by the state and 39 per cent (557,002 houses) by the private sector. It was in the thirty years after the Second World War that the state sector dominated, with local authorities (and to a lesser degree SSHA/Scottish Homes) constructing the vast majority of houses. In its peak year, 1953, the state completed 37,155 houses, and though this number dropped during the later 1950s and early 1960s, there was a later surge of state activity with a second peak of 34,947 houses completed in 1970.[22]

By 1980–1, 83 per cent of Scottish households had a washing machine, and by 1998–9 93 per cent. In the eighteen years between those dates, impressive rises occurred in ownership of dishwashers (from 3 per cent to 22 per cent), and deep freeze/freezers (from 39 to 89 per cent). Home computers were first measured in 1985–6 at 13 per cent of households, and by 1998–9 at 27 per cent. By 1998–9, 26 per cent of households had a satellite dish, 67 per cent a CD player, 78 per cent a microwave, 85 per cent a video – nearly all of these appearing as significant items in the Scottish household in the last fifteen years of the century.[23] Affluence came as a surge late in the century of domestic improvement in scale, fabric and kitting-out of the Scottish home.

CONSUMPTION AND SPARE TIME

With improvements in the structure, size and contents of the Scottish home, there were still areas where the quality of everyday life remained stubbornly behind other parts of Britain and Europe. One was in food intake, with long-standing criticism of a lack of fresh fruit and vegetables and excessive sugary foods. The National Food Survey of 1992 showed that the Scottish divergence continued. Table 1.8 indicates that though Scots drank fewer alcoholic drinks than England (though more than Wales), they consumed significantly more confectionery and soft drinks. Surprisingly, though, Scots ate on average more fruit but significantly less vegetables, fish and fresh meat than in other parts of Great Britain.

How Scots spent their spare time varied enormously during the century. Community forms of leisure had varied fortunes. The cinema rose to be a most important part of the leisure of many adults and children, though especially women. Figure 1.13 shows the rise and fall of cinema admissions, from an estimated 135.5 million in 1933 to a peak of 240.3 million admissions in 1946, to then decline over a very long period to 83.7 million in 1959, to

Table 1.8 *Consumption of food in Britain, 1992; food consumption per head per day (ounces).*

	Scotland	Wales	England
Cheese	3.83	3.77	4.04
Carcase meat	9.28	9.38	10.11
Other meat and meat products	23.85	24.74	23.40
Fish	4.69	4.86	5.03
Vegetables	68.62	79.62	78.09
Fruit	33.57	29.23	32.96
Bread	27.42	28.41	26.41
Soft drinks	30.72	25.07	24.87
Alcoholic drinks	25.77	24.80	31.70
Confectionery	59.72	43.93	50.52

Source: *National Food Survey* 1992, p. 15.

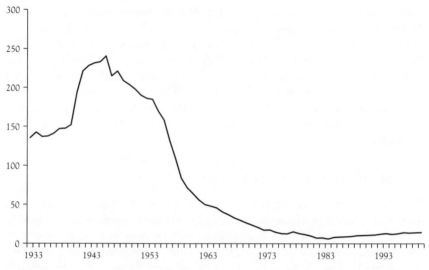

Note: These figures have been computed from the base Great Britain cinema admissions series, collected by the Board of Trade (BoT); separate Scottish figures have not been published. The GB figures have been reduced by applying a moving multiplier, based on known ratios of Scottish/British cinema seats at three fixed points recorded by the BoT (1960 = 14.3%, 1970 = 13.8%, 1979 = 11.6%); to conform to the trends, ratios of 15.0% and 10.0% were attributed to the years 1933 and 2000 respectively, and the gaps between the five points filled by linear extrapolation.
Source: *Annual Statistical Abstract for the UK* n. 98 (1961), pp. 80–1; n. 108 (1971), p. 93; n. 117 (1981), p. 297. *British Film Institute Handbook* 2005.

Figure 1.13 *Estimated Scottish cinema admissions, 1933–2000 (millions).*

73.3 million in 1973, to a low point of 6.1 million in 1984, to revive to 14.3 million in 2000.

Spectator sport rose sharply in popularity in the first thirty years of the century, with world record crowds being set at Hampden Park, while rugby crowds at Inverleith and then Murrayfield reached ground maxima for matches in both sports against England (see Table 1.10). Football club matches also rose sharply in the early decades of the century. Table 1.9 shows the crowds attracted to what became traditional 'derby' matches in Edinburgh, Glasgow and Dundee, indicating the strength of the western city's football allegiances. These were days of immense mass mobilisation of Scottish men. At New Year's Day in 1939, it was estimated that 200,000 people watched football matches in Glasgow, using 200 extra trains, 120 extra trams and 45 extra buses.[24] But in the first fifty years of the century, the numbers drawn to spectate at lower-status events were also huge, and much larger than in the closing decades. These included international matches

Table 1.9 *Football attendances, 1900–50: New Year's Day matches.*

	Celtic v. Rangers	*Hearts v. Hibernian*	*Dundee v. Aberdeen*
1900	31,000 (h)	6–7,000 (h)	
1905		3,000 (h)	
1910	50,000 (h)	10,000 (h)	15,000 (h)
1920	>70,000 (h)	17,000 (h)	18,000 (h)
1925	34,000 (a)	15,000 (a)	10,000 (h)
1931	83,500 (a)	28,000 (a)	
1936	60,000 (h)	16,000 (a)	20,000 (h)
1939	118,730 (a)	44,000 (h)	
1946	50,000 (h)	30,000 (a)	
1950	60,000 (h)	65,000 (a)	

Note: (h) and (a) denotes played at first- and second-named club's ground respectively.
Source: *The Scotsman*, 2 January 1900, 2 January 1905, 3 January 1910, 2 January 1920, 2 January 1925, 2 January 1931, 2 January 1936, 2 January 1939, 2 January 1946, 3 January 1950.

between the Scottish and English Leagues, and the amateur internationals which started in 1928 with what was described as a 'disappointing crowd' of 19,000.[25]

Participation in sport changed significantly during the twentieth century. Before 1950, men's involvement in playing sport was very great; though this is very difficult to quantify, it seems clear that the pressure for provision of playing fields during the 1920s and 1930s represented a very high level of involvement by men of all social classes. But after the Second World War, there were grave concerns in government about the fall in male participation – a fall which went hand-in-hand with a fall in spectating at lower-league football matches. By contrast, the numbers of women participating in sport grew very significantly from a relatively low level in the 1950s – notably in swimming and women's orientated 'keep fit' classes, but increasingly in sports as diverse as golf, athletics and, from the 1970s, football. By the 1990s, in terms of non-commercial leisure, sport took a position beside a range of other activities, as illustrated in Table 1.11.

By the end of a century which witnessed vast improvements in gender equality in most spheres, the home remained stubbornly resistant. In 1998–9, women in Scottish households claimed to do the following tasks 'mostly' themselves: 53 per cent of grocery shopping, 63 per cent of cooking, 64 per cent of cleaning, 77 per cent of washing and ironing, and 64 per cent of childcare, while 'sharing' these tasks was highest for grocery shopping (with 35 per cent of households) and childcare (34 per cent).[26] By 1999, women had the highest television viewing (at an average of 29.5 hours per week compared to men's 27.9), while men listened more to the radio (at 19 hours compared to women's 16.1).[27]

Table 1.10 *Scotland v. England attendances, 1906–50: rugby and football home internationals in Scotland.*

	Rugby	Football
1906	17–18,000	90–100,000
1908	20,000	121,452*
1910		109–111,000
1912	25,000	127,000*
1914	25,000	110–120,000
1921		90–100,000
1923	30,000	80,000
1927	70–80,000	111,214
1929	80,000	110,512
1931	>70,000	129,810
1933	>70,000	134,170**
1935	70–75,000	136,000
1937		149,407
1940		62,000
1941		75,000
1943		105,000
1944		133,000
1945		133,000
1946	60,000	
1948	70,000	
1950	>70,000	

Notes: The rugby matches were played at Inverleith and, from 1925, Murrayfield. The football matches were all played at Hampden Park.

* These figures were challenged in 1925; see *The Scotsman*, 4 April 1925.

** The same edition of *The Scotsman* gave a different attendance of 134,970.

Source: *The Scotsman*, 19 March, 9 April 1906; 23 March 1908, 4 April 1925; 4 April 1910; 18 March 1912, 4 April 1925; 23 March, 6 April 1914; 11 April 1921; 19 March, 16 April 1923; 21 March, 4 April 1927; 18 March, 15 April 1929; 23, 30 March 1931; 20 March, 3 April 1933; 18 March, 8 April 1935; 19 April 1937; 13 May 1940; 5 May 1941; 19 April 1943; 24 April 1944; 16 April 1945; 15 April 1946; 20 March 1948; 20 March 1950.

The backbone of leisure was the consumption of alcohol. Scottish levels of drinking varied by the end of the century from those in England. In 1995, the average Scottish man drank 20.1 units per week compared to 18.3 in England; by contrast, Scottish women drank 6.3 units per week compared to 7.0 units in England. 23 per cent of Scottish men and 8 per cent of women reported themselves as being drunk at least once a week, and 69 and 53 per cent respectively drunk at least once per three months.[28] Alcohol-related deaths were on the rise in the last quarter of the century; in 1979, 641 deaths

Table 1.11 *Leisure activities: usage of facilities within the last week, 1999–2000.*

Library	14.4 per cent
Museums	3.4 per cent
Parks	34.3 per cent
Sports/Leisure	13.6 per cent
Swimming pools	10.5 per cent

Source: Figures calculated from data in the five banded-age 'what we do' tables in SHS at http://www.scotland.gov.uk/Topics/Statistics/16002/shs-search, accessed on 13 November 2008.

were alcohol-related, and in 1993 only 633; but the figure then rose dramatically to 832 in 1995 and to 1,292 in 2000 (and continued to rise to 1,546 in 2006).[29] This rise was accompanied by an increase in the number of liquor licenses in Scotland; between 1980 and 2000, these increased from 13,892 to 17,244, with the biggest increases in numbers of off sales (from 4,899 to 6,368), restaurants (from 921 to 1,476), refreshment (from 34 to 495) and entertainment licenses (from 169 to 828), while the number of public houses rose more modestly (from 4,472 to 5,080).[30]

Finally, newspaper reading by 1999–2000 was dominated by the *Daily Record* (read by 40 per cent of over 15 year olds) followed by the *Sun* (26 per cent), with the quality newspapers being read by very few (*The Herald* 6 per cent, *Scotland on Sunday* 6 per cent and *The Scotsman* 5 per cent).[31]

TRANSPORT

Table 1.12 shows the relative changes in modes of transport in Scotland. While the number of car journeys more than doubled between 1975 and 2000, bus journeys fell by 74 per cent during 1960–2000. Despite fluctuations, the numbers of rail and ferry journeys were about similar at the start and end of the last quarter of the century. But air passenger journeys originating in Scotland grew some fourteen times.

The proportion of households in Scotland without regular use of a car remained surprisingly high until quite late; 49 per cent of households in 1987, falling to 38 per cent in 1996. The percentage of the population with full driving licences stood at 49 per cent in 1985–6, rising to 62 per cent in 1993–6; the number of motor-vehicle kilometres driven in Scotland stood at 18.8 million in 1987, rising to 24.6 million 1998.[32] From 1960 to the end of the century, a continued shift in transport means was evident. Compared to other nations, Scotland had a low level of car ownership; in 1995 it had 372 vehicles per 1,000 population, appearing twenty-second equal (with Northern Ireland) out of twenty-six advanced nations headed by Luxembourg (785), USA (739) and Italy (666), behind England and Wales (453), and ahead of only Ireland (349), Greece (343) and Hungary (259).[33]

Table 1.12   *Transport journeys in Scotland, 1960–2000 (all figures millions).*

	Car	Bus	Rail	Air	Ferry
1960		1,664	65	1.2	
1965		1,417	71	2.3	
1975	9.3*	891	66	4.2	5.28
1985	13.6	671	57	6.9	4.67
1995	20.1	494	58	12.4	6.86
2000	19.9**	436	68	16.8	5.29

Notes:
* = Scottish Office estimate
** = The fall in this figure may be due, according to the Scottish Executive, to local government reorganisation and consequent changes in recording traffic.
Car = Vehicle kilometres on major roads
Bus = Passenger journeys on local services (pre-1975 Scottish Bus Group and four city corporations, and 'may' include Glasgow Trams and Underground)
Rail = Passenger journeys originating in Scotland
Air = Terminal passengers at Scottish airports
Ferry = Passengers on CalMac, P&O Orkney & Shetland, and Orkney Ferries
Sources: Scottish Transport Statistics no. 17, 1997, Historical Series Table 1; ibid., No. 21 2002, Table H1.

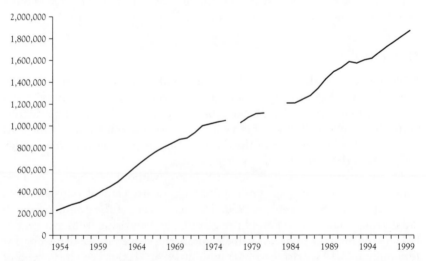

Note: The system of car licensing was conducted by local authorities until 1977, when the DVLA took over. A gap in counting occurred at the point of takeover.
Source: Abstract of Regional Statistics no. 1 (1965), no. 5 (1969), no. 7 (1971), nos 11–16 (1975–82), no. 18 (1983), no. 22 (1987), no. 30 (1995), no. 32 (1997), no. 36 (2001).

Figure 1.14   *Cars with licences in Scotland, 1954–2000.*

Scotland was slower than other parts of the UK in developing car ownership. In Figure 1.14, the inexorable rise of cars on the road is clear, but with
periods of accelerated growth in the mid-1960s and late 1980s. In 1981, 49
per cent of Scots households owned no car, compared to 39 per cent in the
UK as a whole; by 1999, the figures were 34 per cent for Scotland but only
28 per cent for the UK.[34]

CRIME AND POLICING

The twentieth century witnessed telling variations in criminal convictions.
Figure 1.15 shows that the level of convictions in all Scottish courts changed
considerably from year-to-year, but that they were generally declining from
1908 to 1934 (with a low point in 1918 of 49,567 convictions), followed by
a general rise from 1935 to the peak year 1980 (with 243,302 convictions),
after which the numbers of convictions fell to the end of the century.
Within these general trends, there were short-term movements. Both world
wars of 1914–18 and 1939–45 instigated significant falls in convictions,

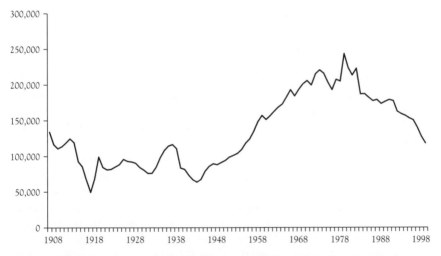

Notes: (a) This series on indictable offences was only published in *Statistical
Abstract* from 1908. Prior to this, numbers of 'criminal offenders convicted' were
given (ranging from 1,835 in 1900 to 2,012 in 1907). (b) In respect of the figure for
indictable offences in 1938, there is an unexplained correction in later editions
(from 14,779 to 15,639); the second figure has been used here.
Sources: *Annual Statistical Abstract for the U.K.*, no. 63 (1917), pp. 412–13; no. 73
(1930), pp. 76–7; no. 83 (1940), pp. 116–17; no. 87 (1951), p. 67; no. 88 (1952), pp.
68–9; no. 98 (1961), pp. 70–1; no. 108 (1971), pp. 80–3; no. 117 (1981), pp. 114–15;
no. 127 (1991), p. 85; n. 139 (2003), p. 177.

Figure 1.15   *Convictions in Scottish courts, 1908–2000.*

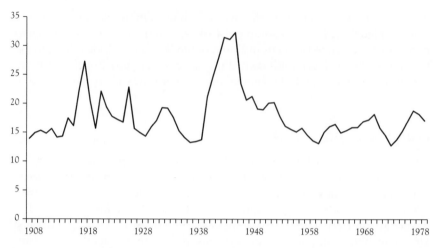

Source: See Figure 1.14.

Figure 1.16   *Indictable offences as percentage of all offences, Scotland, 1908–79.*

while post-war years showed significant surges, and, in the case of the early 1920s, a sustained rise to one peak in convictions in 1926 (at 95,776). But during 1934 to 1939 there was a continuous surge in convictions, evident in the graph with a peak figure of 116,415 in 1938. By comparison to the early part of the century, the middle decades demonstrated much less move‑ment, with a steep and unremitting climb from 1945 until 1980, around which there was considerable fluctuation, before a decline set in for the last eighteen years.

Such a graph is not a clear indication of trends in crime as such. Rather, the graph indicates shifts in both crime *and* policing-cum-prosecution poli‑cies. This view is strengthened by comparing the data with the balance in the proportion of successful prosecutions between indictable offence (more serious crimes) and non-indictable offences (less serious offences). Figure 1.16 indicates that the proportion of indictable offences varied markedly during the century, being especially volatile between 1915 and 1952. At its lowpoint in 1937, indictable offences made up only 13.3 per cent of the total, compared to the highpoint in 1945 of 35.3 per cent. Surges in indictable com‑pared to non-indictable offences seemed to occur during two different types of period: during wartime, and during years of economic or industrial down‑turn. Thus, the peak years were 1918 (27.3 per cent), 1921 (22.1), 1926 (22.8), 1932 (19.3), 1945 (32.3), 1970 (18.2) and 1977 (18.8). It is important to note that the changing proportion of serious to lesser offences was often due to a marked decline in the latter. In the First World War, non-indictable offences fell from 106,942 in 1913 to 36,049 in 1918, while indictable offences were much less changed (at 17,618 and 13,518 respectively). In the Second World

War, indictable offences rose markedly (from 15,227 in 1939 to 21,816 in 1945), while non-indictable offences fell (from 95,492 to 45,701 over the same years). This would seem to indicate that minor offences, though more likely the legal system's pursuit of them, declined during war, while serious offences were more energetically brought before the courts. In 1926, uniquely in the century, there was a massive 47 per cent rise in indictable offences (rising from 14,841 the year before to 21,874, to fall back to 14,585 the following year); one conjectures if this was associated with the miners' and general strikes of that year. From 1959, there begins a steady rise in convictions of both crimes and offences to peaks in 1978 and 1974 respectively.

Within the rise and then the fall in the figures for indictable convictions, there is evidence that Scotland was becoming a more violent society as the century progressed. Homicides recorded by the police rose significantly, mostly between the late 1950s and 1980s, and then very sharply in the later 1980s and 1990s; they stood at around 60 in 1925, falling to 35 in 1950, and rising to 84 in 1985 and to 137 in 1995.[35] Yet, crimes remained dominated by non-indictable offences. By 2000–1, there were 418,494 crimes recorded by the police in Scotland, of which 14,812 were crimes of violence (non-sexual), 5,727 were sexual offences, 253,295 were crimes of dishonesty, and 85,781 were crimes of vandalism and fire-raising.[36]

Despite falling numbers of prosecutions, the prison population of Scotland rose across the century. In 1900–10, it stood around 2,800, and then fell from 1920 to 1950 to under 1,800 in most years. But by 1960 it had risen to over 2,700 and then surged to 4,900 by 1970, at which level it stayed until the late 1990s when it rose again to 5,900 in 2000.[37] Against a background of only modest rise in population, and decline in convictions from 1980 onwards, the prison population doubled in a century. Other forms of punishment diminished; between 1938 and 1964, forty-four people were executed in Scotland, with nine being hanged in 1950 alone.[38]

Far from being an experience solely for a tiny minority, everyday life was for many Scots one of disturbance, anti-social behaviour and crime. In 1999–2000, 7.8 per cent of Scottish households reported noisy neighbours and/or loud parties as very or fairly common, with the proportion rising to 14.4 per cent of those living in social rented houses.[39] People drinking or using drugs was reported as very or fairly common by 23.5 per cent of households, with the figure rising to 34.6 per cent of those in social rented houses; but even among those owning their houses outright, the figure was 12.2 per cent.[40]

Notes

1. For the English evidence, see H. Cook, *The Long Sexual Revolution: English Women, Sex and Contraception 1800–1975* (Oxford, 2004).
2. Men and women: a statistical profile, Chart 2.3, at http://www.scotland.gov.uk/stats/mnw-04.asp#23

3. Table 7.4, http://www.gro-scotland.gov.uk/statistics/publications-and-data/vital-events/vital-events-reference-tables-2005/section-7-marriages.html#table7-6

4. http://www.gro-scotland.gov.uk/statistics/publications-and-data/vital-events/vital-events-reference-tables-2005/section-7-marriages.html#table7-6

5. C. G. Brown, *Religion and Society in Twentieth Century Britain* (Harlow, 2006), p. 281.

6. C. G. Brown, *The Social History of Religion in Scotland since 1730* (London, 1987), p. 73.

7. http://www.scrol.gov.uk/scrol/warehouse/NewWards_ER_N.jsp, Table Cast 07, accessed 28 January 2009.

8. http://www.scrol.gov.uk/scrol/warehouse/NewWards_ER_N.jsp, Table S203, accessed 28 January 2009.

9. Calculated from data in *Catholic Directory Scotland*, 1997 and 2004.

10. A. McIvor, 'Gender apartheid? Women in Scottish society', in T. M. Devine and R. J. Finlay (eds), *Scotland in the Twentieth Century* (Edinburgh, 1996), pp. 197–201.

11. The lowpoints were 1949 (24.6%) and 1950 (24.9%).

12. *Registrar General (Scotland), Annual Report* 1970, p. 360.

13. Ibid., p. 86.

14. *Registrar General (Scotland), Annual Report*, 1980, p. 112.

15. Figures from Scottish Household Survey, http://www.scotland.gov.uk/Topics/Statistics/16002/shs-search, accessed 13 November 2008.

16. Data calculated from figures in *General Household Survey* 1976, p. 149.

17. J. Butt, 'Working class housing in the Scottish cities 1900–1950', in G. Gordon and B. Dicks (eds), *Scottish Urban History* (Aberdeen, 1983), p. 248.

18. C. G. Brown, 'Urbanisation and social conditions', in R. Pope (ed.), *Atlas of British Social and Economic History* (London, 1989), pp. 176–8.

19. Ibid., pp. 178–9.

20. N. Morgan, 'Property-ownership in Victorian and Edwardian Glasgow', End of Grant Report, ESRC Grant D00232126 (1988), p. 16.

21. *General Household Survey* 1976, p. 125; *Scottish Executive: Scotland's People: Scottish Household Survey*, 1999–2000, p. 35.

22. Sources as per Figure 1.12.

23. 2001 Scottish Social Statistics, Table 10.12. http://www.scotland.gov.uk/stats/sss/docs/sss10-05.asp, accessed 13 November 2008.

24. *The Scotsman*, 3 January 1939.

25. Ibid., 30 April 1928.

26. 2001 Scottish Social Statistics, Table 10.13. http://www.scotland.gov.uk/stats/sss/docs/sss10-05.asp, accessed 13 November 2008.

27. 2001 Scottish Social Statistics, Table 10.14. http://www.scotland.gov.uk/stats/sss/docs/sss10-05.asp, accessed 13 November 2008.

28. *Scottish Health Survey 1995: Alcohol Consumption*, at http://www.archive.official-documents.co.uk/document/scottish/shealth/shch5.htm, summary and Table 5.14.

29. http://www.gro-scotland.gov.uk/statistics/deaths/alcohol-related-deaths/index.html, Table 1.

30. *Scottish Executive Statistical Bulletin, Criminal Justice Series*, May 2002, p. 9.
31. 2001 Scottish Social Statistics, Table 10.17. http://www.scotland.gov.uk/stats/sss/docs/sss10-05.asp, accessed 13 November 2008.
32. Data from *Scottish Transport Statistics* no. 17 1997, Tables 1.14, 1.13, 6.1 respectively.
33. Travel Choices for Scotland: White Paper 1998, http://www.archive.official-documents.co.uk/document/cm40/4010/4010.htm, Table 5.
34. *Abstract of Regional Statistics* no. 26 (1991), p. 107. These data for Scotland seem to conflict with the data recorded by *Scottish Transport Statistics* cited above.
35. *Scottish Executive Statistical Bulletin, Criminal Justice Series*, Nov. 2001, chart on p. 1 and Table 1, p. 17. Police-recorded figures for homicides bore no similarity at all to medically recorded homicides. The latter stood at 19 in 1900, 1925 and 1940, rising to 80 in 1980 and then leaping to 301 in 1990 and 316 in 1995; for the latter data, see *Registrar General (Scotland), Annual Reports*, 1900, 1910, 1915, 1920, 1925, 1930, 1935, 1940, 1945, 1950, 1955, 1960, 1965, 1970, 1975, 1980, 1985, 1990, 1995.
36. Data from *Recorded Crime in Scotland 2004/5*, Table 1.
37. *Scottish Executive Statistical Bulletin, Criminal Justice Series*, November 2001, pp. 1, 24.
38. *Statistical Abstract of the United Kingdom* no. 88 (1952), p. 68; no. 98 (1961), p. 70; no. 108 (1971), p. 82.
39. Figures calculated from data at Scottish Household Survey (SHS), http://www.scotland.gov.uk/Topics/Statistics/16002/shs-search, accessed 13 November 2008.
40. Figures calculated from SHS data at http://www.scotland.gov.uk/Topics/Statistics/16002/shs-search, accessed 13 November 2008.

Chapter 2

From Scullery to Conservatory: Everyday Life in the Scottish Home

Lynn Abrams and Linda Fleming

INTRODUCTION

The home is synonymous with the everyday. It symbolises and encompasses those activities which are deemed banal, monotonous, repetitive, even trivial, so much so that its intrinsic value as a measure of social life is regularly overlooked. Yet, home as a concept is imbued with layers of symbolic meaning that on the surface of things have appeared constant: home is about a sense of identity, it is about family and belonging, and whether we like it or not, it demonstrates status. Evaluation of the period since the First World War actually reveals an apparent transformation that has occurred in both the material reality of the Scottish home and in ideas about what home signifies in imaginative terms to Scots. In material terms, at the start of our period, the majority of Scottish households were thought of as being considerably disadvantaged within poorly maintained houses and at the mercy of heartless landlords and housing factors. In 1914, around 90 per cent of Scottish homes were rented. By the end of the twentieth century, an unprecedented number of Scots – 63 per cent – were homeowners.[1]

Despite such dramatic change, some continuity of what Scots desired of their homes was also notable. Here material ambitions operated side by side with ideals about what was important in everyday home life and one has acted as a barometer of the other. The design, size and location of dwellings, and the spatial environment within and around these, influence both aspiration and experience. For example, in 1900 the desire for a separate scullery, which today might be seen as particularly unglamorous, actually reflected high ambitions for greater cleanliness, comfort and decorum in the Scottish home, separating the work of the house from the rest of family life. The hidden nature of the scullery allowed greater public display of home comforts devoid of the accoutrements of hard labour. By the 1990s, the conservatory played a similar role in symbolising the very open attainment of consumerist comforts in a new space which has no fixed function but which is resolutely separate from the work of the house. Thus, Scottish housing can be employed to convey the nature of daily life in the home and the place of the home in everyday life.[2] At the start of the century, the home for most families was a place for work and sleep; by the end, it was primarily a space for leisure though it never stopped being a workplace for some. Consequently, the home needs to be taken seriously as a historical nexus for changes and continuity in the texture of everyday Scottish life, whether at its most banal or most transformative.

In an analysis of the home, class inequalities, gender difference and ethnic cultures are writ large. Increased varieties in housing and more widespread aspirations to home ownership neither created nor reflected a more classless society in twentieth-century Scotland. While acknowledging the extent of material impoverishment in working-class housing, some perhaps equally important components of the Scottish home – notably the middle-class suburbs and the new towns – have been largely ignored by historians. Moreover, the home is a gendered space; indeed, the association that began in the nineteenth century between home and the so-called unproductive private sphere firmly gendered this space as female.[3] Home increasingly symbolised domesticity, family, a haven from work, and a place of both physical and moral regeneration facilitated by the woman of the house. This nineteenth-century concept of home not only survived into the twentieth century, it was further refined and strengthened despite the experiences of two world wars. Indeed, the twentieth-century home was an area where changes in gender relations may be keenly observed through everyday behaviour. One other notable influence on the everyday was the arrival of immigrants. Newcomers to Scottish society had to adapt to the existing styles of Scottish homes while transplanting reminders of other homes from as far apart as the Baltic and the Punjab. In fact immigrant homes, more than most, give a clear indication of how any 'home' is more than just bricks and mortar but is also an imaginative terrain, influenced both by the culture surrounding it and individual family traditions that are brought to it. Across these differences, Scots have displayed through the variety of their homes, hopes and aspirations, or indeed the lack of these; and the backdrop to all of this is of course the inescapability of twentieth-century consumption.

This chapter will approach the history of the Scottish home by using a framework that will include all of these factors, as well as the material and imaginative landscapes of the home. It will focus especially on three areas that encompass both apparently banal realities and lofty aspirations, namely: the spatial arrangement of urban Scottish homes, the work of the home, and lastly, the home improvement and 'ideal home' movements as they impacted in Scotland. Throughout we will try to interrogate the notion that homes in twentieth-century Scotland have been about more than just property and tell us quite a lot about what has been meaningful at the level of everyday life.

THE HEART OF THE HOME? PRIVACY AND SPACE

Twentieth-century Scotland was predominantly urban, with two-thirds of the population living in towns of over 5,000 by 1951 and 21 per cent of these residing in Glasgow.[4] Furthermore, by this same date, fully a quarter of the population continued to reside in one- or two-roomed dwellings.[5] Somewhat unsurprisingly then, the issue that has singularly characterised Scottish home-life has been overcrowding and the consequent lack of either space or privacy for the majority of the population within congested towns and cities. The notorious 'single-end' – a one-roomed apartment in which more than a quarter of Glasgow families lived in 1901 – became a synonym for all that was worst about Scottish urban living. In 1911, almost three-quarters of the Scottish population lived in houses with three rooms or fewer. And a measure of how much this was a singular characteristic of Scottish life can be seen when this residential pattern is contrasted with England and Wales, where 74 per cent of the population had four or more rooms.[6]

Table 2.1   *Total housing stock by rooms (%).*

	England & Wales	Scotland
1 Room	3.2%	12.8%
2 Rooms	8.3%	40.4%

Source: T. Begg, *50 Special Years: A Study in Scottish Housing* (1987), p. 7.

This pattern was pernicious, for despite a rash of official measures, the cramped and reputedly unhygienic conditions of Scottish working-class life were still in evidence well into the twentieth century. In 1961, following a massive building programme and a reduction in the number of one- and two-roomed dwellings by 18 per cent, still 31 per cent of Scottish households had fewer rooms than persons.[7] At the start of the twentieth century, urban tenement homes frequently contained not only a family, but also lodgers; for the most unfortunate it could also be the site of sweated home labour. In comparison, even the modest three-roomed cottage flat that was a frequent example of inter-war social housing, was palatial, and represented a substantial lifestyle change for the better for a lucky few. However, despite municipal efforts, the Second World War fractured the story of twentieth-century progress in this area of Scottish life.

Low and irregular wages meant that many families never knew better than life in one room and expected this standard of accommodation as their lot in life. On the eve of the First World War, the major urban centres of Aberdeen, Dundee and Edinburgh faced similar problems to Glasgow of a huge scale of overcrowding, an existing stock of houses that were too small and, despite regular outcries, only piecemeal measures to address the problems. It was the official response to this intractable crisis after the war that has coloured much of the housing landscape of urban Scotland, not to mention the aspirations of Scots with regard to owning their own homes. Following the report of a Royal Commission in 1917–18, government and municipal intervention became the order of the day.[8] In Scotland in particular, it was felt that the era of the private landlord should be brought to a speedy end and replaced with social housing of an improved standard. It has been argued that this cemented an 'ingrained tenant culture'.[9] This assertion is important when the nature of Scots' expectations with regard to their homes is considered, because an image emerges of many sections of the population as having little or no choice about their housing and consequently limited ambitions for either space or privacy. This image needs further investigation.

The central space that looms large in analysis of overcrowding is ironically the room romantically conceived as intrinsic to the nurturance of family life – the kitchen. This means we must juxtapose the undoubted squalor of single-end living alongside rather more rosy images of the family tackling their mince and tatties around the kitchen table. The place of the kitchen as the heart of the average Scottish home has been reconceived several times in the twentieth century. At the start of the century, the average tenement kitchen associated with the urban working classes could have been the prototype in miniature for the open-plan living so beloved of many sections of the urban middle classes by the end of this period. Both examples favour the kitchen as having multiple functions. Whether in the Glasgow Gorbals or Edinburgh's Tollcross district, life in one room formed the horizons of many urban Scots, and that room was the kitchen.[10]

The conception of what a kitchen was for in Scottish homes is therefore of interest since this room often encompassed all aspects of everyday life. Among the many evils catalogued by those who lobbied for housing reform in Scotland, was the persistence of one- and two-roomed houses that had been erected as such, or made down from larger apartments built in the nineteenth century. Typical inhabitants of the single-end home used their multifunctional kitchen for its usual purposes of cooking and eating, but they also worked, washed, talked, played, argued, conceived children, gave birth, slept and probably died there. The tenement kitchen was all life rolled into one room and represented competing impressions. It was an intolerable burden in terms of its lack of privacy, not to mention the hard work of keeping it tolerably hygienic. Conversely, it conveys an image of working-class family life that was closer and more integrated than that enjoyed in the social housing which succeeded slum clearance.

In tenement life there is much to condemn, but there are also less clear-cut aspects of this lifestyle which raise questions about any wholesale censure. From the point of view of women, the tenement seems to have been both friend and foe. The maintenance of overcrowded tenement homes involved backbreaking, monotonous labour that was mostly the responsibility of women, day in, day out. On the other hand, the support network operated by women in such working-class communities could offset domestic drudgery. Fundamental aspects of everyday life such as the weekly wash were often undertaken communally in Scottish towns and cities. This and the opportunity for stair-head gossiping and shared childcare are elements of the everyday that have been conceived of as positive by gender historians who regard opportunities for female networking as the basis for a female consciousness and, in some cases, political action.[11] With so little space in the interior of homes, everyday life often spilled over into the street. Memories of urban homes often conjure up childhoods spent out of doors where now-extinct street games were played.[12] And for women who were often tied to their homes by the routines of cooking and the care of infants, the Scottish habit of 'windaehinging', where women talked to one another from the vantage points of open tenement windows by leaning on the ledges with their head outside, was a particular way of coping with the strain of containment.[13] On the other hand, women accused of spending too much time windaehinging invited local condemnation for neglecting their domestic duties – a salutary reminder that the community spirit in everyday life came at a price in terms of privacy.

For men, it is commonplace to portray the public house or workingmen's club as an escape from the overcrowding and female-centred home life, whether through intoxication or the companionship of their own sex. The sheer numbers of public houses and licensed clubs in most inner areas of Scottish towns and cities during this period is testimony to the importance of their place as alternative to family life and a home-from-home for working-class men. Yet, the home could also be a space wherein men could regenerate and partake in family activities. Although the stereotype of the working-class husband and father positions him as marginal to home-life in the early decades of the twentieth century, and working conditions for men meant they spent little time there, it is also clear that the home offered an opportunity for men to play a different role. As the daughter of a Glasgow tram conductor who was born in 1906 recalled, 'He helped look after me a lot. I was an awful favourite with him – I was! There was nobody like my Daddy.'[14]

Such overcrowding and the means taken by the working classes themselves to make a life despite this, gave rise to concerns among social observers about the impossibility of any kind of home and family life as the middle classes experienced it. Insufficient ventilation, poor lighting and inadequate food storage and preparation facilities militated against an ordered domesticity. The shared nature of facilities for most personal functions and the sharing of beds within dwellings caused concern for the health and moral well-being of the residents. Yet good or bad, the colourful and memorable aspects of slum life are sometimes difficult to disentangle from either official commentary that blamed the ills of urban life on slum dwellers themselves, or from under a patina of rosy reminiscences found in much personal testimony. As one example, Ralph Glasser's memoirs of life in the Gorbals were a very deliberate attempt to circumvent both of these trends.[15] Glasser depicts squalor vividly, but still shows that it is quite wrong to assume that a home could not exist in such conditions.

People's conceptions of home, then, did not always meet with universal approval. The rhetoric of racism has often invoked the very different styles of immigrant home-life. Criticisms of Irish and Jewish migrants to Scotland at the beginning of the century regularly focused upon their apparent inability or unwillingness to conform to ideals of Scottish respectable domesticity. The Irish were accused of 'intemperance and improvidence' in the conduct of their everyday lives which contradict supposedly Protestant values such as thrift and cleanliness.[16] Jews equally met condemnation for bringing neighbourhoods into disrepute by their inclination to work on Sundays and alleged disinclination to clean common stairs and dispose of refuse.[17] In turn, immigrants often experienced difficulties in obtaining tenancies outside of specific ethnic enclaves that were generally concentrated in run-down localities, thereby compounding problems of racial antagonism. When West Indian migrants arrived in English cities in the 1960s, their family life was described as 'domestic barbarism'. Their tendency to live in large groups and their cultural preferences for different foods, music and leisure activities appeared to contrast the cultural home-life of the 'respectable' English who preferred privacy and quiet.[18] Asian migrants to Glasgow experienced similar prejudice, as Bashir Mann recalled:

> For example, in the Fifties and Sixties, your neighbours used to be very racist. Your Scottish neighbours I mean. If we were cooking and your windows were open your doors would be banged 'close the bloody window, we can't stand this terrible smell of your cooking', you know. Some people got some records from India and Pakistan and if they played records 'Put it off, this bloody bad music you are playing' and things like that. But the funny thing is that the main objection of having a Pakistani or Asian neighbour at that time, to the Scottish people was that smell of their cooking we have to live with and now that smell has become so popular.[19]

However, in some respects immigrants to Scotland found much that was familiar in home-life. For example, in one study conducted slightly before the First World War in Glasgow, an Italian couple who had only one infant child, complained that their two-room home above their chip shop was too big for them! Previously they had lodged in two rooms with another family of seven and this had been preferable.[20] Clearly this style of overcrowding was not only the province of Scots. Indeed, tenement living in Scotland has often been compared to the continental apartment model of housing which differentiates it from most of the rest of the UK. When making comparisons with England, for example, negative commentary on Scottish housing was often concentrated on the notion that 'an uncontrolled system of tenements' invariably led to overcrowding.[21]

Patrick Geddes, innovatory thinker on town planning and housing, criticised the tenement and the conditions found there, advocating the organic
regeneration of cities. More influential though were the ideas of Ebenezer
Howard, father of the garden city movement. In Scotland, this model was
somewhat anachronistic to tenement traditions and initial attempts at it
were either small-scale or short-lived. At Westerton garden suburb in
Dunbartonshire, for example, a 1910 initiative of Sir John Stirling Maxwell
resulted in eighty-four terraced cottages to rent.[22] This planned community
outside of Glasgow survived only into the 1930s, when further suburban
encroachment from private development swallowed up the model community. More successful was the use of the garden city concept for the building
at Rosyth in 1915 of homes for construction workers on the dockyard and
naval base.[23] However, this initiative to build dream homes for a fortunate
few who could afford higher rents lacked sustainability. When Glasgow
council embarked upon the building of council houses in the inter-war years,
around half took the form of tenements and only one-fifth conformed to the
cottage style of the garden city ideal; even then most of these were flatted,
that is divided into four houses in two-storey semi-detached buildings.[24]
This trend was in large part determined by the tension between the massive
need for new housing and the lack of available land and finances to provide
substantial improvements in terms of density and privacy. No doubt also it
was felt that this standard of home-life was neither deserved by the average
slum dweller nor was it something from which he or she would be likely
to benefit. Such variety as existed in urban homes was an extension and
continuation of the belief about a deserving and undeserving poor – for the
latter, tenements would do.

There is evidence, however, that council-built tenements, though much
an improvement on the inner-city version, were no answer to the concerns of
the middle classes nor the aspirations of the working classes. Many families
resented the rules and regulations of this new social housing. These proper-
ties had lower rents than the private sector lets, but were also subject to rig-
orous regulation by the council. Tenements had resident caretakers and were
haunted by the fearsome figures of the 'green ladies', representatives of the
local medical officers for health.[25] The level of intrusiveness by officialdom
into the everyday lives of families was too much for many. In the 1920s, over
20 per cent of Glasgow's Calton district refused to be rehoused out of their
slum dwellings, and a further 10 per cent returned to their slum after having
been rehoused.[26] Such examples demonstrate that home is more than just
property and an indoor toilet could not compensate for other less material
aspects of human dignity and privacy.

During the inter-war years, perhaps as a response to the emergence of
slightly less homogeneity in Scottish houses, attitudes to the tenement did
begin to change among the middle and working classes. The climate of ideas
at this time about women's domestic roles and about family life doubtless

influenced this. Popular literature of the inter-war years promoted very specific gendered roles in respect of home-life, and the dwelling house, which
permitted privacy and a domesticated lifestyle, was seen as a prime factor in
encouraging respectable family life. According to Daunton, 'the emergence
of the private, encapsulated dwelling was a physical demonstration of the
social value attached to the conjugal family and domestic life.'[27]

The ideals of the garden suburb movement appealed to the aspirational
section of the working-class and many lower middle-class families; rather
than wait on the beneficence of city councils, suburbs made up of owner-
occupied and privately let housing provided this group with what they
wanted. Some house builders went so far as to target council-built garden
schemes with leaflet drops advertising the benefits of home ownership,
reputedly with some success.[28] There were very specific amenities desired
in the inter-war suburbs, which can be seen in different urban localities
throughout Scotland. By and large the kitchen now became a site of labour
and not a gathering place for the family – it was renamed the scullery or
kitchenette – and separate dining areas and living rooms provided more
space and at least the illusion of more privacy. In fact, house builders in the
inter-war years like McTaggart and Mickel who designed and built a large
proportion of both municipal and private housing in Glasgow, used a series
of standard designs but described them as 'equally distinctive' to appeal to
aspiring home-owners. Suburban homes now had gardens and these became
one of the ways of making quite uniform housing unique to its owners.

Despite the interruption of the war, the die had been cast in terms of
expectations in Scotland. In 1959 it was claimed that most Scots now wanted
their own street-fronted door.[29] Again though, economy in land costs and
building expenses largely prevented the majority from getting this. High-
rise buildings (1958–70), further suburbanisation, the building of peripheral
estates to the cities such as Drumchapel and Easterhouse in Glasgow and
Wester Hailes and Niddrie in Edinburgh, and the innovation of new towns
(East Kilbride, Cumbernauld, Livingston, Glenrothes and Irvine) were all
employed as solutions in the twenty years following the Second World
War. Tenements were resurrected but designed to minimise population
congestion by being at most three storeys high with two flats to each floor
and were a solution of sorts for the continued problems of homelessness and
overcrowding, which in Scotland was as bad as can be imagined for many
families in the post-war era. Squatting in slums that had survived both inter-
war clearances and wartime bombs became the only alternative to homelessness for many. And the pre-war problem of sub-letting to lodgers with
consequent overcrowding increased yet again.[30] For many Scots, the single-
end was actually a dream too far and home was made in a succession of sub-
lets called 'digs' where tenancy was far from assured. There is no doubt that
over this period many Scots had their hopes raised with regard to the kind
of home they needed and wanted, and had them just as rapidly squashed.

In this climate, local authorities were often forced to pay lip service to the people's hopes and not only the resurrection of tenements ensued. Many Scots entered the era of high-rise living in order that more homes could be provided quickly within limited space.

The uncertainty that the inter-war and post-war housing shortage created had different outcomes, which were dependent on class, gender and ethnicity. For example, during the inter-war years the majority of Scotland's Jewish community managed to relocate from their ethnic enclave in the notorious Gorbals district of Glasgow to the certainly more salubrious suburbs outside the city boundaries, such as Giffnock and Newton Mearns. Those who were too poor, too old or too tied to what had represented security, found themselves trapped in this slum which further deteriorated during and after the war. At the annual general meeting of a large Jewish charity in Glasgow, the condition of many Gorbals families was remarked upon as 'abject misery', with overcrowding, a lack of beds and bedding, and what was alluded to delicately as 'other surrounding circumstances' forming the case for 'an immediate remedy whatever the capital outlay'.[31] The allusion is of course to sanitary conditions and in slums across Scotland the absence of a lavatory or standing bath was still a major feature of everyday life even while the rest of the country 'never had it so good'. In 1961, 13 per cent of non-shared households in Scotland still lacked a private water closet.[32] As one historian has commented, in Scotland the 'queue at the housing department allocation desk became in the late 1940s, the main manifestation of the New Jerusalem.'[33] For the Jews concerned, help did come from Jewish charity, since rehousing by the local authority would have taken them far away from areas of Jewish culture to the new peripheral housing estates such as Castlemilk, which catered for the relocation of slum dwellers. This is a salutary reminder that 'home' is a sentiment that is difficult to pin down. It may mean aspects of wider community and culture beyond nuclear households, but it can also be contained in one room if that place has a degree of permanence and provides emotional security.

It was not only Jews who balked at the prospect of being moved to new peripheral 'schemes'; many inner-city dwellers did too. Not only this, the new towns and designated overspill areas handpicked their prospective tenants from skilled workers and those of good reputation in a reinvention of the garden city philosophy. It has been commented that the new town planning doctrine was 'bound up with a passionate, evangelising belief in the moral, social and visual rightness of the pre-industrial-revolution village, and the evil of the city.'[34] Slum dwellers were seen as unlikely to fit within these new utopias. In any case, as we have seen, in this intensely urban nation many Scots saw the city as their proper home, and some planners supported this with the ambition of maintaining the populations and therefore economies of inner cities. The answer to this was the high-rise flat and there were more than 200 tower blocks containing almost 21,000 flats in Glasgow alone by 1971.[35] A measure of the effect that this move had on everyday life can be seen in the fact that Scotland's very first television soap opera was set in a tower block. *High Living*, an ironic title underpinned by a very Scottish cynicism, was made by Scottish Television and ran from 1968 to 1972 before, like its setting, it eventually disappointed the expectations of the Scottish public. Life in a high-rise was particularly hard on women. In the post-war baby boom, raising a family in a tower block was far from ideal. The buildings were often poorly insulated for noise and dampness rapidly developed, making the homes hard to keep clean. Furthermore, many women became isolated in tower blocks despite their hundreds of near neighbours. 'I never go out' reported one high-rise dweller who had moved to Crescent Court in Clydebank from a prefab. 'We know who the neighbours are but we never see them.'[36] The relief of overcrowding through post-war planning cannot be overlooked, yet many high-rise houses soon failed their tenants, and often became spectacularly unloved homes considered by many Scots as blots on the landscape. Indeed, at the time of writing, a programme of refurbishment for existing social housing in Scotland has entailed the wholesale demolition of many high-rise buildings.

Further social changes that affected everyday home life, for example family size and work practices, also need to be considered. In terms of gender relations, the high-quality social housing of new towns and suburban locations provided a reminder of the social distance many women had travelled from the slums their mothers had to cope with. A better home arguably gave such women 'a certain pleasure from the fulfilment of material goals' and not necessarily the neuroses so often associated with the supposed isolation and ennui of suburban life.[37] Where class is concerned, patterns of owner occupation and the consequences of residential segregation sometimes had different outcomes in Scottish cities. For example, by the 1970s Edinburgh had a residential pattern that was in some ways little changed from a century before. Outlying schemes of social housing have meant that many of the capital's problems are little seen by tourists and high amenity housing is still nearer the centre. In Glasgow, by contrast, the retention of social housing in the inner city is more marked, which is not to say that the notorious schemes associated with Glasgow are any less isolated. Somehow though, they have maintained more of a profile, even if for the wrong reasons. The problems of living in peripheral schemes, which had few of the amenities of everyday life to which their residents were accustomed, such as public transport links, shops and leisure facilities, were evident from early on, as were the class antagonisms they created. In 1959 it was reported that the 'teenage toughs' newly settled in Glasgow's Drumchapel scheme had nothing better to do with their time than invade the private gardens of the nearby and very douce suburb of Bearsden, 'generally leaving the place as though an atom bomb just burst there!'[38] Clearly young people had a need to get away from their new dream homes sometimes, but there was precious little to do in this rather bleak, hilly and isolated location. By the 1960s, part of everyday life in owner-occupied suburbs was the ease of travel and increased privacy afforded by the private motorcar. This was not yet so for the working classes who were often given more space in terms of their housing, but confined to a locality that provided precious little other comforts and trapped them miles away from the dreadful delights they had left behind. Even by the early 1980s, car ownership in Scottish peripheral estates was only between 10 and 15 per cent, making dependence on public transport for work and leisure very much a part of everyday life for significant numbers.[39]

Throughout the twentieth century, owner occupation was generally more popular in the East than in the West of Scotland, a situation thrown into sharp relief when government policy in the late 1970s began encouraging the sale of social housing. Despite the fact that part of the propaganda of this move was to give more choice to ordinary people about how and where they lived, the motives of Scots who bought their council houses appear to have taken little cognisance of this. Council house purchase was a financial decision for most Scots, and one that was sometimes made with a heavy heart: 'I originally thought that council housing was not meant for resale. I thought it was wrong. [But] she [my wife] put a logical argument forward and I had to concede.'[40]

Between April 1979 and December 1983 nearly 49,000 public sector houses were sold to their tenants, the most popular being houses in new towns.[41] And despite many fundamental objections, it was noted at the time that buyers often made cosmetic changes to their houses almost immediately after purchase, as a means of advertising to the world their new status but also perhaps their personal investment in their own home.[42]

We must assume that over the course of the twentieth century, Scots did know what they wanted in a home; a large part of this must have been contained in ideas of what that space should hold. Yet it is difficult to know with any certainty whether people exercised any control over this or simply accepted what they were given. It does seem clear that the garden-city model was not what the majority desired. The renovation of nineteenth-century tenements from the 1970s onwards, and the continued popularity of these with families of all types, seemed to point to the fact that the urban landscape was still preferred by many and the tenement home compares favourably with new builds.

Scotland's population is, after all, largely urban and unlike in England there has been little evidence of nostalgia for the rural idyll. Indeed, for much of the century Scots have increasingly made their home in towns and cities, abandoning the less fertile and more remote rural regions. The decline was most marked in the crofting counties where, as James Hunter argues, since the Second World War expectations of higher living and educational standards resulted in quite dramatic depopulation, resulting in an imbalance in the age structure of the population favouring the elderly.[43] In the last decade of the century, however, the attractions of rural life and the possibilities of making a home there improved as better communications (especially the arrival of broadband internet), greater prosperity, especially among retirees, and a nascent desire for more sustainable living made rural Scotland a viable proposition. Thus, between 1991 and 2001 Glasgow, Dundee and Inverclyde recorded population decreases while Moray, Perth and Kinross, the Scottish Borders and Highland saw their populations increase.[44] However, within the Highlands and Islands more generally, some dramatic differences are evident, contrasting the serious depopulation of the Western Isles in the last decade of the century (declines of between 10 and 30 per cent) with the rapid growth of the city of Inverness.[45] The 'but and ben' so closely associated with the Scottish Highland home was replaced by the eco house and the 'Barratt' home.

KEEPING A CLEAN HOUSE: GENDER AND STATUS IN THE SCOTTISH HOME

Day-to-day life in the home was shaped by the structural and material circumstances in which people lived. It has been mooted that within the Scottish home, by the mid-twentieth century, a 'distinctive, traditional sexual division of labour existed'.[46] This section will therefore examine the different relationship that Scottish men and women had with the home, and if any diversity in experience supports the view of a particularly rigid set of gender distinctions within Scottish life. It will do so by looking at how work was managed in the variety of new homes that emerged over this period. The amount of space, the organisation of that space and the facilities available within the home all particularly impacted upon women's experience of housework and home-making. Moreover, alongside the gender dimensions of housework, the work actually performed differed considerably according to social class.

At least since the early nineteenth century, the discursive and increasingly material separation of home and work has positioned the home as a complementary but secondary space. Since the home is synonymous with the domestic, which in turn is associated with the private sphere, the assumption developed that everyday life in the home was singularly the responsibility of women. Men either reaped the bounties of this, or suffered the consequences of poor domestic management. This gender arrangement was more or less ubiquitous in industrialised countries, but of course impacted differently at the level of the everyday, according to local customs. For example, public discourse in Scotland at the turn of the century had this to say about the relationship between everyday habit and home-life:

> . . . it was further stated that persons of vicious and immoral habits were usually
> associated with dirty and filthy houses, and that their chief vice was that of

excessive drinking . . . Families in receipt of an income capable of maintaining them in comfort were found to be living under indescribably sordid conditions . . .[47]

The preference of Scottish men for escaping from life's travails through drink was deemed the originator of many problems in working-class homes. Nevertheless, it was believed that the ignorance and indifference of women throughout working-class communities in respect of 'house management and domestic economy' compounded the situation and significantly contributed to 'discomfort, ill-health, expenditure in excess of income, and poverty'.[48] For middle-class observers, though men's conduct left much to be desired, only a woman could truly make a home. Thus, the ill-kempt home virtually forced men to take refuge in the public house. If poverty was the fault of the male breadwinner, this did not necessarily absolve the housewife whose skills contributed in an essential way to the well-being and morality of working men. Underlying this concept was the notion that 'housework' was women's work whether performed by the housewife herself or by female servants; real productive work took place away from the home in those industrial and commercial environments that have become emblematic of Scottish masculinity – in everything from the Clyde shipyards to the Edinburgh banks.

For working-class women, possibly more than those of the middle classes, the ability to keep a clean house was not only a private duty, it was also frequently a measure of public worth. Indeed, evidence of a dirty house could be hidden neither from neighbours in overcrowded areas nor, as we have seen, from the prying eyes of officialdom. Life in one room demanded intense and repetitive labour, yet many women rose to the challenge with skill and energy – a fact that was sometimes recognised publicly. In the late 1940s, the Lord Provost of Glasgow in a public speech remarked that on visits to inner-city houses in Gorbals, Cowcaddens and Bridgeton he had witnessed spotless homes: 'Glasgow folk, the great majority of them, are house proud and they keep clean happy homes.' This was despite, as he further commented, 'the difficulties with which these housewives have to contend . . .'[49] On the other hand, the demoralisation of poverty, overcrowding and slum conditions also took its toll:

> Poverty, drink and indifference were at once suggested by the appearance of the first house visited. The tenant said he was a dock labourer. Near the fireplace, on an old couch lay his wife in her ragged workaday clothes; three dirty children were asleep on the bare floor, without covering of any kind. The muscular unkempt father sat on an old soap box blinking with tipsy satisfaction at a jug of stale beer. He was fluent regarding his hardship. 'Only three days' work this week and maybe less next . . . we're starving.[50]

In some instances, no amount of female ingenuity could combat conditions and making a home was a battle fought against the odds for many women. It was homes such as these which were meant to be addressed by inter-war housing reforms, and it was in this period that home-making was raised to the level of both art and science, a situation that presented women with new challenges. Built into new public housing in Scotland were facilities aimed at making housework easier and more effective; while in the new suburban areas that were created for owner-occupation or private let, the science of housewifery was given full reign. In both of these housing models the Scottish tradition of undifferentiated living space was abolished; out went the large kitchen, in came the living room, separate bedroom and the reinvented 'kitchenette', this being a more refined expression of a scullery. Such housing design articulated the tasks expected of women within the family.[51] Cooking, cleaning and child rearing were supposed to be easier and indeed some manuals produced on housework claimed that it could be a health-giving activity: '[S]crubbing is a good example, as it gives an opportunity for the worker to exercise the deep muscles of the back.'[52] The performance of women in keeping a clean house also set new standards of respectability. In the middle-class home the parlour had to be in a state of constant readiness for guests, and in the new inter-war housing 'schemes' the entire house might be examined by municipal inspectors at any time.[53] However desirable these new domestic spaces were, it is doubtful whether they made housework less of a task. With the benefit of hindsight, it is clear that there is no cause-and-effect relation between the mechanisation of homes and changes in the volume and nature of household work.[54] The washing of laundry provides a good example of this conundrum.

Where working-class life is concerned, washday has become the leit-motif of women's experience of everyday in the tenement. Perhaps as a concession to the general grime of urban life, the washing of clothes and linen represented a weekly ritual of cleansing in which both body and soul were involved. The Scottish fascination with the 'steamie' – an institution emblematic of Scottish urban life – has resulted in the prevalence of a dis-course about female solidarity and community networking in the tenement. In her tenement building in Stirling, which housed sixteen families, one woman explained the system:

> You had the washday on the Monday, a fortnight on the Wednesday, and three weeks on the Monday . . . but two or three people went in everyday and it was a happy land they called it, 'the big happy land' and everybody, not like now, everybody helped everybody else.[55]

Clothes washing, whether at the communal steamie or in the backcourt, was extremely heavy work and in fact few women romanticised the task itself. Indeed, there was little choice involved in this collective ritual, for doing a wash in the multi-purpose living space of the single end would have been impossible. Unsurprisingly, in oral histories the move to a home with integral washing facilities was invariably recalled with relief. This woman described how washday has continuously meant a day of hard labour for women:

> I think there was double sinks and she [mother] washed in one of the sinks. I don't think there was a boiler or anything . . . how young people would cope nowadays I don't know . . . you would rub the washing – you soaked it first all night, then you rubbed it on a washing board. Even when I got married [1930s] I had that to do. And then you boiled it, the things that were boilable. The other things you washed in Lux . . . and then you had blue in your water for rinsing your whites and then a lot of the whites had to be starched, so it was a very big job. It was a complete day's work, the washing day.[56]

In a survey completed in the 1940s, communal wash-houses appear to be an aspect of everyday life Scottish people were keen to lose; only a little over 1 per cent of more than 1,500 respondents wanted a communal wash-house in preference to facilities in individual homes.[57] In working-class tenements the clothes-line of immaculately laundered articles in the communal back-court was a public beacon of domestic competence and a woman who was absent from the steamie on her allocated day would set tongues wagging. The nostalgia associated with communal washdays needs to be considered along-side such evidence. Nevertheless, it was not until the 1940s that Glasgow Corporation considered a gas-fitted wash boiler to be an essential item in all council houses.[58] And it was only when she moved to a council house in the 1950s that this woman had a gas boiler and a large garden, and as she said, '. . . the washing was very easy compared to what it had been . . .'[59]

Among the supposedly labour-saving devices of Glasgow's post-war housing schemes, facilities for washing were a great attraction for the new tenants. In eulogising terms one woman summarised such progress: 'For me I was going to have a kitchenette with a BOILER. I don't need to go to the Steamie or down the backcourt wash-house. I also had a bit at the back to hang out clothes. A dream come true.'[60] Although new technology in the form of electric washing machines had appeared on the British market from the 1920s, for most families the new machines were far too expensive and for the majority inappropriate – electricity was not commonplace in urban Scottish homes until the 1930s. In fact, the earliest twin-tub so-called automatic machines still required constant attention and manual labour to operate.[61] Available evidence from personal testimony suggests that washing machines powered by electricity had little impact on this regular chore in Scotland until at least the 1960s.[62]

For middle-class women laundry might be sent out. The relatively small sculleries of inter-war suburban homes and the 'servant problem' of the time rather dictated this. Even in more affluent tenement homes, doing laundry was truly a private activity; washing was either sent out of the home alto-gether or expedited in the privacy of the kitchen. One memoir of inter-war life in genteel, suburban Glasgow recalls that not only the washing of laundry created work, drying articles in rainy Scotland was also a mammoth task. To enable this to be private, the Scottish habit of having a pulley (an arrangement of poles suspended from the ceiling) made drying possible within the home, but it was inconvenient and far from decorous:

> . . . it hung there day and night like a bleeding sword of Damocles. Mother put out newspaper to catch the drips, which made things even worse as we lived in a ceaseless suspension of carbolic and moisture and the slow rat-tat of water on paper.[63]

Taking in the washing of better-off households was a service that was in demand and was one way that working-class women could earn some money without compromising their own respectability by 'going out' to work, and this remained the case in the inter-war years. In suburban housing, whether privately owned or in the new council estates, heavy laundry such as bedding that would have been difficult to manage in a kitchenette, could be sent out. Certainly, commercial laundries were a common feature of Scottish suburban areas and these proliferated until the Second World War.[64] Laundry was a domestic tyranny that permeated the everyday and women were quite prepared to ameliorate this through financial transactions. But the actual domestic environment also influenced behaviour. The high level of attention to domestic conveniences facilitating this was in fact a selling point for new suburban homes, which were marketed as a more socially gracious alternative to the tenement. One 1937 advertisement for villas at Silverknowes in Edinburgh asked, 'Why do Scottish women put up with such bad kitchens?' These homes were said to address 'the servant problem' of the time by simplifying domestic organisation via an 'oblong' kitchenette wherein cooking and storage arrangements were on one side and washing facilities on the other.[65] These suburban houses may actually have increased the amount of housework required of women because housework became individualised and further privatised in contrast with the communal labour more common in shared tenements.[66]

As the twentieth century progressed, the double burden of domestic and paid employment did little to ease many women's ambivalence about facilitating a never-ending supply of clean laundry. Cheaper and more available clothing, and ever-higher standards of cleanliness, made washing a daily task rather than a weekly chore. To this extent, laundry was still labour intensive despite the availability of domestic technology. Since the 1980s, the design of Scottish homes changed again in response to the modern, everyday laundry crisis by building in small 'utility' areas, which replaced the scullery as the site of this task. Yet again, a necessary domestic chore was reinforced in building design as a private task divorced from other areas of everyday life in the home. It remains to be seen, however, whether this synthesis between architecture and domestic work reflects a new gendering of this task.

Throughout the inter-war years and into the 1950s there was no questioning of the home-making role of women, although the material spaces in which they were exhorted to do this were designed by men. On the one occasion when women did have an input into the design of new housing, in the form of the Women's Housing Sub-Committee of the Ministry of Reconstruction in 1918, they concerned themselves particularly with the reduction of the burden of domestic labour, advocating not only improved facilities but also co-operative housekeeping. However, the experience of many Scottish women in sharing domestic labour in the context of tenement living made them reject communality and yearn for improved standards in the privacy of their own home.[67]

Part of the rhetoric of inter-war home-making was that men indulged their home-centredness in the utility areas of the home formed by the garden, often specifically in vegetable growing, and in the tool shed. According to Giles, 'the interior of the home was woman's place, one in which . . . she was increasingly encouraged to exercise her skills of creative homemaking', whereas the garden was seen as the domain of men.[68] The provision of gardens in the new inter-war council schemes was a deliberate attempt to provide working men with a leisure activity when they returned home from work, though gardens feature less frequently in Scottish housing developments owing to the land costs which encouraged high-density housing rather than the garden-suburb model favoured south of the border. Allotments were the solution in more urban areas and around 20,000 allotments were in use in Scotland on the eve of the Second World War.[69] The attempt to wean men away from more traditional male leisure pursuits, which were seen by middle-class reformers as the scourge of Scottish domestic life, seems to have worked in these areas. A 1930s report on preferences for suburban living included the observation that 'a number of wives spoke of improvement in their husbands' habits and sense of domestic responsibility. Gardening, bowls at the local clubs, odd jobs about the house and so on were said to have displaced the public house for relaxation.'[70] It was among the middle-class suburban dwellers though, that gardening really took off as a leisure pursuit evidenced by the popularity of garden and horticultural shows, open gardens, items on gardening in the newspapers and increasing use of landscape garden designers. In 1934, the *Scotsman* reported on the 'widespread development of gardening and the happiness and beauty which gardening brings into people's lives'.[71] By 1940 the woman's section of the paper was recommending the use of the garden as an additional room in the summer months where 'Meals may be taken either on the terrace, in the loggia, or in a shady corner of the lawn.'[72] In Stirling, the wife of a minister commented on her first manse in 1947: 'it had a big garden and fortunate that my husband was very keen in the garden and always had a very delightful arrangement of flowers and some vegetables and worked hard in it.'[73]

This vision of a domestic division of labour is of course a world apart from many, if not most, Scots. For women the everyday experience of housework was of monotonous, often backbreaking labour, in two- or at most three-apartment homes. The possibility of labour-saving devices was probably not even considered by the majority of women, but it should be noted that there was awareness of such innovations. After the Second World War, in a rash of fervent, socially responsible planning for the post-war world, over 1,500 Scottish women and men were asked what appliances they wanted as 'standard' for future homes. Among these, the commonest suggestions were for well-known devices such as electric sockets, electric irons and vacuum cleaners, but perhaps surprisingly other common desires were for showers and telephones. Moreover, over 90 per cent wanted a refrigerator, which was still a luxury item even in affluent Scottish homes.[74] The 1948 report produced from this survey essentially formed a wish list of aspirations which were seldom, if ever, met in full within new social housing, but it is notable that there was majority approval for making housework easier and absolutely no cognisance given to the notion that this would be done by anyone other than a woman. Alongside the reforms brought about by the new welfare state, the arrangements for homes were gendered to suit housewives and the functions of the home separated into a living unit and a working unit. There was no doubt in the minds of the report writers that the housewife would spend most 'of her working day' in these two 'units' or rooms and they should therefore be planned to serve the convenience of such women. The answer recommended to make women's lives easier was to install a 'serving-hatch' to minimise the amount of movement for the housewife.[75] In an effort to be properly appreciative of women's work, however, the committee did firmly come down in favour of separate utility rooms for washing. There was only one dissenting voice against this proposal; Bailie Jean Mann of Glasgow Corporation stated that, 'the average housewife has to keep an eye on the cooking, and watch the children in the living room, answer the door, etc., while she washes. The utility room removes her further . . . and in my opinion makes the task more irritating.'[76] Clearly, in the minds of planners, no amount of labour-saving devices, new housing measures and post-war scientific progress were set to unchain the appropriately irritated Scottish housewife from her proper place in the kitchen!

In his study of everyday life in the modern world, Henri Lefebvre comments on women's relationship to the everyday:

> Everyday life weighs heaviest on women . . . Some are bogged down by its peculiar cloying substance, others escape into make-believe, close their eyes to the surroundings, to the bog into which they are sinking and simply ignore it . . . Because of their ambiguous position in everyday life – which is specifically part of everyday life and modernity – they are incapable of understanding it.[77]

For Lefebvre and others, women's everyday lives are characterised by deadening routine and their existence within the private world that is beyond historical time. By the 1970s, this was a characterisation already familiar to American readers of Betty Friedan, whose description of the 'problem that has no name' expressed the dissatisfaction of middle-class women in the post-war American suburbs.[78] This reading of the beginnings of second-wave feminism has subsequently come to dominate our understanding of women's poverty of experience in the modern home. Yet, the world of the home and of the domestic sphere did not continue time out of mind in the twentieth century. By then it was thoroughly part of the world of science, progress and commerce; women understood very well the weight of the everyday on their shoulders, and the possibilities there were for shaping their situation. The role and identity of housewife illustrated women's consciousness of both the value and the burden of everyday life as it was experienced through domestic labour. Scottish women, like their sisters in most of the western world, can be seen to have made an emotional and creative investment in domestic work. They were encouraged to do so by modern marketing techniques, which set out in this period to invent the ideal home and reinvent the housewife as a brisk, domestic engineer. The following section will examine how this impacted specifically within Scotland.

IDEAL HOMES

The allure of the ideal home is intimately bound up with the twentieth-century identity of the household as a site of consumption. More lately, the different relationships that men and women have had with this development have become of interest. By mid-century, the association between home and women was as strong as it had ever been, although the idealised role of the productive housewife had evolved in favour of consumption rather than production. In the words of sociologist Mark Abrams in 1959, the housewife's role was as purchaser of commodities that would create the modern home, a place that is 'warm, comfortable and able to provide its own fireside entertainment'.[79] Whether this notion of the classless female consumer-come-homemaker was a concept easily applied to Scotland is a question open to debate and will be examined in the following discussion. In this section, we will focus on two types of housing experience, the high-rise flat and the new town, in order to explore how particular models of ideal homes have influenced the experiences of people who have to live in them.

Over the course of the century, home-making and housework began to be separated in public discourse – at least for the more affluent classes. This process allowed men more of a stake in the work of the home, albeit in demarcated areas, and had particular repercussions for the lifestyles of women. It was concluded that a woman could not create the ideal home if she were engaged all her waking hours in manual labour that caused mental stress and physical exhaustion. Just as across Europe a notion of 'idealised domesticity' was propagated in the wake of fears concerning a crisis of the family, in Scotland too women were urged to grasp the opportunities offered by labour-saving devices, scientific invention and rational planning. It was believed that these innovations would relieve the monotony of housework by middle-class women suffering from the shortage of servants, and even ease the drudgery endured by working-class women coping with inadequate housing. Advertising for new homes exhorted women not to feel guilty or selfish about this aim but to spend 'more time in the open air and less time bending over an oven'.[80]

Beginning after the First World War, the Ideal Home Exhibitions held every year in Glasgow and Edinburgh catered to the more affluent housewife. In 1922, for instance:

> The stands showed how to furnish a house artistically, economically, and substantially; how to equip the home with labour-saving appliances; how to light the home; how to heat the rooms; how to decorate the windows; how to cover the floors; how to cook by gas and electricity; how to get the last atom of caloric value out of a wall fire; and how to do all the domestic work of the house with the minimum of effort. Practically every exhibit stood for economy – economy of time, of space, of personal labour; and, compared with the cost of old-fashioned methods, economy in the expense involved. Money spent in eliminating domestic drudgery was an investment, not an expense. The ideal home was the healthy home, and all contrivances for reducing labour had a salutary effect on the health of the family.

Sir Robert Cranston, who opened the exhibition, was 'quite sure that this exhibition would not only appeal to the practical minds of all housewives, but would also be of great benefit to them, as well as to the city.'[81] In an era when tuberculosis was a significant problem in Scotland, the health-giving benefits of such apparently rational truths about the home encouraged large middle-class audiences for exhibitions over successive years in both Glasgow and Edinburgh. Reporting on the London Ideal Home exhibition in 1929, *The Scotsman*'s reporter told the newspaper's readers of the work of the National Institute of Industrial Psychology, which was to 'carry into the home the methods employed by the Institute in factory and office for the most economical use of effort and the best design of appliances and arrangement of working space.'[82] Suburban homes that came equipped with easy-to-clean, fully tiled kitchenettes and bathrooms had definite appeal and Scots were receptive to the message.

The home-improvement movement inevitably influenced those Scots who escaped the congestion of slums during the inter-war years and even more forcefully in the post-war era. For tenants of local authorities, however, there were limits on what could be done to change either the exterior or interior of the average four-in-a-block cottage. Information on the interiors of working-class homes is fragmentary but we do know that material items were just as important to working-class tenants as they were to middle-class home-owners. When Mrs H1 married in 1928 in Stirling, she and her husband moved into a rented house in the town. She recalled in detail the efforts she made to make their first house a home. In addition to pieces of Templeton's carpet bought before they were married when Mrs H1 was working in the carpet factory:

> we had that and there was lino on the floor when we got that wee place and there were a bed. But it was only a rented place but the bed was . . . it was brass and iron, nice and of course I did it all up. I bought lacy curtains, and I put it on each end, made it nice you know and bought the bedding and chairs and table and sideboard that was complete and a wee wireless. It was quite nice and tidy and his mother gave me a leather chair . . . and I got one the same . . . so that was two leather arm chairs, the table and four chairs stuck in and the sideboard and your carpet . . . that was all and it was nice.[83]

This woman's pride in making her first home 'nice' reflected a much more widespread interest in home furnishings and interior.

However, it was not really until after the Second World War that architects and designers paid attention to house interiors. In 1944, *The Scotsman* remarked that women had little choice in the situation of their homes but:

> there is no reason why she should not have as good an interior as the builders can provide. For years she has been crying out for this, that, and the next labour-saving or comfort-providing device, and except in a few lucky instances she has been put off on the ground of expense or pure conservatism. Now, it would seem, is the time to make herself heard, while architects, town planners, and the makers of interior fittings are in a mood to listen to her. The cupboard units between rooms, shelves in the sitting room, and providing a wardrobe for the bedroom, with a supply of drawers in both rooms, will be welcome. So will that kitchen unit comprising, in a neat row, cooker, cupboards, sink, and refrigerator. To have a refrigerator has hitherto been the unattained height of many a woman's kitchen ambition.[84]

To meet these new expectations were furniture makers and retailers such as Wylie & Lochhead who, with their flagship stores on Glasgow's Buchanan Street and Edinburgh's Shandwick Place, as well as their regular appearance at the Glasgow International Exhibition, offered the affluent real choices as to how to furnish their interiors.

For the masses though, the high rises, unveiled with great fanfare in the 1960s, were seen as the answer to Scotland's housing problems. In 1961, the brochure commemorating the opening of Wimpey's 'Royston A' development in Glasgow, consisting of three twenty-storey blocks, extolled the modern design features of the new homes. 'Each flat has a private balcony and each block contains two lifts and refuse chutes.' All the flats had under-floor heating, radiators, hot water and mechanically ventilated bathrooms.[85] In the first few years, residents were broadly satisfied with their new homes. A 1967 survey of high-flat living in Clydebank revealed residents liked their modern apartments, particularly citing the internal facilities and the views as

Figure 2.1   *A family moving into new high flats in Leith, 1969. www.scran.ac.uk*

advantages of living in these tenements in the sky. Women especially appreciated the ease of cleaning. 'I love my home' was said to be a typical response of new tenants, albeit this view was coloured by the length of tenancy and the appalling housing conditions experienced by many in their previous homes.[86]

But the list of dislikes – which was fairly subdued at this stage – presaged the familiar complaints that were to bedevil the high-rise experiment: unreliable lifts, absence of clothes-washing and drying facilities, the wind noise, lack of amenities for children, poor provision of shops and the social isolation.[87] Many women and the elderly became isolated in tower blocks. A 66-year-old retired man missed the 'neighbourliness and inter-visiting' he had been used to in his previous home and particularly commented on the difficulties he experienced taking his dog for a walk – he lived on the eleventh floor and he feared the lifts breaking down. One 65-year-old housewife who lived on the twelfth floor of a Clydebank high rise appreciated the good design and comfort of her flat but admitted she was very lonely. She reported on the archetypal sign of isolation: 'one woman lay dead on this landing and it was only when [she] was being buried that we knew.'[88] Few women could drive and as one woman with two young children noted, 'I couldn't do any travelling with them as I couldn't manage the babies on and off buses.' For her the loneliness in Castlemilk was unbearable.

> I discovered that meeting people in a multi-storey block is not easy. Each house is rather like a warm, comfortable, isolated cell . . . I used to go out to the chute room . . . to empty the rubbish in the hope of seeing some other living soul but invariably there was just no-one . . . I felt like a prisoner, tied to my children.[89]

If the high-rise flats did not conform to many people's idea of the ideal home, the houses in the new towns perhaps came closer and East Kilbride south of Glasgow was originally planned along garden-city lines containing as many cottage-style dwellings as possible. More than 8,000 applications were received for the first tranche of houses to be built, indicating the intense interest in this experiment and the almost universal desire for a traditional house with a garden and a back door.[90] Yet by the mid-1950s, housing density here was dramatically increased to house the increasing numbers moving from Glasgow. By 1971 flats accounted for 42 per cent of all accommodation in the town, including a significant number of high-rise blocks, a pattern more akin to that in Cumbernauld which was planned on urban, high-density principles.[91] One of the consequences of the high-density approach in the first phase of Cumbernauld was lack of privacy. Residents complained the houses were so close together that 'people are looking into your house whichever way you turn'.[92] Clearly, privacy was a key element of the ideal home. People would put up with unconventional design and unorthodox planning but were unwilling to compromise on this hard-won ideal. On the other hand, as early surveys indicated, the home in these new towns became the focus of people's lives, in part because of the absence of other amenities, at least in the early years. This focus on home-life was borne out by ownership of consumer goods which was markedly higher than average in the 1960s. In East Kilbride, for instance, 96 per cent of residents owned a television set and 67 per cent a washing machine compared with 81 and 43 per cent respectively in Britain as a whole.[93]

The demand among tenants in the new towns to buy their homes under council house purchase arrangements after 1979 is testament to the success of these homes in stark contrast to the low take-up rate in the peripheral housing schemes dominated by flats. And in 2001 home ownership in East Kilbride – at 74 per cent – was significantly higher than the Scottish average of 63 per cent and markedly more so than the Glasgow figure of 50 per cent.[94]

CONCLUSIONS

Over the course of the twentieth century the idea of home has remained more or less constant in Scots' imaginations. The home has symbolised and provided privacy, security, comfort and a setting for family life, and for most Scots the home was the centre of their lives. It was the locus for all the everyday activities of the most banal kind: eating, sleeping, caring, sex, housework and leisure. What changed was the physical structure of the home. The major transformation in housing stock in urban Scotland produced for most, more space, comfort and cleanliness. But the material changes in terms of structure and ownership suggest a significant shift away from the home as a place of refuge, to the home as a place of consumption and display. The ideal home exhibitions have symbolised this shift by offering up to consumers of the home new or alternative ideals, whether that be in terms of the organisation of internal space, the ownership of labour-saving gadgets or the gendered division of labour.

Change was not only manifested in structural and material improvements but also in terms of family size and structure, and the patterns of work and leisure prevalent at the end of the century. Yet, gender and class operated hand-in-hand to create everyday reality that fell well short of ideal for many. The quest of families in some of the peripheral housing schemes to create clean, happy, safe homes was probably no less arduous at the end of the century than in the Victorian slums. At the end of the century though, for the more fortunate, the separate scullery no longer symbolised changes in people's experience and expectations of home; this role was arguably taken on by the conservatory. This flexible and aspirational living space signals material consumption that has come within the grasp of quite modest homes. It represents a quest for the ideal home in accordance with contemporary models and thus it represents continuity, for it is symbolic of what has always been the case. And yet the conservatory marks a change in one notable sense; it provides a bridge between outside and inside, public and private, male and female, thus symbolising the greater fluidity of gender roles within the modern home. Home is not only bricks and mortar; it is a hugely potent expression of how material reality interacts with our ideal needs and longings at the level of the everyday while also reflecting gender roles and the spaces associated with these.

At first sight the Scottish home changed dramatically during the course

of the twentieth century, both influencing and reflecting wider structural and
material changes in society which in turn affected people's everyday experiences of home life. Crowded, insanitary and rented homes gave way to more
spacious, hygienic and warm spaces with two-thirds owner occupied; homes
which were once places containing the whole gamut of human experience
became predominantly spaces for leisure and home entertainment (with
the exception of housework and home improvement and a degree of home-
working). On the other hand, the home continued to figure prominently in
everyday experience, perhaps particularly in the lives of women who continued to carry the burden of household chores and childcare. Arguably,
despite the rise in personal autonomy and levels of consumption expressed
in car ownership, access to commercial entertainment and leisure facilities,
and the decline in family size, the home remained the fulcrum of identity for
most Scots.

Notes

1. Scottish Census Results online (SCROL) www.scrol.gov.uk: Table CAS049.
2. R. Rodger, 'Crisis and Confrontation', in R. Rodger (ed.), *Scottish Housing in the Twentieth Century* (Leicester, 1989), p. 27.
3. See J. Giles, *The Parlour and the Suburb: Domestic Identities, Modernity, Class and Gender* (Oxford, 2004), and Giles, *Women, Identity and Private Life in Britain, 1900–1950* (Basingstoke, 1995).
4. T. C. Smout *A Century of the Scottish People, 1830–1950* (London, 1987), p. 32.
5. J. Butt, 'Working-class housing in the Scottish cities 1900–1950', in G. Gordon and B. Dick (eds), *Scottish Urban History* (Aberdeen, 1983), p. 234.
6. Tom Begg, *50 Special Years: A Study in Scottish Housing* (London, 1987), p. 7.
7. *Census for Scotland* 1961 (HMSO, Edinburgh), p. xxii and Table XXV.
8. *Report of the Royal Commission on the Housing of the Industrial Population of Scotland, Rural and Urban* (Edinburgh, 1918). See discussion of Report in Begg, *50 Special Years*, pp. 5–9.
9. Miles Horsey, *Tenements and Towers: Glasgow Working-Class Housing 1890–1990* (Edinburgh, 1990), p. 11.
10. *Census for Scotland*, 1921, p. 81. In 1921 in the city of Glasgow, for example, 18 per cent of all dwellings were single rooms, with the highest figure recorded in Glasgow parish at 22 per cent.
11. James Smyth, 'Rent, peace, votes: working-class women and political activity in the First World War', in E. Breitenbach and E. Gordon (eds), *Out of Bounds: Women in Scottish Society 1800–1945* (Edinburgh, 1992), pp. 174–96; T. Kaplan, 'Female consciousness and collective action: the case of Barcelona, 1910–18', in *Signs* 7 (1982), pp. 545–66.
12. Sean Damer, *From Moorepark to 'Wine Alley': the Rise and Fall of a Glasgow Housing Scheme* (Edinburgh, 1989), pp. 132–3.
13. Damer, *From Moorepark*, p. 134.

14. Stirling Women's Oral History Project (Smith Art Gallery and Museum, Stirling), Mrs N2 (1906). Lynn Abrams, '"There was nobody like my Daddy": fathers, the family and the marginalisation of men in modern Scotland', *Scottish Historical Review* LXXVIII:2 (1999), pp. 219–42.

15. Ralph Glasser, *Growing up in the Gorbals* (London, 1986).

16. 'Report of the Committee on Overtures re Irish Immigration', in *Annual Reports to the General Assembly of the Church of Scotland* (Glasgow, 1934), p. 358.

17. *Minutes of Evidence taken before Glasgow Municipal Commission on the Housing of the Poor*, vol. 1 (Glasgow, 1904), sections: 7401, 7441–3 and 7592.

18. Wendy Webster, *Imagining Home: Gender, 'Race' and National Identity, 1945–64* (London, 1998), p. 45.

19. Strathclyde Oral History Centre Archive (SOHCA): History of University of Strathclyde oral history project, interview with Bashir Mann, 12 May 2003.

20. Dorothy E. Lindsay, *Report upon the Diet of the Labouring Classes in the City of Glasgow* (Glasgow, 1913), p. 25.

21. G. W. Clark, *The Housing of the Working Classes of Scotland* (Glasgow, 1930), p. 8.

22. M. Whitelaw, *A Garden Suburb for Glasgow: The Story of Westerton* (1992).

23. Begg, *50 Special Years*, pp. 43–9.

24. Smout, *Century of the Scottish People*, p. 55.

25. Horsey, *Tenements and Towers*, p. 20.

26. Ibid.

27. M. Daunton, *House and Home in the Victorian City: Working-Class Housing 1850–1914* (London, 1983), p. 37.

28. Miles Glendinning and Diane Watters (eds), *Home Builders: McTaggart and Mickel and the Scottish Housebuilding Industry* (Edinburgh, 1999), p. 71.

29. T. Brennan, *Reshaping a City* (1959), quoted in Smout, *Century of the Scottish People*, p. 39.

30. Butt, 'Working-class housing', p. 226.

31. Suburbs where Jews settled are overwhelmingly in East Renfrewshire; 'Annual General Meeting of the Glasgow Jewish Board of Guardians' reported in *The Jewish Echo*, 24 September 1948.

32. 1961 census for Scotland, Table XXII.

33. Smout, *Century of the Scottish People*, p. 57.

34. Horsey, *Tenements and Towers*, p. 32. For a general factual history of new towns in Scotland, which nevertheless fails to mention how tenants were selected, see David Cowling, *An Essay for Today: the Scottish New Towns 1947–1997* (Edinburgh, 1997).

35. R. Smith, 'Multi-dwelling building in Scotland 1750–1970: a study based on housing in the Clyde Valley', in A. Sutcliffe (ed.), *Multi-Storey Living: the British Working-Class Experience* (London, 1974), p. 229.

36. Glasgow University Archive Services (GUAS), DC 127/1: Pilot study (questionnaire returns) Mrs Bould.

37. Alison Light, *Forever England* (London, 1991), p. 218, here quoted in J. Giles, *Parlour and the Suburb*, p. 64.

38. Horsey, *Tenements and Towers*, p. 36.
39. Duncan Sim, *Clearance in the 1980s: The Experience of Barlanark* (Glasgow, 1984), p. 11.
40. Michael B. Foulis, *Council House Sales in Scotland, April 1979–December 1983* (Edinburgh, 1983), p. 54.
41. Foulis, *Council House Sales*, p. 1; *Housing in 20th Century Glasgow: Documents 1914 to the 1990s* (Glasgow, 1996), p. 161.
42. Foulis, *Council House Sales*, p. 3.
43. James Hunter, *The Making of the Crofting Community* (Edinburgh, 1976), pp. 207–8.
44. www.scrol.gov.uk: 1991 resident population – all people, all council areas.
45. www.scrol.gov.uk: 1991 resident population – Highland and Eilean Siar.
46. A. McIvor, 'Women and work in twentieth century Scotland', in A. Dickson and J. H. Treble (eds), *People and Society in Scotland Volume III, 1914–1990* (Edinburgh, 1992), p. 151.
47. *Glasgow Municipal Commission on the Housing of the Poor: Report and Recommendations* (Glasgow, 1904), p. 9.
48. *Glasgow Municipal Commission on the Housing of the Poor: Minutes of Evidence* vol. 1 (Glasgow, 1904), Section 7401, p. 347.
49. 'Lord Provost's Tribute to Housewives', in *The Scotsman*, 6 October 1949.
50. 'Slums in the Scottish Cities', in *The Glasgow Herald*, 15 November 1907.
51. Giles, *Parlour and the Suburb*, p. 66.
52. Quoted in Mike Brown and Carol Harris, *The Wartime House* (Stroud, Gloucestershire, 2001), p. 65.
53. See A. McGuckin, 'Moving stories: working-class women', in Breitenbach and Gordon (eds), *Out of Bounds*, pp. 197–220.
54. J. Wajcman, 'Domestic technology: labour-saving or enslaving?' in G. Kirkup and L. S. Keller (eds), *Inventing Women, Science Technology and Gender* (Cambridge, 1992), pp. 238–54; C. Zmroczek, 'The weekly wash', in S. Oldfield (ed.), *This Working-day World: Women's Lives and Culture(s) in Britain 1914–1945* (London, 1994), pp. 7–17.
55. Stirling Women's Oral History Project, Mrs B2, born 1907.
56. Stirling Women's Oral History Project, Mrs C2, born 1912.
57. *Planning Our New Homes: Report by the Scottish Housing Advisory Committee on the Design, Planning and Furnishing of New Houses* (Edinburgh, 1948), Appendix 3, p. xxv.
58. Scottish Housing Advisory Committee, sub-committee on furniture (1942), p. 121.
59. Stirling Women's Oral History Project, Mrs C2, born 1912.
60. 'Moving to Castlemilk', in *Housing in Twentieth Century Scotland*, p. 178.
61. See Zmroczek, 'The weekly wash'.
62. Stirling Women's Oral History Project.
63. Chaim Bermant, *Coming Home* (Plymouth, 1976), p. 82.
64. See Linda Fleming, 'Gender, Ethnicity and the Immigrant Experience: Jewish Women in Glasgow 1880–1950' (PhD, University of Glasgow, 2005), p. 292.

65. Quoted in Diane Watters, 'McTaggart and Mickel: a company history', in Glendinning and Watters (eds), *Home Builders*, p. 82.
66. See D. Hayden, cited in A. Blunt and R. Dowling, *Home* (London, 2006), p. 8.
67. L. Christie, 'Gender, design and ideology in council housing: urban Scotland 1917–1944', *Planning History*, 15:3 (1993), pp. 6–13.
68. Giles, *Parlour and the Suburb*, p. 62.
69. *The Scotsman*, 19 July 1950.
70. Annual Report of the Department of Health for Scotland, 1934–5, in *Housing in Twentieth Century Scotland*, p. 18.
71. *The Scotsman*, 13 September 1934.
72. *The Scotsman*, 26 July 1940.
73. Stirling Women's Oral History Project, Mrs P1.
74. *Planning Our New Homes, Report by the Scottish Advisory Committee on the Design, Planning and Furnishing of New Houses* (HMSO: Edinburgh, 1948). Appendix 3, pp. xix–xxxi.
75. *Planning Our New Homes*, p. 27.
76. *Planning Our New Homes*, p. 96.
77. H. Lefebvre, *Everyday Life in the Modern World* (orig. 1971, New Brunswick, NJ, 2002), p. 73.
78. B. Friedan, *The Feminine Mystique* (Harmondsworth, 1965).
79. M. Abrams in *The Listener* 1965, here cited in Giles, *Parlour and the Suburb*, p. 103.
80. Quoted in Watters, 'McTaggart and Mickel: a company history', p. 82.
81. *The Scotsman*, 21 February 1922.
82. *The Scotsman*, 4 March 1929.
83. Stirling Women's Oral History Project, Mrs H1, born 1907.
84. *The Scotsman*, 4 May 1944.
85. GUAS, DC 127/13/5: Programme for opening of Royston A housing redevelopment, 10 August 1961.
86. P. Jephcott, *Homes in High Flats* (Edinburgh, 1971), p. 133.
87. GUAS, DC 127/11/2: University of Glasgow Department of Social and Economic Research – Study of High Flats: Pilot study of Clydebank, 1967.
88. GUAS, DC 127/11/1: Pilot study of Clydebank, 1967: Questionnaire returns.
89. Testimony of a resident in Jephcott, *Homes in High Flats*, p. 93.
90. J. T. Cameron, *East Kilbride: Scotland's First New Town* (East Kilbride, 1996), p. 41 et seq.
91. R. Smith, 'Multi-dwelling building', in R. Smith (ed.) *Multi-dwelling Building in Scotland, 1750–1970: A Study Based on Housing in the Clyde Valley* (1974), pp. 231–5.
92. P. Willmott, 'Housing in Cumbernauld: some residents' opinions', *Town Planning Institute Journal* 50 (1964), pp. 198–200.
93. P. Willmott, 'East Kilbride and Stevenage: some social characteristics of a Scottish and an English New Town', *Town Planning Review* 34:4 (1964), p. 311.
94. Scottish Census Results Online: www.scrol.gov.uk. Comparative household profile (East Kilbride, Glasgow and Scotland).

Chapter 3

Changing Intimacy: Seeking and Forming Couple Relationships

Lynn Jamieson

INTRODUCTION

This chapter is concerned with the kinds of intimacy that ordinary working-class people living in Scotland anticipated when seeking or developing couple relationships, and how this changed over the twentieth century. Intimacy has a range of meanings and its usage changes over time and context. A claim of intimacy between two people might be made because of frequent association leading to privileged knowledge. Often intimacy is used to refer to physical and emotional closeness, including, but not requiring, what used to be called 'carnal knowledge'. It often also signals a connection of care, affection and trust. By the end of the twentieth century, the form of intimacy that is regularly idealised in English-speaking Euro-North-American popular culture involves mutual dialogue, talk, in which each party to the relationship discloses something of his or her innermost self. The emphasis on 'disclosing intimacy' has become a popularised expert recipe for successful personal relationships; it's 'good to talk' to friends and family. Some academic commentators claim that personal life is now centred on this type of intimacy and its pursuit was a key driver of social change in the later part of the twentieth century, advancing equality between men and women, adults and children.[1] I have argued that a more diverse repertoire of ways of constructing intimacy persisted and, in many circumstances of personal life, across all socio-economic classes supportive or caring actions remain as important as talk.[2] This is not, however, to deny any change over the twentieth century in the extent to which some people felt that they needed or wanted to share talk about themselves and knowledge of each other's inner world. However, simplistic uses of 'increased individualism' or 'detraditionalisation' do not effectively capture the change.

The extent of emphasis placed on heterosexual couple relationships as the primary source of companionship and intimacy varies culturally and historically. In the early twentieth century, the ideal working-class household involved marriage between a man prepared to work hard and hand over his income to support the household and a woman prepared to throw her energies into making best use of the income to create a home, look after him and bring up their children. Many working-class women also worked to supplement their husband's earnings. A co-operative division of labour and shared purpose did not necessarily mean intensely intimate everyday relationships were either expected or typically practised. Writing about Victorian and Edwardian middle-class marriages, Eleanor Gordon and Gwyneth Nair suggest that the most companionate marriages involved both a strong emotional bond and an intellectual partnership, but without the expectation of being the sole source of companionship or intimacy for each other.[3] At any one time across the twentieth century there is considerable variation, but evidence presented in this chapter shows that expectations of companionship and intimacy were relatively low for some working-class couples in the early 1900s.[4]

It is beyond the scope of the chapter to make a general case about the distinctiveness of Scottish society or to systematically compare Scotland with elsewhere, but it is possible to infer both a degree of distinctiveness and considerable similarity not only to our immediate neighbour – England – but also to some of the other industrialised and relatively wealthy societies of 'the global north' from comparative analysis of the directly relevant demographic trends.[5] The demographic indicators of couple relationships, such as the proportion of people marrying, age of marriage, birth rates to married and unmarried parents, size of families and rates of divorce, show that the twentieth century was a period of radical reconfiguration of couple relationships across many societies. The common trends indicate that some of the underlying causes of change were much wider than national borders. Much of the economic and cultural restructuring of Scotland in the twentieth century must be seen in the context of the changing salience of the idea of a global economy and culture.

In demographic terms, the most dramatic difference between Scotland and England has been in the extent of out migration. Like the Irish, Scots have been called a diasporic people and, throughout the first half of the twentieth century, Scots continued to emigrate to a much greater degree than the English.[6] It was only in the 1990s that Scotland stopped being a net exporter of people. Relatively little is written about the effect of high levels of migration on everyday personal relationships, but greater awareness of the possibility of mobility and experience of the mobility of others must have had some impact. In the twentieth century the disruptions of wartime, conscription and National Service (1916–18, 1939–60) and children's evacuation have had more recognition than this mass migration of the early decades. However, the heightened willingness to consider leaving friends and family may also have had some impact on approaches to forming couple relationships. Differences in patterns of marrying and having children were not as dramatic but no less persistent.[7] Age of first marriage and the proportion of never-married women remained higher in Scotland than England and Wales until the 1970s but women tended to have more children once married.

Michael Anderson notes that at the aggregate level, Scottish patterns more closely resembled Norway or Sweden than England and Wales.

It is also important to acknowledge the continued significance of more local economies and cultures, and the marked regional diversity within Scotland throughout much of the century, reflecting different practical and imaginable possibilities of a couple getting together and of establishing a household. Andrew Blaikie has argued that exceptionally high rates of illegitimacy that persisted in parts of the north-east and the south-west of Scotland across the nineteenth and into the twentieth centuries reflected specific cultures of sexual behaviour characterised by less condemnatory attitudes to births out of wedlock.[8] He argues that the widespread and regionally specific practice of illegitimate children being brought up by a grandparent must have involved willingness to condone and support unmarried mothers. While much of the material presented here is drawn from urban Scotland, such regional variation must always be borne in mind.

Across the twentieth century, a significant minority of adults have lived without marriage being a centrepiece of their lives. There have always been examples of individuals who derive their main source of companionship and intimacy outside of a marriage-like relationship. It was also always possible to either avoid marriage or fail to achieve an ambition to marry. Throughout the first half of the twentieth century over 20 per cent of the population never married, although again the average marked considerable regional variation with higher levels in most crofting communities.[9] The percentage of women aged 45–49 who had never married fell below 20 per cent for the first time in the 1950s and fell below 10 per cent in the 1970s. Rates of marriage were highest for the cohort of women born in the late 1940s and early 1950s.[10] Hopes and expectations of the heterosexual couple relationship as the primary site of companionship and of an intimacy that involved both loving care and deep understanding were undoubtedly higher in the second than the first half of the century.[11] A relatively invisible, minority world of same-sex relationships has always existed alongside the majority heterosexual world.[12] It became much more visible at the end of the century. By 2000, marriage had become much less fashionable, with the proportion of women aged 45–49 who had never married again above 10 per cent and on a rising trajectory. Some British commentators were predicting the demise of co-resident couple relationships as the ideal centre of adult life.[13] Among the more pessimistic commentators, the breakdown of tradition, the rise of hyper consumption and the ideology of individualism, or a process of individualisation, have been blamed for the negative aspects they see in changes in personal life. I and others have previously argued that the individualisation thesis has little explanatory power with respect to recent rapid change and a similar argument can be made of detraditionalism.[14]

The chapter begins by looking at key changes in the general context in which couple relationships form. It then reviews the evidence concerning sexual intimacy while noting that physical intimacy need not coincide with intimacy in any of its other forms; sexual intimacy among young people at the end of the century did not automatically mean strong emotional bonds, attentive acts of practical care resulting from caring about the cared-for person or the deep knowing and understanding of mutual self-disclosure. This is followed by putting some historical flesh on the bones of the well-established thesis that over the course of the century the typical orientation to becoming a couple shifted from seeking the securities and comforts provided by the institution of marriage to a focus on the relationship, asking how best to characterise the intimacy and quality of the relationship sought.[15] This is elaborated by contrasting pragmatic acceptance of 'the bird in the hand', whoever was readily available as a potential life-partner, with alertness to 'the one' and high expectations of a particular type of partner. Further elaboration is provided by discussion of the extensiveness of time together, of talk and disclosure in the process by which couples got to know each other, and the perceived tension between the commitment to a couple and development of individual identity.

ADULTHOOD, COUPLEDOM AND SOCIAL CHANGE

Eloquent testimony of the factors that shaped couple relationships in the early period of the century is provided in the biographies of Molly Weir, the popular Scottish entertainer and actor, born in 1910 and brought up by her widowed mother in Springburn in the environs of Glasgow, in a respectable working-class family. She sketched the interaction of material circumstances, cultural norms and personal ambitions in her own expectations about marriage in the second of her biographies, *Best Foot Forward.* Writing in 1972 about herself as a young office worker, she described how she and her female friends had a passion for attending fortune-tellers with a particular interest in knowing something of their future marriage prospects and likely husband. She noted, 'We knew well enough it would be years before any of us could think of getting married. Oh we were romantic, all right, but we had first-hand evidence all around us that marriage involved rent, insurance, clothes, and that a house had to be furnished before you could live in it, and furnished from savings at that.'[16] This was written of herself around age nineteen; it was to be another ten years before she married Sandy Hamilton in 1939.[17]

Something of the broad outlines of the process of forming couple relationships are suggested by Molly's relationship with Sandy. They were 'childhood sweethearts', having first met through their church: 'All our romantic attachments were formed with these boys whom we met through the church . . . we could peep across at the lads under cover of our hymn-singing, and later we might join up with them for a few delicious moments on our demure walks over Crowhill Road after evening service.'[18] Describing the time of her engagement, Molly explained their feelings for each other as 'someone in my life who could make my heart turn over, and for whom I seemed to make the sun shine'.[19] Sandy first appears in the book as her 'permanent escort' from home to Sunday school and to college, placing the beginning of their relationship to when she was around age fifteen to sixteen. However, as well as talking of 'the long legendary Scottish courtship' because of the need to save, given cultural norms which 'regarded with horror' any arrangement approximating to hire purchase, she also noted she had no desire to rush into marriage. She describes a visit to the house of a married friend and her son as a quiet backwater out of the swing of things that she was not yet ready to enter.

It is clear that Molly and Sandy spent a great deal of time alone in each other's company, but almost always in public places, often walking. They certainly talked. When at college they shared something of their learning, Weir commented that 'each benefited from the other's studies'.[20] Accomplishment in the practice of retelling events in vivid and entertaining ways was something Molly Weir had acquired early. Her biography suggests it was part of her family culture and, arguably, also working-class Glasgow culture. She no doubt communicated much of the excitement of her early auditions and success to Sandy, who was often waiting outside the studio or theatre door. She and Sandy also clearly talked about their future – for example, carefully planning practicalities and finances on varying timescales, from agreeing short-term trade-offs like a chocolate bar now meant walking rather than taking the tram and long-term strategies like saving for the engagement ring and eventually marriage and a house. However, what is less certain is that their talk routinely involved a dialogue of self-reflection and self-disclosure of the sort postulated as being at the core of intimacy at the end of the century.

Changes in the economic, material and institutional structures of everyday life across the century restructured conventional routes to adulthood, the conditions in which people could establish their own households and reshaped the opportunities for intimate couple relationships as leisure and pleasure. The everyday context in which people imagined, developed and maintained their personal lives was modified by the extension of compulsory schooling, along with post-war expansion of state-provided education, health and welfare, the transformations in availability of housing, including the rise and, at the century's end, decline of council housing, the steady increase in cheap mass-produced goods for personal and domestic consumption, revolutions in travel and communication, and the reconfigured options for earning a living (the credentials required for entry to occupations, wage levels, working conditions and the rise and fall of full employment). In all these respects the courting couple at the end of the century inhabited a different world from Molly Weir. She met her future husband through the church because it structured much of her leisure time in a way that no longer applied to the better-educated, better-off and more secular majority at the end of the century. She and Sandy went walking and met outdoors and in public places because there was no other space for private dialogue. Working-class homes did not generally give young people access to privacy and it was much later in the second half of the century before access to motorcars began to extend to the young of working-class families.

Transformations in material and economic conditions impacted on couples directly and indirectly through interaction with changes in ideas and attitudes. Legal and institutional changes also directly impacted on couple relationships. After 1950, legal aid made divorce economically possible for working-class people and women with no income. In the 1960s and 1970s, educational and employment discrimination by sex finally became unlawful. By the last decades of the century, gendered household divisions of labour between male earner and female housewife were no longer the taken-for-granted ideal or practice. Marriage and motherhood no longer meant long-term withdrawal from paid work and the majority of couple households with children became dual-earner households. Acceptance of earning mothers and fathers was gradually reflected in the expansion of legal and institutional supports such as employee rights to parental leave and the improved public provision of childcare. In 1967, women were given legal access to abortion and the 'pill' gradually became widely available through 'Family Planning Clinics'. While sex between consenting men was decriminalised in England and Wales in 1967, the equivalent legislation in Scotland took until 1980, despite a much lower rate of prosecuting male homosexuals, although there was no such lag in introducing civil partnerships in the early twenty-first century.[21]

Molly Weir was clearly an exceptional woman, creating a sense for herself of more possibilities for doing things with her life than most. This is perhaps reflected in her above-average age of marriage and her childlessness. Even in the 1930s, when more couples delayed marriage, the average age in Scotland of first marriage between spinsters and bachelors was between 25 and 26 for women and 27 and 28 for men. As Figure 3.1 shows, across the twentieth century it was in the 1970s that age of marriage was at its lowest in Scotland.[22]

In the decades after this, age of first marriage rises, not because of the suppression of marriage through difficulties in establishing a household, but because of the pervasive, although not universal, practice of developing a sexual relationship and living together as a couple prior to or without marriage. This reflects a significant shift in norms and values rather than simply changing material circumstances. Developing a sexual relationship and living together have become ways of getting to know a partner and new conventional milestones in the process of constructing a long-term and perhaps life-long partnership.

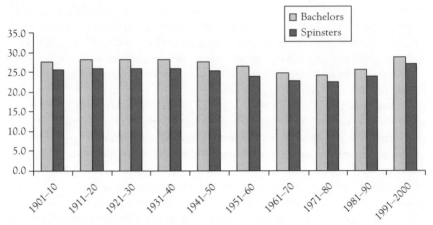

Figure 3.1   *Average age of first marriage by decade.*

SEXUAL INTIMACY AMONG THE YOUNG AND UNMARRIED

By the end of the century the majority of couples who registered marriages in
Scotland had already been living together and, therefore, presumably, sexually intimate.[23] At an aggregate level, notions about the morality or immo-
rality of men and women having sex before marriage, living together before
marriage and of same-sex relationships were transformed, particularly in the
last few decades of the century. This is shown by the British Social Attitude
Surveys conducted since 1983 and the more recent Scottish Social Attitude
Surveys.[24] Although attitudes varied by age, religiosity and sometimes by
gender and region, by the end of the century the secular majority made
little moral distinction between marriage and co-resident couples living-as-
married, particularly if children were not involved. This transformation in
attitudes to the relationship between sex and marriage was also reflected in
the widespread social acceptability of sexual intimacy as an aspect of the
process of becoming a long-term couple. Same-sex relationships did not have
such overwhelming approval, but, by the end of the century, only a minority
believed they were 'always wrong'.

Interviews at the end of the century with young co-resident heterosexual
couples living in Scotland, some married and some cohabiting, found
little hostility to or advocacy of marriage.[25] The majority of interviewees
believed their commitment to each other did not require marriage. Some
clearly stated that their bond as a couple was already adequately expressed
in joint projects, such as buying a house together. For them, marriage made
or would make no difference to their relationship. Nevertheless, many who
were not married planned to marry. Often this was explained in terms of
a special day of celebration focused on them and their relationship; those
who were childless often planned to marry before having children. A few,

and particularly those who were religious, acknowledged getting married as a final step in making a commitment to each other. This was said quite clearly, for example, by Mark and Debbie Thorpe when they were asked why they did not simply continue to live together rather than get married. Debbie remarked, 'Dinnae feel there's the same commitment then.' Mark agreed and said of marriage, 'It's commitment, and it's finally makes it that, eh, taking vows and sticking to they vows.'[26] At the same time, Debbie noted without any condemnation that they had friends who lived together without being married who did not feel the same way as she and Mark did about it. Few interviewees attributed moral weight to a conventional sequencing of marriage and then children.

Nor did all who wanted to get married before having children take steps to ensure this order. For example, Sharon and Bill Noble cancelled their wedding when Sharon became pregnant. They had talked of marriage from an early stage in their relationship and had been living together for about three years when they set a date for their wedding. They were not using contraception but were surprised by the timing of the pregnancy. The idea of Sharon being eight months pregnant simply did not fit with their plans for enjoying their special day. After the birth, competition between the wedding day and other priorities for expenditure became more acute and the effort seemed more pointless.

> Sharon: I think we would like to do it but then we think about the money. I think we would just rather get something. Like we would like to get a bigger TV. I think we would take that rather than get married. . . . It doesn't matter because I think before we really wanted to get it over and done with but now that we have had [baby] we are a bit more relaxed about it now. It isn't like we are going to go anywhere noo, you know, it doesn't matter.[27]

Sharon and Bill's cancelled wedding captures the extent of change over the century; it is the antithesis of the hastily arranged marriages in response to pregnancy that were relatively common in the earlier years of the century. Among sixty-three working-class respondents born around the turn of the century who I interviewed in the 1970s, two of the men and three of the women reported pregnancy as precipitating teenage marriage. These elderly respondents were largely brought up in the central belt of Scotland, in families and communities in which sex before marriage was regarded as wrong and becoming pregnant shameful, but clearly it still happened not infrequently.[28]

When elderly respondents volunteered that marriage was precipitated by pregnancy, few made direct reference to sexual behaviour. One exception was the account given by Belle of her courtship with George. 'You're loving and kissing each other. I said, "Oh I'm terrified." [he said] "Och never hurt, Belle I'll watch. I'll watch."' However, George's watching was clearly not the contraceptive Belle hoped for. She knew she had reason for worry when her period was late. Her mother was also tuned into her periods but because Belle's were often irregular she commented:

> 'I know nothing 'll ever happen to you.' I said 'Oh no, mother.' I should have been truthful but I couldnae tell her. He [George] told his eldest sister and she says, 'I'll tell her.' . . . When I got home from my work my mother said, 'A Mrs X sent for me today.' I said, 'Aye, that's George's sister. What did she want?' I looked up and said 'Oh mother' crying. She said, 'Well.' My dad, he come through. 'What's all the weeping for?' My sisters were all weeping. Oh God. They were all crying, 'What a disgrace on the family. Oh, how to face it' and [one of her sisters] said, 'A perfect disgrace. I've been going for three years and Harry's never even tried anything. You've only been going since the war and this is what happens.' My mother says, 'Now she'll get married but I havenae got much to give her. She'll get blankets and a bedcover. But where they're going to stay, I don't know.'[29]

Stigma and shame remained attached to many unmarried mothers for much of the twentieth century, notwithstanding the regional differences indicated by Blaikie. As late as the 1970s, as Sally McIntyre's interviews with women who were single and pregnant showed, a hastened marriage remained within the repertoire of response to unplanned pregnancy.[30] Only a minority of McIntyre's interviewees saw becoming an unmarried mother as their best option. Others opted for termination or for giving their child up for adoption. Some interviewees seeking abortions did so despite conceiving with a man they expected to eventually marry and have children with, because they wanted to do things 'properly'. This meant a planned marriage before pregnancy and after gathering the appropriate resources for setting up a household. Until the closing decades of the century, in everyday life and in fiction, the best outcome of an unplanned pregnancy experienced by a single woman was widely regarded as being marriage between the father and the mother-to-be, regardless of other cross-cutting romantic ties. [31] This is illustrated by Jimmy's moral tale of how his friend Willie's expectations of marrying Nellie were abandoned when she got pregnant by another man.

> I said to Willie one day, 'You no going out with Nellie this while?' He said 'No'. [I said] 'Have you been misbehaving yourself lad?' He says, 'If anybody else had said that but you, I would have knocked their bloody heid off.' . . . Now Nellie had gone to her auntie's in Hamilton for her holidays and she'd met this boy in Hamilton . . . Jimmy went over [to her house to ask her out] this night as usual. Went to the door. Mother come to the door. She says, 'You'd better come in.' So Willie went into the room and [mother] says 'By the way, when are you and Nellie getting married?' Willie says, 'Oh nae hurray. Let me get my time [as an apprentice] properly out and get some money saved up.' She says, 'Oh you'd better hurry up Willie. Nellie's going to have a baby.' Willie said, 'She can have a baby if she likes but it's nothing to dae with me.' And that's when it came out. So poor Nellie she went away to Hamilton, got married and went away to stay with

this bloke. She only lived about two years. Died of a broken heart. Nice wee girl she was too.[32]

This dramatic ending clearly raises the possibility of embellishment but marriage with little regard for the suitability of the match was not an extraordinary response to unmarried pregnancy. Another woman I interviewed was precipitously married to a man whose obvious fondness of alcohol must have made him of dubious desirability and he, indeed, subsequently proved himself to be not only drunken and unwilling to provide, but also violent and abusive.[33]

Jimmy's morality tale portrayed Willie as mortally offended by the suggestion that he could have ever got Nellie pregnant. Many of the elderly respondents that I interviewed in the 1970s were at pains to stress the chastity of their courting years. For example, Amy, who met her husband when she was twenty-five and got married at age thirty-one, commented, 'We never had any nonsense you know. We knew better.'[34] Similarly, Kate marvelled at the contrast between her courtship and what she knew of courting behaviour of young people in the 1970s: 'I went for four and a half years with my husband, who was a widower and who was sixteen years older than me. Four and a half years. He never once made an improper move or suggestion. It just couldn't happen like that nowadays.'[35] Ina, who married at age twenty-three, hinted at the consequences of such chastity and ignorance of sexual matters for her experience of marriage: 'We were grown up right enough but we didnae know what the kids know now. Oh no. Even when you were married you didnae know. Got the shock of your life when you were married, you know.'[36] Ignorance was sometimes also acknowledged by male respondents. Ronnie commented: 'I remember furtively, I think it was after I was married, buying a book by Marie Stopes feeling that this was a terribly wrong thing to do, but having a need to get at this area of conduct and it was very helpful.'[37]

While the partners of Amy, Kate and Ina, like Jimmy, his friend Willie and Ronnie, were not men pressing for sexual intercourse before marriage, it was obviously not unusual for some men to do so. This was what Belle described George as doing, albeit her reference to 'loving and kissing' suggested the possibility of mutual pleasure. One female respondent, Sheila, blamed her strict upbringing and ignorance of sexual matters for her pregnancy at seventeen, perhaps suggesting she felt ill equipped to deal with men's sexual advances.[38] Betsy Whyte's autobiographical account of her teenage years in Angus described as inevitable that she eventually failed in her efforts to ward off the moves towards sexual intercourse that became relentless once her courtship was established and she was happy to kiss and cuddle.[39] Betsy was from a traveller community, and travellers' codes of morality were no less concerned than the majority population to confine sex to marriage. Her account is uncharacteristically frank about her first experience of sexual intercourse, which she found 'painful and disgusting'.[40] This, in turn, led to a more effective dismissal of subsequent advances but it was already too late to avert a pregnancy. Betsy lacked Belle's knowledge and was amazed to discover this single unpleasant act had resulted in conception. Her initial resistance to her mother's and boyfriend's assumption of marriage as the appropriate rapid response stemmed from her strong dislike of this first sexual experience combined with the impossibility of naming this as the problem, or in any way discussing it or seeking remedy.

Such ignorance and lack of recourse to information had largely disappeared by the century's end, along with much of the stigma and shame of sex and motherhood outside of marriage. But more young people with sexual experience at an earlier age did not automatically mean more sharing of intimacy in the more general sense or more mutual sexual pleasure at the time of first intercourse. In the 1970s, feminists used the term 'double-standard in sexual conduct' to note the greater licence given to men to pursue sexual pleasure than women. This was not simply because women carried the risk of pregnancy but because their moral reputations were judged by their sexual conduct in a way that men's were not. Even at the century's end, it seems that something of the double standard persisted and that sexual encounters without the negotiation of safe sex and sexual pleasure continued to be typical of many first sexual experiences. Young working-class Scottish men in the 1990s had a number of ways of talking about women and sexuality but a common discourse celebrated sexual conquests demonstrating masculinity through mastery over women.[41] A small interview study of sexually active young women at the beginning of the twenty-first century found that the majority regretted their first sexual intercourse; the exceptions were those for whom the experience was in a relationship that had subsequently lasted.[42]

MARRIAGE AS INSTITUTION RATHER THAN RELATIONSHIP?

Interviews I conducted with elderly men and women in the late 1970s about their youth in the first decades of the twentieth century suggest that, for many, marriage was anticipated as much in terms of the normal, sensible, pragmatic arrangement as in terms of a romance and emotional intimacy. Marriage was the route to securing conventional future domestic and familial circumstances. Potential partners were often commented on in terms of their ability to fulfil the conventional roles of male provider and female housewife and mother. In this sense, marriage as an institution was still to the fore rather than marriage as a relationship, albeit more because of taken-for-granted practical arrangements than because of a conscious defence of the religious, legal or moral sanctity of marriage.

Interviewees offered spontaneous comments about the good prospective husband and wife. For example, Mickie talked of being self-conscious about the need to be seen as a good provider, given he had a visible physical abnormality. He reported an adverse comment made to the woman he was hoping to marry by her aunt: 'You better watch what you're doing. That man's got a big hand and a wee one. You want to get a man who'll be able to work for you.'[43] Tina told me that she had broken off with her boyfriend after two years because he was having trouble getting a job: 'I wanted someone more able to support me than that.'[44] Angus referred to his desire for a partner who would look after him. He was thirty-six when he got married and acknowledged that he was hitherto quite comfortable living with his widowed mother: 'But you knew it would be best to be married some time.' He recalled how an old journeyman he worked with asked him, '"Are you coortin?" I says, "No" . . . He says, "That's right. Always remember the best wife you'll ever get is your own mother."' Angus carried on to say, 'I think that often happens that a mother will do more for you than what a wife will.'[45]

This emphasis on marriage as a practical institution is not, of course, to suggest that the norm was an absence of love or the irrelevance of the particular person to whom marriage took place. However, the interviewees born at the beginning of the century sometimes expressed pragmatic acceptance of the available suitor. Pat, for instance, commented:

> I never had any boyfriends, except the one that I married. And I don't think I would have been married either to him if; the point is, I was getting awfie fed up. I felt I was getting a wee bittie tied down, you know. However, I said to him this night, 'Oh Jimmy, I'm no coming out with you again, because my mother thinks I am far too young.' So, I was 16 I think it could be, he says, 'Oh well. You sure?' I says, 'Aye.' I was going to the guild one night so he meets me and says, 'I want to talk to you . . . You told me your mother said you were far too young to be going. I seen your mother and she says, "Oh what a lie. I never said such a thing."'

Pat resumed going out with him till they married when she was in her early twenties, about which she said, 'I suppose we thought the time was coming for it. Well you knew. The point was you couldnae make much more of it. I mean to say that I don't know. I imagine. In fact, I can't tell you how I really felt. I got married anyway, so that was that.' Pat was not able to say with hindsight that she had been in love. Her time of courting was not focused on intimacy or fun. 'Going out' was a relatively passive routine for Pat, but one which she recognised was likely to end in marriage. In time, Jimmy became the 'good enough' choice.[46]

In contrast to Pat's courtship career, involving one-to-one courtship from her early teens, some interviewees had longer periods of more gregarious participation in the youth culture of their time. For example, Nina met her husband when she and her female friends went out in a large group: 'It always seemed to be crowds of boys we went out with. There was a wee gang, like. There was the Leith boys, the Gilmerton boys and the Southside boys. We used to trip around with the lot, all in a bunch, dancing . . . theatre

Figure 3.2 *Young people at a dance hall in Perth, 1955. www.scran.ac.uk*

and pictures [cinema].'⁴⁷ Young people working in large works and factories were often in the company of other young people, albeit often in sex-specific tasks and spaces. Many large employers organised social events including mixed-sex dances. For those reporting more sociability and fun, a history of several boyfriends or girlfriends seemed to be typical. Nina explained she had planned to marry a young man that she had been out with four or five times. When he had to leave town, their relationship continued by letter writing. He came to visit her for a fortnight's holiday and confided in her husband-to-be, at the time just one of the group of her male friends, that it was not yet possible to get married as he didn't have enough money: 'I don't know if that put anything into my husband's head or not but the next time he [the former boyfriend] came back I was engaged [to future husband].' Nina's account indicates that the possibility of marriage could be on the agenda despite a relatively modest period of 'going out with' somebody, and before the declaration of intention signalled by engagement. At this stage, however, Nina's choice of partner could be easily reworked. Even 'getting engaged', of course, did not always settle the matter. For example, Kate described herself as having had 'dozens of boyfriends' and having been engaged thrice before she married at age twenty-four. Getting engaged on two occasions seems to have simply consisted of being presented with a ring.⁴⁸

Going to dances was one of the most common ways of spending leisure time in mixed-sex arrangements. It was an entertainment form that celebrated the formation of heterosexual couples. Eileen explained that when she went to dances with other girls from her work, 'When I went oot with the other girls and we could get a click. . . That's what we used to say, "We'll get a click". But that was a'. You just left them.'[49] In other words, she and her friends were looking for a male partner who would take an interest in them, at least for the evening. This use of 'click' spanned several decades and I can testify that 'Did you get a click?' was still being asked of embarrassed teenagers by older relatives in the 1960s. The notion of 'a click' at a dance encompasses everything from a dancing partner with whom you exchange a few civil words to the moment of the beginning of a romantic/ sexual relationship. The conventional first move extending the interaction beyond the dance hall was through the device of the boy walking the girl home, perhaps then followed by the making of 'a date', another arrangement to meet.

Spending time with friends at the dancing might have been about having fun rather than consciously seeking a partner but, in the early 1900s, dancing meant the orderly pairing off of young men and women into couples. Dance classes were often regarded as a necessary prerequisite and they did not just involve learning dancing steps, as Angus explained: 'You were taught how to approach a girl. . . . And you must escort the girl back to her seat.' On the first occasion of meeting his future wife at the Plaza club in Edinburgh, she sold him a ticket for the annual dance at her own workplace. For many dances and private parties, young people were required to attend in couples with a partner. This institutionalised heterosexual match-making. For example, when Eric was invited to a wedding dance and did not have a pre-existing partner, the bride-to-be arranged that a girl from her work would be his partner for the dance.[50] The consequence was he started to 'go out with' this girl.

Jimmy described how his twenty-first birthday was organised in couples; in some cases they were paired for the occasion rather than established courtship relationships. His own courtship with his wife started when the game of spin the plate disrupted the pairs that had been set for the evening.

> Now being my twenty-first birthday party I had my pals and they'd all girlfriends. I'd invited big Polly a girl that I was friendly with and I invited Meg as big Jimmy L's partner. However, during the time of these forfeits . . . 'This belongs to a lady, [Meg] what is she to do?' and her forfeit was to kiss the boy she wanted to take her home that night. [Meg kissed Jimmy not Jimmy L] . . . So there was some trouble. So I said, 'Right. The deal's on.' So I took Meg home and big Jimmy L had to take Polly home. So eventually I married Meg.

Arrangements which require people to be sorted into couples never completely disappeared from young people's sites of leisure, but by 2000 they were the exception in the commercialised mixed-sex and gay leisure scenes. The constrained opportunities for observing the opposite sex afforded by some of the larger factories and works of the early 1900s became a more universal and immediate experience as growing proportions of young people remained in mixed-sex classrooms throughout more of their teenage years.

A study of a sample of young people in their twenties living in the Kirkcaldy district of Fife at the end of the century asked about how they saw their future. The overwhelming majority wanted a marriage-like arrangement involving co-residence with a life partner. This included those who were not yet living with a partner, about half of the sample, and half were already living as a couple, claiming commitment and a long-term relationship. As could be expected, given that sociologists have been claiming a shift from marriage to relationship since the 1950s, companionship, a quality of the relationship, was rated much higher as an advantage of a partner than practical arrangements. However, economic security was important to more women in the sample than men. In interviews the importance of gathering resources, getting established in employment, having a house and creating a suitable environment for children were issues raised by men and women, both as an explanation for delay in co-resident coupling and as evidence of commitment to each other by co-resident couples.

Those without relationships spoke in the romantic language of 'the one', the idea of a unique ideal other person whom they would come to recognise as their special life-partner. Alongside their sense that they would eventually find 'the one', many wanted time out first, before 'settling down'. Gender differences again emerged in the sample, with men more likely to emphasise a period of fun and freedom and women to talk in terms of self-development or self-recovery following a breakdown of a previous relationship. Both talked of the need to consolidate career and gather resources. Just over half of those without co-resident partners (therefore just over a quarter of the whole sample) said they were not looking for a long-term couple arrangement at the moment, although they ultimately wanted such an arrangement. This group included those without a boyfriend or girlfriend who described themselves as 'not looking' and those who saw a current boyfriend or girlfriend as short-term. There were more young men than young women in the latter category and the larger numbers of women who said they were 'not looking' artificially created a sense of equal numbers of men and women actively wishing to postpone a relationship. Interviews revealed that women were typically open to a relationship and were only 'not looking' because of a self-protective rule against organising their lives around 'looking'.

> I never go out looking for 'Mr Right' or to find anybody. I think, I just don't think you can do that. I go out to have fun and if I meet somebody fine. If I don't, then I'm still having a good laugh. I think if you go out with the expectation you're gonna meet somebody and you don't you're disappointing, you're . . . you're having a bad night 'cause you're looking for something. But I think, I mean I've, I'm quite positive that I will meet somebody.[51]

BECOMING A COUPLE: GETTING TO KNOW YOU?

The amount of unsupervised time that courting couples spent together in the early 1900s was often quite constrained by lack of privacy, community surveillance, parental curfews and the long hours of paid and unpaid work. Many young working-class women went from their day job to a share of the domestic duties at home, creating restrictions on their leisure time that were not shared by their brothers.[52] Some working-class sons as well as daughters were expected to be home by the time their parents went to bed, usually just after ten o'clock, or they would find the door locked or barred and find themselves having to knock and get somebody up to let them in. Rules of conduct meant that young women's reputations were often more guarded than men's. Women in domestic service had curfews placed on them by their employers. George's future wife was in domestic service in Colinton, Edinburgh and therefore he could only see her once a week on her day off because otherwise she was resident in her employer's house. He noted that the conventional employers' discouragement of boyfriends visiting was relaxed when he could be used as an extra worker. 'No wonder they allowed you into the house. You worked harder there than what you did at your work through the day, you know, giving a hand. . . . huge functions at night in the last house [before marriage] she was in. . . . The result is you used to be allowed in, you see. But they kept an eye on you. You know what I mean?'[53] Parental concerns to exercise some supervision over young people's romantic and sexual behaviour, and particularly that of girls, persisted across much of the twentieth century, even if notions of appropriate age-specific activities changed. Christina Hall's comments about her teenage years in the 1950s when she attended dances in South Uist in the school holidays described a more widespread practice: 'We had to come straight home after the dance. If we had a boy in tow, we brought him in and gave him a cup of tea before sending him on his way with a quick goodnight kiss if he was lucky. Somehow my father was always around to check up on what he called "camp followers".'[54]

The degrees of freedom that most young men and women have to come and go, their access to and control of private space, were radically different by the end of the century. While we know that practices of physical intimacy have changed, it is much harder to assess change in what couples mean to each other and what they seek in terms of the quality of their relationships with each other. The song 'Getting to Know You' (Rodgers and Hammerstein 1951) was part of my own childhood in the 1950s and 1960s in Scotland because it was frequently played on the 'wireless', although I knew nothing about the musical from which it came or this famous American song-writing duo. The lyrics 'getting to feel free and easy when I'm with you' and to know 'beautiful and new things about you every day' were delivered by a teacher talking to her new pupils. However, its popularity on request programmes was as a romantic song pointing to the pleasures of growing intimacy in the development of a couple relationship.

Accounts of young adulthood in the early 1900s suggest that talk was not necessarily an important aspect of initial encounters. Then as now, alertness to the possibilities of romance and the physical attractiveness of others was part of the social world that many young people inhabited. Potential partners were often 'fancied' before ever being spoken to. Tilly, for example, knew her husband from her work in an Edinburgh envelope factory where she was a folder and he was a cutter. He was 'always the man I fancied, fae the very first day I saw him'.[55] Their relationship did not start at work; she and her female friend encountered him and his male friend when they went to hear the band at the bandstand in the Meadows. 'And we walked home and it was from that, we went out together.' Walking together was a conventional way of spending time together, and a boy walking a girl home expressed attentiveness and a conventional gender order in which men were chivalrous to women. What is unclear in the many accounts I was given of walking home or being walked home is how much talk there was on the walk. It seems that occasions and places visited are spontaneously remembered more than what was said. It is also clear that sometimes initial interest was communicated entirely non-verbally. Betty met her husband on the promenade at Portobello where she was brought up. Families went there after church and groups of young men and women promenaded on Sunday evenings. Speaking of the boys from neighbouring Musselburgh she said, 'They were always in a crowd . . . I've seen them many a time, if you were walking along the promenade, you know, throwing you off the prom onto the [beach]. Of course, it wasnae high. This was the way things started.'[56] In other words, the way things started was that romantic/sexual interest was expressed physically not verbally.

The relative absence of verbalisation of expectations and feelings left plenty of scope for misunderstanding. In his biography, Molly Weir's brother Tom Weir reported a mistaken presumption that walking out together would lead to marriage.

> During my army service in Kent I had become friendly with a Land Army girl in Canterbury . . . I had a kind of calf love for her. Nothing ever happened between us. We went for walks. Both of us were virgins when we parted. Our final meeting was when she came all the way from Kent to see me in Edinburgh. I had never talked about marriage with her. In Kent, once when I was due to go on leave, she suggested coming to Scotland and spending it with me. I put her off, because I wanted to go climbing and not moon about with her. In Edinburgh, I had to be truthful and be as blunt as I could about domesticity not being for me. I won't forget her stricken face. I have often wondered what became of this simple, trusting girl.[57]

Given that walking with little by way of self-disclosing talking was a common pattern of courtship, this misunderstanding was, in fact, very understandable. A practice of relatively silent courtship among some young people raises the possibility of people marrying who did not really know much of each other, at least as judged by the standards of the later part of the century. In 1977, Janet Askham asked twenty wives and twenty husbands in the Aberdeen area, half working-class and half more affluent, how well they knew their partners. The older, longer-married working-class couples were the most likely to confidently assert complete knowledge of the other person, saying things like 'I can read him like a book' or 'I know her every move'.[58] Younger couples often described their knowledge as growing rather than complete, indicating that it takes a very long time to know someone. On the other hand, a few older middle-class couples suggested that complete knowledge of each other was not sought because it would not be a good thing to lose all possibilities of being surprised by the unique individuality of one's partner.[59] The majority of couples talked to each other regularly and had a sense of personal things that they would only discuss with their partner and no one else, as well as topics that they would avoid because they were outside of their shared interests. The exceptions included two couples whose relationships seemed to be unravelling, but also one older working-class couple, Mr and Mrs G, who described themselves as having a very close relationship that did not require talking. Mrs G said, 'Sometimes we don't speak for hours – when we're together we often have nothing to discuss', as well as 'we just live for one another'.[60] As Askham pointed out, communication does not always require talk, similarly neither does intimacy. It is and was possible for people to feel special and close 'living for one another' and be of very few words, even if this became increasingly unusual in the closing years of the century.

By the end of the twentieth century, the majority of young people would get to know each other by being verbally and physically intimate, and through co-residence. Sharon and Bill Noble, introduced earlier as cancelling their wedding when Sharon became pregnant, effectively got to know each other by living together. They were aged twenty and twenty-one when they first met and Sharon was already living with but in the process of 'breaking-up with' a boyfriend. They moved in together almost immediately and Sharon said, 'When I met him, I knew, "That was him; he was the one".' Consistent with this conviction, she described herself in the individually completed survey, conducted some months before a more in-depth joint interview, as seeing her co-residence with Bill as a 'permanent arrangement' from the very beginning. Bill, on the other hand, more cautiously described this in terms of 'try and see', but like Sharon he gave 'love' as his motivation and he also indicated 'I wanted to commit myself'. At the time of interview, Bill described their relationship in terms of being 'daft about each other' and 'made for each other'.[61]

Many parents had become relatively relaxed about such arrangements, in some cases sanctioning sexual activity under their own roof and unmarried co-residence even at a relatively early age. Mary Hutton was only sixteen years old when she moved in with Greg, who was then aged twenty-three. She had been going out with Greg for three months when he asked her to move in with him. Mary explained what happened when she asked her mother's permission: 'We were gonna leave it a wee while before we moved in. And, em, my mum was like, "Well, if you are moving in, you may as well do it this weekend", eh. So, that was that.'[62]

Askham's study was designed to explore how couples managed the balance and tension between nurturing their own individual identities and the stability of their relationship. Not all the research participants, however, had much sense of such a tension. While all were able to talk of constraints as a result of marriage, as Askham reported, these did not typically weigh heavily. Certainly, a notion of such tension did not typically arise for many of the much older respondents that I interviewed in the 1970s. Their pragmatic view of marriage did not compete with ideas about the development of personal identity. A tension between personal identity and nurturing a relationship, however, was a concern that most certainly made sense to many of the respondents in their twenties interviewed at the end of the century, and particularly, perhaps, to young women. Both young men and young women who were not yet 'settled' often talked about their own development, but while young men were more likely to emphasise having some time to enjoy the 'good life', young women talked in terms of 'personal growth' before settling into a relationship. For example, Jane's concern to 'better herself' and 'do things for me' meant being careful not automatically to follow the conventional partnership sequence: 'I don't want to just fall into a routine, you leave school, you get married, you have children, I never wanted that.' She suggested that self-confidence would help her negotiate a good relationship when she found the right person. At the same time, she recognised that she had become quite fussy and that there were not many suitable candidates. So while remaining emphatic that she would find somebody, she anticipated difficulties and was rehearsing the kind of self-account given to researchers by interviewees reconciled to living alone.

> Jane: I feel a lot of people are threatened by my independence in a lot of ways. . . . well my success really in my job, they feel threatened by it. Whereas I think in all honesty to be with somebody I'd need somebody on an even level intelligence-wise em, no disrespect to anybody else but I feel I, I need to sit down and be able to talk to somebody who understands what I'm talking about. Em, have an intellectual conversation as it was. Em, so I need, I think I'd need to find somebody on an even scale. Em, but it, I think as you get older it does get harder. Em, because I expect an awful lot, . . . I'm quite particular I think I'm quite fussy. That's probably why I'm still single.[63]

Her observation that 'people' are threatened by her independence and success is, of course, a gender-specific worry about heterosexual partnership that indicates continued difficulties in negotiating relationships of gender equality.

CONCLUDING REMARKS

By the end of the century, in the context of romantic relationships, the ways in which many young people expected to go about 'getting to know each other' included a fairly rapid transition to sexual intimacy. In developing long-term relationships, most young couples, heterosexual and same sex, were doing so against a backdrop of heightened knowledge and expectations of sexual pleasure and were unlikely to silently bear the discomforts reported by Betsy Whyte in the inter-war years. The picture of change has primarily been built through focusing on the beginning and end of the century. However, it cannot be presumed that a straight line can be drawn from one to the other; change was unlikely to be either linear or uniform across Scotland.

There are important continuities as well as radical change. While the social acceptability of sex as part of the process of 'getting to know you' was alien to the respectable working-class culture that was inhabited by Molly Weir, it was not without any precedent. The nineteenth-century statistics on exceptionally high rates of illegitimacy and births within eight months of marriage in agricultural districts of the north-east and south-west have been used to argue otherwise. Also, even when clear taboos on sexual behaviour outside of marriage existed, as they clearly did for many women, it remained commonplace for a minority to fail to honour the taboos. Teenage sex is no longer taboo but some stigma has remained attached to teenage pregnancy. Attitudes echo the type of practical concerns expressed by Belle's mother, if not the moral concerns of her weeping sisters, and the repertoire of standard socially organised ways of reacting has broadened from hastily organised marriage to termination, unmarried motherhood or trial-and-error cohabitation.

There are also continuities in gendered aspects of sexual conduct. It was generally men who took the lead in initiating sex and in so doing were following a persistent script. Fear of sexually predatory men 'taking advantage' of women and the notion that masculinity is expressed through seducing women is a long-running discourse that continued to shape the first sexual experiences of some young men and women at the century's end. By then, women had the means of effectively separating sex and reproduction, greater possibilities of sex outside of marriage-like relationships without stigma and were more empowered to negotiate sexual pleasure. However, gender differences in the possibilities of calling morality into question by reference to sexual conduct had not entirely disappeared. Unpleasant or unpleasurable first sexual experiences remained the norm for women and regretted first sex may have become more not less common than at the beginning of the century.

It is important not to misunderstand the shift over the course of the century in the typical orientation to becoming a couple from marriage as an institution to the companionship of a relationship. In the approach to marriage as an institution of many working-class couples at the beginning of the century, pragmatic acceptance of the practicality of this arrangement was more to the fore than a sense of the moral sanctity of marriage. Over the century, a shift from emphasis on practical institution to loving relationship has occurred, but it has not been a total shift. It has involved higher expectations of emotionally communicative if not talkative intimacy, more fluid divisions of labour, and expectations of greater equality of responsibilities for caring and providing in co-resident partnerships. Nevertheless, the institutional aspects of co-resident coupledom that made marriage the obvious practical endpoint ever in sight from the beginning of courtship in the early years of the century were re-created in living together during the later years. The practice of living together allows people to build commitment to each other through their practical arrangements, their shared belongings, their jointly paid-for residence and their children rather than through a declaration at the outset that these will follow.

The need to settle with a partner before having children remains a very widely held ideal. It is impossible to know for sure whether the hesitating unpartnered who were still seeking 'the one' at the end of the century were warier of co-resident partnership than their counterparts in the early 1900s. The general presumption has been that the involuntary single predominated over those avoiding marriage at the beginning of the century, particularly in times and places characterised by 'surplus of women'. At the end of the century, in at least one study, young unpartnered men and women in their twenties both claimed to be enjoying a freedom each characterised rather differently. Although single women were using an individualistic discourse of personal development, they also often had detailed understandings of the need to work at a relationship and openness to abandoning their time of 'not looking' for a partner if 'the one' for them should appear.

Jane's end-of-century observations that she may accidentally remain single because of being 'fussy', wanting a partner who is her intellectual equal and being unwilling to act as a subordinate, contrasts with Pat's observations that her marriage in the early 1920s, to the first boy she went out with, was despite her own lack of enthusiasm. There may also have been women like Jane in the early 1900s and marriages like Pat's at the end of the century; the case presented is that each was more typical of their own period than of each other's. These different paths illustrate the transformation of women's opportunities to establish independent households. Jane was living in her own home, something Pat would have found almost impossible to have achieved. While it may have remained a struggle for working-class women to form their own independent households, the changes in context described in the first section of the chapter made this much more possible by the end of the century. Yet, Jane and Pat both expressed an element of resignation and recognition that all was not as they would have wished. Perhaps both had romantic ideals that were not being met, and Pat too would have recognised the dilemma of seeking an ideal partner versus risking having none.

Notes

1. A. Giddens, *The Transformation of Intimacy* (Cambridge, 1992).
2. L. Jamieson, *Intimacy: Personal Relationships in Modern Societies* (Cambridge, 1998); L. Jamieson, 'Intimacy transformed? A critical look at the pure relationship', *Sociology* 33 (1999), pp. 77–494.
3. E. Gordon and G. Nair, *Public Lives: Women, Family and Society in Victorian Britain* (Newhaven, CT, 2003), p. 105.
4. Since Elizabeth Bott's observations in the 1950s, sociologists have considered that the emotional weight and closeness of a couple relationship is related to the types of wider social networks which the individual participants inhabit; men and women who separately inhabited close-knit gender-segregated social networks tended to develop couple relationships as systems of separate complementary roles and maintain greater emotional distance than couples who inhabited loose-knit overlapping social networks. E. Bott, *Family and Social Network: Roles, Norms and External Relationships in Ordinary Urban Families* (London, 1957).
5. For a good summary comparing Scotland with England and Wales across the twentieth century, see M. Anderson, 'British population history 1911–1991', in M. Anderson (ed.), *British Population History: from the Black Death to the Present Day* (Cambridge, 1996).
6. T. M. Devine, *The Scottish Nation 1700–2000* (Harmondsworth, 1999), see Chapter 20.
7. M. Anderson, 'Why was Scottish nuptuality depressed for so long?', in I. Devos and L. Kennedy (eds), *Marriage and the Rural Economy: Western Europe Since 1400* (Turnhout, 1999), p. 50.
8. A. Blaikie, 'A kind of loving: illegitimacy, grandparents and the rural economy of Northeast Scotland 1750–1900', *Scottish Economic and Social History* 14 (1994), pp. 41–57; A. Blaikie, 'Scottish illegitimacy: social adjustment or moral economy?' *Journal of Interdisciplinary History* 29 (1998), pp. 221–41.
9. See Figure 3.3 derived from census data provided by Michael Anderson in L. Paterson, F. Bechhofer and D. McCrone, *Living in Scotland: Social and Economic Change since 1980* (Edinburgh, 2004), p. 36. Note that averages mask considerable regional variation in the earlier period. In the 1911 census, the proportion of women aged 45–49 who had never married varied from 11.4 per cent in West Lothian to 36 per cent in Shetland. However, it was above 20 per cent in all counties except the Central Belt counties of West Lothian, Lanarkshire, Dunbarton, Ayrshire, Stirling, Renfrew and Fife – see M. Anderson and D. J. Morse, 'High fertility, high emigration, low nuptiality: adjustment processes in Scotland's demographic experience, 1861–1914, Part II', *Population Studies* 47 (1993), pp. 319–43.
10. In Scotland's Census 2001, Table S02 only 9.1 per cent of women aged 45–49,

6.6 per cent of women 50–54, and 5.8 per cent of women aged 55–59 were never married. This compares with 13.4 per cent of men aged 45–49, 10.6 per cent aged 50–54 and 9.0 per cent were never married. http://www.gro-scotland.gov.uk/files1/the-census/stan001-014.pdf

11. J. Finch and P. Summerfield, 'Social reconstruction and the emergence of companionate marriage 1945–59', pp. 7–32, and D. Morgan, 'Ideologies of marriage and family life', pp. 113–38, in D. Clark (ed.), *Marriage, Domestic Life and Social Change: Writings for Jacqueline Burgoyne (1944–88)* (London, 1991).

12. B. Cant, *Footsteps and Witnesses: Lesbian and Gay Lifestories from Scotland* (Edinburgh, 1993).

13. See S. Roseneil (2006), 'On not living with a partner: unpicking coupledom and cohabitation' and the editorial introduction, in L. Jamieson, D. Morgan, G. Crow and G. Allan, 'friends, neighbours and distant partners: extending or decentring family relationships?', *Sociological Research Online*, 11 (2006).

14. Such pessimistic commentators include Z. Bauman, *Liquid Love: On the Frailty of Human Bonds* (Cambridge, 2003); U. Beck and E. Beck-Gernsheim, *The Normal Chaos of Love* (Cambridge, 1995). For specific discussion of individualism with reference to family change in Scotland in the twentieth century, see L. Jamieson, 'Theories of family development and the experience of being brought up', *Sociology* 21 (1987), pp. 591–607. For an early critique of the individualism thesis, see A. McFarlane, *The Origins of English Individualism: the Family, Property and Social Transition* (Oxford, 1978). For critique and reworking of the detraditionalisation thesis, see N. Gross, 'The detraditionalization of intimacy reconsidered', *Social Theory* 23 (2005), pp. 286–311.

15. One of the earliest formulations of this thesis was by the American authors E. W. Burgess and H. J. Locke, *The Family: From Institution to Companionship* (New York, 1945). It has been reappropriated and reworked over the decades since, with shifting claims about the precise timing, extent and drivers of change.

16. M. Weir, *Molly Weir's Trilogy of Scottish Childhood* (1996), p. 319.

17. Obituary 2 December 2004, *Telegraph*, http://www.telegraph.co.uk/news/obituaries/1477976/Molly-Weir.html

18. Weir, *Molly Weir's Trilogy*, p. 285.

19. Ibid., p. 421.

20. Ibid., p. 374.

21. R. Davidson, '"The Sexual State": sexuality and Scottish governance, 1950–1980', *Journal of the History of Sexuality* 13 (2004), pp. 500–21.

22. General Registrar Office for Scotland, www.gro-scotland.gov.uk/files1/stats/07t7-3.pdf

23. The Registrar General of Scotland does not publish the percentage of marriages at which brides and grooms have an identical address, as has been the practice for England and Wales. However, it can be presumed that the trend in Scotland is similar. See J. Haskey, 'Identical addresses at marriage and premarital cohabitation: results from linking marriage registration and census records', *Population Trends* 59 (1990), pp. 20–9. The Registrar General does publish the proportion

of births outside of marriage that are to unmarried parents living at the same address, showing that by the end of the century at aggregate level the majority are to co-resident parents but again there is considerable regional variation. See Registrar General's Review 2006 Figure 2.10, http://www.gro-scotland.gov.uk/ files1/stats/06-chp2-all-figs.pdf

24. See the published annual reports and in particular M. Phillips, 'Teenagers on family values', in A. Park, J. Curtice, K. Thomson, C. Bromley and M. Phillips (eds), *British Social Attitudes: The 21st Report* (London, 2004); A. Barlow, S. Duncan, G. James and A. Park, 'Just a piece of paper? Marriage and cohabitation.', in A. Park, J. Curtice, K. Thomson, L. Jarvis and C. Bromley (eds), *British Social Attitudes: the 18th Report – Public Policy, Social Ties* (London, 2001); K. Hinds, L. Jamieson, 'Rejecting traditional family building?: attitudes to cohabitation and teenage pregnancy in Scotland', in J. Curtice, A. Parks and L. Paterson (eds), *New Scotland, New Society?* (Edinburgh, 2001); C. Bromley, J. Curtice and L. Given, 'Attitudes to discrimination in Scotland 2006' (Scottish Government, 2007).

25. This was a study of 20–29 year olds living in the Kirkcaldy district of Fife. L. Jamieson, M. Anderson, D. McCrone, F. Bechhofer, R. Stewart and Y. Li, 'Cohabitation and commitment: partnership plans of young men and women', *Sociological Review* 50 (2002), pp. 354–75.

26. Ibid., p. 366.

27. Ibid., p. 365.

28. Pregnancy was also the likely cause of the small number of cases of teenage marriage reported by respondents. Although talking about events that had happened decades earlier, my own reticence, or sense of theirs, prevented me from directly asking when no explanation for relatively unusual teenage marriage was offered. The interviews were conducted for my PhD thesis (L. Jamieson, 'A case study in the development of the modern family: urban Scotland in the early twentieth century', PhD, University of Edinburgh, 1983), which is based on interviews with 37 women and 26 men brought up by working-class parents; 12 women and 3 men with middle-class fathers in professional or managerial occupations; 6 women and 2 men with parents who were small-business proprietors. The bulk of interviewing was in Edinburgh in 1977. I used a semi-structured interview format and was influenced by the work of Paul Thompson. Respondents were contacted through a range of facilities and clubs for older people, including lunch clubs run by a church in the Craigmillar area, Dalry House, several local authority sheltered housing schemes and Abbeyfield housing. Most of the interviews were conducted in people's own homes on a one-to-one basis. The material was tape recorded on reel-to-reel machine and then transcribed on a typewriter partly verbatim and partly summarised. The tapes were never archived and, after careful storage for many years, to my abiding regret, a set were lost at the time of my department's move from Buccleuch Place to the Adam Ferguson building, along with the later tapes that formed the book *Country Bairns*. The remaining PhD tapes have been transferred to CD but not yet catalogued for archive. They are also playing at a

slower than the original speed due to a quirk of the original tape machine. All respondents were promised anonymity, pseudonyms are used and the original details of names and addresses have not been preserved. The material presented here is from my original typewritten transcripts.

29. Belle was interviewed on 27 April 1977 in her sheltered housing. Born 1900. Her father was a shoe maker working in a factory during the day and 'for the toffs' in the evening. Youngest of a family of fourteen brought up in two rooms and a kitchen in Stewart Terrace, Edinburgh. Started work at fourteen in golf bag factory till going to work in a munitions factory during the First World War.

30. S. Macintyre, *Single and Pregnant* (London, 1977).

31. For example, Tom, the hero of Neil Gunn's *The Serpent* (1943), pursues the absconding minister's son to try to force him to marry his love, Janet, on discovering she is pregnant as a result of her relationship with the minister's son. There was no other imaginable and desirable possibility. Note that Gunn came from the north-east but this novel gives no sense of any tradition of socially acceptable illegitimacy.

32. Jimmy, born 1903, interviewed 24 June 1977, brought up in West Kilbride, Ayrshire. Youngest of seven. Father was a mason/builder. Mother died before he was two. Left school at fourteen and started as an apprentice joiner after a summer job.

33. Meg interviewed at her home in Craigmillar, date not recorded but early 1977. She was the illegitimate child of a maid brought up in the Canongate by a middle-aged couple who ran a small dairy. Worked in a printing works feeding paper into a lithograph machine. Met her husband when out on Sunday with other girls to Portobello. Had seen him before as he worked in the bottle factory near her work.

34. Amy interviewed in her Abbeyfield housing, date not recorded but it may have been conducted with a later batch of middle-class interviews in early 1979. Born 1894 in Leith, brought up in Balfour Street. Her father was a foreman book binder in Andrew Whyte's, Easter Road. Second oldest of seven children. Worked as a clerkess from age fourteen.

35. Kate interviewed 12 May 1977 in her sheltered housing. Born 1908 in Wishaw, Lanarkshire. Middle child of three. Two other children died as babies. Father was a steel erecting engineer in British Steel works. Father was English and mother from a middle-class Irish family. Stayed at school till fifteen then worked as a children's nurse.

36. Ina interviewed 26 April 1977 in her sheltered housing. Born 1904. Father died when she was an infant. At age six, she and her mother moved from the High Street to Leith on her mother's remarriage. Had four half-brothers. This new dad was a brass finisher. He died when she was fourteen. Worked from age fourteen, first in a boot shop then in a printers.

37. Ronnie interviewed 22 March 1979, location not recorded. Born 1897 in Glasgow. Parents Ulster Scots who wanted to bring up their children in Scotland. One of five children. Father was a police sergeant but died when Ronnie was five. He said to me that I should read Molly Weir's book because she had the same kind of background as he had. Started as an office boy at River Bolton Nut company

at fourteen and studied at night classes, eventually passing civil service exams. While in the civil service, continued studying and achieved his ambition of going to university to study for the ministry.

38. Sheila interviewed 8 March 1977 in her sheltered housing. Born 1889, one of thirteen children. Mother had a small fruit shop and her father was a miner. Her mother was in the Plymouth Brethern.

39. B. Whyte, *Red Rowans and Wild Honey* (Edinburgh, 2000).

40. Ibid., p. 134.

41. D. Wight, 'Boys' thoughts and talk about sex in a working-class locality of Glasgow', *Sociological Review* 42 (1994), pp. 702–37; Wight, 'Beyond the predatory male', in Lisa Adkins and Vicki Merchant (eds), *Sexualizing the Social* (Basingstoke, 1998).

42. E. Gillian, 'In love or just curious: exploring young women's experience of first sexual intercourse', *CRFR Briefing* 16 (2004), http://www.crfr.ac.uk/reports.rb16.pdf

43. Mickie interviewed 28 March 1977. Born 1895 in Tranent in a family of five. Father was an Irish Catholic miner and mother born in Scotland to Irish parents. Started in the pit himself at age thirteen.

44. Tina interviewed 1977, date not recorded. Born 1903, near Glasgow. Father from Galashiels. They moved a lot as a child. Father took children away from mother because she was alcoholic. Second in family of six. Mother died when she was age twelve. Father was a miner. Worked as a spinner and piecer in woollen mill.

45. Angus interviewed 29 March 1977 in his Edinburgh home. Born 1902 and brought up in Sauchtonhall and Stenhouse outside Edinburgh. Parents were Highlanders. Father was a tailor. Youngest of three. Went to Boroughmuir higher grade school to take 'intermediate courses' and then an apprenticeship in marine engineering but switched to an insurance office, being an insurance agent after the First Word War.

46. Pat interviewed 26 April 1977 in her sheltered housing. Born 1903 in Dundee, where her parents had a second-hand shop, but her mother moved back to Edinburgh when she was nine and her father died. Pat moved to stay with her grandmother in Gifford when she was aged twelve because she did not like her mother remarrying. She worked in the fields at fourteen and then as a domestic servant before returning to her mother's home in Edinburgh and working in a biscuit factory.

47. Nina interviewed 2 May 1977 in sheltered housing. Born 1903, sixth in a family of ten brought up in Edinburgh's Southside. Her father was a plumber. At fourteen she had a short period in a Leith tobacco factory before starting an apprenticeship in printing which she left to be a children's nurse.

48. Kate, see n. 35.

49. Eileen interviewed 13 May 1977. Born 1901 in Edinburgh, oldest of six surviving children of ten. Her father was Irish, a storeman for the Burgh Engineers and in the army during the First World War. She was a dye stamper in a printing works. Her mother died when Eileen was sixteen and she then went into digs.

50. Eric interviewed 20 June 1977. Born 1905 in Edinburgh. Father a brewery driver,

died when Eric was six weeks old. Mother worked as a cleaner. He worked from age fourteen as a labourer in the rubber mill.

51. L. Jamieson, R. Stewart, Y. Li, M. Anderson and D. McCrone, 'Single, 20 something and seeking?', in G. Allan and G. Jones (eds), *Social Relations and the Life Course* (London, 2003), pp. 135–54, here p. 145.

52. L. Jamieson, 'Limited resources and limiting conventions: working-class mothers and daughters in urban Scotland circa 1890–1920', in Jane Lewis (ed.), *Labour and Love* (Oxford, 1986), pp. 49–69.

53. George interviewed 27 April 1977 in sheltered housing. Born 1900 in Edinburgh. His father was a railway foreman porter. Last child of seven. He worked from fourteen as a van driver for the railways.

54. C. Hall, *Tales from an Island* (Edinburgh, 2008), p. 155.

55. Tilly interviewed 2 May 1977 in sheltered housing. Born 1890 in Edinburgh. Her father was a brass finisher. Ninth child of ten. Worked as a folder in an envelope factory.

56. Betty interviewed 5 May 1977 in sheltered housing. Born 1905 in Bonniebridge near Falkirk. An Irish immigrant miner's daughter. Fourth of nine children. Left school at age thirteen in order to help her mother at home.

57. T. Weir, *Weir's World: An Autobiography of Sorts* (Edinburgh, 1994), p. 42.

58. J. Askham, *Identity and Stability in Marriage* (Cambridge, 1983), p. 33.

59. Ibid., p. 35.

60. Ibid., p. 46.

61. L. Jamieson, M. Anderson, D. McCrone, F. Bechhofer, R. Stewart and Y. Li, 'Cohabitation and Commitment', p. 362.

62. Ibid., p. 361.

63. L. Jamieson, R. Stewart, Y. Li, M. Anderson and D. McCrone, 'Single, 20 something and seeking?', p. 146.

Chapter 4

The Realities and Narratives of Paid Work: The Scottish Workplace

Arthur McIvor

'Labour is a law of life' commented an Irish cleric in a eulogy to ten Irish migrant labourers, 'martyrs to duty', who were tragically killed in a bothy fire in Kirkintilloch near Glasgow in September 1937.[1] These few words indicate what one narrator perceived as the centrality of work in people's lives in the 1930s. We might expect such an observer to emphasise the work ethic (the moral principles or standards associated with paid employment) in these terms, given its incubation within religious belief. But was this the way that ordinary workers represented and understood their employment – as a Christian 'duty'? Did the work ethic endure or change over the course of a twentieth century that witnessed such a radical transformation in the nature of employment?

Before going any further, however, we should make it clear what is meant by 'work ethic'. Michael Rose has noted that 'the term *ethic* implies that individuals have a moral involvement in work' – an 'inner need' – and he highlights several features of this: firstly, employment commitment: 'duty' to work, as opposed to dependency; secondly, work centrality and career orientation: work is more important than any other aspect of life – 'the prime source of meaning and personal identity'; thirdly, deferment of gratification: work comes first; and fourthly, conscientious effort ('something is not worth doing unless it is going to be done well'), irrespective of the financial rewards.[2] In the UK these ideas go back to the work of Samuel Smiles in the 1850s and the pioneering research of Max Weber who famously associated the Victorian period with a strong work ethic linked to Protestantism.

Much of what we know about work focuses on experience rather than perception. The latter is important, so this chapter explores the significance of work for Scots, using personal accounts of workers to investigate the meanings and material realities of labour, as well as the ways that work was remembered and represented in discourse and language within such personal accounts. What do these personal participant testimonies reveal about work culture – the pleasures, satisfactions, frustrations and connotations of work in twentieth-century Scotland? Oral testimony can provide a *barometer* of the changing meaning of work to Scots between *c*. 1900 and the 1990s, and the accounts used here are revealing and valuable. While work remained remarkably consistent as a site of social and cultural power and a fundamental aspect of Scots' lives, its significance in everyday life varied across different individuals and groups, and mutated over time. In the first half of the twentieth century there may have been a dominant (or hegemonic) work ethic connected to the 'breadwinner' ideal or duty, but the meaning of work varied widely across space, gender, class and ethnicity. The work ethic, in other words, had many diverging manifestations, and work experience was capable of incubating multiple, intersecting identities. This provides an opportunity to engage with wider understandings of work in the twentieth century – both positive (facilitating job security and enrichment, known as 'upskilling') and negative (the idea that work became progressively degraded and dehumanised within modern capitalism, also known as 'deskilling'). What is clear from the evidence is that there was no universal degrada-tion of work in Scotland, or wholesale 'abandonment' of traditional work values. Rather, the work ethic survived relatively intact, especially for those working-class men for whom there was a continuity in terms of masculine identity in their relationship to work, at least until the 1970s. (This is a topic examined in Hilary Young's chapter in this volume.)

Work has been a persistent theme tackled by British oral historians, from Paul Thompson's pioneering early studies of the Edwardians in the 1970s through to Penny Summerfield's seminal analysis of women's wartime oral narratives.[3] The workplace has also featured heavily in Scottish oral history, though in the main this has remained in the 'reconstructive' rather than 'interpretive' mode. Ian MacDougall's impressive body of work is evidence of this, as is Helen Holmes' fine study of the potato pickers, Neil Rafeek's recent investigation of women in the Communist Party in Scotland, Stephenson and Brown's analysis of working in Stirling, and Hutchison and O'Neill on work in Springburn.[4] There remains much potential for using oral sources to develop our understanding of workplace culture and, perhaps, for a more critical reading of both new interviews and the extensive extant oral recordings in Scotland to focus on the underlying narratives and (as Paul Thompson has done for the English Midlands car industry) to re-examine and challenge stereotypical hypotheses such as the deskilling/ degradation meta-narrative.[5] There is also the potential for a more synthe-sised approach, incorporating 'a materialist oral history used to study social relations' in tandem with the post-modernist concerns with linguistics and discourse.[6] To be sure, oral narratives are both informative and interpretive in quality, representing people's own subjective interpretations of the past and reflecting discourses, *as well as* informing us about real people and real material circumstances.[7]

What follows is a brief exploration of some different types of orally transmitted narratives concerning work: Edwardian narratives *c.* 1900–14; the activist, class-oriented narrative; gendered and migrant narratives; and the 'modern' professional narrative. To contextualise, I start with a brief comment on some of the key ways in which work changed in the twentieth century.

THE CHANGING CONTEXT AND FORM OF WORK

Scotland was an economy based on manual labour in 1900, with around 70–75 per cent of the workforce employed in 'blue collar' occupations, including agriculture, coal mining, metal manufacture, shipbuilding, engineering, heavy chemicals, textiles and clothing manufacture. For women, domestic service was the largest single employer, followed by textiles and clothing. Many of these jobs were dangerous and could extract a high toll on the body, through fatigue, injuries and disease (including rampant respiratory ailments associated with the inhalation of dust at work). The twentieth century witnessed a fundamental shift from such manual work to services, involving a change from working with materials and objects, to working with people and creative occupations.[8] Clerical work, shops, managerial and administration jobs and the professions were all significant growth sectors. By 2001, 63 per cent of Scottish workers were employed in service industries (excluding transport).[9] So, Scottish workers were located in very different spaces and work environments in 2000 compared to 1900.

The time people spent in paid work decreased proportionately over a lifetime (from around an average of 60 hours a week in *c.* 1900 to around 40 by the end of the 1990s), resulting from the raising of the school leaving age, the expansion of further and higher education, the introduction of a statutory retirement age, rising life expectancy and the contraction in weekly working hours. This, combined with the structural changes in the types of work undertaken (and other factors), contributed to a marked fall in the number of work injuries and occupation-related deaths, though stress levels may well have increased and the evidence relating to industrial diseases (such as asbestos-related disease) is more ambiguous.

The gender composition of the paid workforce changed radically through the course of the twentieth century, with the feminisation of the formal economy. In 1900 the labour market was sharply segregated by gender, and marriage usually marked the transition point for women from paid employment to domestic labour in the family home. This pattern broke down in the second half of the twentieth century, though vestiges of gender inequality in employment persisted, including some segregation and a marked gender gap in earnings. But the net result was an increasing proportion of workers were women, and women's greater penetration into skilled and white-collar occupations.

Workers became better represented and protected at work – with the growth of trade unions, the expansion of state intervention (directly through state ownership of some sectors and indirectly through the development of labour laws providing, for example, for rights for trade unions, unemployment benefit, redundancy pay and a minimum wage). Union membership grew from about 10 per cent of those in work in 1900 to peak at a little over 50 per cent by the 1970s, dropping back thereafter to around 35 per cent by 2000.[10]

Mechanisation and the application of science and technology transformed labour processes, bringing the fragmentation and specialisation of manufacturing jobs (epitomised, perhaps, in motorcar manufacture) and, in turn, service sector jobs. The last quarter of the century perhaps witnessed the most fundamental change in this respect with computerisation and automation.

At the end of the twentieth century there was a growth of a secondary, casualised workforce, often working on temporary, part-time and self-employed contracts. A two-tier labour market emerged, encouraged by government policies of deregulation and a return to market forces – with a more secure and privileged segment contrasting with the more unstable, 'flexible' forms of working. Such changes contributed to erosion in trade union strength and changes in work identity, including the fracturing of traditional modes of working-class consciousness.

But what did all this mean for ordinary workers and for Scottish society? Did this lead to a collapse of the traditional work ethic and the emergence of a more instrumental attitude towards work – as some commentators have hypothesised?[11] How did these developments impact on different individuals, groups and communities, on associational activity and class consciousness? How did this affect the work identities of men and women? There is much debate about the extent to which such developments resulted in improvement or deterioration in work. For some, technological change, scientific management, computerisation and the refragmentation of employment represented the death of the traditional crafts, resulting in deskilling, a loss of control and fundamental changes in work culture.[12] For others the emphasis was on upgrading or 'upskilling', with evidence such as attitudinal studies in the 1980s and 1990s – which invariably showed that people *felt* their jobs were becoming *more* meaningful and not less skilled – and the decennial census data, which shows that the number of higher status and creative jobs had risen markedly; for instance, those employed in the professions, in 'creative' work and as managers and administrators rose from about 8 per cent of the total workforce in 1931 to about 34 per cent in 1991.[13] But what is the evidence of these changes as the workers themselves reported on their everyday experience of work?

ORAL NARRATIVES AND THE MEANING OF WORK, c. 1900–14

The interviews conducted in Scotland in the early 1970s for the pioneering *Edwardians* project provide a good benchmark for an exploration of what work meant to Scots in the early twentieth century.[14] One recurring motif in these interviews of family and work life is the extent to which paid work dominated men's lives before the First World War. The testimonies also tell us much about the emotional and physical costs of employment in this era. As one Edinburgh man (born 1897) noted about his father: 'When he come home from his work he was dead tired.'[15] Robert Ferguson (b. 1891), a clerk in Glasgow, lamented that overwork had contributed to his publican father's premature death at just thirty-five: 'He never had time for anything . . . he was tired when he got home at night . . . the hours were too much for him.'[16]

Similarly James Luke (b. 1891) put his father's lack of affection down to his overwork: 'He was too tired, just popped into bed and that was that . . . we never seen very much of Dad through the week, up 'til Sunday.'[17] His father was a steel furnaceman working twelve-hour shifts. James Luke's narrative about his own working life as a furnaceman typified a craft discourse emphasising the independence and autonomy he was privileged to enjoy in the workplace (describing himself as 'the gaffer as far as the rest is concerned') and his deeply embedded work ethic. He counterposed his love of the craft and pride in his 'intuitive' knowledge of the labour process against the indifference of fellow workers: 'there were few of them interested in their work'. An important message embedded in Luke's testimony was *sacrifice*: he gave up a job as a bookkeeper to earn more money as a furnaceman (following his father's trade) – on 'millionaire wages' – to help his parents – entering a career that sapped bodily capacity: 'Well it certainly restricted my life tremendously, because you were working twelve hours . . . there wasn't much time to do anything else . . . I'd no time to go out I was that jolly tired when I got home.'[18] While he made conscious and informed choices about his career, his testimony reveals the extent to which these were constrained by prevailing culture: the notion that the eldest boy should help support the family; the dictum (passed down from his father) that a man should be independent and never resort to the state for handouts (not taking anything that hadn't been earned); and the breadwinner ideal which placed a stigma upon his wife undertaking paid work after marriage (something which Luke regarded revealingly as 'insulting').

For somewhat different reasons, Robert Ferguson's life was also work-centred. He was a clerk for a printing firm, and gave up his love of boxing because it was not compatible with his image of 'respectable' work where he wore a bowler every day to his office: 'My job didna suit it you see. If you get marked it looks terrible the next day.' Interestingly he stressed with evident pride at two points in his interview that he 'broke a record' for being fifty-two years in the same job. Ferguson lived to work, saying: 'If you were off your work a day you'd be fed up . . . it gets under your skin'. He was a politically conservative freemason whose working life distanced him from the 'labouring class', providing a very individualistic work narrative that was overtly critical of trade unions as 'dogmatic', 'too powerful', 'cause unemployment' and responsible for 'anarchy'.[19]

The identification with and attachment to work was markedly less evident in other Scottish Edwardian work narratives – especially those generated by lesser skilled men and female workers. Hard, physical, repetitive and monotonous labour under the close supervision of others, such as craftsmen, foremen and other 'gaffers', brought few rewards beyond the wage packet and a diminished attachment to the job. A low-paid Glasgow railway worker found himself taking on another part-time job in a theatre in the evening 'just for to – get that little bit together – to cause independence'.[20] This was more of a 'stoic' narrative of tolerating a lifetime of hard physical labour. He stressed with evident pride never being unemployed in his life, but indicated a degree of ambivalence when asked how he felt about his working life: 'Oh it was all right. I liked the railway or I wouldn't have been so long as I was on it.' Jean McKillop (b. 1894) noted the constrained choices of working-class women and lamented that she disliked the job of machinist in a boot and shoe factory that her father had got her into, commenting: 'Didn't like it at all. No. I'd rather have been in a shop or something.'[21] She continued: 'You were just put in there and you stayed . . .' By contrast, Kath Skeffington (b. 1901) was among the minority of women in Scotland who continued in her paid employment in hotel catering beyond marriage. Her experience also indicates that fatigue from long working hours was not just confined to Scottish men in the Edwardian period; she had suffered exhaustion in one spell of work as a servant working from 6 a.m. to 12 midnight, resulting in medical treatment and a long period for recuperation.[22]

Thus, while different people drew out diverging meanings from work and the plurality of experience was evident even within this small sample, these oral narratives of Scottish workers do illustrate several characteristics of employment in the Edwardian era: the gendered nature of work, the prevalence (and deeply embedded nature) of a work ethic, the prevailing inequalities in the labour market (based on class and gender) and the centrality of paid work and unpaid domestic labour in men's and married women's lives respectively. To what extent though is it possible to distinguish and identify specific work narratives, messages and discourses within oral testimony? And what can these tell us about how work culture, attitudes and mentalities changed over time?

ACTIVIST, EXPLOITATION AND CLASS-BASED WORK NARRATIVES

One of the dominating theories among scholars of the history of twentieth-century work is the way that common (and negative) experiences in employment forged class consciousness, politicising and radicalising a generation of workers and contributing to the growth of trade unions and socialism. This has particular resonance in Scotland because of the phenomena known as 'Red Clydeside' and the persistently left-wing orientation of Scottish voters through much of the century. Many prominent 'Red Clydesiders' and trade-union activists wrote autobiographies and some have been interviewed. In these narratives they recall their working days and, frequently, the lifetime mutations from working the tools to full-time employment as union officials, activists and/or politicians. Harry McShane, a leading Glasgow communist and activist in the hunger marches, spoke his reminiscences to Joan Smith who wrote them in the form of a memoir. This is a particularly good example, telling us much about the role of work in the forging of McShane's Marxist-humanist politics. Ian MacDougall provides many other examples in his extensive oral interviewing among labour movement veterans in Scotland, including miners, dockers, Spanish Civil War veterans and inter-war hunger marchers.[23]

Such class-based, 'activist' oral history narratives range massively in scope. However, there are frequently recurring themes within them. They invariably depict a workplace where conditions are degraded and dehumanised, with work changing under the inevitable dynamics of exploitative profit-orientated production, especially with technological change causing deskilling and unemployment. 'Slavery' and 'hell' are common metaphors. Workers' bodies are exploited in this relationship and suffer physical and mental degeneration as a consequence (boredom; fatigue; injuries; chronic disease). Employers and management are empowered and authoritarian and frequently depicted as the villains of this narrative. Victimisation is a recurring motif. An example would be Newtongrange miners recalling the dictatorial regime of the infamous Lothian Coal Company manager Mungo Mackay. James Moffat commented of the 1920s:

> He says to me one day, 'ye'll do what ye're told or ah'll put ye out of your house
> . . .'; if ye gane back to yer faither and mither we'll pit them out the house too
> . . . Ah can remember miners that were actually pit oot their hoose by Mungo
> Mackay. There was Bobby Gordon an' George Letham . . .[24]

Conflict and confrontation characterise social relations in such narratives. The memories are invariably framed within a battle – a class war of inequalities, injustices, struggle and strife. As one Ayrshire miner and trade-union activist recalled: 'men and management in general were always at loggerheads in the coal mining industry. Men and management . . . If you were a weak man you would have did what the boss said.'[25] These narratives often depict the heroes of the piece as the trade unions and/or political organisations that fight the bosses, win concessions and improve work conditions and wages, thus humanising the labour contract. Frequently at the centre of these reminiscences are the individuals themselves, recalling their personal contribution to the struggle in wresting improvements from recalcitrant bosses or achieving key legislative changes.

These kinds of testimonies tell us a lot about work regimes, prevailing power relationships at work and the rise of a workers' movement which played a vital role in transforming an intensely exploitative situation. Undoubtedly, many workers' everyday lives in Scotland were critically affected by routinised exploitation at work, a powerful work ethic and a prevailing productionist culture, though individual experiences varied widely by occupation, skill, region, gender and ethnicity (we come on to these shortly). Work was capable of destroying lives. This was illustrated starkly in disasters such as coal-mine explosions and fires (the worst in Scotland in the century being at Auchengeich pit in September 1959 in which forty-seven men died), the disaster on the *Piper Alpha* oil platform in July 1988 (in which 167 died), the pneumoconiosis epidemic and the currently unfolding asbestos tragedy. Accelerating death rates from mesothelioma are the consequence of an historical legacy of neglect within a productionist, profit-oriented and machismo work culture.[26]

Such activist narratives from early in the century tell us much about the ways in which work experience could cultivate collective and political identities, providing part of the explanation for 'Red Clydeside' and the more radical political culture of Scotland compared to England.[27] While other experiences beyond the labour process (such as housing and health) could also radicalise, exploitation at work undoubtedly acted to forge class consciousness. These oral testimonies also frequently illuminate the craft culture, rituals and world view of the artisans and the miners – the bedrock of the labour movement in Scotland in the first half of the twentieth century. However, these types of narratives neglect vast swathes of experience and oversimplify industrial relations, often into a 'them versus us' dichotomy which misses much of the grey hues and nuances of social relations.

Moreover, the processes of recall and the political agendas of the respondent and interviewer can lead to implicit (and explicit) reconstruction – with management 'dirty tricks' exaggerated and working conditions overgeneralised within unregulated private enterprise capitalism. The recurrent use of the 'hell' metaphor in work narratives illustrates this, as in this example from an interview with a worker from Turner's Asbestos Factory in Clydebank: 'I'll never forget till the day I die the first impression of that place. It was like walking into Dante's inferno without the fire. It was just hell. . . .'[28] Contradictions within group interviews also starkly illustrate the ways some activists misrepresent the 'facts' to paint a blacker picture and/or to reach personal composure, as for example in the misremembering of pit ballot results in favour of the Miners' Strike of 1984.[29] Recalling work as 'hell', moreover, occurred in retrospect, with the narrator influenced by what had changed in the interim, including the reform and regulation of employment conditions. This prompts the question: would the same narrator have described her/his work like this at the time?

Despite their obvious value, activist narratives can also be limiting, with the class paradigm that clutter these personal accounts obscuring other, no less important, dimensions of the labour experience, milieu and culture of work. They may say little of substance about the other divisions within the working class based on religion, gender, skill and the ways in which work nurtured alternative identities – such as those associated with masculinity and femininity – and how in turn ethnic and gender identities could influence the moral dimension of work. This may have been as much to do with the questioning of interviewers (who brought their own 'baggage' of interests, preconceptions and politics into the interview arena) leading respondents into telling their stories of oppression, class struggle and conflict. In other words, the interviewers' subjectivity was influential here in shaping the responses, manufacturing, circulating or hybridising these narratives of exploitation and activism.

GENDERED AND ETHNIC NARRATIVES IN ORAL TESTIMONIES: FEMININITY, MASCULINITY AND ETHNICITY IN THE WORKPLACE

A number of oral history projects from the 1980s have focused much more explicitly on the gendered nature of work and how employment experience contributed to and impacted on other divisions and inequalities, such as that associated with ethnicity. This shift has mirrored wider changes within the historical discipline, with the crisis in Marxist-driven history and the emergence of social, cultural and post-modernist approaches. Among the key developments in such work has been the sharper sensitivity towards sexual difference and gendered experience in employment, including the ways that work experience forged feminine and masculine identities.

The Stirling Women's Oral History Project was designed to provide life history narratives from what were in the mid-1980s an extremely neglected group of workers. The insights into work culture are significant, with the testimonies illuminating the frustrations linked with discrimination against women in the workplace, the internalisation of separate gendered roles, the prevalence of the marriage bar, unequal pay and subordination. However, as Stephenson and Brown postulated, these narratives also demonstrate that the work ethic of women was more similar to men than had been previously thought, contrary to the interpretations of other scholars.[30] Women in the first half of the twentieth century gleaned much satisfaction and joy from their paid employment, and much pride and self-esteem in the use of their skills. Key issues that emerged from the oral testimonies of Stirling were the camaraderie and sociability aspects of work. This was a site for socialising, song and gossip, of friendships and contact which was much missed in later life, and recalled wistfully and positively in oral interviews. When asked how she felt about her work, one Stirling department store worker (a clerk and cashier) said: 'I liked it very much. I must admit I thoroughly enjoyed all my years. . . .'[31] Evidently, there was a conflict between the material reality of structural and deep-rooted subordination of women at work within

Figure 4.1   *A woman textile worker at New Lanark mills in the 1950s. www.scran.ac.uk*

an intensely patriarchal capitalist economy and society, and the ways that women actually perceived and narrated their working lives.

Other female Scottish work narratives enable further consideration of these ideas about the meanings of work. For example, Ian MacDougall interviewed eleven female textile workers in Peebles. These testimonies are witness to a rich and varied work experience – though the length of interviews, from less than 3,000 words to almost 30,000 words, signifies much about the differing performances and power of recall of narrators. One thing that is evident is that up to the 1970s the type of job you did conferred a certain status and meaning; there was a distinct pecking order of jobs in the female labour market, with professional occupations (e.g. teaching) and clerical and shop jobs at the top, with textile working of intermediate status and domestic service at the bottom. As one Borders textile worker pointed out: 'they used tae say if ye worked in a shop ye were kind o' posh, in these days'. She hastened to add: 'But the wages werenae good.'[32]

The Peebles narratives are suffused with a great deal of job satisfaction. Effie Anderson worked in the mills from the early 1940s to around 1980. Her narrative identifies gendered job segregation and subordination in employment (no female supervisors), the tendency towards work intensification in the 1960s and 1970s with changing technology and the requirement to work more looms (from one to four), as well as the increasing insecurity of the work as time went on (she was made redundant in her mid-fifties). Nonetheless, she indicated in her testimony that she wished for no other work (she had hated domestic service in her early teens) and had found the job financially rewarding and intrinsically satisfying: 'Ah enjoyed ma work. Ah did enjoy ma work.'[33] Similarly Myra Little noted: 'Ah thoroughly enjoyed ma stake warpin'. Tae me that wis an experience, it really wis. But ah like a' these sort o' complicated things that you've tae think on. Somethin' that you're goin' tae achieve somethin' at the end o' it.'[34] These were not narratives of alienation, but rather very positive stories, frequently with detailed descriptions of the labour processes and friendships forged in the factory. In textile communities such as Peebles, Stirling, Dundee and Paisley, women workers were more upbeat about their memories of work and its importance to them.

To what extent are these stories typical or representative? Other female work narratives were more critical and markedly less affirmative. Domestic servants, for example, frequently articulated a sense of estrangement, linked to their literal servitude and marked lack of work control, hence the recurrence of the 'slavery' and 'cage' metaphors in oral narratives.[35] A prevailing theme in the testimonies of manufacturing and extractive industry workers was the erosion of skill and fragmentation of the labour process with mechanisation and changes in ownership, management and work regimes. Margaret Gray, employed as a skilled point seamer then a quality inspector in Peebles hosiery mills for over forty years from 1949, is an example. This respondent emphasised her interest and enjoyment of the work in her first twenty years or so, though a recurring theme in her narrative was the degeneration of work over the course of time: 'Aye, I enjoyed it. It was a very happy atmosphere in the place 'cause everybody got on well. We used tae sing at oor work an' things like that. It was nice. It was good. It changed through the years of course, you know.'[36] Several of the Peebles respondents recalled the disconcerting process of mill closures and redundancies which threatened their livelihoods, while automation and more-loom working were also key themes. Wilma French commented that she had enjoyed her working life from the 1950s but noted that stress had increased over time, commenting in 1996: 'the mill nowadays wants everything yesterday'.[37] Margaret Gray went on to identify the changes in company ownership and the different managerial regimes that were imposed. These mutations, together with changing technology, affected her entrenched sense of quality and craft: 'Ah mean, ah had standards,' she opined. Frustration and resentment over encroaching depersonalisation and a loss of control and autonomy was wrapped up in these developments, as Margaret articulated it:

> An' ah jist didnae like the changes. They sort o' forced you into doin' things that you wouldnae do normally . . . It went against the grain. . . . They didnae seem to

bother about ye. The atmosphere was different. You wis jist a number in the end, jist a number, and they couldnae hae cared less.[38]

This sense of alienation was sharpened by a feeling that the 'outsiders' did not have *experience*, did not know how to run the company ('hadn't a clue'), and a deep sense that the personal and paternalist touch in management was gone and that the workers were no longer valued:

Ah mean, they would walk through the shop floor and they would never look right or left or say good morning or anything, which, it doesnae take much to say good morning, ye know . . . They looked upon you as if ye were dirt at times. As ah say, ye wis jist a number.[39]

This repetition of the 'number' metaphor, evoking dehumanisation, speaks volumes about the changes in the meaning of work for a significant group of people employed in the declining manufacturing industries in post-war Scotland. What is significant, however, is that even with these experiences (together with insecurity and short-time working in textiles), Margaret Gray ended her narra- tive on a very positive note, commenting that she would not have done anything different and stressing the intrinsic job satisfaction and the economic value of what she had done: 'Ah did what ah wanted to do. We've made a good living out of it.' These textile workers spoke with pride about their long years of employ- ment and clearly had a deep attachment to the job. As another female Peebles worker noted with pride, 'ah wis hardly ever off ma work'.[40]

The 'number' metaphor recurs in other narratives. For example, Duncan Adam, a Peebles mill manager, reflected on his first contact with one of the company owners, Sir Henry Ballantyne: 'He says, "your father was a warper." . . . He had known ma father, he wasn't jist a number. He'd known ma father and he was welcoming me into the business. It was quite nice.' Interestingly this mill manager shared aspects of the degradation narrative, describing the new owners as 'ruthless' and bemoaning the shift from paternalism:

Ballantyne had been a family business. . . . He knew ma father. . . . You could approach anybody. . . . After, the whole thing was divorced. They weren't inter- ested in the shop floor. All they were interested in was money. And anything that was in the way of making money – chop.[41]

Reflecting on this passage, one gets a sense of a degree of inevitability in this kind of critique of change in work narratives of individuals reflecting back in older age, and, invariably, after retirement from work. There are several possible ways that this might influence the way narratives are con- structed. Firstly, people tend to become more conservative and set in their ways with the passage of time: invariably a 50- or 60-year-old will distrust changes in the nature of work that would have been warmly embraced in their youth. Duncan Adam articulated this when asked what he felt about the changes in his working life:

Sad. Sad. Sad to see the decline and as you get older you resent change. You know, the changes in the mill, rationalisation and all that, everything, you know, you saw it as progress and it was a necessity. But there's something inside ye, ye resented it a wee bit.[42]

Recalling work days in an oral interview some time after retirement might also influence the way narratives are constructed. The actual experience of alienation and/or joy through work may have receded somewhat, while the events are being recalled through the prism of contemporary experience and the knowledge of what has happened to work conditions in the interim. Experiencing relative isolation and perhaps social exclusion in older age, for example, may lead respondents to emphasise the positive socialising and cameraderie aspects of work.

The extent to which wartime constituted a discontinuity in working lives has been the subject of much debate. A key research question has been whether wartime experience replicated patterns of class and gender subordination at work, or marked an emancipatory episode, altering fundamentally the meaning of work in women's lives. To Summerfield, the Second World War was a cathartic experience for many women, though experiences varied across a spectrum from 'stoic' to 'heroic'.[43] Some welcomed the opportunities war brought – as with Maisie Gordon in the North British Loco.[44] To others, it was a case of having to put up with it – 'it was jist a case of you having to do it', noted a female wartime worker in the Borders.[45] One of the few female journalists in post-war Scotland summed up the contradictory impact of wartime experience neatly:

I know a lot of people hated it, loathed every moment they were away. But I can't say I did. I made a lot of good friends, I had some very interesting experiences, and as I say, I gained a lot of self-confidence. . . . And I think if it hadn't been for that, I wouldn't have been able to do the job of a journalist. I'd have been far too shy.[46]

This is a more modernist narrative, transgressing traditional ideas of gender normative behaviour. It also points to an important meaning of work – how it can forge self-esteem. The respondent went on after the war to develop a career as a journalist in a male-dominated sphere. Even where workers appeared to have little control over their jobs in wartime, there could be choices. Margaret Lavin told a story of a friend who took direct action to get out of an unpleasant wartime job, taking cigarettes deliberately into the TNT section to invoke dismissal.[47]

The growth of part-time employment opportunities after 1945 for women broke a long pattern and was one factor which drew more women into the formal, paid economy. While they may have lacked rights in such subordinate part-time positions, for some this represented a liberation of sorts. This was expressed by Margaret Crawford who took a part-time job as a local librarian, initially working eighteen hours a week because this fitted with her family responsibilities (she was married with two children). She was an untrained library assistant who worked alone running the local library at Hurlford, Ayrshire, and described her work in very positive tones, using phrases like 'rewarding' and 'satisfying'. Positive elements for her were the contact with the public and especially with school children, the joy she got from encouraging reading, the 'service' to the community and the control she exercised over her own work environment:

> I found, well, you can have the place the way you liked it. I mean, especially the first few years really, there was nobody pressurising in any way, nobody standing over you . . . As long as things were going OK you were left just to run it the way you did.[48]

The development of the library service after the 1918 Education Act provided a field where middle-class women found some employment security and decent promotion prospects. Dorothy Milne recalled a number of deputy and chief librarians who were women in the 1940s and 1950s and she herself rose from assistant librarian in Aberdeenshire to chief librarian in West Lothian in 1941.[49]

Masculinity at work has also recently been brought under the spotlight in a series of oral history projects that have focused specifically upon male-dominated industries in Scotland, including engineering, shipbuilding and coal mining.[50] This work has been revealing in demonstrating the persistence of workplace rites of passage from boyhood to manhood and in showing how toleration of danger and risk-taking at work were construed to be manly attributes. Such values were passed from father to son and from journeyman to apprentice. Some oral respondents clearly revelled in the 'hard man' or 'he-man' image, emphasising the honed body, showing pride in the scars from work injuries, and stressing toughness in the face of risky, dirty and exhausting work. This is evident in testimonies ranging from agricultural workers to coal miners. For craftsmen, 'respectable' masculinity could be celebrated in their achievement of the 'family wage' – enabling them to afford to keep their wives at home. For manual labourers, manliness was forged from the capacity for sustained heavy labour in energy-sapping work environments, such as the heat of the steelworks or navvying in inclement weather. Competition between workers was endemic, a feature of workplace culture often neglected by labour historians and not much in evidence in the 'activist' oral narratives. Miners struggled to cut the most coal or advance the most tunnel yardage, while shipyard workers revelled in riveting and welding contests (and the telling of epic tales, such as the riveter who banged a rivet in so hard that it supposedly flew across the Clyde and killed a sheep on the other side!). Competitions punctuated the agricultural calendar; Bill Brack proudly recalled his physical prowess in his record-breaking tree planting in the Ae forest, reaching 2,400 in one day.[51] Frequently respondents affirmed their masculinity by asserting the primacy of work and their breadwinner role. As one Clydeside shipyard worker put it:

> The filth that we worked in right fae 14 years of age. And being a man with no education, the only thing you had was the muscle in your arm and what experience you got with metal, and a very willingness to work. I would go in and say to people, 'Yes I'll do that in that time'. And whatever it took to do that [job] I would do it. Silly now, looking back through the years, you know.[52]

Another noted how he realised asbestos was dangerous at the time, but felt compelled to work in Turner's asbestos factory because of his family responsibilities: 'When you have two of a family to bring up it was better than walking the streets.'[53] Here again is the resurfacing of the 'sacrifice' motif.

Miners undertook what was among the most dangerous of all jobs and their work fostered machismo attitudes. Their oral narratives could be suffused with a discourse of manliness: 'Yes we were a bit macho . . . and we thought we were the greatest and we knew that was the case . . .'[54] Similarly:

> That's what you done till aince you got a place eh on the run ken among the men ken. . . . I was drawing when I was 18 year old. . . . I was drawing 100 hutches a day. No kidding you, I was like steel. I was a hard man then. . . . Oh we were down there first go in the morning and last away ken. Aye we made good money then ken.[55]

And the transition to primary wage earner marked the coming of manhood and conferred a privileged position within the home:

> Once you were a producer, ah think it's maybe like something similar tae the animal kingdom, now the lion has tae get the grub first. Ah think once yi' wir a producer and handing in, contributing more tae the household you got maybe a wee bit better treated than a younger brother or whatever you know or a sister.[56]

One other consistently recurring theme in life and work narratives of Scottish manual workers was about an injury to the respondent, or about a colleague or relative injured or killed on the job. These 'trauma' narratives have a purpose. They locate the narrator within a dangerous environment, hence enhancing his masculinity, raising his esteem as a man and perhaps also legitimising through such 'sacrifice' the sexual division of labour and traditional empowerment of the male provider in the household.[57] That is not to suggest that such work was not intrinsically hazardous, or that female workers were not also exposed to dangerous work practices (which were common enough, for example, in textile factories), and risk was certainly heightened for female workers during wartime in 1914–18 and 1939–45.[58] However, that said, quantitative evidence confirms that men were around four times more likely than women to be killed, receive a serious injury or contract a life-threatening chronic disease while at work. This was part of the adverse trade-off linked to macho behaviour and attitudes within an intensely patriarchal society (reflected, for example, in Factory and Mines legislation which restricted female employment).

Oral testimonies suggest this discourse of danger was played upon by male narrators to enhance their manly identities in such practices as refusing to wear protective helmets, harnesses, goggles, clothing and respirators. On the one hand, perhaps the telling of these stories of bravado and risk taking helped to compensate for the emasculating experience of unemployment, redundancy, encroaching old age and physical decline. On the other hand, they also evoked very real experiences, recounting an almost lost world of trauma, wounded bodies and encroaching occupation-related diseases (such as pneumoconiosis and mesothelioma) and disability that characterised heavy industry and mining communities in the twentieth century. This was no empty discourse divorced from reality. When miners used the metaphor 'blood on the coal', this represented real material circumstances, not just empty rhetoric. Male workers in the heavy industries were exploited by a profit-oriented management but also found themselves the victim of peer pressure, including a tough, highly competitive, 'he-man' machismo work culture where high productivity and high earnings were placed on a pedestal. Taking risks and earning big money were exalted masculine values. An example would be the much-lauded 'big hewers' who existed in almost all Scottish mining communities.[59] What this meant to such workers steeped in the breadwinner ethos could be starkly illustrated when working lives were over – whether as a consequence of retirement, ill-health or redundancy. As one miner commented: 'I worked a' my life . . . but it was a big blow to me to be told that I'd never work again. Eh, your pride's dented, ken. I mean when you're out and your wife's to come out and say to you "Come on I'll get that . . ." It definitely hurts your pride.'[60]

Other oral testimonies elaborated on the male-only domains of a pretty rigidly segregated workplace in mid-twentieth century Scotland, and not just in the heavy industries. One example would be journalism, which was a very macho world of heavy-drinking and -smoking reporters and editors, operating in a stressful environment to tight deadlines. On the *Edinburgh Evening News* the only women involved in the fifties were a couple that worked specifically as features writers on the women's page, significantly termed 'Eve's Circle'.[61] One of the jobs such female journalists were given was the 'church notes', a practice that reflected the gendering of religious belief.[62] Exceptions might be rationalised as being masculinised, as one male reporter noted: 'Any women reporters that I ever did come across on jobs, they always seemed kind of hard to me. [laughs] . . . They had the sort of hard crust. . . .'[63] One of these 'transgressors' was Nancy Williamson who was a journalist for fifteen years from 1947. While she noted the clear division of labour (female reporters did not do Saturday sport or the court reporting in the 1950s and early 1960s), she did not express resentment towards this and went on to deny any overt discrimination.[64] Again, there is a contradiction here between the evident structural subordination of women in the Scottish labour market and the more positive recollections of those narrating their experiences of employment.

The experience of work and the meaning of employment were also refracted through ethnicity. Scotland may well have been less of a melting pot than many other societies; nonetheless there were waves of migrants that were drawn to Scotland to work – notably the Irish, Europeans (particularly Poles, Lithuanians and Italians) and latterly south Asians, Chinese and, the largest single migrant group in the twentieth century, the English. The oral narratives of such workers tell us much about the receptivity of a host society to immigrant labour, including the nature of discrimination and prejudice against the 'other', about migrants' coping strategies in the workplace, and about the pace and processes of assimilation, erosion of sectarianism and inequality.

Experiences and how they were narrated ranged widely. The English, for example, commonly migrated to Scotland to fill places at the upper echelons of the economy. Their work narratives tend to be more affirmative, stressing the creativity and autonomy of work in the professional, managerial and financial sectors, as well as the rewards of highly paid and meaningful jobs.[65] The experience of the Irish historically depended on religion, with the Protestant migrants invariably moving into the better-paid jobs, such as the skilled and supervisory positions in the ironworks and shipyards, while the Catholic migrants populated the less-skilled and poorer-paid jobs. Vestiges of discrimination based on religion persisted long after statutory race discrimination legislation, notoriously evident in the Scottish practice of asking at interview or in job application forms about the name of the school attended (from which the religion of the applicant was usually revealed). An asbestos insulation lagger, Hugh Cairney, recalled how jobs in the shipyard communities prior to the 1950s were clearly demarcated by religion:

> When my father was a young boy, sixteen and that, looking for work, if you were a Catholic in the shipyards you didnae get employed. You got employed as a labourer or something like that but you didnae get employed to learn a *trade*, and the only thing at that time going was the insulation, you can go to that – we werenae a trade, *we're still no' a trade*.[66]

The diverging work trajectories of other migrant communities in Scotland have also been investigated in oral interviews, including Asians, the Italians, and the variations in experience within the Glasgow Jewish community that took them from their initial base in tailoring and other manual occupations in the Gorbals in Glasgow to professional and financial sector jobs and relocation to more affluent communities, including Giffnock and Newton Mearns.[67] Unlike the 'activist' narratives, collective activities and camaraderie appear less in evidence in migrant work testimonies, and frequently the villains are not solely or even predominantly employers and management but neighbours and fellow-workers. This is how a Pakistani immigrant, Bashir Maan, narrated the nature of discrimination when he came to Scotland in the early 1950s:

> I started peddling too with them, because there was no other way, no other job available . . . . most of them were in peddling in the fifties, but in the late fifties what happened was that the country was going through a very prosperous spell, this country, and people here, the indigenous population was moving on to better jobs, jobs with social hours and better pay. They were leaving the jobs with less pay and unsociable hours, so there was a vacuum there, so the employers needed labour and they couldn't get their own labour, so they were forced to recruit immigrants.[68]

Maan commented on how south Asians moved into work in chemical factories and the buses because of the unpopularity of these jobs and, later, moved into local retail despite initial prejudice:

> Now the trouble they found was that no customers would come in during the day, so they had to keep their shops open till late at night to make a living. During the day if a person saw, at that particular time, a black face behind the counter, they would walk out.

In some of these oral testimonies, a strong 'self-help' narrative can be detected where the emphasis is on personal struggle to overcome an alien and inhospitable culture and to succeed in the face of intense discrimination. Clearly some migrant groups (including Jews and Asians) brought greater levels of work attachment, and diverging and more individualistic work ethics with them, and sometimes this could clash with different, more collectivist work cultures.[69]

MODERNIST AND PROFESSIONAL WORK NARRATIVES: INSTRUMENTAL VERSUS MEANINGFUL LABOUR

What can be said about oral narratives of working in the 'new' sunrise industries, the rapidly growing service sector, the professions and creative industries in the second half of the twentieth century? One of the prevailing theories is that with mechanisation, automation and 'scientific' management systems (associated with Taylorism, time and motion study and ratefixers), work lost its meaning to many people and, stripped of opportunities to express themselves through employment, they adopted increasingly an instrumental attitude towards their everyday work.[70] As a cleaner at Ferranti in the 1970s commented: 'Ye didnae have to think, ye know, ye just did it.'[71] A female watch assembler at Timex, Dundee, expressed this sense of alienation crisply when she commented: 'you were like a battery hen'.[72] What has been argued in some of the literature is that increasingly people responded to such changes by prioritising the wage and working to live, rather than living to work. In other words, the traditional work ethic evaporated as work lost its moral dimension and the economic element became uppermost.

From the typing pool to the car assembly plant, people worked in order to gain the cash to sustain lifestyles that were increasingly leisure-oriented and consumerist. Doris Gibbs explained why she worked in the 1960s: 'When the children were very small, *we didn't have any money* . . . my mother looked after the baby and it bought us a new carpet and took us on holiday and things.'[73] An office cleaner, interviewed in 2002 just eighteen months before her retirement, articulated a sharp sense of changing work culture and in her occupation a diminution in younger workers' attachment to and pride in the work: 'They've not got the same interest in their job now that they did. You kept working and kept an interest in your job. . . . You come in here, you take a pride in how you scrubbed that room "Oh that looks nice". They don't do that now.'[74] To this respondent the meaning of work had altered from her generation to the next – the moral dimension had eroded. She recognised the improvements in wages and productivity that came with mechanisation of the cleaning job, but still looked back nostalgically to the more interesting, sociable days in the 1960s when the work was simpler and less stressful: 'Everybody kind of all worked together. . . . They were happy days then, they were happy days then. You looked forward to coming to your work in those days, so you did.' Among the compensations for deskilled toil (at its extreme, repeating a work cycle every few seconds on an assembly track) was a decent wage, and the wage in turn became fetishised. The motorcar assembly perhaps epitomised this vision, and car workers' oral testimonies not infrequently incorporated this work-as-drudgery narrative.[75]

It appears clear, however, that work had multiple meanings (often not mutually exclusive), and that for many Scots in the later twentieth century work continued to hold significance beyond the wage packet. Moreover, inter-generational change was invariably in the direction of job enrichment, rather than denigration. There continued, right through to the end of the twentieth century, to be a moral dimension to work with attitudinal surveys showing that people felt jobs were becoming more skilled and expressed a wide range of reasons for working beyond the financial rewards – such as a sense of achievement, independence and creativity.[76] Clearly for many people, and probably proportionately more than in 1900, work continued to be *enjoyable* and to provide dignity, self-respect, satisfaction and a sense of worth.

Nowhere was this more evident than amongst the burgeoning ranks of professionals whose work narratives often clash sharply with those recalling their working lives of pre-1950, or those of their parents.[77] Given the radically changed job profile of men and (particularly) women in Scotland by the 1990s compared to the 1900s, this is hardly surprising. For women, inter-generational shifts from domestic service to the factory and shop work, and from there to the office and into the professions, increasingly via higher education, were often (and not surprisingly) articulated in a positive light. The dehumanisation of work thesis was very male-centred. Despite persisting inequalities, historically the direction for female labour has undoubtedly been towards more status, power and independence in employment over time, as well as towards access to a wider range of jobs and higher positions. To Scottish women, paid labour was much more important and meaningful to their everyday lives in the 1990s compared to *c.* 1900. Access to and working within higher education provides an example. Ann Mair, employed as a programmer in the early years of computerisation in the late 1960s at the new University of Strathclyde, represented a female worker benefiting from the creation of new skills with the coming of computers.[78] Similarly, Karen Morrison took advantage of strong demand for labour in the 1960s and 1970s to enhance her career, becoming a university academic department secretary, explaining: 'It just promised probably a better career, a better working environment, *more interesting*, I mean I was bored to tears where I was.'[79] Morrison's narrative is that of an articulate woman who progressed from routine office work to department secretary and then department administrator: 'I forged the way if you like.' Despite being forced to leave her job temporarily at a university in 1968 when she was pregnant (because there was no provision then for maternity pay), she went on to a fulfilling career. She commented:

> It was just kind of tacit, that a secretary was a secretary and you were, you know, my phrase is 'I'm only paid up to here', under my chin, I'm not paid to think from there to there. . . . So I increased my involvement and was allowed to do so which has been very rewarding for me and I think, *I think*, I hope to the benefit of the department. I can't say in the sixties that I would have been able to do what I'm doing today, I don't think I would have been given the opportunity. I would think it would have been seen that only an academic could do this.

The growth of the service sector and professional jobs, as well as the significant expansion of public sector employment in Scotland, also altered perceptions and experiences of work. The resulting workplace environment was much safer and less health-eroding (at least in a physical sense), and for many the work involved the application of complex skills and long training after several years in further and higher education. The son of a joiner, Willie Dewar trained as a draughtsman, undertaking his apprenticeship during the Second World War. In his narrative he articulated a close attachment to the work and to the product:

> Some people said they would have quite willingly worked for nothing in the locomotive industry because it was an interesting, interesting trade to be in. And the loco, I always say a locomotive is a living thing. You know it spits back at you, it throws oil at you . . . it burns you and it will also kill you.[80]

Widening higher education admission and upward mobility provided access to creative and enriching careers for a larger segment of the offspring of the working classes. Alan White, born in 1938 and raised in Edinburgh, was the first of his family to enter librarianship from a manual working background. He reflected in 1996:

> I liked working with the public . . . I reckoned in my modest way I was quite good at it, I got a lot of fun out of it, I enjoyed myself, I enjoyed the variety that working with a wide cross-section of the public can bring. And to the day that I retired, I retained that liking. I was very, very lucky. I mean, I landed in doing something that I enjoyed doing and I enjoyed doing it with a wide cross-section of people. And I've never regretted my decision whatsoever.[81]

His narrative emphasised his pride in doing the job well and being recognised by his peers (he became President of the Scottish and UK Library Associations). However, he never joined a trade union and his work testimony is almost the antithesis of the 'activist' or 'alienated' narrative. Other librarians never joined a trade union; it was clearly not part of their culture and tradition, and may have breached entrenched notions of respectability linked to their work ethic. As one local librarian in Ayrshire (Margaret Crawford) noted: 'I wasn't a union member . . . And I'm saying, "I can't go on strike. Imagine my Brownies passing the library and the library's closed because Mrs Crawford's on strike." [Laughs] So I didn't go on strike.'[82]

Similarly the draughtsman cited earlier commented that 'the union' was 'the problem' in North British Locomotive in Glasgow; the 'communistic element' meant that 'you had to obey the union or you were in trouble'.[83] In his early days as a journalist Ron Thompson signed the non-union pledge at D. C. Thomson in Dundee with no hesitation as he explained he had no union tradition in his family (his father came from an army background) and was brought up in a non-political, non-religious household; trade unionism, such a key motif in the 'activist' narrative, had no meaning to him in this period of his working life. Thompson's narrative stressed his love of journalism, the romance of getting the 'scoop' or 'exclusive' and his enjoyment of the range and variety of the work and, in later years, his independence and autonomy as he moved into television journalism with Grampian TV.[84]

For some professionals, such as lecturers and librarians, there were increasing frustrations linked to work intensification, rising stress levels and the increasing bureaucratisation of the job. One male librarian reflected critically on committees and administrators more interested in resources than providing a service (for example when the mobile libraries were scrapped). Nonetheless, his positive work narrative stressed the pleasure he derived from over forty-five years working in the public library service in the Lothians.[85] For some of these workers, employment was injected with meaning and significance by a sense that they were providing a service to the public and to society as teachers, social workers, nurses, doctors and civil servants. Respect was earned as valued members of the community. Witness, for example, the excitement embedded within this comment by a trainee economist on Glasgow as an environment in which to work:

> I felt for someone who's interested in doing Economics it [the city] seemed a living laboratory of economics in action in terms at least of the kinds of *real problems* that economists should be interested in; unemployment, inequality, poverty, poor housing, social problems in general. . . . I loved it, it was what I wanted to do and I just blossomed.[86]

Concurrent with these articulations of job satisfaction and enrichment were countervailing tendencies linked to two major inter-linked structural changes in the economy and labour markets: deindustrialisation and casualisation. An increasing proportion of older Scottish workers in manufacturing faced redundancy and the inability to adapt to different types of employment in the second half of the twentieth century. The 1980s and 1990s also witnessed a rise in temporary, part-time and more 'flexible' employment contracts which provided less job security and more routinised work. The vast growth in call centres would be an example. As an ex-textile mill manager, Duncan Adam commented: 'There's no jobs for young folk, compared wi' my day . . . Ye can't get a permanent job.'[87] How workers negotiated and understood their employment (or lack thereof) in such demoralising contexts and the extent to which a meaningful dimension to their work survived such experience remains to be seen. What appears evident is the persistence by 2000 of a multi-tiered labour market in which the fortunate and privileged contrasted with the poor and deprived, with age, social class, ethnicity and gender continuing to influence and limit employment opportunities. In turn, this shaped workers' attitudes, and the ways in which they narrated their working lives as participants, drawing out different messages, discourses and signifiers from their labour.

CONCLUSION

At a very fundamental level paid employment had considerably less meaning to Scots at the end of the twentieth century compared to the beginning. In 1900 employment provided virtually the only means of survival, whereas a century later the state provided a comprehensive welfare safety net to cushion the effects of unemployment and poverty. Nonetheless, while work is no longer a prerequisite for survival, both the material and moral dimensions of work retain much significance. At the material level, employment provides the means to participate in an increasingly consumer-oriented society, with those without work on state benefits or in casual, irregular employment experiencing relative poverty and degrees of social exclusion.[88] Beyond the wage, the work ethic has also meant different things to different groups of workers, depending on age, social class, gender and ethnicity, among other things. While the moral dimension of work may well have eroded, with the work ethic less in evidence in oral testimonies in the second half of the century, work narratives persistently encapsulate the essential dualism of work – the joy and the degradation. Nostalgia for a lost past of creative, skilled work and a 'job for life' intermingles in these narratives with a sense of progress and positive change with more opportunities, more education, more choice and less hard, health-eroding and dangerous physical graft. What is evident is that at the end of the twentieth century work retained a deep and elemental meaning in people's everyday lives, giving structure, self-esteem and much intrinsic satisfaction. Talk of the 'abandonment' of the work ethic has been premature. The scourge of unemployment and the mental health problems associated with loss of work over the long term are testament to the importance and meaning of work in Scottish society. Undoubtedly the Scottish economy encapsulated a wide range of experience, a plurality of mutations and trajectories over time. The oral evidence can be contradictory and may be difficult to 'read' but it does not support the supremacy of any single narrative of change – either ameliorative or degenerative.

More research is necessary, however, before we can give any kind of definitive answer on the moral dimensions of work. Even taking into account the recent tendency towards more casualised and flexible working, employment for most Scots in the 1980s and 1990s was much more secure, much better rewarded materially in real terms – as regards both remuneration and non-wage benefits – much less dangerous and took up much less time than before 1939. Having said that, expectations change with each new generation, and there are plenty of contemporary voices critical of the high stress levels, the intensity of labour, the drudgery, the persisting inequalities, the insecurity, the deleterious effects of new technology, the depersonalised nature of work and the loss of camaraderie. Paradoxically, there existed a lingering sense of loss of power and autonomy at work at the end of the twentieth century, linked perhaps to a range of changes: the disciplining effects of an overstocked labour market characterised by high unemployment, deindustrialisation since the late 1970s, and the changes in labour law and the empowering of management which came with Thatcherism (and its carefully remobilised notion of the Victorian work ethic), and globalisation. In the last quarter of the twentieth century, there was an unmatched dichotomy between the sense of job satisfaction and enrichment felt by the privileged majority in employment (an increasing number of which had been educated to degree level) and the feeling of insecurity, hopelessness and powerlessness among those unemployed and underemployed victims of deindustrialisation, casualisation and deregulation. In this sense, as in 1900, it appears work continued to hold different meanings for different individuals and groups within Scottish society, with oral narratives reflecting and perpetuating how work continued to be a site for conflict, for struggle over power, and for varying degrees of moral significance.

Notes

1. I. MacDougall, *Voices from Work and Home* (Edinburgh, 2000), p. 557.
2. M. Rose, 'Attachment to work and social values', in D. Gallie (ed.), *Employment in Britain* (Oxford, 1988), pp. 132–4.
3. P. Thompson, *The Edwardians* (London, 1977); P. Summerfield, *Reconstructing Women's Wartime Lives* (Manchester, 1998).
4. See I. MacDougall, *Voices from Work and Home*; H. Holmes, 'As Good as a Holiday' (East Linton, 2000), N. Rafeek, *Communist Women in Scotland* (London, 2008), J. Stephenson and C. Brown, 'The view from the workplace', in E. Gordon and E. Breitenbach (eds), *The World is Ill-Divided* (Edinburgh, 1990), G. Hutchison and M. O'Neill, *The Springburn Experience* (Edinburgh, 1989).
5. P. Thompson, 'Playing at being skilled men', *Social History* 13, 1988. The dehumanisation of work thesis goes back to Marx and perhaps the most well-known twentieth-century manifestation of the thesis is H. Braverman, *Labor and Monopoly Capital* (New York, 1974).
6. J. Sangster paraphrasing Louise Tilly in 'Telling our stories', in R. Perks and A. Thomson (eds), *Oral History Reader* (Abingdon, 1998 edn), p. 96.
7. For development of this view, see R. Johnston and A. McIvor, 'Oral history, subjectivity and environmental reality: occupational health histories in twentieth Century Scotland', in G. Mitman, M. Murphy and C. Sellers (eds), *Landscapes of Exposure* (OSIRIS, vol. 19, 2004), pp. 234–49.
8. For more detail, see W. Knox, *Industrial Nation* (Edinburgh, 1999) and M. Mulhern, J. Beech and E. Thompson (eds), *The Working Life of the Scots*, vol. 7 of *A Compendium of Scottish Ethnology* (Edinburgh, 2008).
9. R. W. McQuaid, 'Employment and employability', in Mulhern et al., *The Working Life of the Scots*, p. 69.
10. A. McIvor, 'Trade unions in Scottish society', in Mulhern et al., *The Working Life of the Scots*, pp. 450–7.
11. See, for example, J. Goldthorpe, D. Lockwood, F. Bechhofer and J. Platt, *The Affluent Worker in the Class Structure* (London, 1969).
12. For an example of this argument, see W. W. Knox and A. McKinlay, 'Work in twentieth century Scotland', in Mulhern et al., *The Working Life of the Scots*, pp. 48–66.
13. For an overview of the 'upskilling' argument, see D. Gallie, 'The labour force', in A. H. Halsey and J. Webb (eds), *Twentieth Century British Social Trends* (Basingstoke, 2000).
14. See P. Thompson, *The Edwardians*.
15. Timothy Cox, interview 374 of the *Edwardians: Family Life and Work Experience*

oral history project (Economic and Social Data Service, Qualidata Archive, Essex, www.esds.ac.uk/qualidata/online). Hereafter cited as *Edwardians* (ESDS Qualidata Archive).

16. Robert Ferguson, interview 260, *Edwardians* (ESDS Qualidata Archive). While this concept of death by overwork is not widely accepted in Western culture, it is elsewhere – such as in Japan, where 'karoshi' is legally defined and victims' families can get financial compensation.

17. James Luke, interview 307, *Edwardians* (ESDS Qualidata Archive).

18. Ibid.

19. Robert Ferguson, interview 260, *Edwardians* (ESDS Qualidata Archive).

20. Mr MacDougall, interview 305, *Edwardians* (ESDS Qualidata Archive).

21. Jean McKillop, interview 306, *Edwardians* (ESDS Qualidata Archive).

22. Kath Skeffington, interview 308, *Edwardians* (ESDS Qualidata Archive).

23. See, for example, I. MacDougall, *Militant Miners* (Edinburgh, 1981); *Voices from the Hunger Marches* vol. 1 (Edinburgh, 1990), vol. 2 (Edinburgh, 1991); *Voices of Leith Dockers* (Edinburgh, 2001).

24. Ian MacDougall, *Mungo Mackay and the Green Table: Newtongrange Miners Remember* (East Linton, 1995).

25. Interview with Alec Mills, Coal Miners Project, Scottish Oral History Centre (University of Strathclyde) Archive Deposit C1/ 017 (subsequently cited as SOHCA).

26. See R. Johnston and A. McIvor, *Lethal Work: A History of the Asbestos Tragedy in Scotland* (East Linton, 2000); A. McIvor and R. Johnston, *Miners' Lung* (Aldershot, 2007).

27. For a stimulating recent contribution to this debate, see W. Kenefick, *Red Scotland! The Rise and Fall of the Radical Left, c. 1872–1932* (Edinburgh, 2007).

28. Owen Lilly, Interview A19, Asbestos Project, SOHCA 016. This was referring to the 1960s.

29. Steffan Morgan, 'Masculinity and the 1984–5 Miners' Strike in South Wales' (PhD, University of Swansea, 2008).

30. J. Stephenson and C. Brown, 'The view from the workplace'.

31. Ibid., p. 24 (citing respondent Mrs X2 remembering the 1930s/40s).

32. Wilma French, b. 1938, interviewed 6 December 1996, Scottish Working People's History Trust (hereafter SWPHT) Collection (Peebles Textile Workers). I am indebted to Ian MacDougall for permission to cite from these interviews.

33. Effie Anderson, b. 1925, interviewed 28 November 1996, SWPHT Collection (Peebles Textile Workers).

34. Myra Little, b. 1936, interviewed 18 December 1996, SWPHT Collection (Peebles Textile Workers).

35. See G. Braybon and P. Summerfield, *Out of the Cage* (London, 1987).

36. Margaret Gray, b. 1933, interviewed 31 January 1997, SWPHT Collection (Peebles Textile Workers).

37. Wilma French, op. cit.

38. Margaret Gray, op. cit.

39. Ibid.

40. Margaret Lavin, b. 1919, interviewed 12 November 1996, SWPHT Collection (Peebles Textile Workers).

41. Duncan Adam, b. 1916, interviewed 8 November 1996, SWPHT Collection (Peebles Textile Workers).

42. Ibid.

43. See Summerfield, *Reconstructing Women's Wartime Lives*.

44. Hutchison and O'Neill, *The Springburn Experience*, p. 69.

45. Margaret Lavin, op cit.

46. Nancy Williamson, b. 1921, interviewed 28 October 1996, SWPHT Collection (Scottish Journalists).

47. Margaret Lavin, op. cit.

48. Margaret Crawford, b. 1936, interviewed 3 March 2002, SWPHT Collection (Scottish Librarians).

49. Dorothy Milne, b. 1911, interviewed 10 May 1999, SWPHT Collection (Scottish Librarians).

50. See, for example, A. McKinlay, *Making Ships, Making Men* (Clydebank, 1991); R. Johnston and A. McIvor, *Lethal Work*; A. McIvor and R. Johnston, *Miners' Lung*.

51. Bill Brack in I. MacDougall, *Voices from Work and Home*, pp. 239, 246.

52. Interview A9, Asbestos Project (SOHCA 016).

53. Interview A25, Asbestos Project (SOHCA 016).

54. Interview with Tommy Coulter, Coal Miners Project (SOHCA C21/017).

55. Interview with Thomas McMurdo, Coal Miners Project (SOHCA C20/017).

56. Interview with Tommy Coulter, op. cit.

57. For a study of manliness in the domestic, family context, see L. Abrams, 'There was nobody like my Daddy', *Scottish Historical Review* 78 (1999), pp. 219–42 and see H. Young, 'Hard man, new man: re/composing masculinities in Glasgow, c. 1950–2000', *Oral History* 35, no. 1 (2007), pp. 71–81.

58. R. Johnston and A. McIvor, 'The war and the body at work', *Journal of Scottish Historical Studies* 24 (2004), pp. 113–36.

59. See in particular McIvor and Johnston, *Miners' Lung*, Chapters 8 and 9, pp. 237–308. For an important Scottish social-anthropological study that explores masculinity and its mutations through deindustrialisation and unemployment, see D. Wight, *Workers not Wasters* (Edinburgh, 1993). Wight stresses the lack of fulfilment and alienation from work evident in this declining coal-mining community (pp. 111–12, 232–3).

60. Interview with Billy Affleck, Coal Miners Project (SOHCA C2/017).

61. Bill Rae, b. 1928, interviewed 3 September 1996, SWPHT Collection (Scottish Journalists).

62. Ron Thompson, b. 1929, interviewed 7 July 1999, SWPHT Collection (Scottish Journalists).

63. Bill Rae, op. cit.

64. Nancy Williamson, b. 1921, interviewed 28 October 1996, SWPHT Collection (Scottish Journalists).

65. See M. Watson, *Being English in Scotland* (Edinburgh, 2003).
66. Hugh Cairney, Asbestos Project, interviewed by Neil Rafeek, 26 March 2005 (SOHCA/016).
67. See L. Fleming, 'Jewish women in Glasgow: gender and the immigrant experience c. 1880–1950' (PhD, Glasgow University, 2005); W. Ugolini, 'The Second World War and the Italian community in Edinburgh' (PhD, Edinburgh University, 2006); W. Ugolini, 'The Italian community in Scotland', in J. Beech, O. Hand, M. Mulhern and J. Weston (eds), *The Individual and Community Life*, vol. 9 of *Scottish Life and Society* (Edinburgh, 2005).
68. Interview with Bashir Maan (by Neil Rafeek), University of Strathclyde 1945–75 Project, 9 May 2003, SOHCA.
69. See D. Yankelovich, *A World at Work* (New York, 1985) for international comparisons of the work ethic.
70. D. Wight, *Workers not Wasters*, pp. 235–8.
71. Margot Russell in I. MacDougall, *Voices from Work and Home*, p. 136.
72. Interviewed October 1994 (Dundee), cited in Knox and McKinlay, 'Work', in Mulhern et al., *The Working Life of the Scots*, p. 60.
73. Interview Neil Rafeek with Doris Gibbs, 18 December 2002, SOHCA (University History Project).
74. Interview Neil Rafeek with Nan Stevenson, 28 November 2002, SOHCA (University History Project).
75. See H. Beynon, *Working for Ford* (Wakefield, 1973) and A. Gilmour's forthcoming PhD (University of Glasgow) on working at the Linwood car factory in Renfrew near Glasgow.
76. D. Gallie, 'The Labour force', in A. H. Halsey and J. Webb (eds), *Twentieth Century British Social Trends*, pp. 289–90.
77. For an example, see Interview Neil Rafeek with Pat Fraser, 4 December 2002, SOHCA (University History Project).
78. See Interview Neil Rafeek with Ann Mair 23 December 2002, SOHCA (University History Project).
79. Interview Neil Rafeek with Karen Morrison, 25 November 2002, SOHCA (University History Project).
80. Willie Dewar, b. 1924, interviewed by A. McIvor, 9 December 2008, Reserved Occupations Project (SOHCA).
81. Alan White, b. 1938, interviewed 22 August 1996, SWPHT Collection (Scottish Librarians).
82. Margaret Crawford, op. cit.
83. Willie Dewar, op. cit.
84. Ron Thompson interviewed 7 July 1999, SWPHT Collection (Scottish Journalists).
85. Andrew Fraser, b. 1917, interviewed 23 May 1997, SWPHT Collection (Scottish Librarians).
86. Interview Neil Rafeek with Roger Sandilands, 1 November 2002, SOHCA (University History Project).

87. Duncan Adam, b. 1916, interviewed 8 November 1996, SWPHT Collection (Peebles Textile Workers).
88. See, for example, A. Sinfield, *What Unemployment Means* (Oxford, 1981); J. Seabrook, *Unemployment* (London, 1982).

Chapter 5

Being a Man: Everyday Masculinities

Hilary Young

INTRODUCTION

Across the twentieth century men have experienced a number of significant challenges to their masculine identities both at home and in the workplace. This has resulted in both continuities in, and changes to, the experience of manhood, and to its representation in popular culture. In few places has this been as significant as in Scotland. In relation to health, employment, home-life, fatherhood, psychological illness, war and leisure, the nature of manhood was constantly under the microscope. The condition of the Scottish man seemed to be a litmus test for the state of the country.

A lot of criticism fell on Scottish men. Hard drinking and heavy smoking were taken as 'strong symbols of male virility and machismo in Scottish culture.'[1] A report published in 2000 identified alcohol and the cult of the 'hard man' as key factors behind Scotland's high murder rate. Between 1985 and 1994 there were an average of 19 killings per million people in Scotland, compared to 11 per million in England and Wales put together. In his response the Scottish Justice Minister said: 'The real problem is one of young men, drink and knives. We need to educate young people away from the "hard man" approach to life which results in a man in Scotland being more than twice as likely to be murdered as a man in England and Wales.'[2] This was nothing new, as these had been aspects of Scottish life for many decades.[3] At the same time, men were vulnerable. According to *The Scotsman* in 2006, 'in the period 1998–2004 the ten UK areas with the highest suicide rates for men were all in Scotland, with the highest rate of 47.5 per 10,000 found on the Shetland Islands.'[4] Men were susceptible to distinctively 'male' illnesses; in the early twentieth century this included tuberculosis, but later in the century this had changed to conditions such as prostate cancer and coronary heart disease.[5]

Much of the explanation for this picture of Scottish manhood was to be found in the workplace. Prior to the First World War employment was relatively stable and ensured that men were able to base their sense of masculine identity on their role as breadwinner for their families. During the inter-war period this became more difficult as unemployment soared due to the Depression. With it men's role as the economic provider or 'breadwinner' was questioned both by a failing ability to provide for the family and the chance to test their masculinity within the workplace. In addition, what were perceived as 'less manly' forms of masculinity became more visible after the First World War as veterans returned from the front with horrific physical injuries which clearly undermined their role as active, independent, healthy men. Psychological illnesses acquired as a result of battle were less visible but were no less damaging to masculine identity. Conscientious objectors' passive reaction to war also appeared to undermine men and women's definition of masculinity and how a man was supposed to behave. But the Second World War and the affluent post-war period allowed young and older men to enjoy the benefits that came with full employment, improving housing conditions and the advent of a welfare state. However, their definitions of self which were clearly defined by work and their position within the family were challenged in the 1960s and 1970s (as perhaps they had been in 1918 and 1928 with the suffrage campaigns) by the feminist movement that questioned conventional gendered power relationships. Widening access to divorce and birth control, as well as a growing female labour force, squeezed men's hold on traditional sites of Scottish masculinity within the family, at work and in society in general. A final straw seemed to come in the last quarter of the century as the process of deindustrialisation, accompanied by the ravages of the miners' strike of 1984–5 and high unemployment, hit hard at many working-class Scottish men and their sense of identity.

By the end of the century, the concept of the male breadwinner was a shadow of its former self. From 1997 the male unemployment rate in Scotland was higher than the female rate. The 2001 census showed the unemployment rate across Scotland to be 7 per cent, but the rates varied geographically. Seven council areas including East Ayrshire, Dundee City, Glasgow City, Inverclyde, North Ayrshire, the Western Isles and West Dunbartonshire had male unemployment rates of between 10 and 14 per cent; in contrast Aberdeenshire and the Shetland Islands had male unemployment rates of 4 per cent. Yet, common to all council areas was the fact that a lower per-centage of women were out of work compared with men.[6] Massive changes within the Scottish labour market with the loss of heavy industries, the shift to more service-based concerns, the rise in female employment and the femi-nist movement have meant that traditional arenas for men to express their masculinity have shrunk or disappeared altogether.

It is timely at the beginning of the twenty-first century to consider the history of men and different experiences of being a man in Scotland in the light of these concerns about Scottish men's health and employment. Historians of Scottish labour, leisure, religion and culture have begun to consider masculinities as identities continually in flux and have added a range of male voices and a variety of experiences to the record. The employ-ment of oral history techniques as a tool to explore changing histories and constructions of masculinity across time is beginning to flourish. However, exploring everyday masculinities historically is less well established. This chapter examines everyday sites such as the home, work and street where men lived and worked and ultimately expressed, or 'performed', their masculinities. Taking age and the life cycle as a structure, this chapter attempts to plot across the century the changing nature and everyday practice of masculinity from boyhood through to old age.

BOYHOOD LEISURE

Masculine identity was first formed in boyhood. Time spent playing in the street at lunchtime, after school, at weekends and in the holidays was vital for young boys to hone their boyhood identities. Until the latter decades of the century, when concerns for traffic and child safety became greater, the street was a main site where new identities were experimented with and initiation was performed. Role models for boys were to be found among family and friends, but of great importance were the role models found in literature. Reading, though not always synonymous with ideal masculinity, was yet part of many working-class and middle-class boys' daily and weekly routines. The reading materials were influential in shaping identities for boys.

During the late nineteenth and early twentieth centuries, boys' story magazines like *Boy's Own Paper* were crammed with athletic, chivalrous, aristocratic public-school boy heroes whose manly virtues were combined with their upper-class position, superiority and moral rectitude which were then tested in the British Empire. These papers emphasised moral obligations and exploited middle-class parents' anxieties and concerns about the nature of boyhood.[7] At the turn of the century the *Magnet* (1908–40) and *Gem* (1907–39) appeared on the market and challenged the tradition by introducing a number of stories set in more local environs. School stories such as the 'Greyfriars' series featuring Billy Bunter by Frank Richards were popular among *Magnet* readers. By the 1920s lower middle-class and artisan protagonists such as factory workers, engine drivers and clerks began to play central roles in the stories in order to acknowledge the growing working-class readership of the periodicals. These more 'democratic heroes' were more community focused, compared to the individual superiority of their aristocratic predecessors.[8] By the inter-war years, however, these publications began to falter and a new brand of boys' story-papers appeared that was to take over the boys' story-paper market for the remainder of the twentieth century.

In 1921 the first of Dundee-based D. C. Thomson's story-papers, *Adventure*, aimed at the male juvenile market, was published, and was quickly followed by *The Rover* (1922–61) and *The Wizard* (1922–63); *Skipper* then appeared in 1930 until it ceased publication in 1941, while in 1933 *The Hotspur* was added to the D. C. Thomson stable. This collection of story-papers was fondly known as 'The Big Five'. With each one, young readers would receive a tabloid-size journal full of vivid stories including detective, science-fiction, adventure and sporting tales featuring superheroes such as Wilson, Morgyn the Mighty and the Black Sapper. But during the mid-twentieth century, D. C. Thomson responded to public concern surrounding male youth by introducing anti-heroic, male working-class characters into their story-papers for boys. The most famous of these, Alf Tupper, The Tough of the Track, 'was regarded as a hooligan' in *The Rover*.[9] The label 'hooligan' produced the image of a rough working-class youth, a sign of moral decline and cultural disintegration, who required control and regulation. Despite this, in fact because of this, the character Alf Tupper grew in stature for young working-class males. The Tupper series focused on this young man's hard-fought achievements in athletics. Set in a fictional northern, industrial working-class manufacturing town called Greystone, Alf, who was a plumber by trade, took on and beat athletes from privileged 'posh' schools. This story line contrasted with previous boys' sporting stories set on the playing fields of public schools and those concerned with superhuman characters.

The story-papers, followed by their comic versions in the 1950s and 1960s, were immensely popular. *The Rover*, *The Wizard* and *The Hotspur* accounted for between half and two-thirds of all story-papers bought by twelve-year olds, while through the 1930s the weekly circulation for *The Wizard* alone was 800,000.[10] With other papers like *The Dandy* (1937) and *The Beano* (1938), the market was crowded with more than twenty leading boys' papers. Acquiring them and reading them was well remembered in memoir and oral history testimony. Sometimes deemed a high-brow, feminine, lazy, solitary, indoor leisure pursuit, reading was a difficult pastime from which to create a suitable masculine identity, as Ralph Glasser who grew up in the Gorbals in Glasgow in the 1930s recalled:

> [My] Father was well read in politics and in the nineteenth-century novelists, Dickens and Trollope being his favourites. But his reading nourished the sour scepticism that deeply possessed him. One day, when I was about fifteen, he said to me sharply, a shade enviously I afterwards thought, 'Why d'you waste your time with all this reading? It won't get you anywhere!' 'I don't know,' I answered. 'I can't help it.'[11]

Even if reading was encouraged, it was not always an easy activity to pursue. Reading material, books or story-papers were outwith some working-class families' budgets. Yet boys developed a variety of tactics to overcome these financial restrictions as Ronnie Paterson who grew up in the East End of Glasgow in the late 1940s and early 1950s recalled:

> most of the working-class kids had the idea of raking midges [pile of rubbish in a tenement backcourt]. And you often found comics, you know thrown out with newspapers. So you would get quite a few comics like that or you would,

you might, might find empty booze bottles. There was always a few people who had parties. And the different bottles you could get money for them [pause] two pence a bottle. And you could get tae the cinema. You could maybe go errands for people and maybe get a thruppenny bit [3d. coin]. Well that was how much it would cost for a *Dandy* or a *Beano.*[12]

The freedom to choose a comic and the routine of reading was taken away from the 'midge raker' in this context. But the action of acquiring money through innovative strategies overcame the financial restrictions and widened the reader's choice. The adventure and entrepreneurial skills involved in such exploits helped create boyhood identities. Other boys recalled how they would regularly run errands for people in their street and earn a penny or two to satisfy their reading habit. These men's memories of reading are habitual – in other words, they place reading within their wider everyday routines as a normal activity. They were involved either by raking midges or going on an errand. The boys' participation in actively seeking reading material was represented as routine and collective; they made comments such as: 'most of the working-class kids had the idea of raking midges and you often found comics'; and 'three or four of us each took a turn'. Despite the financial restrictions and time taken to convert their bounty into money to buy story-papers, even if they were not the latest editions, reading was a central everyday experience for these working-class readers.

Story-papers and comics presented myriad characters and plots for young boys to act out in their play. While some boys made do with home-made props or freebies from comics, Ken Doran recalled his father carefully making his make-believe costume and props. Born in the Townhead area of Glasgow in 1940, Ken was a keen cowboy fan as a boy. He recalled afternoon and weekend trips to the cinema to watch westerns, and reading the western cartoon strip 'Jeff Arnold Rider of the Range' in the *Eagle* at home after school. Ken's father was a cabinetmaker to trade

and had the skills to make the pistols from wood which were then painted black, leather holsters and belt were made from the leather of the aprons that electric welders used, as at that time my dad was working as a welder in Howdens. The wristbands and the chaperos (leather over trousers) came from the same source and they were decorated with metal discs down the legs made from tin, as was the sheriff's star to pin on the cut down waistcote [sic] with fringes stitched on. The hat was a felt trilby like a Stetson with a hat band made of leather. Most of the material was scrap from the Howdens workshop.[13]

By making a make-believe outfit for his son, Ken's father encouraged his son to identify with a specific masculine ideal. Some fathers revelled in the opportunity to use their skills, normally deployed in the shipyard, mine or factory, to make childhood games and accessories at the end of the working day or at the weekend.

The energy of boyhood games based on reading is palpable within some oral history interviews. While talking about the escapism he experienced reading comics Ronnie Paterson recalled children pretending to be cowboys:

> The kids would run down the street wi' one hand holding the reins and the other hand slapping their arse! [*Narrator stands up slaps his thigh*] . . . You know, that's them slapping the horse! And there'd be 'gunfights' all over the place![14]

Such recollections emphasised the physicality of boyhood play. The 'gallop', for instance, was central to the acting out of the cowboy role in childhood and in the acting out of its memory. The kinetic energy of boyhood play and the spaces where the boys performed were significant to the feeling of action and creation of suitable boyhood roles.

For most boys the family household and surrounding area would be the first space that would be utilised as a site of everyday play.[15] Ken transformed the family flat into somewhere to read by getting 'two chairs back to back and put poles across them and then drape a blanket and that became a den, so you would sit in there in the hallway and read the comics'.[16] As boys grew older their boundaries widened. Hamish Fraser recalled 'playing at Dan Dare' every lunch-time with a school friend, initially in a derelict smithy in his back garden.[17] Other respondents recalled how local monuments or bombed landscapes were utilised as backdrops to their make-believe because 'air raid shelters in the garden would make ideal castles.'[18] Ken Doran emphasised that 'make believe took place [in] the house, the street and in the air raid shelter [. . .] as long as it was devoid of adults.'[19] These memories of where boys read and enacted their games emphasised the importance for boys to separate and colonise distinct adult-free spaces in order to play out their fantasy and escapism. These spaces contrasted significantly with the official sites of reading such as the school, library and parental home which were governed by adult control: 'I didn't read them in libraries, you certainly weren't allowed to read them in school, ah mean you wouldn't read them in the organizations you went to.'[20]

ADOLESCENT LEISURE, APPRENTICESHIPS AND NATIONAL SERVICE

Attention to male adolescents in twentieth-century Scotland has tended to focus on 'problematic youth', and primarily boys' involvement in youth gangs and their subsequent punishment.[21] The 'hard man' was an archetypical construction of masculinity in Scotland and has more often than not been associated with Glasgow. Alec McArthur and H. Kingsley Long were among the first to make the association between the 'hard man', gangs and Glasgow in their 1935 novel *No Mean City*. Other 'hard men' have also taken centre stage in the fiction of contemporary Scottish writers such as Alasdair Gray, James Kelman, William McIlvanney and Irvine Welsh.[22] Glasgow gangs have predominantly been at the centre of historians' attention due to their notoriety fuelled by these literary representations and extensive media coverage in the 1930s, 1950s and 1960s. Vociferous critiques of the transition from post-war austerity to 1950s affluence sharpened concern about male youth. In 1945, the Scottish Youth Advisory Committee, focused on post-war reconstruction, connected juvenile delinquency to changes in the wider culture rather than to war conditions. According to the report, youths showed contempt for any type of education and were 'simply under developed', craving passive forms of leisure in gambling, sex, the dance hall and the cinema.[23] In 1951 'A Study of Glasgow Boys' based on the experiences of 1,349 Glasgow lads was concerned with their future prospects. The report indicated that despite the numerous social organisations 'run by churches, social agencies, and other autonomous bodies, and supplemented more recently by a Youth Service provided by Education Authorities and led by Youth Service officers [. . .] there is a failure to guide the interests and ambitions of youth into channels of social usefulness and their mental and physical energies into productive work.' 'Glaring' records of 'hooliganism and gangsterism' were cited as evidence of the youth problem.[24] While this kind of camaraderie merits attention, other 'rites of passage' were negotiated daily by boys while they were growing up.

The transition from boyhood to manhood was not straightforward, and as boys got older their everyday leisure patterns and routines also changed. Ceasing to read comics represented the shift from boyhood to manhood and was often hastened by experiencing more traditional rites of passage such as work or courting girls. The point at which boys negotiated this transition differed significantly. Roland Marshall, born in the Govan area of Glasgow in 1935, discussed the various jobs he had while still at school from his first one, aged ten, as a stable hand for his neighbour, to carrying coal aged fourteen. Roland emphasised the gap between boyhood and manhood that comics represented:

Roland: So ah would say when ah went tae look after the horses in the stable in Harmony Row, the comics finished then.
Hilary: *Could you say a little bit more about that?*
Roland: Well, just as easy, ah was in among the men, the men group there. Ah was looking after the horses and the men didnae read comics [laughs] so it could have just been that.[25]

At the age of ten Roland viewed reading as an indoor, private pursuit, in stark contrast with the outside, fully masculine and active world of work. He explained that a comic was something he would turn to 'when I was sitting in the house, you know, well just one room. Nothing tae dae. So you may as well occupy, so you had a comic that you liked tae read sort of thing.'[26] He explained the division in his youth between boyhood and manhood: 'In they days the men didnae take anything tae dae with the weans. The weans was women's work. They wouldnae even talk tae them outside, you know.'[27]

John Tosh notes that boys' 'qualification for a man's life among men [. . .] depends on their masculinity being tested against the recognition of their peers during puberty, young adulthood and beyond.'[28] Therefore, in order to project the image of manhood instead of boyhood, Roland had to negotiate the division and reject the everyday paraphernalia of boyhood that might have undermined his aspiring masculinity.

Age and their place in the job market is a significant marker of time used by men to structure their narratives of boyhood and manhood. John Cooper started working at the age of sixteen and explained that: 'Oh no when ah was working ah wasnae interested in anything like that [comics] then.' Instead, John detailed the novels and specialist magazines pertinent to his new employment.[29] The consumer power acquired with the prestige and masculine identity as a young wage earner allowed John to traverse the transition from a boyhood reading identity to a suitable manly reading identity. Courtship was another significant rite of passage during the mid-twentieth century when marriage was viewed as the 'norm'. Claire Langhamer argues that at this age courting superseded all other forms of leisure.[30] Alex Thomson's experience exemplified the tension between financial restrictions of young manhood and courting: 'I stopped buying it [the *Eagle*] because I couldn't afford it, because although it got paid with the family papers it came out of my pocket money and then I got interested in girls.'[31]

Until 1947 the school leaving age was fourteen. Older men interviewed in the mid-1980s recalled how they could not wait to leave school at the age of fourteen or fifteen, however difficult the work was. As one man said: 'you were brought up to work.'[32] The enthusiasm to leave school was not felt by all as they came to terms with the economic realities of education versus working. For more better-off boys the ritual of school and homework was a prolonged experience as they continued secondary education through to higher education.

The daily routine changed abruptly for young boys starting work often with only a night or a weekend between the two routines: rising early in the morning often with an hour lunch break before returning home in the evening. Often working a six-day week meant the nature and time spent with family and friends changed. After a day seeking work in the shipyards with his father, a fourteen-year-old 'gulped down his tea [and] rushed into the back-courts to tell his tenement friends' about what he had experienced while they had been in school:

> They rallied, a charmed, envious circle, while he narrated, a little Homer of the back-streets. He had seen a dead man and the highest crane on the Clyde! His da had knocked a man 'right oot' over the table! – by now his father's adversary had attained prodigious proportions – and he had got a job in the 'Yards' with 'big money'. Suddenly he broke off importantly with: 'Well, I'll have to be gettin' home now. I've got to be up gey early for my job, ye know!' and swaggered away.[33]

Having started work, young men often assumed a new position within the family as the second 'breadwinner', if their father was still in employment. They were usually no longer requested to help with the daily chores, if they had previously, and were allocated more preferential treatment at meal times.

Young lads starting work in heavy industries were quickly introduced to the harsh nature of their new working environments and the routine of injury and death. The introduction to fishermen's work culture, for example, was strenuous and fraught with dangers for new recruits. At the age of fourteen a young boy was expected to cook all the meals for the crew, do the washing up, polish the ship brass and scrub the decks. Jock Bruce, a fisherman for fifty years who had started out as a cook at the age of thirteen in 1928, explained: 'You hadn't only the cooking, you had the coiling of the ropes, almost a mile of rope would shoot out with the herring net and you were down there in a square box and you'd to coil that rope so it would run itself clear.'[34] Young boys who started their fishing career as cooks were not included in the 'manly' body of the crew: 'If the crew were at their food or they were in the cabin and you were down there, you'd to be seen but not heard, you weren't allowed to chip in.'[35] It was not until after a year and a half as cook that Jock 'got a step up to deck hand, doing the men's work'.[36] Once a boy had completed his apprenticeship he was deemed to have crossed the boundary between boyhood and manhood, which was reflected in his treatment and new-found respect both at work and in the home.[37]

The skills of a trade and the inside knowledge of the work culture were prerequisites to a full-blown masculine identity and inclusion within the male working community. Young men's physique, which was crucial to performing well down a mine or in a shipyard, was maintained and honed during their daily and weekly leisure activities: Tommy Coulter was born in 1928 and started work on the mine surface in 1943. His personal time was occupied pursuing physical activities that not only honed his physique but were also a stark antidote to working twelve hours a day in a pit:

> When we went tae work in the coal face yi', well we were strong lads, you had to be. And yir lifestyle was such that if you werenay producing coal you were playing football, or boxing or dancing or walking, mainly engaged in physical pursuits. Ah mean ah used to walk twenty-five miles every Saturday and Sunday and that was, ah done that fir years and years.[38]

Daily life for young men working in reserved occupations during the Second World War changed again. Mr Donaldson, who was fifteen in 1939 and living in Cambusnethan in Lanarkshire, explained that during the war he became

> fed-up with home life, I was fed-up with working in the foundry and I was eventually fed-up with doing twelve or fourteen hours in a foundry and coming home

and the hooter going at night and you had to get oot your bed [. . .] If you werenae in the army you still had to do voluntary service, fire watch and home guard and things like that. And if you did fourteen hours work in the bloody foundry you werenae [exempt].[39]

Working overtime as well as contributing to the war effort on the home front rigidly defined and structured a man's working day and significantly depleted his leisure time. National Service continued to have a fundamental impact on the structure and routine of everyday life for all young men after the Second World War.

Emblazoned across the front page of the revolutionary comic *Eagle* every week from 1950 until the mid-sixties was the editor Marcus Morris's timely ideal of masculinity – 'Dan Dare, The Pilot of the Future'. Morris was primarily concerned about the morality of youth and wanted to create a wholesome comic 'founded on strong Christian principles as a counter to the American crime and horror comics which were beginning to flood the country.'[40] Dare was a skilled pilot, competent and brave, who went on missions into space fighting enemies and saving the world through daring feats of endurance. A natural leader, 'who inspired those around him to give of their best', he was diplomatic when faced with problematic situations of good versus evil.[41] He would not resort to brute violence to get himself out of situations but preferred to negotiate himself out, and if that failed he would attempt to outwit his enemy. Recalling stories of Dan Dare and other RAF fighter pilots he had read as a young boy, Richard Ingram stated, 'We were going into the services anyway, I had no choice in the matter, you were going, [into] the National Service.'[42]

Fresh wartime memories combined with the maintenance of military conscription made the negotiation of 'manhood' a difficult process in the fifties.[43] Young men were expected to undergo basic military training and military service for a period of two years under the terms of The National Service Act of 1948. Leaving home often for the first time meant young men had to cope with changing environments both physically and mentally. Once again their everyday routines of work and leisure were disrupted as they fell into step in military fashion. Some men felt National Service helped them grow up as they learned discipline and new skills. Other men felt it was an unwelcome interruption at a crucial point in their life when they were trying to carve out a career for themselves after earning a low wage on a five-year apprenticeship. Recognition as a skilled man with a full-time job and marriage had to be put on hold until they returned from National Service.

WORKING AND UNEMPLOYED MEN

In Scotland, where for nearly two centuries national wealth was dependent on heavy industry, the routine of manual labour for the working-class male reaffirmed his masculinity. Of those insured in Scotland in 1913 only 1.8 per cent were unemployed, in contrast to 8.7 per cent in London.[44] High employment rates in Scotland prior to the First World War, in physically demanding industries such as shipbuilding, mining and agriculture, guaranteed men's ability to maintain their masculine prowess. As McIvor and Johnston have shown, with reference to Clydeside between 1930 and 1970 and the range of heavy industrial jobs on offer, work and work cultures provided a number of opportunities for men to learn, perfect and reproduce macho values.[45] The physicality of work in industries such as coal mining, shipbuilding, steel foundries and fishing placed an emphasis on an 'ideal' masculinity, one which was muscularly strong and full of stamina in order to be able to endure the physically demanding labour. The dirt, noise and monotony of a job were challenges to be overcome by strength and self-discipline. Displays of emotion were to be avoided.

Along with the physical nature of the work which honed men's physiological power, earning a living wage and being able to provide for your family as the man of the house were central to the definition of working-class masculinity. A man's wage was a measure of his masculinity: 'the hard worker was a "big earner"'.[46] The piece-rate system of payment in some workplaces meant there was an important emphasis on high production. In some cases, to ensure the wage they wanted and needed, some men would forego safety equipment which could impede their work rate and reduce their pay packet.[47] Moreover, the wearing of protective clothing and goggles was sometimes viewed as a sign of weakness and was deemed 'unmanly'. But generally the pressure of having dependants at home would force men to push themselves and their bodies to extremes, working in difficult conditions with dangerous materials in order to be able to take home enough money. However, the physicality of the work and the exposure to hazardous working conditions made men's labour a potentially dangerous element of their masculinity.[48]

The First World War was a crisis point in the history of masculinity and impacted significantly on previous concepts of masculinity. Employment was fairly secure throughout the duration of the war, allowing concepts of masculinity to be based on waged labour. However, the dismembering of male bodies in battle and the psychological scars severely impeded a strong masculine identity.[49] During the inter-war period and in the later twentieth century unemployment threatened not only men's potential to provide for their family but 'the sudden economic deprivation and emotional stress of joblessness was devastating'.[50] As a 1940s report noted, prolonged unemployment and continual inability to find work resulted in 'frustration and lowered personal value'.[51]

Deskilling and structural changes within the workplace undermined men's ability, pride and opportunity to showcase their skill. Scottish unemployment averaged 14 per cent between 1923 and 1930. Unemployment rates were higher in the west of the country: in 1936, Edinburgh 12.3 per cent, Greenock 20 per cent, and Airdrie 30 per cent.[52] In the summer of 1937 there were 8,273 young men between the ages of eighteen and twenty-three inclusive registered as unemployed in Glasgow alone.[53] The impact of unemployment on masculinity was stark. Edwin Muir's *Scottish Journey* in 1934 took him through Hamilton, Airdrie and Motherwell. He recalled: 'It was a warm, overcast summer day; groups of idle, sullen-looking young men stood at the street corners; smaller groups were wandering among the blue-black ranges of pit-dumps which in that region are the substitute for nature; the houses looked empty and unemployed like their tenants.'[54] Muir continued: 'Everything which could give meaning to their existence in these grotesque industrial towns of Lanarkshire is slipping from them; the surroundings of industrialism remain, but industry itself is vanishing like a dream.'[55] With the decline of industry at this time, the opportunity for Scottish men to parade their masculine identity based on work declined sharply, restricting them 'to very unstable conditions from which to draw a sense of manly identity'.[56]

The impact of unemployment on a family was immense due to complex and increasingly restrictive benefits systems. Men's ability to provide for the family and to maintain a suitable masculine identity for themselves was weakened and tested in this period. Young men, who were able to find work possibly for the first time, were sometimes in a position where they now threatened their father's own authority and sense of masculinity. Alec Miller was born in 1919 in Lanarkshire. His father had been 'an iron and steel dresser [who] took whatever he could get. That was his main job. He worked in the foundry for a while too and he worked in the quarries.'[57] In the early 1930s Alec got his first job but at that time his father was unemployed. He recalled: 'I started work and I was only quite young you know and I was getting tuppence ha'penny an hour and I discovered after a while that what I earned my father lost because he was on the dole.'[58] Another oral history respondent, William Young, born in 1927 in Hamilton, explained that 'any time my father was out of work it was just a case of signing on the buroo (dole) to get so much money and that sort of kept him going. He was a bit independent (laughs), it got to the extent that things were desperate.'[59] He continued to explain that 'that was one of the reasons I left school at fourteen. I started work on my fourteenth birthday. (laughs) [. . .] The folk my mother used to work for, they had a shop in Hamilton, so I went down and I got a job.'[60] Some young men who had been destined to be skilled labouring men and were now at a risk of having no work found themselves entering employment in what had traditionally been deemed feminine spheres, namely shops and offices. For other young men unemployment was endemic and since leaving school at fourteen 'had matured [to the age of eighteen] against a background of unemployment, in some cases slight, in other cases entirely devoid of any pattern of work as part of life'.[61]

Some men attempted to cope with unemployment by maintaining the structures of their everyday routine. Older men who were unemployed in the 1980s tried to sustain their daily routine by replacing their job with job hunting. They would get up at their usual time and look for work at the Job Centre, scour newspapers in the library or try to secure work through local contacts. However, while maintaining one aspect of their daily routine, older unemployed men tended to withdraw themselves from their social activities at night-time in the pub or club as they did not want to attract a stigma when unable to join in the traditional male preserve of buying a round of drinks. From previous research on male unemployment both in the 1980s and earlier during the inter-war period, there is little evidence to suggest that working-class male unemployment transformed daily gendered roles in the home. Although dislocated from participating in traditional male social activities in the pub through lack of money, standing outside pubs during the day in a group was a compromise between withdrawing altogether from male interaction and the alternative of staying at home which was regarded as a female sphere.[62]

Other men attempted to hold onto a routine of work that defined the breadwinner role by supplementing what 'buroo' money they received with other means. Working in an allotment was one way men were able to use their day-time productively while producing much-needed food for their family. Jack Donaldson recalled men working in their gardens: 'Oh aye, oh well, I don't think there were that many professional gardeners but everybody was a gardener more or less because you had to have a garden to feed the kids, you know big families and you couldn't afford the produce.'[63] Other strategies and routines were also pursued. Alec Miller could remember that 'the men used to go out at night and go round the farms and pick some potatoes and a turnip or something. But they didn't make a mess, they didn't destroy anything . . .They would get enough to feed their family and go away. And a lot of farmers knew that.'[64] A less respectable means of providing for the family during times of unemployment throughout the century was to collect fuel from the surrounding area. The public act of 'coal howking' from abandoned open-cast sites and carrying the sack of coal home could have undermined a man's identity as a provider and his family's respectability within the community. However, the physical nature of the dig for the coal and the close association to work and routine were also deemed positive.

The decline of manufacturing, heavy industries and artisan trades since the 1970s has impacted again on the construction of Scottish masculinity. Simultaneously, the rise of second-wave feminism, the demographic revolution in the nature of the family, and the rise of 'the new man' have done much to erode the presence of, and sympathy for, the 'hard man' of British urban folklore.

FATHERS AND HUSBANDS

The nature of the historical relationship between working- and middle-class
men and the home has come under scrutiny recently. Ranging from awkwardness, reluctant participation through to absenteeism, the working-class father
has often been portrayed as a distant figure expected to play only the most
minor role in looking after the children on a day-to-day basis.[65] A distinct
imbalance in the allocation of responsibilities within women's and men's
roles, with Scottish men sharing little of women's domestic life, is depicted
in common discourses throughout the twentieth century. Tom Brennan's
1959 survey of home-life and work in Govan acknowledged that 'Men are
very rarely seen in food shops, are never seen wheeling a pram, and would
feel ridiculous if they had to carry home a bunch of flowers. [. . .] In Govan
such men would be very rare indeed and furthermore the typical Govan wife
would not expect her husband to behave like this.'[66] One male oral history
respondent explained that 'men pushing prams was thought soft. As a man
he wouldnae want to be seen by his pals, pushing a pram, or he would be
referred to as a sissy, that's a woman's job.'[67] According to Lynne Segal, for
the husband to maintain his status and prestige in his social life with his peers,
he had to conspicuously distance himself from his wife and children.[68]

The 'new man' who was willing to stay at home and look after the children, take an equal share of the household chores and be kind and consider-
ate due to understanding his feminine side, is cited by many commentators
as appearing in the late 1980s. This new location of male activity and male
interest has been seen in recent sociological work as a new phenomenon.[69]
Yet if the historian extends the gaze backwards, it is possible to find both
working-class and middle-class men taking part in the familial daily routines
at home.

Recently the distinction between gendered roles for women and men
in the family in twentieth-century Scotland has been subject to reappraisal among historians. The 'separate spheres' model which privileged the
woman's role in the domestic home and the man's role in the public world
of work has been re-examined in order to better identify and appreciate
fathers' roles in the family home. Despite the supremacy of the 'separate
spheres' discourse, Eleanor Gordon argues that it 'is by no means clear that
a sharp demarcation of gender roles based on a male breadwinner and a non-
working wife had become the established norm by the twentieth century'.[70]
In the late nineteenth and early twentieth centuries the demand for a 'family
wage' for the 'breadwinner' by the trade unions meant that the husband who
worked and who should be able to provide for his non-working wife became
the benchmark of working-class respectability.[71] However, the instability
of the working environment coupled with poor wages meant that the ideal
was far from the reality. The numbers of married women working varied
across Scotland geographically and across classes. In Glasgow and Edinburgh

married women working in the economy matched the national average, yet in Dundee (known as a 'woman's town') and Shetland (also a 'woman's world') the numbers were dramatically higher.[72]

The 'separate spheres' discourse disguised the role men played as fathers, by diluting their participation in the lives of their children to that of the provider. Middle-class fathers have generally been represented as distant figures in their children's lives, yet Gordon and Nair challenge this with reference to (albeit late nineteenth-century) correspondence from fathers to their children showing that they were interested and active in their children's lives and development.[73] Middle-class Glaswegian masculinities were easily defined as husband and father as well as businessman and industrialist.[74] Lynn Abrams demonstrates, with reference to oral histories, autobiographies and records left by child-welfare organisations, that 'working-class fathers were as affective, indulgent and involved with their children as their middle-class counterparts'.[75] Indeed in his study of Govan, Brennan conceded that in 1959 'even in working-class areas at least a few men would be found who would help with the shopping, take the baby out or buy their wife some flowers.'[76]

Some men in work struggled to spend more time with their families. Fishermen fought for recognition as fathers and husbands against capitalist pressure from owners and skippers of boats. In 1914 the Aberdeen *Fishing News* called for an urgent need to 'put a stop to the wholesale delaying of trawlers by members of the crew.'[77] At the end of trips that had lasted about a week it was usual for the skipper to ask his crew if they wanted to sail with him on his next voyage. Men who had already been at sea for a prolonged time often declined this offer in order to spend more time at home on shore. This had the potential to delay the turnaround of the ship and ultimately its ability to make money. In 1919 a concession was introduced that allowed men who had been on trips longer than ten days the right to one day ashore without pay.[78] One Great Line skipper, George Leiper, who fished between 1934 and 1961 and had two children in 1940 and 1942, 'was away – on the average trip I'd be away – three weeks. Twenty-one, twenty-two, twenty-three days was the usual time.' He continued to explain that prior to going back out he would spend 'three days back at home [which] wasn't much time for home life.'[79] Another fisherman, Andrew Craig, who was thirty years old in 1910 and the skipper of an Aberdeenshire line boat, would often be away from home for long periods of time also. He would maintain contact with his family by sending postcards home. While these postcards were often formal acknowledgements detailing the weather conditions and the catches landed, Andrew would also include more personal phrases and tell his family he missed them. On one occasion he wrote to his son: 'I feel strange for want of your loud voice to break the monotony.'[80]

After the Second World War new demands were placed on women, as wives and mothers, due to a soaring birth rate and attitudes to working women being largely hostile. But women were no longer isolated in their

Figure 5.1   *Men with children at Edinburgh Zoo, 1972. www.scran.ac.uk*

interests and preoccupations: the man's place was also in the home. After 1945 improved housing conditions and smaller families facilitated the transition of male recreation from the pub to the home. New expectations of the comforts and the pleasures of home had been forged on the battlefield. A new 'togetherness', domestic harmony and equality between the sexes was being promoted.[81] There was also a growing belief in equality between partners, with husband and wife playing different but complementary roles, as an important element of the 'companionate marriage'.[82] The stereotypical representation of the working-class husband of days gone by was apparently to be replaced by a new partnership in marriage. Michael Young and Peter Willmott affirmed the end of the absentee husband in the fifties: 'In place of the old comes a new kind of companionship between man and woman, reflecting the rise in status of the young wife and children, which is one of the great transformations of our time.'[83] Although, if notions of masculinity were to be found to have progressed by the fifties, what was expected of them within it, according to some, had changed very little.[84]

In 2000 *The Independent* reported that 'Burchill steps in as Dodds takes paternity leave'. Billy Dodds took leave from the Scottish football team to attend the birth of his first child ahead of the team's World Cup qualifier match against Croatia in Zagreb. Dodds was supported by his employer in his decision.[85] In response to the discovery of the 'new man' who attends the birth of his child and plays a role in childcare since the 1990s, one of the most significant political changes that has impacted on men's everyday routines has been the introduction of their legal right to paternity leave and statutory paternity pay in the form of the Work and Families Act (2006). Currently men are entitled to one or two weeks' paternity leave paid at the same rate as statutory maternity pay. This acknowledges men's role in looking after their children. Yet crucially, it provides a base for the Scottish Government to continue developing its Gender Equality Scheme that aims to address disadvantages that both men and women face at home and in the workplace in Scotland today.[86]

MEN AND MASCULINITY IN THE 2000s

The trials and tribulations of two fictional Glaswegian pensioners have recently taken centre stage in BBC Scotland's sitcom *Still Game*. From discussions ranging from death to sex, the two elderly protagonists Victor and Jack play with media representations of urban Scottish masculinity with much tongue-in-cheek hilarity. In social and historical research an awareness that gender intersects with age is important. However, there is still little research on older men's masculinities or older men's own perceptions of masculinity. Studies that do exist focus on biomedical aspects of aging such as disease and disability or the effects of retirement. Older men are rarely seen as individuals and are often invisible 'as men' in contemporary society. One reason for this is that women's life expectancy is higher than men's and therefore women make up a large proportion of the older population. In this sense, old age has been more synonymous with women. Glasgow has the highest male mortality rate in Scotland, with male life expectancy in some areas as low as sixty-three.[87] Socially constructed images of older men usually feature asexual, sedentary figures, genderless and thus not really 'men' at all.

Historians Arthur McIvor and Ronnie Johnston have explored the relationship between masculinity and occupational health. The oral history interviews they conducted with men previously employed in shipbuilding, construction and mining industries highlighted many examples where machismo culture exposed men to dangerous working practices that undermined their health and subsequently their masculine identity in old age. Some of the men interviewed constructed a set of changing identities for themselves: young, active, healthy and strong men in the past, retired men suffering debilitating illness due to dangerous working practices in the present.[88] Loss of physical ability, agency and freewill, combined with personal feelings of inadequacy, make reconciling present and past selves difficult. The physical and psychological effects of working hard from an early age sometimes created a sense of flux and loss in working-class men's narratives of their later lives.

Older men in the late twentieth century grappled with changing gender roles.[89] Discourses of the 'new man' or 'new father' became more acceptable, signalling changing constructs of masculinity that older generations of men came to face in the last quarter of the century. Mrs Murray who married in 1963 recalled: 'It's strange as men get older, ah mean ma husband the now, he'd do a washing, he'll hang the washing out in the back garden and he'll bring it in again. He'll do the –, he'll iron and yet years ago if he –, when we were first married there was hell to pay if I didn't have his shirts ironed for going out at night.'[90] Social class also cut across experiences of masculinity and age. In their study of older Scottish men born in the 1930s, Hunt and Emslie showed that 'men who were upwardly mobile were much more egalitarian in their views about the gendered division of labour in the household than those in either stable middle-class or stable working-class households'.[91]

CONCLUSION

Contemporary concern about young Scottish males dominates headlines. The media report boys' underachievement in school, their poor health, their high suicide rate, their resort to violence and murder, and their involvement in gangs. The Scottish *Daily Record* headline 'Glasgow "Has As Many Gangs As London"' in February 2008 was based on a report commissioned by the Centre for Social Justice, 'Breakthrough Britain', that highlighted the importance of combating social deprivation, failing education and intergenerational worklessness in Glasgow.[92] Schemes across the city such as The Green Bridge Initiative in Pollok, part of YMCA Glasgow's Calm Project, aim to give young people a louder voice in tackling trouble on the street. Yet such initiatives still lack suitable facilities and the opportunities to provide young people with a stake in running groups.[93] This idea has as much historical precedence as gangs themselves. In 1968 pop singer Frankie Vaughan got involved with gangs in Easterhouse and together they established a self-managed site in the area for young people to use as long as local authority subsidies were provided.[94]

The practice of men's everyday lives changed throughout the twentieth century. Although boys' and men's life courses were by 2000 still dominated by school, work, marriage and retirement, daily experiences and routines were altered and disrupted by aging, changes in social class, and increasing individual responsibilities in home and family across the period. Listening to men talk about their lives showed that there were numerous ways to be a man, and that external social and political factors impacted throughout the century on the making of the Scots man.

Notes

1. K. Mullen, *A Healthy Balance: Glaswegian Men Talk about Health, Tobacco and Alcohol* (Aldershot, 1993), p. 177.

2. http://news.bbc.co.uk/1/hi/scotland/664845.stm
3. K. Soothill, B. Francis, E. Ackerley and S. Collett, 'Homicide in Britain – A comparative study of rates in Scotland and England and Wales', *Crime and Criminal Justice Research Findings* (2000) no. 36.
4. *The Scotsman*, 31 August 2006.
5. A. Chapple and S. Ziebland, 'Prostate cancer: embodied experience and perceptions of masculinity', *Sociology of Health and Illness* 24 (2002), pp. 820–41.
6. 'Reporting progress against the social justice milestones and targets. Milestone 13: Reducing the proportion of unemployed working age people', Social Justice – a Scotland where everyone matters: Indicators of Progress 2003, The Scottish Government Publications, website publication date 17 December 2003, http://www.scotland.gov.uk/Publications/2003/12/18693/31063
7. John Springhall, *Youth, Popular Culture and Moral Panics: Penny Gaffs to Gangstarap, 1830–1996* (Basingstoke, 1998).
8. Kelly Boyd, 'Knowing your place: the tensions of manliness in boys' story papers, 1918–1939', in M. Roper and J. Tosh (eds), *Manful Assertions: Masculinities in Britain since 1800* (London, 1991), p. 145.
9. *The Rover*, 18 June 1949.
10. K. Carpenter, *Penny Dreadfuls and Comics: English Periodicals for Children from Victorian Times to the Present Day* (London, 1983), p. 89.
11. Ralph Glasser, *Growing Up in the Gorbals* (London, 1986), p. 33.
12. Strathclyde Oral History Centre Archive, Representation and Reception Study (subsequently cited as SOHCA/RR. Other collections held by the SOHCA and used in this article are named after the SOHCA prefix and abbreviated in subsequent citations), SOHCA/RR/15/Ronnie Paterson, p. 3.
13. Correspondence with author from Ken Doran, 8 June 2005.
14. SOHCA/RR/15/Ronnie Paterson, p. 5. Annette Kuhn's interviewees also recalled the 'gallop home' after watching a cowboy film, A. Kuhn, *An Everyday Magic: Cinema and Cultural Memory* (London, 2002) p. 102.
15. Graham Dawson, *Soldier Heroes: British Adventure, Empire and the Imagining of Masculinities* (London, 1994), pp. 251–8.
16. SOHCA/RR/07/Ken Doran, p. 8.
17. Correspondence with author from Hamish Fraser, 14 June 2005.
18. SOHCA/RR/12/Richard Ingram, p. 6; correspondence from Ken Doran to author, 8 June 2005.
19. Correspondence from Ken Doran to author, 8 June 2005.
20. SOHCA/RR/07/Ken Doran, p. 8.
21. Andrew Davies, 'Street gangs, crime and policing in Glasgow during the 1930s: the case of the Beehive Boys', *Social History* 23, 3 (1998), pp. 251–67; David Smith, 'Official responses to juvenile delinquency in Scotland during the Second World War', *Twentieth Century British History* 18, 1 (2007), pp. 78–105.
22. Alec McArthur, *No Mean City: a Story of the Glasgow Slums* (London, 1935); Alasdair Gray, *1982 Janine* (London, 1984); James Kelman, *How Late It Was, How Late* (London, 1994); William McIlvanney, *The Big Man* (London, 1985); Irvine Welsh, *Trainspotting* (London, 1993).

23. Smith, 'Official responses to juvenile delinquency', p. 90.
24. T. Ferguson and J. Cunnison, *The Young Wage Earner: A Study of Glasgow Boys* (London, 1951), pp. 24–5.
25. SOHCA/RR/14/Rowland Marshall, p. 16.
26. Ibid., p. 16.
27. Ibid., p. 4.
28. John Tosh, 'What should historians do with masculinity? reflections on nineteenth-century Britain', *History Workshop Journal* 38 (1994), p. 184.
29. SOHCA/RR/06/John Cooper, p. 5.
30. Claire Langhamer, 'Love and courtship in mid-twentieth-century England', *The Historical Journal* 50, 1 (2007), pp. 173–96.
31. SOHCA/RR/19/Alex Thomson, p. 9.
32. Daniel Wight, *Workers Not Wasters, Masculine Respectability, Consumption and Unemployment in Central Scotland: A Community Study* (Edinburgh, 1993), p. 101.
33. Edward Gaitens, *Growing Up and Other Stories* (London, 1942) p. 15.
34. National Sound Archive British Library QD8/Fish/79/Jock Bruce.
35. Ibid.
36. Ibid.
37. Keith McClelland, 'Masculinity and the "representative artisan" in Britain, 1850–80', in Roper and Tosh (eds), *Manful Assertions*, p. 81.
38. SOHCA/Tommy Coulter, p. 7.
39. SOHCA/Lynn Sinclair/02, p. 12.
40. *The Times*, Frank Hampson, Obituary (10 July 1985), p. 14.
41. N. Wright and M. Higgs, *The Dan Dare Dossier: Celebrating the 40th Anniversary of the Pilot of the Future* (London, 1990), p. 16.
42. SOHCA/RR/12/Richard Ingram, p. 5.
43. Lynne Segal, *Slow Motion: Changing Masculinities, Changing Men* (London, 1990), p. 18.
44. Christopher Harvie, *No Gods and Precious Few Heroes, Twentieth Century Scotland*, 3rd edn (Edinburgh, 1998), p. 2.
45. Arthur McIvor and Ronnie Johnston, 'Dangerous work, hard men and broken bodies: masculinity in the Clydeside heavy industries, c. 1930–1970s', *Labour History Review* 69, 2 (2004), pp. 135–51.
46. Wight, *Workers Not Wasters*, p. 139.
47. McIvor and Johnston, 'Dangerous work', p. 145.
48. Ibid.
49. Anne-Marie Hughes, 'Domestic violence on Clydeside between the wars', *Labour History Review* 69, 2 (2004), p. 174.
50. Joanna Bourke, *Working-class Cultures in Britain, 1890–1960* (London, 1994) p. 131.
51. C. Cameron, *Disinherited Youth: A Report on the 18+ Age Group Enquiry Prepared for the Trustees of the Carnegie United Kingdom Trust* (Edinburgh, 1943), pp. 65–9.
52. Harvie, *No Gods and Precious Few Heroes*, p. 47.
53. Cameron, *Disinherited Youth*, p. 3.

54. Edwin Muir, *Scottish Journey*, first published in 1935 (Edinburgh, 1979), p. 1.
55. Ibid., p. 2.
56. Hughes, 'Representations and counter-representations', p. 175.
57. SOHCA/LS/07, p. 2.
58. Ibid.
59. SOHCA/LS/08, p. 3.
60. Ibid., p. 7.
61. Cameron, *Disinherited Youth*, p. 65.
62. Wight, *Workers Not Wasters*, pp. 199–204.
63. SOHCA/LS/02, p. 3; SOHCA/LS/07, p. 12.
64. SOHCA/LS/07, p. 7.
65. Lynn Abrams, '"There was nobody like my Daddy": fathers, the family and the marginalisation of men in modern Scotland', *The Scottish Historical Review* LXXVIII, 2 (1999) p. 227.
66. T. Brennan, *Reshaping a City: a Case Study of Redevelopment in Glasgow* (Glasgow, 1959), p. 101.
67. SOHCA/Hard Man New Man/03/Ronnie Paterson.
68. Segal, *Slow Motion*, p. 8.
69. Andrew Singleton and Jane Maree Maher, 'The "New Man" is in the house: young men, social change, and housework', *The Journal of Men's Studies* 12, 3 (2004), pp. 227–40.
70. Eleanor Gordon, 'The family', in Lynn Abrams, Eleanor Gordon, Deborah Simonton and Eileen Janes Yeo (eds), *Gender in Scottish History since 1700* (Edinburgh, 2006), p. 252.
71. Colin Creighton, 'The rise of the male breadwinner family: a reappraisal', *Comparative Studies in Society and History* (1996), pp. 310–37.
72. Gordon, 'The Family', p. 252; Lynn Abrams, *Myth and Materiality in a Woman's World: Shetland 1800–2000* (Manchester, 2005).
73. Eleanor Gordon and Gwyneth Nair, *Public Lives: Women, Family and Society in Victorian Britain* (New Haven and London, 2003), p. 61.
74. Ibid., p. 58.
75. Abrams, 'There was nobody like my Daddy', p. 230.
76. Brennan, *Reshaping a City*, p. 101.
77. Cited in Paul Thompson, *Living the Fishing* (London, 1983), p. 142.
78. Ibid., p. 143.
79. QD8/Fish/128/George Leiper.
80. Thompson, *Living the Fishing*, p. 133.
81. Segal, *Slow Motion*, p. 3.
82. L. Davidoff, M. Doolittle, J. Fink, K. Holden, *The Family Story: Blood, Contract and Intimacy* (London: Longman, 1999), p. 190.
83. Michael Young and Peter Willmott, *Family and Kinship in East London* (Harmondsworth, 1962), p. 30.
84. Segal, *Slow Motion*, p. 3.
85. *The Independent*, 10 October 2000.
86. Scottish Government, *Gender Equality Scheme 2008–2011*, consultation for

Scottish Government published June 2008, http://www.scotland.gov.uk/Publications/2008/06/12114733/0

87. Centre for Social Justice, Breakthrough Glasgow Report, 5 February 2008, p. 5.

88. McIvor and Johnston, 'Dangerous work'.

89. Hilary Young, 'Hard man, new man: re/composing masculinities in Glasgow, c. 1950–2000', *Oral History* 35, 1 (2007), pp. 71–81.

90. SOHAC/HMNM/01/Mrs Murray.

91. Carol Emslie, Kate Hunt and Rosaleen O'Brian, 'Masculinities in older men: a qualitative study in the West of Scotland', *Journal of Men's Studies* 12, 3, March (2004), p. 223.

92. The Scottish *Daily Record*, 'Glasgow "has as many gangs as London"', 5 February 2008.

93. *Glasgow Evening Times* Online, 'Rapping to beat the gangs', 26 December 2006.

94. Angela Bartie, 'Moral panics and moral enterprisers: Frankie Vaughan and Glasgow gangs, 1965–1970', Independent Study Project, History Department, University of Strathclyde, no. 1022, 2001.

Chapter 6

Spectacle, Restraint and the Sabbath Wars: The 'Everyday' Scottish Sunday

Callum G. Brown

THE BATTLEGROUND

On 2 July 1905, two thousand people gathered after Sunday worship on the promenade in Lerwick in Shetland outside the ice-cream and aerated-water shop run by Harry Corrothie, an Italian Catholic immigrant. They were led there by the ministers of the Church of Scotland, the United Free Church, the Baptists and the Congregationalists, the last bringing with them a large cart drawing a harmonium. They proceeded to hold a service with hymns and speeches condemning ice-cream shops for 'the injurious effect they had upon the youth of every town where they were planted'. Meanwhile, inside the shop were members of the British Socialist Party, who were particularly strong in number in Lerwick, and by siding with Harry Corrothie they started a saga which, over the ensuing eight years, led to a plebiscite on Sunday closing of ice-cream shops and the formation of a 'Sunday-closing party' that had four candidates elected to the town council in 1913, opposed by two socialists who lost. 'To me', wrote one of the victors of the anti-ice-cream campaign, 'the contest appeared to be the Churches of Lerwick versus Socialism. The philistines have been routed before the Ark of the Lord.'[1]

Battles like that in Lerwick continued to rage in Scotland during the twentieth century. On 7 February 1946, Edinburgh Corporation decided on a contentious vote to open the Ross Bandstand in Princes Street Gardens on Sundays – but only for the use of religious services. Described by one councillor as 'the thin end of the wedge to make Edinburgh a pagan city', this move had split councillors and attracted banner headlines in *The Scotsman*.[2] Two decades on, in June 1965 the *Daily Record* reported that at Kyleakin in Skye three hundred protestors prayed and sang psalms as they pressed against a big police cordon in an attempt to prevent the first Sunday ferry from landing at the slipway. The first car, driven by an American couple, rolled off with an escort of twenty-five police, but was then stopped by a line of human bodies; fourteen people were arrested, including the Revd Angus Smith of the Free Church who said; 'It is a sad, sad day for this God-fearing island of ours.'[3] And on a momentous day, Sunday, 27 October 2002, the same Revd Angus Smith, known for his actions in 1965 by some as 'the Ferry

Figure 6.1 *The arrest of the Revd Angus Smith of the Free Church of Scotland, after trying to prevent the first car from rolling off the initial Kyle–Kyleakin Sunday ferry in 1965. www.scran.ac.uk*

Reverend', was reported by the *Sunday Herald* as 'the living embodiment of a Calvinist Scotland that may be all but extinguished as the first regular Sunday flights arrive in Stornoway today'.[4] Seven years later, on Sunday, 19 July 2009, the iconic Stornoway–Ullapool ferry route witnessed scheduled Sunday sailings for the first time in seventy years.

From Sunday ice creams to Sunday air flights, these are four examples of how the Sabbath endured as a contentious issue in twentieth-century Scotland. Some historians have tended to focus on the erosion of 'traditional' sabbatarianism as a result of the two railway 'Sabbath Wars' of the 1840s (which closed some railway lines) and of 1865–6 (which reopened them).[5] But this may underestimate the power of sabbatarianism in the following century. Equally, many writers take the Sabbath to be a distinctively twentieth-century Scottish attribute, but this too may be a misjudgement.[6] One analysis is that a 'secularised Sabbath' survived British de-Christianisation from the 1960s; certainly, as Clive Field has shown in a recent survey of opinion-poll data, as many as 75 per cent of British people in the 1980s and 1990s thought Sunday should be 'a special day'.[7] The Introduction to this volume considered the theory of the everyday; this chapter should be read in the context of the theory, and the conclusion will return to it. But the chapter starts by summarising the legal aspects, before recounting the place of Sunday in people's memory, and then examining sabbatarian campaigns during the century.

THE SABBATH IN THE LAW

Ironic as it may seem, sabbatarianism was initially strongly opposed by John Knox, and even when the *First Book of Discipline* enjoined in 1561 that 'Sunday must straitlie be keipit, both before and efter noon, in all tounies', it was speaking primarily of the hours of public worship. The Sabbath remained a fairly liberal affair for decades, with Sunday weddings and funerals commonplace, and a 24-hour Sabbath only being proclaimed in the Westminster Confession of Faith of 1638. It was from the 1640s that the full vigour of sabbath-keeping descended on the country, but enforcement varied – poorly in Edinburgh but better in Glasgow and western towns, and from the 1730s commerce and industrialisation took their toll; ecclesiastical prosecutions for sabbath-breaching tailed off between 1740 and 1780 in the Church of Scotland, though Seceders continued to be disciplined severely by their kirk sessions for several decades. But civic enforcement increased in the 1780s, with a revival of sabbatarian ideology in the 1800s leading to intensifying observance of the Sabbath from 1815 by factory owners, shopkeepers and social leaders. This was followed by vigorous legislative measures (notably Sunday closing of Scottish public houses from 1853) and campaigning pressure (especially over Sunday trains in 'the Sabbath War' of 1865–6). The Victorian Sabbath was a fairly strict affair across Scotland (and much of England[8]), with few opportunities for pleasures and constant harassment of commerce, and increasingly so in the Highlands where the Free Church imposed a new harsh discipline. Yet, civic Scotland was willing to compromise on the Sabbath, signalled in 1889 by the opening of Edinburgh Botanic Gardens on Sunday afternoons – a move which surely did much to legitimate 'tourist promenading' as 'observance'.[9] But the battle over the Sabbath was far from over. By 1900, Scottish families had got used to a new culture of respectability wrapped up in Sunday observance. In truth, it was in the twentieth century, not before, that what campaigners slightly misleadingly called 'the old Scottish Sabbath' came to perish. Indeed, along with the century's sexual revolution, Sabbath decline was to be one of the greatest changes in everyday behaviour and morality of the last three hundred years.

The enforcement of this Sabbath was ironically mostly not the product of legislation. Scottish ecclesiastical law had been the mainstay of Sabbath enforcement in Scotland's parishes in the seventeenth and eighteenth centuries, but since these were no longer used at all by 1900 against even church members, the ecclesiastical system was now defunct. There had been a variety of acts of the Scottish Parliament from the reign of Queen Margaret in the 1070s to 1701 which sought to prohibit a long series of specific activities on Sunday. But a flurry of sabbatarian legislation between 1691 and 1705, generally enforcing earlier acts, showed little success. Two critical cases established the Scottish position on travel and retailing. In 1828, a civil prosecution of a steamboat operator (*Jobson* v. *Lambert*), plying one Sunday between Dundee and Broughty Ferry, was abandoned when it was brought as a civil case, and successfully appealed in the Court of Session on the grounds that it was a criminal offence. And the case of *Bute* v. *More* of 1870, heard before the House of Lords, found that the law could not be used to force shops to close on Sunday; a further case brought by the magistrates of Rothesay in 1898–9 showed that magistrates in Scotland did not have the right to close ice-cream shops on Sundays. A rare victory came in 1835 from Dundee when an apprentice barber (in *Phillips* v. *Innes*), who refused to shave customers on a Sabbath on grounds of religious conviction, was successfully charged before the magistrates on breach of indenture; the finding was disputed through three courts, finally finding for the apprentice in the House of Lords; this ruling was taken to disable compulsory labour on Sunday in Scotland. Sabbath prosecutions were generally failing between 1880 and 1900. By 1900, legal opinion was that the old Scottish laws on Sabbath enforcement had fallen into desuetude, and that no procurator fiscal would now start a prosecution; this was acknowledged in 1906 when the Scottish Law Revision Act repealed most of the laws of the old Scots parliament against Sabbath profanation.[10] But there remained specific activities that were subject to Sunday control by national legislation or local authority discretion – the licensing laws, cinemas, use of municipal spaces (such as parks, playing fields, golf courses and streets) and shows and exhibitions.

The consequence of this was that in the 1960s and early 1970s, when the social pressure for the opening of facilities such as shops grew very rapidly, there was no legal impediment in Scotland, and, unlike in England and Wales, there was an almost total cave-in by the Sabbath-keeping system. For this reason, the Scottish Sabbath went from being unusually strict before 1960 to being after 1980 one of the most liberal in the whole of Europe. This change was for most of Scotland an uncontested dissolution of tradition; only in isolated pockets, mostly in the Highlands and Hebrides, were there some interesting confrontations – some of which still go on to this day – between conservative presbyterians of an older stamp and liberal Scots both religious and secular. This fight has been rapidly lost, notably over Sunday running of ferries to, from and between the islands. Today, Scotland has a far more liberal Sunday than England, Wales, France, Germany or most of the Nordic countries, where laws and various complex pressures (few of the them strictly 'religious') keep Sundays as anything but ordinary.

THE SABBATH IN MEMORY

Towards the end of the twentieth century, elderly Scots highlighted the ways in which the Scottish Sunday of their youth was special and different. Throughout lowland and highland Scotland, urban and rural, they recalled with very little deviation a day of marked contrast to the other days of the week and to the more liberal Sunday that prevailed from the 1960s onwards.

First and foremost among Sabbath reminiscence is the place of religious activity. For adults, Sunday church-going was already diminishing in Protestant lowland Scotland by 1900, but continued strong for Roman Catholics, in the Highlands and Hebrides, and for children. One series of calculations places Scottish Sunday church attendance as high as 36 per cent in 1851, 18 per cent in 1959, 17 per cent in 1984 and 11 per cent by 2002.[11] In an oral history survey in the late 1980s, 27 per cent of children reported that in the first three decades of the century both parents went to church every Sunday, a further 40 per cent said 'regularly', 11 per cent that their fathers went regularly or every Sunday, and 9 per cent their mothers; only 13 per cent reported that neither parent attended church.[12] For children, attendance at church services, Sunday schools and bible classes, often twice and for many three times per day, was widespread until the late 1930s, and though diminishing somewhat thereafter, Sunday morning attendance remained a norm in the 1940s, 1950s and early 1960s.

When asked in the late 1980s how they spent Sundays in their youth, Scots born early in the century typically responded:

> Very, very quiet. Well, as I said, you went out walking, with my father. I went to church, went to Sunday School, the church and then Sunday School, and you'd come home and you had your meal. Well if it was a wet day you didnae get out. You'd to sit and read your books, sit perched up on the chair, read your books. Sunday was held as the Sabbath day, there was nothing done at all that day. And well some of them, they had music at night if they had a piano, played the piano.

Some of them had visitors on a Sunday, sometimes went visiting, they went visiting friends. We would go away, there was buses then, we could go away in the buses, either, – visit one another you know.[13]

The religious observance of children was almost universal; as one oral history respondent from Scotstoun in Glasgow recalled: 'There wasnae the same division of some folk go to Sunday School and some folk don't bother, you know . . . everybody went to the Sunday School in these days, as a matter of course.'[14] In some families there would be private religious services in the evening, with hymn or psalm singing (sometimes round a piano) and with bible reading. A lady, born 1899 and brought up in Montrose, recalled how her father was away working in Aberdeen and her mother conducted a small service each Sunday evening in the home: 'every Sunday night she held just a small service on her own, singing hymns and read out of the Bible and everything like that'.[15] For some the Sabbath was completely dominated by religion: 'Sunday, Sunday was a day off; morning was church, in the afternoon Sunday School, at night would be the Mission Hall, that was our Sunday.'[16] A woman from Kilmacolm recalled:

. . . you see mother gave us a Sunday School talk or read to us out of a book, or something, you see. She did that every Sunday, I mean there was no question of that she gave it up because somebody was there, she was particular about that, we got our lesson and, – so we did that. So I think probably by the end of that time we were quite tired, all the different things, having done the walk, you see, as well as going to church.[17]

Church attendance declined gradually during the century, but for some people it was a life-long attachment and routine. One elderly woman from Dunblane recalled in 1988 of her church: 'I've sat in that cradle for seventy-four years under six – five ministers, five beadles and three organists, and I hope to see the sixth minister.'[18]

The second common recollection was the banning of pleasures on Sundays. One woman from Cupar in Fife remembered:

. . . we were never allowed to have any ball, any games at all on a Sunday. That was one thing, we were never allowed on a Sunday, even after we came to Stirling. But sometimes we used to, – in the house, and you would hear the voice, "Who's got the ball?" You thought you would try it up off the wall, "Put the ball away!" So what I mean, we were never encouraged on a Sunday, that's why we were told to go out, Sunday was the Sabbath day and that was it.[19]

Many recalled a very strict home Sabbath, including those from Lowland urban areas:

Sunday! You wouldnae dare lift a pair of scissors to cut your nails. My mother used to say that all the Sundays of the world would come down on your head if you cut your nails on a Sunday. Oh, – what! No. We came home from the Sunday

School, – no, we went to church with my mother then we went to the Sunday School. We had to come home and take off our good things. And this used to be a big park right round here and it would go over, – we used to call it Dobbie's Park, and play there with our old clothes on. You werenae allowed to go out with your Sunday things.[20]

Ball games by boys in public places were particularly frowned on both by the community and by patrolling bobbies. Bob Crampsey, brought up in a Catholic family in Glasgow, recalls how Sundays were days of Protestant sub-jugation, and how he and other lads were restrained from breaking taboos; he was banned from playing football by his mother because the neighbours would object, and the family had to 'go for a nice walk' instead.[21]

Yet, practise varied, with some leisure activities conducted out of sight of community censure. One family went pearl fishing in a glass-bottomed boat on the river Forth, while from the 1920s for many families there was the reading of newspapers, predominantly the *Sunday Post, Sunday Mail* and *Pictorial* which between them dominated Sunday newspaper sales in Scotland – where, interestingly, until the launch of *Scotland on Sunday* in 1988, there was no broadsheet 'quality' Scottish paper.[22] The Sunday papers changed habits; a woman brought up in the Baptist Church in Alloa remem-bered: 'You know, I remember when the Sunday papers came in first – and a lot of folk wouldn't buy them. Oh it was terrible if you read a Sunday newspaper at first, 'til folk began to get used to them. But, I mind when oh, that was terrible if you bought a Sunday newspaper.'[23] One Sunday activity was going to the countryside. One woman from Morningside in Edinburgh recalled that five boys and five girls who went to church together used to do a lot of walking together: 'I remember we got an older man in the church to come with us and we did a moonlight hike over the Pentlands and we had a picnic on the top of the Pentlands. I think there was the ten of us and this older man, he was our chaperone, and we came into Edinburgh at six o'clock in the morning. It was dead quiet at that time you know, there was no trams or buses or anything like that because it was Sunday morning. We did it on the Saturday night and came in on Sunday morning.'[24] With the spread of the motorcar to middle-class families between the 1930s and 1960s, Sunday afternoon jaunts into the country were common though, apart from tea at an hotel, there was frequently little to do when they got there.

The third big recollection, notable in working-class families, was of special diets on Sundays. The most crucial difference was at breakfasts where, for the other days of the week, porridge was the staple diet, but on Sundays was exhilaratingly different. One woman brought up in Hamilton at the turn of the century recalled:

Q. So can you remember what kind of meals you had when you were wee?
A. Well we'd always have soup, potatoes and vegetable, – and very often a milk pudding.

Q. And did you have anything different on Sundays?

A. Yes. It was the only day sometimes that we were all together, the only day for the week, and we always had something special on Sunday. Very often it was ham and egg. My mother made pancakes and scones.[25]

A woman from Stirling recalled:

I remember getting lovely steak on a Sunday. Sunday morning we used to get the steak, Sunday morning. It was lovely steak my mother cooked, and I don't say my mother was a terribly good cook, but she did cook, and she did cook this and lovely soda scones or something. And the fat was lovely on the meat, not like you get nowadays, but I remember that.[26]

Fathers were often given breakfast treats; in Glasgow a favourite dish was a Finnan haddock served with bacon.[27] But for children a common feature was that Sunday breakfast was the only day of the week to get ham and egg, or stew, while lunch or dinner was when meat was put on the table – often roast beef or steak pie, dumpling and chips, or, for poorer families, a meal of kale (broth soup). Some families had relatives in the country who regularly sent meat: 'My grandmother stayed with friends in the Highlands and she would send us down a good portion, a good chunk of venison, or pheasants, or mince, – make mince patties or, – Oh we were well fed.'[28] In this way, as in the rest of Britain, Sunday was recalled as a day for a special diet of nourishing treats.

A fourth characteristic recollection was of particular happy memories for women (though less so for men): Sunday-best clothes. Women recalled with great intensity learning as youngsters to rehearse their femininity through wearing fine dresses, coats, hats and gloves to go to church. One woman who grew up in Cowie in Stirlingshire in the 1920s is typical:

When I was small! Well, Sunday was my day because Sunday I was up and I was born, I mean brought up as Protestant, but on a Sunday morning I got dressed. You had a Sunday outfit you see, you only wore it on a Sunday, no other day except a Sunday. Well I went to my two pals, they went to the Catholic Church, so I went with them to mass on a Sunday morning so's I'd have my Sunday clothes on. When I came home I'd go to the church with my mother and then when I came home from that I kept on my clothes because I was going to the Sunday School, and then we went to Bible Class at night. And the reason I went to all that was because I got wearing my Sunday clothes. As soon as I was finished from the Bible Class you'd to take them off, hang them up and put on your ordinary clothes. You weren't allowed to wear your Sunday best for playing about with. So the one that I looked forward to is a Sunday just for that. Keep my Sunday clothes on.[29]

Preparation for Sunday took up much of Saturday night. As children, many recalled they had to polish shoes, press dresses and, for the girls, prepare their hair for attending church the next day. Boys were cocooned in sailors' suits or Eton collars, and banned from their ball games; Dugald Semple, studied by Steven Sutcliffe in another chapter in this volume, reported: 'I came to look on Sunday as a day of horror.'[30] Sunday throughout Britain was a woman's day when parading to and from church, and in afternoon promenades in streets and parks, matched female poise and elegance to the sanctity of the day.

Moreover, the church service was widely recalled as an event of great drama. The theatricality of the revivalist preacher, and of the call to the saved to come forward, appears frequently as the attraction for those who normally went to the Church of Scotland or United Free (UF) Church to attend special independent evangelical services. Molly Weir wrote of the attraction of Jock Troup's tent preaching in Springburn in Glasgow between the world wars. He was such 'great value' that he could 'make the flames of hell so real, we felt them licking round our feet, and the prospect of heaven so alluring we often stood up to be saved several times during the week'; on returning home, she re-enacted the service to her Grannie.[31] The 'tent preachers' and their distinctive hymns with 'jolly-going choruses'[32] were widely mentioned by oral respondents remembering the inter-war period. The evangelical call to be saved was widely remembered. At the Salvation Army in Stirling in the 1920s, one woman recalled:

> I used to belt out, 'A sunbeam, a sunbeam, Jesus wants me for a sunbeam'. (laugh) The Salvation Army people were always wanting to convert you and they used to say, 'Now put up your hand anybody that wants to be saved.' So you would look along the line to see who wanted to be saved and if you thought you were safe you would put your hand up and you'd go forward. Sometimes you were all embarrassed but still you went forward and they put up a prayer for you, and you were saved.[33]

The revival events of Dr Billy Graham attracted almost two million attendances in Scotland in 1955; one teenage boy recalled of the Edinburgh Tynecastle meeting the tension of Graham's sermon – on the theme of a mountaineer swinging on a rope, trying to catch hold of the rock – and his rising at the call to go forward.[34]

A fifth recollection was of Sunday work. Many adults had to undertake waged labour in Scotland in the early part of the century. In 1910, the post office delivered Christmas parcels on Sunday mornings (but not letters) seemingly on the grounds that the latter were routine (or everyday), while parcels were special and clogging up post offices.[35] Works which could close generally did. Shipyards on the Clyde remained routinely closed until 1914, but many other industrial works were functioning. A Church of Scotland survey in 1901 showed that, in the east of Scotland, Sunday work involved 20 per cent of workers in Mid Calder, but only between 1.8 and 3 per cent of those in pit villages. In Glasgow, the Corporation provided figures showing 50 per cent of the police on Sunday duty, 75 per cent of the fire brigade, 650 out of 685 lighting staff, 50 per cent of gas workers, 30 per cent of tram workers (with 74 per cent liable to be called out), but only 9 per cent of cleansing staff and 5 per cent of sanitation workers. In Hamilton presbytery, blast furnaces required Sunday labour, while in the north and east of Scotland the spread of fishing and fish processing on Sunday was growing (including on Lewis).[36] For women, Sunday work both waged and unwaged was standard. This was especially the case for domestic servants who were expected not just to work on Sundays but often to attend church.[37] Women cooked Sunday lunch (and often missed church for that reason).[38] Home work was frowned on in many families, but in a few it was permitted. One woman from Blanefield to the north of Glasgow recalled: 'I think I would spend my Sundays, sewing, patching, darning, looking after my clothes that I had. And looking after my sister. That's how Sunday was spent.'[39]

Oral history respondents recall change to Sunday's rules in the 1930s, with things getting a little less strict.[40] But there is a strong strain of memory concerning the dourness of the Scottish Sabbath after 1945. Despite considerable challenge to Sunday rules during the war years (to which we return later), an Edinburgh Sunday in the mid-1950s was recalled as 'grim and cheerless', with groups of the 'denied generation' of young people moving round the few open cafes (mostly at the railways stations, museums and other public venues) looking for some diversion. Teenagers in 'the soul-less Sabbath' would walk round and round the Royal Scottish Academy and the Chambers Street museum 'looking for a click until we were almost dizzy, and not know how to entertain one even if we scored'. It was regarded as 'bliss' when in the later 1950s the Scottish Office allowed one cinema in each town to open for free on Sunday evenings to show 'health films', with queues stretching to legendary proportions and needing police to control them.[41]

In the later 1960s and 1970s, the Lowland Sabbath was destroyed with remarkable speed. Games began in parks, there were widespread parties and socialising, and DIY stores and supermarkets opened for business. It was part of a wider challenge to authority and the establishment, as well as part of a tremendous collapse in church membership and religious rites of passage.[42] Yet, not everything was immediately liberalised. In 1965, when the House of Lords debated Sunday observance in England and Wales, Lord Belhaven told the house that he 'lived in the land of Sabbath gloom' in which the fourth commandment 'was cited as the reason for making the Sunday a misery for everyone'. But he lived in the countryside, he said, where nature observes no Sabbath and 'one is not subjected to the unbearable pall of gloom that hangs over our towns'.[43] In 1978, Jack Maclean, a *Scotsman* columnist, wrote: 'It is difficult for tolerant, liberal-minded chaps like myself to grasp the reason why the majority of Scots, non-church-goers, should have, with the connivance of the state, a close-mouthed, eighteenth-century Presbyterianism so heavily imposed upon them.'[44]

But in the Highlands, things remained different. The Free Church and

Free Presbyterian Church, and even the Church of Scotland, had a strong hold of Sabbath sanctity, and little could be done on Sundays in public. Sunday labour was strictly confined to acts of 'necessity and mercy', and public transport was rare. Children going on overseas trips were specifically prohibited by the Western Isles Council from participating in Sunday sport.[45] But by the late 1990s, Stornoway was much transformed, described on a Saturday as a hotbed of drink and violence for bored young people, and by 2000 children could be found out on bikes, kicking a football in the streets and on play equipment in the public park. Though the Sabbath was observed by most people in Lewis and Harris, with few stirring from church or hearth,[46] 80 per cent of people in the Western Isles said in a poll in 2002 that they would use Sunday ferries or planes if services existed. This was taken by some to indicate a major sea change in public opinion in the Outer Hebrides, and suggestive of the imminent collapse of the Sabbath.[47] Two years later, the Council removed its blanket ban on Sunday entertainment licences in the Protestant islands of Lewis, Harris and North Uist, in part because of legal advice that rejection of an application from a paintballing venue might contravene human rights legislation. By 2007, Stornoway Golf Club was so confident of the change in public opinion that it was willing to go to court to get restrictions on Sunday opening removed, though two years later it was not yet open.[48]

The people's experience of Sundays changed enormously through the century. For the bulk, it was a transition concentrated into the years after 1970, for, despite some liberalism during the Second World War, there was an air of retrenchment in the late 1940s and 1950s. The Sabbath war was not readily surrendered.

BATTLES FOR THE SABBATH

In his review of the year 1901, *The Times* Scottish correspondent opined that there had been 'a silent revolution' in the liberalisation of the Sabbath in the first year of the new century in Scotland. He wrote that 'Perhaps the increasing elasticity of Sabbath observance is the most noticeable feature of the year from the religious standpoint.'[49] Professor Robert H. Story, a leading Church of Scotland liberal and principal of Glasgow University, had controversially spoken at the Church Congress in favour of the Sunday opening of museums and galleries, lending his support to the decision of the Secretary for Scotland to throw open the Edinburgh Chambers Street Museum. This resulted by 1902 in Sunday attendances varying between 4,472 and 7,615 – 40 per cent higher than on week days when the opening hours were more than double. And Edinburgh, Ayr and Greenock joined Glasgow in starting the Sunday-running tramways, while Aberdeen rejected this innovation.[50] Some liberals in the churches supported an easing of Sabbath strictness. This was not an organised movement, and one in which few like Principal Story took a public lead. One elder in the United Free Church Presbytery of Edinburgh in 1902 fought against some of the stricter brethren, opposing condemning churchgoers for using tramcars on Sunday as he had done to get to church – a confession for which he was harangued with shouts of 'shameful' by other members of the presbytery.[51]

Liberal moves produced apoplexy among the traditionalists in the United Free Church and the smaller conservative Protestant churches, instigating a decade and a half of strong sabbatarian campaigning.[52] Their hope for a Britain-wide legislative onslaught on Sabbath-breaking was propelled by a series of successful campaigns in England; a group of Jewish bakers in London in 1901 were fined three shillings with two shillings costs for baking on the Sabbath within ten miles of the Royal Exchange, while two years later the Working Men's Lord's Day Rest Association claimed to have stopped the Sunday running of the trams in Newport, Monmouthshire, and in Southport in Lancashire through a ratepayers' vote (which it won by 3,600 to 1,800 votes); and campaigners claimed to have shut all shops on Sundays in Crewe and reduced Sunday trading in many northern towns (including Doncaster, Huddersfield and Hull).[53] The abolition of unnecessary Sunday labour was a major target of campaigners in Scotland. The fulminations of the sabbatarians were rich and loud in 1901 and 1902, infecting the Church of Scotland where, in 1901, the general assembly established its first committee on the observance of the Lord's Day in response to west of Scotland protests about rising industrial work, and Sunday trains and trams.[54] But by and large there seems to have been no major change during these years.

The 'secularisation of the Sabbath' was a constant refrain on the lips of ardent supporters of the special Sunday. The 1901 United Free Church Assembly clamoured for reduction in both Sunday work and leisure (especially cycling and golf), in large part to assuage highland parishes considering staying in the 'Wee' Free Church.[55] There were already campaigning groups: The Lord's Day Observance Association of Scotland (founded 1848), and local bodies like the Edinburgh Christian Sabbath Society.[56] But new organisations were mushrooming: The Sabbath Alliance of Scotland (1902) represented the six largest Protestant churches, while the Imperial Sunday Alliance (1909, formerly the Sunday National Movement) created an English-based group that was to last for half a century. These lobbying groups monitored Sabbath-breaking closely and reported them to the press. They made great play of monitoring the Sunday behaviour of members of the royal family and British sportsmen playing overseas, and continued to campaign relentlessly for civic institutions like Chambers Street Museum to close on Sunday.[57]

From 1900 to 1960, four themes dominated sabbatarian campaigning: leisure (especially golf, motoring, ice-cream shops and cinemas), the railways, shopping, and the armed forces. These were to form the core areas of conflict and political agitation. In 1906, the main battles over the rise of Sunday golf were in England, where the Evangelical Free Churches' Council lambasted railway companies and golfers jointly for the spoliation of Sundays.[58] In Scotland, golf was mostly unknown on Sundays before 1914. *The Times* golf correspondent in 1926 wrote an eloquent tirade against the Scottish Sabbath, after travelling up from London to St Andrews on a Saturday to play (for no trains went on Sundays), and then of having to wait out Sunday with scores of other would-be golfers who roamed the Old Course, swinging their walking sticks in frustration at not being able to play: 'I am on fire for this eternal Sabbath to end.'[59] In 1926, golfing was reported as becoming more restricted in England on Sundays where town courses were largely shut. The English urban middle classes were banned from playing on their local courses, so they took to country courses 'when they can break the Sabbath discreetly shrouded by trees'. One newspaper reporter found a Scots golfer who travelled to an English country course to play golf on Sundays: 'Wild horses shall drag no more from me lest his cook, resenting the glare of publicity, should give him notice.'[60]

Sunday leisure was a growing target generally for sabbatarian ire. The rich were targeted by many critics. In Lewis the Presbytery of the Church of Scotland saved its greatest wrath for the shooting tenants 'who drive on the Sabbath to the Druidical stones in Callernish [sic]' – the pagan destination compounding their neglect of Christian ordinances.[61] There was particular furore with 'the idle rich of Edinburgh' for Sunday leisure.[62] A. H. Dunnett, a leading figure in the Church of Scotland in the early 1930s, attacked the rich man who played golf or drove his motorcar on Sundays: 'His soul is in darkness, selfish and arrogant and carrying off his heathendom on the wings of a prosperous independence.'[63] The working classes were also subject to criticism. Working men's clubs were a new fad, which had started in some small towns and were spreading to the larger ones. Hawick was a particular pioneer of these clubs, starting up in the late 1880s. By 1902 there were six with 190 members, each paying a subscription of ten shillings for entry mornings and evenings on Sundays when drinking and other pastimes were allowed. In 1900, it was estimated one Sunday that 1,380 were entering similar clubs in Edinburgh.[64]

Ice-cream shops were a particular target of sabbatarians. In a Church of Scotland survey in 1901, 110 ice-cream shops were found to be open (each fifteen hours on average one Sunday) in Hamilton presbytery, and worse, all the employees were Italian Catholics: 'they are a source of demoralisation to young lads and children and give an unhappy publicity to godless frivolity'.[65] The churches successfully badgered the authorities to harass such shops, including raiding them on Sundays to discover if they were storing or serving alcohol.[66] Stirling police regarded these places as 'dens of iniquity', dealing with a suspicious death in one and a riot at another.[67] Edinburgh Town Council was reported slower than other councils by 1913 in closing these down, though it had intimated to the Free Church Presbytery its keenness to accomplish this. One Free Church College professor lambasted the owners: 'they allowed foreigners to come into this Christian community, not only to trample upon the religious convictions of the people, but practically to be a law unto themselves. It showed how utterly regardless these people were of the Christian sentiment of the nation where they were allowed to settle down.'[68] In the Glasgow area in 1912, the United Free Church pressed local authorities to close these shops as they 'were conducted by foreigners, who had been brought up in a quite a different atmosphere from Scottish children', the vast majority of them Roman Catholic, an 'illustration that Romanism was indeed part of gold and part of clay'.[69]

Attacks on Roman Catholics for being 'weak' on Sabbath observance were a sustained feature of sabbatarian arguments. For observance of the seventh day it was necessary to have what the United Free Church called 'a healthy and vigorous spirituality'.[70] But as the threat to the Sabbath increased, and the battle became little-by-little apparently weakened every year, what might be termed the 'secular' arguments for its value increased. Rising crime was blamed on Sunday work and play.[71] A second argument, which was by no means new but was now used with increasing frequency, related to workers' rights. The rise of Sabbath working was portrayed as infringing on the worker's right to freedom to Christian worship and observance of the Lord's Day. As the century progressed, this argument became increasingly one about protecting the worker's right to a day of rest. At the forefront was the running of trains (and trams) on Sundays. In 1901, the Amalgamated Society of Railway Servants looked with alarm upon the increasing running of Sunday trains and the increasing work demands upon its members.[72] By 1925, Sunday train travel had expanded considerably, though still much restricted in Scotland. A complaint was raised on the floor of the Church of Scotland General Assembly, to which an elder, William Whitelaw, chairman of the London and North-eastern Railway Co., responded: 'It was the business of the Church to prevent that demand from arising.'[73]

A second area of sabbatarian campaigning was over retail shops. One of the surprising features of the early twentieth century in Scotland is the extent to which retail shops were open. In various surveys conducted by the churches, it was clear that the shops concerned were almost all 'small', and were usually located on what were described as minor or small streets. The shops were invariably in working-class areas, and were described as supplying the needs of the poorer parts of society at times when their need to shop access was greatest because of the long hours of work on the rest of the week. Shop opening on Sundays was reported as increasing in 1913 and was widespread in England in the 1920s, averaging 80 per cent in London boroughs in 1924.[74] This suggests that there was freer Sabbath shopping in the 1920s than later in the century, certainly in England and perhaps also in Scotland.

One of the most controversial areas of contention was the role of the royal family and of the armed forces. The visit of Edward VII to Scotland in May

1903 resulted in one transformation of the Sabbath when, the day before, some 40,000 Volunteer soldiers detrained hourly at Waverley station on Sunday afternoon and night, and thousands thronged to see the spectacle. 'It has been almost Continental in animation', wrote one reporter, 'an effect which many elements have combined to produce.' A kilted regiment marched five hundred strong through the old town, resplendent in scarlet tunics, and after thousands of citizens went to church in the morning, they came out in the afternoon to enjoy the spectacles of a bonfire on Arthur's Seat and flags fluttering everywhere, with the courtyard of Holyrood palace converted into a tropical garden of palms and flowers.[75] Sabbatarian defenders complained loudly. In 1904, the Free Church complained again about the army's behaviour and that of the King, who with his family was accused of being 'prominent offenders in the matter of Sabbath desecration'.[76] Complaints against the army were persistent; Sunday rifle shooting was widespread at army ranges in the early 1910s,[77] while territorial army camps were regarded as a particular problem; in the words of one Free Church presbytery, 'the quietness of the Lord's Day [was] utterly destroyed by these camps'.[78]

The extent of the 'quiet revolution' was brought home by church inquiries. An inquiry in 1911 by the UF Presbytery of Haddington and Dunbar showed that no member of the church in the presbytery had been disciplined for Sabbath desecration; most kirk sessions repudiated the idea of such discipline as 'impractical or impolitic'. The fear was that declining Sabbath reverence led to wider de-Christianisation: 'when their non-attendance at the House of God becomes exceptionally bad, and remonstrances proved abortive, their names were dropped from the roll. They lapsed into the ruck of the non-churchgoing, in whom apparently the spark of spiritual life has died.'[79] Some were the rich, 'sending their motor-horn or their golf ball nonchalantly through all that was dear in the Sabbath quiet'.[80] By 1914, the decline of Sunday evening services in Edinburgh was much lamented in the Church of Scotland; churches were reported to be half-empty, and W. P. Paterson, divinity professor at Edinburgh University, called for some rethinking:

> Worship and moral culture should come first, but there was room for the development of the intellectual and aesthetic nature, for reading, reflection, and discussion, for looking at pictures and objects of interest, and for the study of scientific and philosophical works which would develop the God-given intellectual and aesthetic powers. The principle of visitation might be developed on a much larger scale on Sunday, which should be a day of development and the fostering of family life.[81]

Such liberal views were also backed up by practical critics of the sabbatarians. Those complaining of working men's clubs were considered off-beam by some; they weren't 'lost' church goers: 'A man does not spend part of his Sunday in church and another part in a Sunday drinking-club.'[82]

Certainly, there appeared to be reduced vigour in sabbatarian campaigning by the 1910s. This was marked in 1911 and 1912 with the winding up of the special Sabbath committees of both the Church of Scotland and the United Free Church in favour of the work of a Scottish Churches' Lord's Day Association representing ten denominations.[83]

The approach of the First World War changed affairs. Already in 1912, Sunday working was creeping into shipyards at Greenock because of lucrative incentives in government contracts, while Sunday trawling was growing in the north of Scotland and leisure booming on Sundays – notably picture houses, whippet racing, birdwatching, and the motorcar, the last of which was reported as giving 'a great impulse to the craving for the wild excitement of Sunday excursioning'. Sabbatarians in the United Free Church deprecated the growth of people using Sundays for 'friendly visits' and of 'listless loafing of men who spend the day reading Sunday newspapers, and discussing, not always quietly, the latest sporting events'.[84] The quickening of the economy from 1914 had a major impact. By 1916, it was reported of the shipyards on the Clyde: 'There is neither dawn nor sunset, week-day nor Sabbath, on the Clyde now, till victory comes.'[85]

The coming of peace brought conflicting pressures, but liberalisation was strongly opposed by a rising tide of Puritanism. Local veto plebiscites came into force in June 1920, marking a new mood dominated by fierce evangelical campaigning in Scotland. And alongside prohibition campaigning came sabbatarian campaigning. Support arose in high places. In 1924, Prime Minister Ramsay MacDonald addressed an evangelical Free Church assembly in Brighton. 'There was', he said, 'over-indulgence in recreation to-day. There was an incapacity to spend a quiet Sunday.' He was amazed at a great many of his friends, who said that the old Scottish Sabbath was a burden. He was reported as saying that he would like 'to see a state of society where every man and woman preferred the old Scottish Sunday to the modern French one'.[86] A few days later, when challenged by the press that he had said he wanted to re-establish the old Scottish Sabbath, he denied it: 'but I did say that I wished to recreate the men who could undergo with cheerfulness the penalties of the Scottish Sabbath. Now that was a very fine distinction, and nobody but a Scotsman could make it.'[87] Ten years' later in 1933, MacDonald was criticised in the Free Church General Assembly for holding more cabinet meetings on the Sabbath than any of his predecessors.[88]

By the late 1920s, sabbatarians in the United Free Church were quite despondent. Their cause had been downgraded twice within the committee structure of the General Assembly, making them a minor sub-committee, and their campaigning had virtually ceased. By 1929, on the eve of union with the Church of Scotland, they seemed to write an epitaph:

> The Scottish Sunday, as we have known it, exists no longer, and the Church must make up its mind to face the fact that it has to function in a new environment.

It has become increasingly clear that to adopt a merely negative attitude on the Sunday question is futile, as well as a confession of weakness. Protests have achieved little, and we have been unable to check in any marked degree the ever-increasing inroads of one kind and another made upon the sanctity of the Lord's Day.[89]

Breaches of the Sabbath were piling up in the 1930s. A Sunday Theatre Society was formed in Edinburgh in 1939 to hold meetings in the Lyceum after church service hours on Sunday nights; the Corporation agreed the proposal and let the theatre.[90] A badminton competition was held on a Sunday in 1939, and this caused opposition from the Baptist Union, United Free Church and the Free Church.[91] The arrival of an RAF base at Montrose in 1936 led the town council to consider allowing Sunday sport.[92] In Dundee in 1935, the Town Council permitted Sunday concerts so long as the proceeds were all for charity. The Church of Scotland reckoned in 1935 that at least 10,000 shops were open in Scotland on Sundays – 5,273 in Glasgow, 1,998 in Edinburgh, 884 in Dundee, 738 in Aberdeen and 180 in Greenock. Unusually, the Revd D. H. Soutar of Tayport defended Sunday football, saying he himself had played on that day, but his was a rather lone voice in his Presbytery.[93] In 1934, Glasgow Corporation – by forty votes to thirty-six, four abstaining – voted against allowing golf courses, tennis courts and bowling greens to open for play on Sundays. It was supported by the Socialist group, but was opposed by the Scottish Protestant League and the Moderates. Some things had already been conceded – music in parks, skating at Crossmyloof, the opening of children's swings and roundabouts, boating at Rouken Glen, Hogganfield Loch and Loch Lomond. A dozen private golf courses were open on Sundays in the west of Scotland.[94] But in the following year, Glasgow Corporation changed its mind, voting in favour of Sunday golf; opponents said the pressure was coming from 'Romanists'.[95] But other councils refused; Paisley rejected Sunday golf in 1936 by a 2 to 1 majority, while in Edinburgh the Town Council by thirty-seven votes to twenty-six refused permission for Merchants Golf Club at Craiglockhart (which was on council land) to play golf on Sundays. All the private golf courses around Edinburgh permitted Sunday golf – the first being Baberton Golf Club which on a series of votes which split its membership, agreed to allow Sunday golf in 1926.[96]

A raft of new legislation in the 1930s established a new sabbatarian standard in England and Wales, banning the sale of all but certain specified goods (like newspapers, newly cooked food and milk), and controlling the opening of cinemas and banning theatres. Yet attempts to copy it for Scotland failed. In March 1934, a petition of 45,000 signatures was presented to Parliament in favour of restricting Sunday trading in Scotland. The government thought the growth of Sunday trading was modest, and for this reason did not support a bill seeking to establish this, and it was talked out of the Commons on first reading.[97] This presents us with an anomaly in our understanding of the Sabbath in British history, which we think of as a Scottish-led affair. Part of the reason may be explained in terms of party politics; most Scottish Socialist MPs were broadly opposed to sabbatarian laws, and were able to influence the Scottish votes in that direction. But there is a wider issue that Scottish civil, legal and indeed many church leaders had been agreed since the nineteenth century that it was inappropriate to legislate the Scottish Sabbath. The duty in this regard was left in the care of Scottish local authorities who had a free rein to introduce bye-laws on key issues – the opening hours and days of licences of regulated premises (public houses, cinemas, theatres, restaurants and all shows and exhibitions, and of sports activities on its property, and in the streets and thoroughfares). Moreover, police had powers to curb games anywhere, and these powers were used in suppressing Sunday games. In 1937, twenty-six men and youths were arrested in Prestonfield in Edinburgh one Sunday charged with playing football, gambling and breach of the peace. Seven who admitted the charges were fined £2 or twenty days imprisonment.[98] In this regard, the Scottish battle for the Sabbath was conceived as a local one.

The absence of definitive legislation in Scotland left the topic open to contention, and even the Church of Scotland was unclear what its attitude should be. In 1944, the General Assembly asked the Sabbath sub-committee of the Committee on Christian Life and Work to prepare a 'Pronouncement' on the Sabbath for the Scottish people, but a division between liberals and conservatives emerged over the core issue of the origins of the Lord's Day as a Christian institution. Because the church could not agree, the pronouncement did not finally appear until 1948, and was largely ineffectual.[99]

This might seem indicative of the secularisation of the Sabbath that sabbatarians feared. And indeed the Second World War had initially changed the Sabbath dramatically. As well as troop movements on Sundays, pressure quickly grew to enable troops to enjoy Sunday leisure. When the RAF sought Sunday opening of cinemas in England, the Free Presbyterian Church's northern presbytery sent a resolution to Sir Archibald Sinclair, Secretary of State for Air, saying: 'Satanic trifling with God's law incurs righteous judgment. At war for a principle, we should hold fast to divine institutions.'[100] When in late 1942, military authorities repeated their request for cinemas to be open on Sunday evenings, most local authorities agreed, though only permitting the opening of sufficient cinemas to meet demand. Yet in the midst of war, sabbatarianism achieved successes. While Edinburgh Corporation agreed in 1941 to rotational opening of six cinemas around the city on Sundays, with proceeds going to charity,[101] attempts in 1941 and again in 1944 to open theatres and music halls on Sundays were defeated by a narrow parliamentary vote, and Glasgow Corporation successfully prevented a bowling club from opening on Sundays.[102] There was constant sniping by minor Protestant churches (notably the Free Church, the Free Presbyterian

Church and the Reformed Presbyterian Church) against invasions of the Sabbath by the military, councils and the public during wartime; the Scottish Education Department was accused in 1944 of encouraging popular talks, debates, discussion groups, brains trusts and concerts on Sunday evenings for children in the rural areas of the north of Scotland.[103]

This trend to some relaxation continued in the two to three years immediately after the war ended. In 1946, Aberdeen Town Council started to consider providing sports facilities for children on Sundays for the first time; demand was so high that the Council said it did not expect more protests from the Church of Scotland.[104] In the same year, Edinburgh Corporation opened Portobello Swimming Pool on Sundays, and extended the hours the following years; but the Corporation was split 39–20 on this issue, and pressure from the churches to sustain restriction was unrelenting.[105] The Edinburgh International Festival, founded in 1947, became the target for Free Church criticisms for its Sunday concerts.[106] But the official festival had a strong religious credo underlying its civic foundation in the late 1940s and 1950s, and this was reflected in the immensely popular closing religious service held in Princes Street Gardens. With Sunday services at Ross Bandstand permitted from 1946, the closing festival service in 1948 witnessed the whole of the Gardens, Princes Street, the Mound and Ramsay Terrace being thronged with tens of thousands of people in 'a hopeless congestion'.[107] In this way the Edinburgh Corporation combined art and Sabbath sanctity even though stricter sabbatarians objected. The Corporation was not liberalising its policy; indeed, on many other aspects of Sabbath bye-laws the Council reaffirmed the status quo, refusing in 1948 by thirty-six votes to twenty-five to allow the use of music halls on Sunday evenings for political meetings, and two years later refusing permission for golf to be played on Sundays on municipal courses. [108] Though cricket matches were being tried in the late 1940s in various Scottish towns (including Glasgow) and seemed not to arouse much opposition, there was an adamant opposition by sabbatarians to Sunday football.[109]

By 1950, a new line seemed to have been drawn. Though private golf courses were often open on Sundays, and a few other minor sports without serious spectating or large numbers of participants were taking place, the liberalisation of the Sabbath did not take place in Scotland with the speed or breadth that many anticipated. One cause was the renewed vigour of sabbatarian campaigns. The Scottish-based Lord's Day Observance Association, founded in 1847, united with the LDOS in England in 1947, and from this date kept up a steady pressure on local authorities over Sabbath observance.[110] They also kept a very close watch on professional football. Any hint of football clubs breaching the Sabbath were leapt on with alacrity. A case in point arose in 1950, when the Church of Scotland's attention was drawn to a proposal for Aberdeen Football Club to sell cup-tie tickets for a match against Heart of Midlothian on a Sunday, and they opposed this with much publicity.[111] The result of the pressure was that local authorities found it difficult to change local bye-laws. In relation to cinemas, for instance, it had become a general rule among Scottish councils in the 1950s that cinemas could only hold Sunday showings in aid of charity; very few councils broke this rule, one being Greenock in 1958 which on a split vote agreed to grant general opening for a trial period of nine months.[112] Another exception was the Edinburgh International Film Festival which by 1954 was showing films on Sundays when the ordinary cinemas were banned from opening except for charity shows.[113] These examples aside, there was in the 1950s a general reimposition of Sabbath enforcement as part of a wider reinvigoration of the long-standing campaign for rational recreation in Scotland: the suppression of sports and unregulated pastimes associated with gambling, drink and mayhem in the streets.[114]

But in the 1960s the rules started to fall apart. Popular behaviour on Sunday changed appreciably, with large numbers of young people parading on Sundays without the decorum and restraint expected. Police action against Sunday games appears to have ceased, and by the later years of the decade Scotland was feeling the winds of a cultural and moral change – not just on Sundays, but in the behaviour of youth in relation to popular music and fashion, in arts and drama, and the rise of a large student population with the formation of new universities.[115] Against this backdrop of considerable change, the traditional Scottish Sabbath became indefensible in most of the country, and in the 1970s Sunday football, cinema and pub-drinking (by the Licensing Act of 1976) all became commonplace.

The central focus of sabbatarian conflict in the second half of the century narrowed to a small number of high-profile causes. Leading among these were the Sunday running of ferries, largely to the Hebrides. And the cause was one that had already achieved great success. Sunday steamers were a known quantity in early twentieth-century Scotland. In 1902, the Lewis Presbytery of the Church of Scotland complained of steamers leaving Stornoway on Sunday evenings 'blowing the whistle when not necessary'.[116] An attempt by the Liberal MPs for the Western Isles and Ross & Cromarty to get a clause in a transport bill banning steam and railway transport to the West Highlands on Sundays was rejected in 1928.[117] In 1939, the 11 p.m. Sunday steamer was still sailing, and the Stornoway Town Council had resisted protests from the Free Presbyterians for years over this; the FPs felt that the sailing time prevented many islanders from using a service on conscientious grounds. The service had always left at this time to make the connection with the trains from Kyle and Mallaig. But now a new faster steamer was to be introduced, and the Town Council was removing its objection to a later sailing so long as the ferry made the connection.[118] In 1938, the Free Church presbytery in Lewis collected a 10,000-signature petition against the running of the Sunday night mail steamer, but Stornoway Town Council refused to accept it, imputing that it was not a fully proper petition.[119]

In these ways, the Sunday ferry ban was something recent, not old, when it became in the 1960s a touchstone for conflict, and remained so until the 2000s. Proposals from liberals for ferries between Skye and the mainland, between Raasay and Skye, and between Ullapool and Lewis, were the subject of constant dispute during these decades. Liberalisers tended to be reluctant to organise and appear within their communities to oppose the churches and ministers, and the promoters of change were seen to be lowlanders and above all Caledonian MacBrayne, the principal ferry operator. But groups of campaigning liberals did emerge, especially in the late 1990s and early 2000s, and with pressure from incomers, second-homers, young people, commerce and people from the southern isles desperate to be able to make Sunday visits to sick relatives in the Western Isles Hospital in Stornoway, the pressure for change looked irresistible. By 2008, Sunday ferries had been trialled to the sabbatarian stronghold of Raasay and were extended in early 2009 to inter-island routes. Then, on Sunday 19 July 2009, the last island was connected by a Sunday ferry when the MV *Isle of Lewis* sailed the Stornoway – Ullapool route. Long the litmus test for the sabbatarian cause, the first service was cheered by 200 people but met by only twenty-four protesters. [120]

CONCEPTUALISING THE SABBATH AS EVERYDAY

In the introduction to this volume, the editors reflected on theories of the everyday. What issues arise in relation to the twentieth-century history of the Scottish Sabbath?

First, the Sabbath represents a conundrum. It is on the one hand a pretty everyday thing – it happens every seventh day, and stands as a repetitive, regular event, one for which the rules of behaviour the citizens know full well, fulfilling one of the key characteristics put forward by Michel de Certeau to satisfy the notion of the everyday.[121] On the other hand, it is *not* everyday in the sense that it is meant to be, in Christian theology and in practice, *different* from the 'everyday'. It is to be the antithesis of days open to work and play. It is a day in presbyterian polity to be set aside for the worship of the Lord, at home or in church, and with no tasks done other than those of necessity and mercy. For much of the century, this made the day something else. With church worship a scene of display and even high drama (including the sermon and the evangelical 'call'), the day was one of spectacle, and of observable and clear observance of strict patterns of behaviour. Families, individuals and communities were on show for the day – even if that meant *not* being on show, by hiding in the home and doing nothing. It also gave rise to the spectacle of protest against Sabbath-breaking. It became a battleground for resistance and contest.

Second, at the beginning of the twentieth century the Scottish Sabbath was a device to keep out the secular in the midst of the religious. It was part of a containment of a world known and familiar, the temptation within,

that had to be controlled and prohibited. It was a day that stood to represent self-restraint, inner discipline and conformity, very much as evangelical Christians demanded such virtues more widely. But by the end of the
century, the Scottish Sabbath had changed to be something almost entirely
limited to the world of the Gael, mostly in Harris, Lewis and Raasay. And
the battle was no longer about the evil within, but concerned the evil without
– the devil at the door, the arrival of the everyday with television, the motorcar and fast roads, the Sunday ferries and planes, and by the internet and
youth culture. The danger to the Sabbath was not now inner temptation but
cultural invasion.

A third observation is that sabbatarianism appears as a totalising ideology for behaviour. It totalises the world against the fragmenting power of
the everyday. It brooks no place for *la fête*, or for the mundane. And yet, in
its closing down of pleasure, it does from another perspective impose a new
mundane-ness. Sabbatarianism 'sets up' the everyday Sunday of the secular-
ist or backsliding Christian as a fictional enemy; sabbatarianism defines the
everyday in terms that imply that it is a totalising ideology of hedonism – an
ideology that proclaims the self is everything, and that the enjoyment of the
self is depriving God of the right to be praised by human sacrifice of the
desires of the self on this one day. The self is seen in sabbatarian ideology
(as in other Puritan ideologies) as the desire for indulgence – in enjoyment,
hedonism and removal of restraint. Sabbatarianism demands a (temporary)
denial of the self.

Throughout everyday life theory, there is a tension between submission
and contest. And one can apply this to sabbatarianism which, within it,
has the idea that the keeping of the Sabbath is the denial of the everyday
– the refusal to adopt the routines, workaday needs and the pleasures of
the ordinary day. The ordinary day covers all human needs and emotions.
The Sabbath is to deny all of these, to make it empty of the everyday, to
ensure that none of the usual repetitions and sins of the flesh go on. But of
course this is the irony, because the Sabbath imposes its own everyday. It
reduces the day to a lowest common denominator of activities, and absence
of desires. It sublimates the self. It sublimates reality as well. It is the denial
of both. To do this, the ideology erupts in constant fight to maintain itself.
There is no respite from the struggle. It is a constant battle for and against
the everyday.

A fourth observation is that at the start of the twentieth century the
Sabbath was the symbol of orthodoxy, of the establishment and of conformity, and, through the adherence of capitalist Christians, of modernity and
industrial success. All successful businessmen were, or were expected to
be, or sold themselves as, good keepers of the Sabbath.[122] By the 1960s, the
decline of the Sabbath was shifting the ideology from orthodoxy to extrem-
ism. Sabbatarianism was by then the opponent of modernity, the opponent
of liberty, and the gaoler of the young. In the same way, the notion of

resistance shifts over the Sabbath between 1900 and 1970. In 1900, resistance was by the libertarians and by Catholics in Scotland, and by socialists. The campaigns of those who stood by Harry Corrothie and other ice-cream parlour owners are one of the great and forgotten causes célèbres of Scottish liberals. Lefebvre's fête was there in the resistance to the hegemony of the Sabbath in the towns of Scotland. By 1965, the boot was on the other foot; resistance was on the part of sabbatarians who sat down in front of the Cortina car arriving in Skye by ferry on a Sunday, and the echo of the American civil rights movements in the USA is perhaps no accident.

Fifth, the irony for sabbatarians was the sense of the fête concerning the Sabbath found everywhere in oral testimony and autobiography. Many children had revelled in the special diet and clothes of the Sabbath, and the outings to parks and, increasingly for many, by car or tram to public and country parks. For children the Sabbath was a day of fête rather more for girls than for boys. Herein lies yet another irony. On the one hand, Sunday was a woman's day when she was chaperoned to church in her Sunday-best finery, the wonderful feminine dress on show. Much testimony makes plain the degree to which the church on a Sunday, in all Christian denominations, was a woman's place where men, even if placed in a patriarchal place of power, were nonetheless outnumbered, and out-moralised by the display of woman's virtue in Sunday church. Women almost always outnumbered men as churchgoers; in 1984, of Scotland's 853,700 churchgoers, 63 per cent were women.[123] Yet, on the other hand, Sunday was the day when women had to organise and work extremely hard at Sunday lunch, the great meal that embodied the moral virtues of family respectability, feasting and cohesion. For the early twentieth-century middle classes, of course, the domestic servant (again a woman) would be the cooker and preparer of the Sunday lunch. So, in this way, the gendered nature of the Sunday placed the nature of the fête in a difficult and confused location.

Sixth and last: at the start of the twentieth century, there was a joke that 'Scotchmen keep the Sabbath and everything else they can get'.[124] Dourness and meanness were seen as two defining features of the country. But it is important not to overlook the extent to which the Sabbath became harsher in other nations – in England, Northern Ireland, Norway and Germany – where legislation hindered Sunday commerce and many pleasures for the rest of the century. It would be improper to hold up sabbatarianism as something invented by Scotland, or something with unmatched intensity and longevity, for neither was the case. From about 1970, Scotland became one of the most liberal countries for pleasures on Sunday and indeed on any day of the week. By 2000, outside of the Western Isles, there was virtually no activity that could not be undertaken on a Sunday. In a survey in 2001, 55 per cent of Scots said that they never went to a place of worship, 11 per cent less than once a year, and only 9 per cent said they went every week.[125] The LDOS, now renamed Day One Christian Ministries and based

in Leominster, spends more campaigning time defending sabbatarian legislation in England than in Scotland. With all the ferries running on the Sabbath
by 2009, the Sabbath war seems finally to be over.

Notes

1. B. Smith, 'Temperance, Up Helly Aa, socialism and ice cream in Lerwick
   1890–1914', unpublished lecture to Shetland Civic Society, 1984; I am grateful to the author for permission to use this material. In writing this chapter, I
   am extremely grateful to Norman Campbell of BBC Scotland for directing my
   attention to a series of sources on the Highlands and Hebrides.
2. *The Scotsman*, 8 February 1946.
3. *Daily Record*, 7 June 1965.
4. *Sunday Herald*, 27 October 2002. For more background on Angus Smith, see
   F. Macdonald, 'Scenes of ecclesiastical theatre in the Free Church of Scotland,
   1981–2000', *Northern Scotland* vol. 20 (2000), pp. 125–48.
5. C. J. A. Robertson, 'Early Scottish railways and the observance of the Sabbath',
   Scottish Historical Review vol. 57, 1978, pp. 143–67; R. D. Brackenridge, 'The
   "Sabbath war" of 1865–66: the shaking of the foundations', *Records of the
   Scottish Church History Society* vol. xvi (1966–8).
6. Day One Scotland describe Scotland as 'the land of the Christian Sabbath' where
   'Sabbath keeping was a national characteristic'. www.dayonescotland.org
7. C. D. Field, '"The secularised Sabbath" revisited: opinion polls as sources for
   Sunday observance in contemporary Britain', *Contemporary British History* vol.
   15, no. 1, Spring 2001, pp. 1–20 at p. 4.
8. J. Wigley, *The Rise and Fall of the Victorian Sunday* (Manchester, 1980).
9. R. D. Brackenridge, 'Sunday observance in Scotland 1689–1900,' unpublished
   PhD thesis, University of Glasgow, 1962, esp. pp. 2–47, 57–8, 68–78, 123–50;
   182–248; L. Leneman, '"Prophaning" the Lord's Day: Sabbath breach in early
   modern Scotland', *History*, vol. 74 (1989), pp. 217–31; for the theological aspects
   of the early period, see J. Carter, 'Sunday observance in Scotland 1560–1605',
   unpublished PhD thesis, University of Edinburgh, 1957.
10. Brackenridge, 'Sunday observance', pp. 29–32, 188–206; Report by Revd Dr
    Hewison on the civil and ecclesiastical law of Scotland concerning the Sabbath,
    in Committee on the Observance of the Lord's Day, *Reports to the General
    Assembly of the Church of Scotland* (hereafter RGACS), 1902, pp. 1129–46.
11. Children are excluded from the 1959 figure. The figure for 2002 may be on the
    high side. C. G. Brown, 'Religion and secularisation', in A. Dickson and J. H.
    Treble (eds), *People and Society in Scotland volume III 1914–1990* (Edinburgh,
    1992), p. 55; P. Brierley, *Turning the Tide; The Challenge Ahead: Report of the
    2002 Scottish Church Census* (London, 2002), p. 15.
12. C. G. Brown and J. D. Stephenson, 'Sprouting wings? Women and religion in
    Scotland, c.1890–1950', in E. Breitenbach and E. Gordon (eds), *Out of Bounds:
    Women in Scotland 1800–1945* (Edinburgh, 1992), p. 100.
13. Mrs A3 (born 1913) from Fallin in Stirlingshire; Stirling Women's Oral History

Collection, Smith Art Gallery and Museum, Stirling, CD-ROM (hereafter SWOHC).

14. Mrs K3 (1906) SWOHC.
15. Mrs O2 (1899) SWOHC.
16. Mrs Y3 (1901) SWOHC.
17. Mrs V3 (1903) SWOHC.
18. Mrs X3 (1903) SWOHC.
19. Mrs X2 (1920) SWOHC.
20. Mrs R2 (1905) from Cambusbarron, SWOHC.
21. B. Crampsey, *The Young Civilian* (London, 1988), p. 175.
22. Mrs Y3 (1901) SWOHC.
23. Mrs D2 (1907) SWOHC.
24. Mrs C2 (1912) SWOHC.
25. Mrs X1 (1897) SWOHC.
26. Testimony of sister of Mrs U1; SWOHC.
27. Mrs I3 (1904) SWOHC.
28. Mrs T2 (1899) SWOHC.
29. Mrs V1 (1914) SWOHC.
30. Quoted in S. Sutcliffe, 'After "the religion of my fathers": the quest for composure in the "post-Presbyterian" self', in this volume.
31. M. Weir, *Best Foot Forward* (London, 1972), p. 69.
32. Mrs G1 (1924) SWOHC.
33. Mrs W1 (1913) SWOHC.
34. He was restrained by his aunt; comment to the author by his cousin, Ranald Graham, 1998. On the drama of the church, see Macdonald, 'Scenes of ecclesiastical theatre'; and idem, 'Towards a spatial theory of worship: some observations from Presbyterian Scotland', *Social & Cultural Geography* vol. 3 (2002), pp. 61–80.
35. *The Times*, 23 December 1910.
36. Committee on the Observance of the Lord's Day, RGACS, 1902, pp. 1059–128.
37. J. D. Stephenson and C. G. Brown, 'The view from the workplace: women's memories of work in Stirling c. 1910–c. 1950', in E. Gordon and E. Breitenbach (eds), *The World is Ill-Divided: Women's Work in Scotland in the Nineteenth and Early Twentieth Centuries* (Edinburgh, 1990), pp. 13–15.
38. C. G. Brown, *The Death of Christian Britain* (London, 2001), pp. 159–61.
39. Mrs I3 (1904) SWOHC.
40. Mrs S1 (1912) SWOHC.
41. John Renwick, *Edinburgh Evening News*, 27 December 1986.
42. C. G. Brown, *Religion and Society in Twentieth-century Britain* (London, 2006), pp. 224–77.
43. *The Times*, 18 March 1966.
44. *The Scotsman*, September 1978.
45. Ibid., 19 November 1987.
46. Ibid., 24 June 1997, 24 June 2000.

47. *The Herald*, 16 February 2001.

48. Ibid., 13 June 2003, 8 December 2007.

49. *The Times*, 24 January 2003.

50. Ibid., 8 October 1901; Committee on the Observance of the Lord's Day, RGACS, p. 1128.

51. *The Scotsman*, 8 January 1902.

52. Ibid., 23 May 1902; Report of the Committee on Sabbath Observance, *Reports to the General Assembly of the United Free Church* (herafter RGAUFC), 1902, p. 2.

53. *The Times*, 20 July 1901. The case went to appeal on the ground that the bakers closed on their Sabbath, but was lost. Ibid., 9 November 1901, 4 January 1904.

54. Committee on the Observance of the Lord's Day, RGACS, 1902, p. 1058.

55. *The Times*, 4 May 1912, 5 March 1918.

56. *The Scotsman*, 15 December 1900.

57. Ibid., 24 May 1906, 30 April 1913.

58. *The Times*, 8 March 1906.

59. Ibid., 27 August 1926.

60. Ibid., 10 December 1926.

61. Committee on the Observance of the Lord's Day, RGACS, p. 1126.

62. *The Scotsman*, 29 May 1906.

63. A. H. Dunnett, *The Church in Changing Scotland* (London, 1933), p. 63.

64. Committee on the Observance of the Lord's Day, RGACS, 1900, pp. 1150–2.

65. Committee on the Observance of the Lord's Day, RGACS 1901, p. 1085.

66. One such raid in Glasgow's Gallowgate is reported in the *Glasgow Herald*, 20 November 1907.

67. *Stirling Observer*, 26 December 1906, 7 October 1908.

68. *The Scotsman*, 30 April 1913.

69. Ibid., 23 May 1902, 10 April 1912.

70. Report of the Committee on Sabbath Observance, RGAUFC, 1902, p. 1.

71. Francis Peake, *The Times*, 24 January 1903.

72. Ibid., 5 October 1901.

73. Ibid., 28 May 1925.

74. Ibid., 22 February 1936 [sic on the dates]; 23 September 1913.

75. Ibid., 11 May 1903; *The Scotsman*, 11 May 1903.

76. *The Times*, 18 September 1905.

77. *The Scotsman*, 10 April 1912; *The Times*, 28 July 1910. Similar complaints extended to the territorials firing on Sundays; ibid., 4 March 1912, 4 November 1912.

78. *The Scotsman*, 30 April 1913.

79. Report of the Committee on Church Life and Work and Public Morals, RGAUFC, 1912, p. 5.

80. *The Scotsman*, 6 December 1911.

81. Ibid., 7 May 1914. Overture approved after a split.

82. Committee on the Observance of the Lord's Day, RGACS, 1902, p. 1152.

83. Ibid., RGACS, 1912; Report of the Committee on Church Life and Work and Public Morals, RGAUFC, 1912.

84. Report of the Committee on Church Life and Work and Public Morals, *RGAUFC*, 1912, pp. 6–7.
85. Alfred Noyes, *The Times*, 4 September 1916.
86. Ibid., 7 March 1924.
87. Ibid., 17 March 1924.
88. Ibid., 26 May 1933.
89. Report of the Committee on Church Life and Social Problems, *RGAUFC*, 1925, pp. 3–4; 1929, p. 9.
90. *The Scotsman*, 4 May 1939.
91. Ibid., 15 February 1939.
92. Ibid., 29 February 1936.
93. Ibid., 3 October 1935.
94. Ibid., 30 March 1934.
95. Ibid., 8 February 1935.
96. Ibid., 30 October 1926, 16 September 1936, 4 March 1938.
97. *The Times*, 10 March 1934.
98. *The Scotsman*, 14 September 1947.
99. Committee on Christian Life and Work, *RGACS*, 1945, p. 276; 1946, pp. 244–5.
100. *The Scotsman*, 2 April 1941.
101. Ibid., 10 April 1941.
102. Committee on Christian Life and Work, *RGACS*, 1940, p. 386; 1941, p. 356; 1942, p. 295; 1943, p. 247; 1944, p. 281; *The Scotsman*, 2 April 1941.
103. Ibid., 25 May 1944.
104. Ibid., 21 September 1946.
105. Ibid., 4 April 1947.
106. Ibid., 21 January 1950.
107. Ibid., 13 September 1948.
108. Applied for by the Cooperative Association and the Communist Party; ibid., 1 October 1948, 23 May 1950.
109. Ibid., 11 May 1948.
110. Ibid., 19 March 1947.
111. Ibid., 11 October 1950.
112. *Glasgow Herald*, 13 August 1958.
113. *The Times*, 18 August 1954.
114. See C. G. Brown, 'Popular culture and the continuing struggle for rational recreation', in T. M. Devine and R. J. Finlay (eds), *Scotland in the Twentieth Century* (Edinburgh, 1996), pp. 210–29.
115. A. Bartie, 'Festival City: arts, culture and moral conflict at the Edinburgh Festivals 1947–67', unpublished PhD thesis, University of Dundee, 2007; C. G. Brown, A. McIvor and N. Rafeek, *The University Experience: An Oral History of the University of Strathclyde 1945–1975* (Edinburgh: EUP, 2004), pp, 182–230.
116. Committee on the Observance of the Lord's Day, *RGACS*, 1902, p. 1126.
117. *The Times*, 11 December 1928.
118. *The Scotsman*, 15 March 1939.

119. Ibid., 12 March 1938.
120. *The Herald*, 20 July 2009.
121. M. de Certeau, *The Practice of Everyday Life* (Berkeley, 2002).
122. One who failed this test was Lord Overtoun, a leading figure in the Free Church, who in 1899 was exposed by Keir Hardie as a hypocrite for promoting sabbatarianism while demanding his employees work in his factories on Sundays; Brown, *Religion and Society in Scotland*, p. 127.
123. Calculated from data in Table 4.4, Brierley, *Turning the Tide*, p. 53.
124. A *Times* leader suggested that this showed the Australasians as 'intensely Scotch' – 'because they close their hotels on Sunday and seize all the accumulated sinking funds', *The Times*, 16 November 1900.
125. *The Scotsman*, 30 April 2001.

Chapter 7

After 'The Religion of My Fathers': The Quest for Composure in the 'Post-Presbyterian' Self

Steven Sutcliffe

INTRODUCTION

This chapter investigates the shadow cast by 'the religion of my fathers' on the formation of self-identity in everyday life in modern Scotland. It uses a critical biographical method to identify the role of religion in the narration by modern Scots of a viable and acceptable sense of self. The overall aim is to examine new senses of self which emerge as the century unfolds, but which exist in tension with more traditional models. The pluralisation of religious elements in Scotland available for identity construction has been insufficiently recognised in existing historiography, which has tended to overlook the influence of non-presbyterian sources in the formation of a sense of 'Scottish self'. Other selves have been more widely imagined than has been assumed. Although the formative influence in social life of broadly 'Presbyterian' values has been profound, cultural pluralisation has opened up the 'Presbyterian psyche' to new possibilities of resistance and experiment.

This chapter examines possibilities of articulating a different sense of self in modern Scotland – for good or ill – through three biographical case studies: Dugald Semple (1884–1964), Sheena Govan (1912–67) and Ronald Laing (1927–89). Spanning the period from the late-Victorian world to post-modernity, their subjectivities simultaneously challenge, yet defer to, traditional attributions of 'Presbyterian culture' in general and the 'Presbyterian Scot' in particular. In their struggles to achieve composure of identity by modifying these widely perceived attributions, each biography inadvertently displays the tenacity of these traditional identities.[1] Four areas of tension are marked: the relationship with parental and especially paternal authority; changing expressions of gender; breakdown and innovation in work and career; and the relativisation of religious tradition through secularisation and pluralisation. New sensibilities of self emerge at these flashpoints which erode the authoritative transmission of 'the religion of my fathers'[2] – a phrase which symbolises the authority of cultural tradition – without yet crystallising into a replacement tradition of substance.

I have selected these testimonies to illustrate different positions within the 'respectable' culture of the middle classes, since these are the groups with the economic, educational and cultural capital most conducive to self-examination. My questions are, first, what new elements are folded into these identities? Second, to what extent do these narratives succeed in achieving the composure they seek? And, third, do they mount more than a passing challenge after all to the subjectifying power of 'Presbyterian' identities? The manifest turbulence in the lives of the three subjects may in fact represent an 'inner', psychological clash between incorporated traditional values and the new cultural sources which have emerged with the relativisation of Presbyterianism as a social and political institution. In other words, although pluralisation has uncoupled the traditional relationship between church and nation, a 'Presbyterian self' may persist in the wider culture as a bundle of attributes – moral, emotional and intellectual – which continue to address or to 'interpellate' Scottish subjects.[3] Following Giddens' assertion that 'self-identity is created and . . . continually reordered' amid the 'shifting experiences of day-to-day life',[4] I argue that this 'quest for composure' in self-identity is a quite ordinary, reflective enterprise which occurs within a range of groups of individuals who have the motivation and capital to invest in self-reflection. We should avoid projecting a 'virtuosic' or 'heroic' register into these narratives. For many people, reconstructing the self 'after the religion of my fathers' is the stuff of everyday life.

BIOGRAPHY OF RELIGION AS CRITICAL 'LIFE WRITING'

John Dryden famously defined 'biography' as 'the history of particular men's lives'.[5] More recently Thomas Carlyle declared that 'the history of the world is but the biography of great men'.[6] Feminist and Marxist historiography, influenced by demotic sources and oral history methodology, has understandably criticised these self-serving, patriarchal models; for example, Stanley derides 'the near-obsession of modern biography with the "great" and "in/famous"'.[7] Hence biography as a narrative about an isolated male ego (of superior status) has been displaced by biography as a socially mediated, ongoing narrative of 'who I am' in which all persons are to some extent engaged. On this approach biography is the act of 'storying the self' in speech or writing, in which the construction of the personal 'I' occurs in the context of wider social relationships.[8] Kadar proposes the term 'life writing' as an alternative, since it can include 'less "objective", or more "personal", genres such as letters and diaries' as well as 'oral narratives and life testimonies, and anthropological life histories'.[9]

If the anthropological ground of biography has become clearer, its moral tenor as a character-forming exercise lingers on. Biography in popular understanding is at least implicitly a didactic genre: the exemplary life is invariably 'linear, chronological, progressive, cumulative and individualist'.[10] On this model an 'unexemplary' life episode will be deleted at source by the narrator, or else presented as an opportunity for *post hoc* rationalisation of mistakes made and bridges burned. If a productive critical method is to be distilled from treacherous ground, we must become sensitised to traces of Carlylean 'heroism' within traditional biography, and alert to our own predisposition to continue to render 'life writing' in a 'heroic' register even as we locate new sources.

This is particularly salutary when dealing with the concept 'religion'.[11] A biographical approach helpfully restores the element of 'personal religious identity' lost when the scholar, as so often, adopts a 'stunted' model of religion defined merely as a function of church membership.[12] But in the process of becoming aware that a spectrum of 'religious' elements may be incorporated into personal identity beyond the once-a-week act of attending or not attending a church service, we must beware of succumbing to pressures of confession and pedagogy – close to the Carlylean 'heroic' – which traditionally inform 'religious' biography, and which emphasise the struggle of piety and virtue over forces of inertia and error.[13] For a critical 'life writing' approach finds mixed motives and unrealised goals in the content of a life, and impurity and contradiction in its narration. As Summerfield argues, because 'personal narratives are the products of a relationship between discourse and subjectivity' there can be no 'clear space out of which voices can speak'.[14] This is because the narrator's subjectivity is moulded by wider discourses even as it 'acts back' upon them, creating a 'feedback loop'[15] between personal subjectivity and dominant discourse. Attaining biographical 'composure' lies precisely in balancing out 'external' discourse with robust articulation of 'internal' subjectivity. The 'external' discourse in my exemplar biographies is the attributed model of a 'Presbyterian self' which addresses or interpellates the subjects. Its cultural authority compels them to heed its call, even as they test its plausibility for new circumstances by exploring other sources and resources.

Summerfield plays upon two meanings of the verb 'to compose': first, the 'process of creating accounts of experiences'; second, achieving 'equilibrium', accomplished by 'constituting oneself as the subject of those stories'. Self-esteem is an important factor. Healthy selfhood is created by 'reiterating stories which prove [the subject's] worth and the value of the past in their lives', the aim being to articulate a comfortable, viable sense of self.[16] Summerfield underscores the role played here by the 'real or imagined audience': that is, a 'storied self' is 'the product of a relationship between a narrator and a recipient subject'.[17] An important condition of achieving composure is simply that one's story is recognised and affirmed by others. The narrative must be comprehensible not only 'internally' to the self, but 'externally' to others: that is, it must make 'social' sense. This in turn requires shared cultural values between narrator and audience. When these are uncertain or in flux, composure becomes that much more elusive. The

articulation of 'who I am' in early to mid-twentieth-century Scotland forms
an ideal case study.

'A GREAT UPSURGE OF NON-CHRISTIAN RELIGION':[18]
DEVELOPING A 'POST-PRESBYTERIAN' HISTORIOGRAPHY

In order to be a productive method, then, critical biography must reject
veneration of heroic lives for examination of the complex, messy, 'storied
selves' of modern subjects. The wider context for this 'devolution' in self-
identity from grand narrative to unfinished project is an emerging 'post-
Presbyterian' historiography. This pays attention to the new institutions
which are beginning to be constituted in Scotland in reaction to (yet display-
ing continuing deference towards) traditional 'Presbyterian' attributions of
church going, family life, education, work ethic, temperance and thrift. We
will see examples of new institutions flickering in and out of focus in the
three life stories which follow. While self-consciously seeking new ways of
thinking and acting, these remain constrained at their point of origin by the
burden, experienced by the three subjects, of traditional religious roles and
expectations. These 'new' selves ferment at a psychological and emotional
level as a function of a wider 'post-Presbyterian' turn in Scottish history and
sociology. Both levels of articulation, the sociological and the psychological, exhibit the same unresolved dynamic of resistance-cum-deference to the
attributes of Presbyterian tradition.

   When traditional historiography found cultural difference, it often
modelled it in terms of a 'Caledonian antisyzygy' – a mysterious psychological disposition said to unite a distinctively Scottish sensibility through
the mutual attraction of opposite qualities (from the Greek words *anti* plus
syzygia, union).[19] The phrase was coined by G. Gregory Smith in the opening
chapter of his modernist study of Scottish literature, appropriately entitled
'Two Moods'. Despite impressions of cohesion and uniformity, Smith
argues that Scottish literature, 'under the stress of foreign influence and
native division and reaction', presented 'almost a zigzag of contradictions'.
Smith dubbed the resultant 'combination of opposites' the 'Caledonian
antisyzygy', a dialectic which reflected 'contrasts which the Scot shows at
every turn, in his political and ecclesiastical history, in his polemical restless-
ness . . ., [and] in his practical judgement, which is the admission that two
sides of the matter have been considered'.[20] The model allows Smith to find
'incongruities' to be evidence of 'synthesis' and 'breaks and thwarts' to be
signs of 'continuity' (rather than dissolution) of tradition.[21] He presents this
'mixture of contraries' as the motor for the tradition of violent argument or
'flyting', the 'sheer exhilaration of conflict' which produces the 'warp and
woof' of Scottish literary tradition.[22]

   Translated into the religious sphere, this model of a conjunction of
quarrelsome opposites lends itself to the historiographical stereotype of

'Catholic' *versus* 'Protestant'.[23] One problem with this interpretation is that it reduces the complexity of Scottish Christian identities alone to an artificial polarisation between 'indigenous' (Scottish, equalling Presbyterian) and 'alien' (non-Scottish, equalling Catholic) formations.[24] John Highet's *The Scottish Churches* of 1960 qualified the picture by picking out real doctrinal and liturgical differences among reformed congregations.[25] But it was not until the end of the century that a fuller inventory was attempted. For example, Whaling noted that non-Presbyterian Christian traditions in Scotland, such as Orthodox Christianity, could be differentiated along multiple ethnic-cultural lines.[26] Similarly, Irish, Italian and Polish minorities significantly complicated the profile of 'Scottish Catholicism'; Chinese and African Christians were increasingly active; Muslims, Hindus, Sikhs and Jews had developed important histories; forty new religions were identified from the mid-1970s; and the 2001 census revealed Buddhism to be the fastest-growing religion in Scotland.[27] Nevertheless the historiography of 'religion' in Scotland continued until very recently to be equated largely with Christianity in its many 'reformed' varieties.[28]

In fact 'non-reformed', 'post-Presbyterian' traditions such as Spiritualism and Theosophy have played significant roles as religious resources for lower middle and middle social groups. The Findhorn colony on the Moray Firth coast is a case in point. By the early 1970s it encapsulated the interests of 'an increasing number of groups interested in borrowing from any religion or none for the purpose of developing the potential of the individual'.[29] Set up as a small colony in 1962 by an English family and their Canadian friend, Findhorn had grown into an internationally recognised 'new age' colony by the mid-1970s, leading to advice in one Church of Scotland report that 'most unchurched people in Scotland today are more likely to construct their worldview from aspects of the New Age outlook than from elements of mainstream Christianity'.[30] The report described 'the active promotion of New Age ideas and practices in Scotland' through 'well organised and business-like communities' supplying 'courses and literature dealing with astrology, alchemy, the occult, tarot, aromatherapy, I Ching, reflexology, the paranormal and reincarnation'.[31] By the 1980s and 1990s, practices such as T'ai Chi, Reiki and meditation were on offer in church halls and community centres, spreading the popular idea of an unchurched 'spirituality'.[32]

This evidence must differentiate historiographies of 'religion' in modern Scotland which are either monocultural or couched merely in terms of the 'Caledonian anti-syzygy'. It reveals greater plurality in the religious landscape at all levels, particularly in the cities. It also qualifies the big picture of secularisation by showing the persistence of religion as an element of individual subjectivity and psychology in which traditional, alternative and popular influences interact. In the light of 'post-Presbyterian' historiography, the biographies of Semple, Govan and Laing appear less as exotic specimens than as hard-grafted indigeneous responses to a sea change in Scottish culture and religion.

DUGALD SEMPLE (1884–1964): THE 'SIMPLE LIFE'

Dugald Semple's advocacy of the 'simple life' was what 1960s hippies would call 'dropping out', and 1990s 'greens' would call 'downsizing'. Semple was born in 1884 to a large family in Johnstone near Paisley, in the hinterlands of 'radical Renfrewshire'.[33] His mother was from a Beith farm; his father worked as a tailor.[34] Semple won a bursary to Paisley Grammar School, then served his apprenticeship as an engineering draughtsman.[35] In 1907, inspired by a combination of freethinking, dietary reform and the romantic cult of nature, Semple moved into a tent, and later into an old omnibus, on Linwood Moss. In 1910 he left his job to fashion a frugal living as public speaker and journalist, working as Secretary for the London Vegetarian Society during the First World War. He applied for exemption from war service on grounds of conscientious objection in 1916, and was excused on condition that he continue lecturing on food economy.[36] Later he worked a smallholding in hill country near Beith with his wife, Cathie, and continued public speaking and journalism. Following Cathie's death, he retired to Fairlie where he died in 1964.

As a young man Semple described himself as an 'ardent socialist' and 'keen vegetarian'. His published accounts of his 'experiment in living' express a shrewd moral individualism captivated by the natural world. He makes regular use of abstract models of the divine pitched ambiguously between deism and pantheism, and urges on his readers the physical and moral virtues of leading a 'healthy' lifestyle. The 'question of religion', as he puts it, preoccupied him from an early age. It became 'the great obstacle' in his family relationships, precipitating 'long arguments . . . after family worship on Sabbath evenings'. His father, a Sunday school superintendent, threatened to burn his Rationalist Press books, while local ministers 'tried to corner me with their quotations from scripture'. 'At times', Semple writes, 'it was little short of persecution.' A staunch, critical individualism emerged in response: 'their religion, I could see, was not a matter of individual conscience, but simply a sophisticated method of defending the *status quo*'. He, in contrast, 'was inclined to question . . . the actual meaning of life'. Semple writes: 'I came to look on Sunday as a day of horror.'[37] Having left church and Sunday school, he now left the family home.

His antipathy towards organised religion is confirmed by dissenting and anticlerical comments scattered through his writings: for example, 'Sabbaths and Bibles are . . . for the priest-ridden' and 'whenever a man buttons his collar behind instead of in front [wears a clerical collar], he is usually going that way himself'.[38] In a chapter called 'A Simple Religion' in *Living in Liberty*, he decries 'Bible fetishism' and rejects the 'God of Calvin' whom he

describes as 'a God of anger who elects His children to everlasting punishment'.[39] When he anticipates the retort from his elders that 'you are despis-
ing the teaching of your great-great-grandfather', Semple adds provocatively
'as if he had anything to do with the present'.[40]

Later, however, Semple organised a Scottish No-Stipend League against
the Church of Scotland's practice of levying a tithe on landowners for
the minister's stipend. This practice offended Semple's voluntarism,
since it appeared to demonstrate the politically 'established' nature of the
Presbyterian church:

> Reader, do you not think with me . . . that this stipend business is a disgrace to
> the name of religion? Think on how our covenanting forefathers suffered for the
> principles of religious tolerance . . . To compel a Jew, Catholic or Agnostic to
> support one particular faith because he happens to be a landowner is not religion
> but intolerance of the worst kind.[41]

However, in invoking the Covenanters, Semple appeals to Presbyterian
ancestry, a strategy which underscores the Presbyterian moral character of
his principled protest even as it travels in a 'post-Presbyterian' direction.

Meanwhile, his ambiguous relationship with indigenous Presbyterianism
is tempered by naïve curiosity towards more exotic positions. Thus he
admires local Quakers for 'their simple sincere faith', Swedenborgians
for their 'New Church principles', and his father-in-law, a Bridge of Weir
Unitarian minister, for 'his broad outlook'.[42] Later he met and corresponded
with a series of alternative religionists including Theosophists, Buddhists
and Sufis, nature cure practitioners, vegetarians and fruitarians, co-operative
socialists and anarchist individualists, and charismatic activists like Edward
Carpenter and Mohandas (Mahatma) Gandhi.[43]

Semple's dynamic mix of deference and dissent towards tradition is
symptomatic of the modern quest for composure. Despite his rebellious-
ness, a feature of his method is emphasis on virtues of conscience, sobriety,
plain living, frugality and self-reliance which were widely attributed to the
'reformed' tradition. The content and style of his 'simple life' also shares
similarities with Scottish vernacular or 'kailyard' literature of the period,
blending traces of moral probity (Semple opposed theatre, football and
drink) with descriptions of kenspeckle characters and intensely realised local
landscapes. He became increasingly conservative in respect of social reform,
emphasising instead the need to improve everyday habits and one's personal
disposition. 'The real problem is mostly with ourselves,' he wrote in 1915;
we must 'get right within first'.[44] His moral individualism rings out when he
contrasts those who are 'priest-ridden' with the 'healthy religious person'
who expresses 'a code of his own making'.[45] Hence, in a play on his surname
(encapsulating his moot relationship with patriarchal tradition) he warns his
readers against the inference that 'the simple life means the Semple life'. On
the contrary: 'no one is called upon to tell others what they should do'.[46]

Thus while initially sympathetic to the co-operative socialism which was then challenging Whiggish liberalism in Renfrewshire,[47] Semple recasts 'reform' as an ecology of personal moral relationships. For example, it is more in keeping with Presbyterian family culture than communism that Dugald and Cathie worked their smallholding in the traditional social unit of husband and wife.[48] Semple seems to have foreseen this turn as early as 1911, when he wrote that, although he remained a 'convinced Socialist' in legislative matters, 'we are as much the slaves of our own bidding as to that of any taskmaster'. It followed from this that 'to know reform you must live reform'.[49] This method of conscientious reflection clearly moulded Semple's principled objection to war service. But it also helped to make sense of the cacophony of religious traditions to which Semple had exposed himself through his 'post-Presbyterian' adventuring, allowing him to posit that, ultimately, it was personal and not institutional change which mattered most: 'it is not another Messiah that is needed but more obedience to the living voice within'.[50]

Semple's sobriety was, however, tempered by a carefree romanticism. His ecology of personal relationships found room to breathe in the countryside, in 'the life of the open air'.[51] He cites with approval George Borrow's popular works *The Romany Rye* and *Lavengro*:[52] thus, a Romany caravan appears as a plate or cover design in many publications. In a typical passage he writes:

> One of my ambitions of boyhood was to be a Romany and enjoy life in the fresh air of heaven. Often I have envied the gypsy as he wheeled past in his yellow-painted caravan with arched roof, leaving civilization far behind.[53]

In this love of 'fresh air', Semple anticipated the vogue in the 1930s and 1940s for the 'outdoor life' and 'nature watching'. A new genre of broadcasting emerged such as *Out with Romany* on BBC's 'Children's Hour' and *Hutman of the BBC* on Scottish 'Children's Hour'.[54] Semple's 'simple life' seceded from the 'iron cage' produced by modern economic and social rationalisation.[55] To abandon his skilled engineering trade to pursue amateur botany, and to follow the wisdom of the 'living voice within', at the expense of Kirk tradition, was both practically and symbolically to renounce his apprenticeship and its immediate context in the industrialisation and urbanisation of Clydeside and greater Glasgow.[56] Apart from a brief period in London, Semple lived all his life in the North Ayrshire and Renfrewshire countryside. Travelling the Clyde coast on his first public speaking tour in 1911, he describes a 'most depressing journey through Port Glasgow, with its long rows of tenements buried at the foot of a hill, swarming with dirty children in narrow streets with an atmosphere that would do justice to a plague'.[57] This Blakean representation of 'dark Satanic mills' starkly contrasts with the pastoral vision, on the closing pages of his final book, of a 'happy free life under the great blue sky with all nature as companion'.[58]

Yet against Semple's ringing declaration of self-composure in nature must be weighed evidence of everyday pride and defensiveness. The intense Sabbath arguments and the rift with his parents took an early toll. 'My health weakened', he writes, 'I felt forced to leave home for the sake of all concerned'.[59] The relationship was still strained when they attended his first public lecture, which was in Johnstone town hall, 'sitting right in the front seat next to the platform'. With palpable relief, Semple notes they are now 'most friendly'.[60] He also shows concern lest certain career developments be interpreted by cynical readers as diluting his ideals. Thus when the *Evening Times* describes his new wife Cathie as 'a charming Kilmacolm widow, the owner of a large house and grounds', Semple notes testily that she only owns 'a half villa'. He switches to the cause of gender equality to counter perceptions that he might be marrying into money: 'every girl or woman who marries should have money of her own'.[61] And he is quick to defend the changed circumstances of his old age: 'some are very surprised to learn that I live now in a modern cottage and that until recently I owned a motor car and toured like gents of the open road'; 'evidently', he continues with prickly rhetoric, 'I owe to society a full account of my doings, although I never asked anyone for a similar request'.[62] This emphasis on personal moral probity over the uncertainties of social and cultural change reformulates the principled dissent and self-reliance inculcated in his father's Sunday school.

SHEENA GOVAN (1912–67): THE LABOUR PAINS OF THE 'NEW AGE'

Sheena Govan shares Semple's preoccupation with 'the light within' which carries over a sense of Calvinistic election and destiny into 'post-Presbyterian' subjectivities. But Govan introduces a more transgressive element into the process of self-composure: she regenders the divine. In the Glasgow *Sunday Mail* in 1957, her husband Peter Caddy called her a 'World Teacher': 'God, in his infinite love and mercy for mankind, has, at the eleventh hour, sent Sheena to save the world', he announced. She is 'a Redeemer in the form of a woman'.[63]

These claims about Govan's incipient divinity came at the high water mark of twentieth-century Scottish church membership. The fervour of these statements would be recognisable to *Sunday Mail* readers familiar with the 1950–2 'Radio Missions' of the BBC in Scotland and the 'All Scotland Crusade' of Billy Graham in 1955.[64] But the attribution of divine authority to a middle-aged woman of uncertain denominational standing is arresting. As early as the 1930s women had entered the eldership and ministry in the Congregational Church, and in liberal quarters of the United Free Church, but they were unable to train as ministers in the Church of Scotland until after 1968.[65] No commensurable role was available in the Catholic Church. As a female 'Redeemer', Govan had closer affinities with the exercise of

Figure 7.1   *Sheena Govan interviewed by reporters in the Queen's Hotel, Bridge of Allan,*
January 1957. Courtesy of Daily Record.

women's charisma in Theosophy and Spiritualism, and with traditions of
devotion to Mary and motherhood in popular Catholicism. She also anticipates the diffusion of women's authority as healers and teachers in 'new age'
and 'holistic' networks from the late 1960s onwards.[66]

Unlike Semple and Laing, however, Govan left no memoir. Apart from
two columns under her name in the popular press, there is no unmediated
public account of her life. Parts can be reconstructed from the memories of
a small group which gathered around her in the 1950s, but since these are
themselves marked by internal disagreement and ultimately schism, a critical
biography of Govan presents particular challenges. At the same time it satis-
fies the turn towards less accessible life writings advocated by Stanley and
Kadar. I will assemble Govan's biography from three sets of representations:
primary and secondary sources about the Faith Mission, the Protestant
organisation into which Govan was born; 'tabloid' newspaper stories about
the so-called 'Nameless Ones'; and memoirs of the founders of the Findhorn
colony. That these accounts of Govan were themselves produced as part of
a struggle to articulate new identities in a hostile environment, further indicates the complexity of composing the 'post-Presbyterian' self.

Govan's birth in Edinburgh in 1912 is recorded by her older sister, Isabel,
within her biography of their father, John Govan, and the Faith Mission.[67]

The Faith Mission is a Protestant 'home mission' organisation founded in 1886 in Glasgow. The organisation evangelised provincial populations, its itinerant 'pilgrims' holding meetings in villages and small towns in Scotland and Northern Ireland. Their intention was to stimulate revival in existing denominations rather than to found new churches, aiming for participants to become 'fully saved, cleansed from sin, and receive the power of the Holy Spirit'.[68]

Sheena was the last of four children, and the youngest by twelve years. After noting her birth, her sister's biography immediately returns to the gruelling schedule of 'The Chief', as their father was known, who 'superintended the work, and fulfilled engagements all over the country'. Although readers are assured that 'The Chief' was 'a good deal with his children', Sheena's birth seems a passing entry in her father's busy diary.[69] Sheena then disappears from public view for over twenty years. When she resurfaces, it is again through the representations of others; initially, also, under the wrong name, compounding the impression of identity stress. A January 1957 story in the *Daily Record* describes a 'mysterious religious group' in Oban. This is a 'group of people of all denominations . . . Catholics, Presbyterian, Episcopalian . . . who have given up everything for God'. The newspaper reports in sensationalist fashion that an English travelling salesman called Fred Astell has joined the group, and that his wife, Sylvia, is under pressure to 'join sect or lose husband'. The story hints that the leader of this 'sect' is 'Mrs Sheena Gowan [sic]' who 'says she is Christ resurrected'.[70] Three days later the *Scottish Daily Express* takes up the story, leading with a photograph of Govan, now correctly named (although incorrectly aged) and identified as leader of 'The Nameless Ones' – a melodramatic but fitting title for these displaced seekers.[71] The article portrays her as 'a quiet, shy woman' who is 'unobtrusively gathering followers'. Her group is based on the idea that 'God is Love' and that the 'second coming' is imminent, but it has 'no name, no headquarters, no book of doctrine'. Group members describe Govan as 'the new Messiah', but she herself is more equivocal, explaining that 'anyone is a Messiah to the person who finds God through him or her'.[72]

In May 1957 the *Sunday Mail* ran a four-part centre spread on 'The story of the woman they call the Messiah'.[73] The first instalment introduced readers to Sheena's seven 'disciples': her 'children of the new age'. They in turn testify to her status: she is 'the Redeemer of Mankind' and 'God's Beloved'.[74] Govan herself contributes a ghost-written feature entitled 'My childhood days'. Here she traces her intense nature to the strain of being brought up between two worlds: the everyday secular school environment 'where everybody lived quite happily as though they had no souls', and the 'religious instruction' of her family life in the Faith Mission, which 'led me to believe that everybody who had not had a personal experience of conversion . . . was making straight for the hell fire'. She confesses that the resulting 'emotional conflict' produced a nervous breakdown. A strong thread in the story is her description of herself as an 'afterthought' to her parents' career. This leads her to urge readers to put their children first, for they need to know 'they are wanted' by their parents. She also paints an intimate picture of closeness to her father which seems to contrast with her feeling of being an 'afterthought': 'I never went to bed . . . without his coming to read to me, to hear my prayers and to kiss me goodnight . . . I was more devoted to him than to anyone else'.[75]

A sense of conflict and loss continued in 'The Anguish of a Mother', Sheena's second feature for the *Sunday Mail*. Beginning with her mother's death when Sheena was twenty-one, leaving her without either parent as she entered adulthood, the column narrates a broken engagement and Sheena's pregnancy. The story carries a photograph of her cradling the baby whom she is reported to have given up for adoption. Using capital letters to indicate the strength of her emotion, she describes this decision as 'THE ONLY REGRET OF MY LIFE'. She advises other unmarried mothers against it: 'the world won't last much longer', she writes, 'be happy with [your baby] and God will be with you and will help you'.[76]

A refrain is Sheena's desire for security: 'I know now why so many people make unfortunate liaisons in the search for the love they have been starved of in childhood.'[77] The agitated response to the 'Nameless Ones' within the Govan family must have reinforced this sense of rejection. Her sister Isabel describes the group in the *Scottish Daily Express* as 'the work of the devil', the only consolation being that it will 'fade out like all other such heresies'. Isabel also suggests that Sheena is trading on their father's good name by proselytising in a region – the West Highlands – where the Faith Mission was well known. Her closing words are sharp: 'ask her [Sheena] when was the last time she attended a meeting of the Faith Mission'.[78]

The *Sunday Mail* mixed awe with hostility in equal measure. 'WHAT IS THE POWER? IS IT GOOD OR EVIL?' shouted one editorial.[79] Unsurprisingly, readers' letters were 'highly critical'.[80] Locally, Sheena was satirised by Mull poet Angus Macintyre in verses on the 'queer goings-on' in Oban:

> Where pressmen, jostlin', shovin'
>   Besiege the Nameless Sect
>   To talk wi' Sheena Govan
> Who says she's Heaven's elect
>
> But her looks are so bewitchin'
>   Her voice like music runs
>   In no time man, you're itchin'
> To join the Nameless Ones[81]

When the story petered out, Govan again disappears from the public record. She only re-enters history posthumously: in 1975, in an early account of the Findhorn community which depicts Sheena as a relentless critic of her 'disciples', teaching them the 'crucifixion' of the personality.[82] Her severe method of instruction, exacerbated by recurring migraines, renders her 'sharp and irritable'.[83] The author acknowledges that this portrait of Govan is mediated by the recollections of one of her followers, Eileen Caddy.[84] These change little in Caddy's own memoir, where she describes Sheena as 'very severe' and 'aloof', 'moody and silent'.[85] 'I didn't understand Sheena', Eileen writes, 'I was terrified of her and felt I couldn't trust her.' In one episode Eileen describes herself as being 'at the mercy of Peter's wife', a turn of phrase which suggests that personal feelings as much as spiritual discipline fuelled her portrayal, for Eileen had succeeded Sheena as Peter Caddy's partner.[86] Eileen describes Sheena in her final years as a 'lonely, unhappy old woman' who 'had nothing'. Just as the newspapers misrepresented Sheena's name and age, Eileen gets her place of death wrong.[87]

Another member of Sheena's group, the Canadian writer and teacher Dorothy Maclean, is more eirenic. Maclean suggests that the fact that Sheena's 'inner experiences' were 'difficult for her to interpret within the framework of traditional Christianity' created particular 'problems and pressures'. These became 'intolerable' for the rest of the group when Sheena 'imposed upon herself the impossible mission of changing the world'.[88] Maclean acknowledges her debt to Sheena, but her formulation of the group's relationship with Sheena at the end remains equivocal: 'she died . . . still misunderstanding, unfortunately, our seeming denial of her'.[89]

Like Maclean, Sheena's husband Peter Caddy continues the trail of biographical errors in describing the Faith Mission as a 'Quaker' organisation; like Eileen Caddy, he also gets her place of death wrong.[90] Yet with generosity he also describes her as 'one of the most remarkable and loving women that I have ever met' without whom the Findhorn community 'would never have come about'.[91] But Peter is also prone to self-justification, repudiating Sheena in a late encounter:

> She was angry. She hit me in the face . . . She had said to me that in the end, I would be so close to God that I would turn against her . . . Now it was happening, just as she'd prophesied, and I watched with great sorrow the lonely figure of the woman I had loved and served walking away down the frozen drive.[92]

The sources are clearly fragile, but allow us to draw provisional conclusions relevant to the theory put forward here concerning critical biography and the problem of identity formation in a newly transitional culture. Sheena Govan was a flawed charismatic leader who could sustain neither her leadership nor her followers' loyalty, eventually coming to grief in an 'extraordinary tangle of relationships'.[93] She proved unable or unwilling to represent herself convincingly in the company of equally strong-willed and independently minded individuals. The claim that this intense and anguished woman was the 'new Messiah' is perhaps the most controversial religious utterance in modern Scotland. Yet Sheena Govan is known, if at all, almost entirely through the representations of others. And these are at best equivocal, at worst unflattering, especially those made by the two organisations in which her life was most strongly implicated: her father's Faith Mission, and her husband's Findhorn Foundation. The only surviving examples of self-representation, her columns in the *Sunday Mail*, may themselves be ghost-written, and as such continue to place her reputation in the hands of others.

In a 1965 letter to a mutual acquaintance, Caddy writes that 'Sheena had failed in her mission'.[94] In contrast, the evidence suggests that a series of groups and institutions – the Faith Mission, the 'Nameless Ones', the Findhorn colony – failed in their care for Sheena. The different roles in which she was cast – charismatic prophet, ill person, single mother – shared a fragility of identity which required recognition and support from patient companions. The sensational press coverage of 1957 ultimately made Sheena a burden for a group of displaced individuals who were also desperately seeking composure in an unsympathetic culture. Sheena Govan thus became a casualty of the internal conflicts of 'post-Presbyterian' identity formation. Had she been born a generation later, she might have flourished as a 'new age' prophet or healer. Her frailties in the 1950s symbolised the labour pains of a new culture, in which female leadership and single motherhood would no longer automatically draw suspicion.

R. D. LAING (1927–89): THE PSYCHIATRIST 'TOSSED AND TURNED'

R. D. or 'Ronnie' Laing exemplifies the promise and peril of 'post-Presbyterian' self-expression among an occupational group who might be expected to 'know better' – psychiatrists. Where Semple was a skilled artisan and Govan a lower middle-class evangelical, Laing was a university-educated medical professional. His significance for either intellectual or cultural historiography is not immediately self-evident. Writing in the late 1990s, Kotowicz claims that Laing is intellectually problematic. In his view, Laing became increasingly polemical and rhetorical in the 1960s, an attitude which spoiled the scientific cogency of his best-known argument: that 'schizophrenia' is a social construction rather than a natural datum. More importantly from my approach, Kotowicz entirely dismisses the 'complicated personal life', the 'financial difficulties' and the 'drunken stunts' for which Laing gained notoriety. His assessment is stark: 'Just as quickly as he rose to prominence, Laing faded away.'[95]

This focus on Laing as a scientific 'backslider' is not untypical of a secondary literature often preoccupied with his professional shortcomings.[96] But critical biography (and cultural history more widely) is as interested in Laing's 'complicated personal life' as in Laing the peer-reviewed theorist.

Playing down Laing's 'life' at the expense of his 'work' introduces a private/public split which obscures the holistic fashioning of personal identity.[97] The task is complicated by an additional factor which sets Laing apart from Semple and Govan: the existence of a large commentary, both critical and adulatory. Where Semple is unnoticed and Govan unknown, Laing is famous – indeed, infamous. This chapter therefore assumes familiarity with the basic chronology of his life. At the same time, the task of critical biography is complicated by the quantity of opinion and speculation. This has produced a mythography of Laing which he himself did not discourage. For example, Adrian Laing describes his father as 'raw with jealousy' when Colin Wilson, one of the loose group of English 'angry young men', published his existentialist bestseller, *The Outsider*, in 1956; Laing hoped that his first book, *The Divided Self*, would 'put Colin Wilson and John Osborne in their places'.[98] He goes on to describe his father's 'fame trip' in the 1960s which culminated in a 'guru image' and a booming 'R. D. industry'.[99]

In this chapter's approach, Laing is not a problematic 'thinker' who requires rehabilitation into a canon, but a complicated modern Scotsman whose biography is a lightning rod across the modern private/public divide. His traverse across the face of cultural identities – from lower middle-class Presbyterian respectability, through European existentialism, to countercultural subjectivities – is a striking response to the 'discursive bereavement' (the grief at the cultural loss of religious certainties) experienced mid-century by Christians under the twin developments of secularisation and religious pluralisation.[100] Laing sought to make ambiguities and conflicts in human experience the data for both professional and personal enquiry, beginning with the disturbed experience of his patients, but increasingly confessing his own conflicts. The objective 'clinical' problems pursued by Laing were thus biographically charged: as much 'personal' as 'professional'. This point is underscored by ambiguity over whether his own analysis, required as part of his professional training, was satisfactorily discharged.[101] According to his son's biography, Laing and his analyst both agreed that the analysis avoided tackling Laing's depression.[102] His difficult relationship with his mother is well known, but less addressed is his relationship with his father. In professionally locating the aetiology of schizophrenia in the nuclear family, Laing was obliquely addressing family tradition and descent in his own biography. Because this was patrilineal and Presbyterian, Beveridge and Turnbull's rhetorical question deftly encapsulates Laing's quandary: 'What does the religion of my fathers mean to me?'

Laing's contributions to the critique of the family and other bourgeois institutions, and his general empathy with psychological outsiders and underdogs, made him a hero for the British and American counterculture of the 1960s. However, a powerful current in Laing's biography, as with Govan and to a lesser extent Semple, is self-discomfiture: uneasiness inhabiting his own skin. In contrast to the aspiring 'redeemer' and the 'simple life' *refusenik*,

Laing's quest for composure was played out within the privileged professional domain of psychiatric medicine. This would prove personally demanding: abundant evidence suggests his unease when operating within the institution. In his early training, he describes how, instead of resorting to an injection, he tried 'hanging out' with a manic patient in a padded cell; 'I felt strangely at home', he writes, 'lounging on the floor . . . without bothering to make sense of it'.[103] Two late oral exchanges articulate the nature of his difficulties. In 1985 his fellow psychiatrist, Anthony Clare, asked him 'what if I said to you that you were too sensitive to be a doctor?' Laing admitted: 'I haven't been able to do what a lot of doctors are able to do . . . which is to keep their sensitivity within a fairly formally ordered frame of conduct. I get tossed and turned.'[104] The second exchange puts the issue in the vernacular, using the language of the 'rough' male culture with which Laing periodically identified. Immediately after suffering the cardiac arrest that was to kill him, he was asked if he wanted a doctor: his 'last words' were 'Doctor, what fucking doctor?'[105]

We get an idea of the many responses Laing could make to Beveridge and Turnbull by first scanning his indigenous cultural heritage. In 1970 he described his upbringing as 'lower-middle-class Lowland Presbyterian, corroded by nineteenth century materialism, scientific rationalism and humanism'. He imagined himself as a 'native' specimen, viewed by anthropologists as 'some idealistic barbarian . . . living before the Enlightenment, exhibiting in frayed but recognizable form the primitive thought forms of the savage mind'.[106] In an essay entitled 'God and Psychiatry' he described himself as 'a negative theologian', by which he meant 'I can define God only by what he is not'. Difficult as defining 'God' was, he admitted to 'much more difficulty' in defining the second term in his essay title – the one which defined his profession.[107]

But Laing was also sensitive to modern religious plurality. The full range of his references to 'religion' include comparative religion and existentialist theology as well as his own mystical expositions. For example, he claimed that behind his iconic countercultural text *The Politics of Experience and the Bird of Paradise* (1967) lay the joint influence of a Jewish colleague, Joseph Schorstein, and George Macleod, leader of the Iona Community. Laing later called this book a synthesis of 'Scottish Presbyterian Celtic Calvinism and elements of Hasidism'.[108] Laing's religious interests could be homely as well as metaphysical, alluding to his upbringing in the south side of Glasgow which led him to recall as a young man 'how startled I was to meet for the first time . . . people of my age who had never opened a Bible'.[109] In his address to the Congress on the Dialectics of Liberation in 1967, he used an act of petitionary prayer as his example of how an unusual behaviour could always be explained in context: 'Someone is gibbering away on his knees, talking to someone who is not there. Yes, he is praying.'[110] He traced his own, apparently exotic, practice of Buddhist meditation and yoga to 'the time I was taught to say my prayers at night'.[111] And he explained to Anthony Clare that his choice to study medicine was personally driven: 'I'd got myself into quite an intensely painful, spiritual, religious quandary over the issue of the existence of God which assumed almost life and death proportions.'[112]

These diverse references show the range of Laing's cultural explorations between 1950 and 1970. He moved from the Abenheimer-Schorstein group meetings at Glasgow University in the 1950s at which European existentialists were discussed, to describing an LSD trip in his iconic prose poem, 'the Bird of Paradise'. This concludes with the well-known line: 'If I could turn you on, if I could drive you out of your wretched mind, if I could tell you I would let you know.'[113]

In 1972, Laing published *Knots*, a collection of poems inspired by the confused 'double bind' communications of his patients which he thought showed affinities with the paradoxes of Zen Buddhist *koans*. He described these poems as his attempt to delineate 'a Linnaeus of human bondage'.[114] The essence of the double bind – a type of confused social intercourse named by the American anthropologist Gregory Bateson in 1956 – was the coexistence of contradictory messages in intimate communications between couples and families. The first poem in *Knots* makes plain the tortuous effects of the double bind:

> They are playing a game. They are playing at not
> playing a game. If I show them I see they are, I
> shall break the rules and they will punish me.
> I must play their game, of not seeing that I see the game.[115]

The second poem spells out further logic of the double bind: that the self's dependency on the approval of the other in intimate relationships prohibits disparity between their experiences. Uniformity of experience is required in 'double bound' relationships:

> They are not having fun.
> I can't have fun if they don't.
> If I get them to have fun, than I can have fun with them.
> Getting them to have fun, is not fun. It is hard work.[116]

The poem imagines the indignant response by the double binding 'others' to the narrator's 'hard work':

> How dare you have fun when Christ died on the Cross
> for you! Was He having fun?[117]

It is difficult not to interpret the anonymous third person – 'They' who are 'not having fun' – as the patriarchal guardians of Presbyterian tradition. This group might also include the local ministers who 'tried to corner' Dugald Semple 'with their quotations from scripture', or Sheena Govan's father, 'The Chief' of the Faith Mission.

Laing's oscillating identity can be understood at least in part as an oversensitised response to such perceived 'double binds' of Presbyterian tradition. In *Sanity, Madness and the Family*, his co-authored study of the families of schizophrenics, he writes that one particular family 'expressly define their spiritual-carnal human condition as a double bind'.[118] Exposure to the new cultural order of the 1960s, in which sensation and subjectivity were given their head over reason and tradition, would only reinforce this sensitised experience of the human condition among those suitably prepared. Laing's expression of masculinity is illuminating in this regard. If evangelical Christian discourses had traditionally represented women as domesticated 'angels' and men as feral 'heathens',[119] Laing reinvested the male role with a passionate agnosticism. His versions of the flyting, drinking and brawling common in Scottish male 'rough culture' were effectively an expression of 'muscular Calvinism'. This behaviour undermined his professional status and was a factor in his resignation as a psychiatrist from the General Medical Council in 1987.[120] There are many accounts of 'Ronnie's' public drinking, with the replacement of the formal initials 'R. D.' with the intimate 'Ronnie' signifying the shift into vernacular culture.[121] For example, when they met to record an instalment of the radio programme *In the Psychiatrist's Chair* in 1985, Clare noted that Laing 'was not in good physical shape' and 'had been drinking heavily'. In the interview itself, Laing described himself as 'quite depressed' and a 'seasoned drinker', linking this to a recurring pattern on his father's side of the family which he called the 'Scottish Calvinist involutional melancholic type'.[122] Drinking brought out machismo as well as confession in Laing. As part of a general dismissal of the post-war American 'human potential' movement, he remarked witheringly that the 'person-centred' psychologist Carl Rogers 'wouldn't last two minutes in a Glasgow pub'.[123] And in a literal, physical example of 'muscular Calvinism', Laing and the Revd Donald N. MacDonald reputedly held a 'wrestling match . . . for Laing's soul' on the island of Iona in 1986. MacDonald even claimed that, as a result, Laing 'made his own personal confession of faith' and rejoined the Church of Scotland.[124]

Collapsing the public/private split employed in traditional historiography allows us to gauge the depth of the convergence between personal and professional issues in Laing's biography. Ironically, the professionalisation of psychiatry was designed to manage and ultimately to prevent such cross-contamination. Laing's critique of his profession sawed at the branch on which he sat. His 'tossed and turned' self shows the crisis in the authority of his profession as its perceived 'scientism' came under fire from the kind of countercultural critique, or flyting, in which Laing himself excelled.

CONCLUSION: COMPOSING THE MODERN SELF

In their analysis of Laing's place in modern Scottish culture, Beveridge and Turnbull argue that his biography emerged from 'a strongly moral-religious milieu' reducible to the question which gives this chapter its title.[125] Their analysis is incisive not only for Laing and fellow 'justified sinners' of the 1960s counterculture, but for Semple and Govan, and for modern Scottish subjectivities in general.[126] Through their various engagements with this question – often conflicted, sometimes successful but ultimately unresolved – the experiences of Semple, Govan, Laing and their peers dramatise a quest for 'composure' in self-narration that is illustrative of the experience of a significant demographic cohort in modern Scotland, and arguably in Protestant Europe more widely. Through grappling with parental reticence and disapproval, expressing new roles in work and gender, and incorporating an expanded religious spectrum into their subjectivities, each biography reveals the emotional excitement which has attended the rise of 'post-Presbyterian' sensibilities. To achieve composure under these circumstances is no mean feat. If Brown is correct to argue that the period can be defined in terms of the displacement of authority from traditional, 'visible' institutions to 'the more demanding power that individuals exerted upon themselves', then the lives of Semple, Govan and Laing amply demonstrate how this brought both opportunity and burden, blessing and curse.[127]

My overall goal has been to take 'religion' out of its traditional ecclesiastical framework and reframe it as an ordinary, everyday component of identity where the line between 'religion' and 'culture' is as porous as that between 'private' and 'public'. Warning against indulging in naïve and heroic biography, Stanley reminds us that 'the apparently referential and unique selves that auto/biographical accounts invoke are actually invocations of a cultural representation of what selves should be'. In other words, biographical narratives are 'not descriptions of actual lives but interpretations within the convention'.[128] The 'convention' in this case has been until recently the attributed 'Presbyterian self' of tradition: composed, assured and self-controlled. The critical biography of Semple, Govan and Laing shows us that 'what selves should be' and what 'convention' might mean became open questions as Scottish subjectivities began to devolve from tradition in mid-century or thereabouts. Who or what now hailed or 'interpellated' modern Scots was no longer self-evident.

Notes

1. On 'composure' in autobiography, see P. Summerfield, *Reconstructing Women's Wartime Lives: Discourse and Subjectivity in Oral Histories of the Second World War* (Manchester, 1998), p. 16.
2. I owe this phrase to C. Beveridge and R. Turnbull, *The Eclipse of Scottish Culture: Inferiorism and the Intellectuals* (Edinburgh, 1982), p. 111.
3. The term 'interpellate' derives from the work of Louis Althusser. The classic example is a police officer 'interpellating' a person by shouting 'Hey you!'; as the person addressed instinctively turns round, s/he identifies as the subject of the address.

4. A. Giddens, *Modernity and Self-Identity* (Cambridge, 1991), pp. 185–6.
5. Cited in M. Kadar, 'Coming to terms: life writing – from genre to critical practice', in M. Kadar (ed.), *Essays on Life Writing: from Genre to Critical Practice* (Toronto, 1992), pp. 3–4.
6. T. Carlyle, 'On history', in *Critical and Miscellaneous Essays* (London, 1837); see also T. Carlyle, *On Heroes, Hero Worship and the Heroic in History* (London, 1841).
7. L. Stanley, *The Auto/biographical I: the Theory and Practice of Feminist Auto/biography* (Manchester, 1992), p. 8.
8. R. Finnegan, 'Storying the self', in H. Mackay (ed.), *Consumption and Everyday Life* (London, 1992); R. Jenkins, *Social Identity* (London, 1992).
9. Kadar, 'Coming to terms: life writing', pp. 4–5.
10. Stanley, *The Auto/biographical I*, p. 12.
11. For a historical introduction to problems in use and meaning of the term, see J. Z. Smith, 'Religion, religions, religious', in M. Taylor (ed.), *Critical Terms for Religious Studies* (Chicago, 1998).
12. On the 'stunted' model, see C. G. Brown, *The Death of Christian Britain: Understanding Secularization 1800–2000* (London, 2001), p. 182.
13. K. Knott, 'Autobiography and biography: an overview', in S. Young (ed.), *Encyclopedia of Women and World Religion* (New York, 1999), pp. 76–9.
14. Summerfield, *Reconstructing Women's Wartime Lives*, p. 31.
15. Ibid., p. 17.
16. Ibid., pp. 17–18.
17. Ibid., p. 20.
18. Subtitle quotation from B. Wright and C. Worsley (eds), *Alternative Scotland* (Edinburgh, 1975), p. 114.
19. It has been suggested that the Calvinistic duality of the 'Caledonian antisyzygy' forms the model of (male) psychic division in J. Hogg's *The Private Memoirs and Confessions of a Justified Sinner* (London, 1824) and R. L. Stevenson's *The Strange Case of Dr Jekyll and Mr Hyde* (London, 1886), reappearing in the mid-twentieth century in R. D. Laing's *The Divided Self* (London, 1960) and A. Trocchi's *Cain's Book* (New York, 1961).
20. G. Gregory Smith, *Scottish Literature: Character and Influence* (London, 1919), p. 4.
21. Ibid., p. 5.
22. Ibid., pp. 20, 40.
23. Compare T. Devine (ed.), *Scotland's Shame? Bigotry and Sectarianism in Modern Scotland* (Edinburgh, 2000) with S. Bruce et al. *Sectarianism in Scotland* (Edinburgh, 2004).
24. The following paragraphs draw on material in S. Sutcliffe, 'Unfinished business: devolving Scotland/devolving religion', in S. Coleman and P. Collins (eds), *Religion, Identity and Change: Perspectives on Global Transformations* (Aldershot, 2004), pp. 85–106, and S. Sutcliffe, 'Alternative beliefs and practices', in C. MacLean and K. Veitch (eds), *Scottish Life and Society. A Compendium of Scottish Ethnology, Volume 12: Religion* (Edinburgh, 2006), pp. 313–31.

25. J. Highet, *The Scottish Churches: a Review of Their State 400 Years After the Reformation* (London, 1960).

26. F. Whaling, 'Religious diversity in Scotland', in *Soundings II: Proceedings of a Day Conference for the Methodist Church in Scotland* (Edinburgh, 1999), pp. 18–21.

27. See references in Whaling, 'Religious diversity in Scotland' and Sutcliffe, 'Unfinished business'.

28. See, for example, C. G. Brown, *Religion and Society in Scotland since 1707* (Edinburgh, 1997); S. Brown and G. Newlands (eds), *Scottish Christianity in the Modern World* (Edinburgh, 2000).

29. Wright and Worsley, *Alternative Scotland*, p. 114.

30. J. Drane, 'Coming to terms with the New Age movement', in *Report of the Church of Scotland Board of Social Responsibility* (Edinburgh, 1993), pp. 54–7.

31. 'Young people and the media', in *Report of the Church of Scotland Board of Social Responsibility* (Edinburgh, 1993), p. 44.

32. S. Sutcliffe, *Children of the New Age: A History of Spiritual Practices* (London, 2003), Chapters 6–8; J. Macpherson, *Women and Reiki: Energetic/Holistic Healing in Practice* (London, 2008), Chapters 4 and 6.

33. For a poetry anthology and a study of popular politics respectively, see T. Leonard (ed.), *Radical Renfrewshire: Poetry from the French Revolution to the First World War by Poets Born, or Sometime Resident in, the County of Renfrewshire* (Edinburgh, 1990) and C. M. M. MacDonald, *The Radical Thread: Political Change in Scotland. Paisley Politics 1885–1924* (East Linton, 2000). Neither, however, mentions Semple.

34. There are brief references to Semple in J. Twigg, 'The Vegetarian Movement in England, 1847–1981: a study in the structure of its ideology' (London School of Economics: unpublished PhD thesis, 1982, available online at http://www.ivu.org/history/thesis/index.html) and in Anonymous, 'History of the Scottish Vegetarian Society' (available online at http://www.ivu.org/history/societies/scottish.html, n.d.). Semple's writings can be consulted in Paisley Central Library, the National Library of Scotland in Edinburgh, and the British Library in London.

35. D. Semple, *Joy in Living: an Autobiography* (Glasgow, 1957), p. 12.

36. Ibid., pp. 49–50.

37. Semple, *Joy in Living*, pp. 13–14.

38. D. Semple, *Joys of the Simple Life* (London, 1915), p. 79; Semple, *Joy in Living*, p. 121 (quoting an American self-help philosopher).

39. D. Semple, *Living in Liberty; or, the Wheelhouse Philosophy* (Paisley, 1911), pp. 125, 128.

40. Ibid., p. 121.

41. D. Semple, *Scottish No-Stipend League: an appeal for freedom* (The Author, 1935), n.p.

42. Semple, *Joy in Living*, pp. 14–15.

43. Semple, *Joys of the Simple Life*, p. 76; Semple, *Joy in Living*, p. 52; D. Semple,

A Free Man's Philosophy (London, 1933), pp. 14, 120–5. On diet and natural health, see D. Semple, *Be Your Own Doctor: Natural Cures for Common Ailments* (Glasgow, 1945), *A Scots Health Cookery Book* (Glasgow, 1949), *The Sunfood Way to Health* (London, 1956); Cathie Semple, *Wheelhouse Good Health Recipes* (London, 1938).

44. Semple, *Joys of the Simple Life*, pp. 12, 26.
45. Ibid., p. 79.
46. Semple, *Joy in Living*, p. 111.
47. MacDonald, *The Radical Thread*, Chapters 1 and 6.
48. Semple, *Joy in Living*, pp. 58–9.
49. Semple, *Living in Liberty*, pp. 151–2.
50. Semple, *Joy in Living*, pp. 142–3.
51. Semple, *Joy in Living*, p. 15.
52. Semple, *Joys of the Simple Life*, pp. 28, 30.
53. Semple, *Joys of the Simple Life*, p. 31.
54. 'Romany' (George Bramwell Evans, 1884–1943) was a Methodist minister whose mother was a Romany. Evans wrote ten books, from *A Romany in the Fields* (London, 1929) to *Out with Romany by Moor and Dale* (London, 1944), the first three under the earlier pseudonym 'The Tramp': see www.romanysociety. org.uk. The 'hut-man' was Gilbert Dempster Fisher, author of *The Hut-man's book* (London and Edinburgh, 1938) and *Adventure in the Hut Country* (London, 1939).
55. The 'iron cage' metaphor is from M. Weber, *The Protestant Ethic and the Spirit of Capitalism* (London, [1904–5] 1930).
56. Ironically Linwood Moss, where Semple first practised the 'simple life' in 1907, became famous for its automobile manufacturing from 1963 until 1981.
57. Semple, *Joys of the Simple Life*, p. 33.
58. Semple, *Joy in Living*, p. 149.
59. Ibid., p. 14.
60. Ibid., p. 49.
61. Ibid., p. 50.
62. Ibid., p. 111.
63. *Sunday Mail*, 5 May 1957, p. 13; 12 May 1957, p. 11.
64. Brown, *Religion and Society in Scotland since 1707*, p. 163.
65. Ibid., p. 203.
66. Macpherson, *Women and Reiki*; Sutcliffe, *Children of the New Age*, pp. 219–21.
67. I. Govan, *Spirit of Revival: a Biography of J. G. Govan, Founder of the Faith Mission* (London and Edinburgh, 1938).
68. T. Warburton, 'The Faith Mission: a study in interdenominationalism', in D. Martin (ed.), *A Sociological Yearbook of Religion in Britain 2* (London, 1969), p. 76.
69. Govan, *Spirit of Revival*, p. 164.
70. 'Amazing Drama of a Mother's Dilemma', *Daily Record* (Glasgow), 14 January 1957, p. 9.

71. The story is summarised in 'The Nameless Ones', in Jack Campbell, *A Word for Scotland* (Edinburgh, 1998), pp. 113–16.

72. 'Now Mrs Astell flees to her mother', *Scottish Daily Express*, 17 January 1957, pp. 1–2.

73. *Sunday Mail*, 12 May 1957, pp. 10–11.

74. *Sunday Mail*, 5 May 1957, pp. 12–13.

75. Sheena Govan, 'My Childhood Days', *Sunday Mail*, 5 May 1957, p. 12.

76. Sheena Govan, 'The Anguish of a Mother', *Sunday Mail*, 12 May 1957, pp. 10–11.

77. 'The Anguish of a Mother', *Sunday Mail*, 12 May 1957, p. 10.

78. *Scottish Daily Express*, 17 January 1957, p. 2.

79. 'Good – or Evil?', *Sunday Mail*, 12 May 1957, pp. 10–11.

80. 'Astell's story', *Sunday Mail*, 19 May 1957, p. 14.

81. 'The Nameless Ones', in A. Macintyre, *The Compleat Angus: the Life and Works of Angus Macintyre of Taynuilt and Tobermory* (Gartocharn, 1989), pp. 56–7.

82. P. Hawken, *The Magic of Findhorn* (Glasgow, [1975] 1990), pp. 66–8.

83. Ibid., p. 72.

84. Ibid., p. 217.

85. E. Caddy, *Flight into Freedom* (Shaftesbury, 1988), pp. 31, 38.

86. Ibid., pp. 29–30. Caddy seems to acknowledge this in a later remark: 'I had turned Sheena into a monster in my mind and had been incapable of seeing her as she truly was' (p. 83).

87. Ibid., pp. 83–4. Sheena Govan died in Dumfries (not in Edinburgh) on 10 October 1967: Dumfries Register of Deaths 1967, district 821, entry 415.

88. D. Maclean, *To Hear the Angels Sing* (Forres, 1980), pp. 13, 34.

89. Ibid., pp. 34, 38.

90. P. Caddy, *In Perfect Timing: Memoirs of a Man for the New Millennium* (Forres, 1996), pp. 73, 207. Cf. Maclean, *To Hear the Angels Sing*, p. 13.

91. Caddy, *In Perfect Timing*, p. 73; Caddy, *Scottish Daily Express*, 17 November 1970, p. 12. For a fuller account of Govan's role in the formation of Findhorn, see Sutcliffe, *Children of the New Age*, Chapters 3 and 4.

92. Caddy, *In Perfect Timing*, p. 146.

93. Ibid., p. 113.

94. Sutcliffe, *Children of the New Age*, p. 64.

95. Z. Kotowicz, *R. D. Laing and the Paths of Anti-psychiatry* (London, 1997), pp. 1, 7.

96. See, for example, D. Holbrook, 'R. D. Laing and the death circuit', *Encounter*, August 1968, pp. 35–45, and E. Friedenberg, *Laing* (London, 1973). A. Laing, *R. D. Laing: a Biography* (London, 1994) is equivocal. More positive are J. Clay, *R. D. Laing: a Divided Self* (London, 1996) and D. Burston, *The Wing of Madness: The Life and Work of R. D. Laing* (Cambridge, MA, 1996). A good introduction focusing on Laing's intellectual significance is G. Miller, *R. D. Laing* (Edinburgh, 2004).

97. Helpful insights are provided by Laing's memoir, *Wisdom, Madness and Folly: the Making of a Psychiatrist 1927–1957* (London, 1985) and his reminiscences in B. Mullan, *Mad to be Normal: Conversations with R. D. Laing* (London, 1995).

There is an extensive archive of Laing's case notes, diaries and correspondence in the University of Glasgow Library Special Collections: http://special.lib.gla. ac.uk/collection/laing.html

98. A. Laing, *R. D. Laing: a Biography*, pp. 61, 68.

99. Ibid., pp. 90ff, 161, 163.

100. Brown, *The Death of Christian Britain*, p. 184.

101. Laing, *R. D. Laing: a Biography*, p. 63: 'He treated the whole time-consuming process as a necessary hassle in order to gain his badge'; Clay, *R. D. Laing: a Divided Self*, p. 66: 'with hindsight, the question arises as to how successful this analysis was'.

102. A. Laing, *R. D. Laing: a Biography*, p. 63.

103. Laing, *Wisdom, Madness and Folly*, p. 95.

104. A. Clare, *In the Psychiatrist's Chair* (London, 1992), p. 209.

105. Clay, *R. D. Laing*, p. 1; cf. A. Laing, *R. D. Laing: a biography*, p. 236.

106. R. D. Laing, 'Religious sensibility', *The Listener*, 23 April 1970, pp. 536–7.

107. R. D. Laing, 'God and psychiatry', *Times Literary Supplement*, 23 May 1986, p. 559.

108. R. D. Laing, *The Politics of Experience and the Bird of Paradise* (Harmondsworth, 1967); R. D. Laing, 'A note on "The Politics of Experience": from the psychopathology of everyday life to the pathology of normalcy', *Edinburgh Review* 84, 1990, pp. 120–1.

109. Laing, 'Religious sensibility'.

110. R. D. Laing, 'The Obvious', in D. Cooper (ed.), *The Dialectics of Liberation* (Harmondsworth, 1968), p. 17.

111. Mullan, *Mad to be Normal*, pp. 228–9.

112. Clare, *In the Psychiatrist's Chair*, p. 209.

113. J. Rillie, 'The Abenheimer/Schorstein group', *Edinburgh Review* 32, 1978–9, pp. 104–8; Laing, *Politics of Experience and the Bird of Paradise*, p. 156.

114. R. D. Laing, *Knots* (Harmondsworth, [1970] 1972), foreword, n.p.

115. Ibid., p. 1.

116. Ibid., p. 2

117. Ibid., p. 2.

118. R. D. Laing and A. Esterson, *Sanity, Madness and the Family* (Harmondsworth, [1964] 1970), p. 180. The family in question are described as 'fervent Nonconformist Christians of fundamentalist leanings', ibid., p. 178.

119. Brown, *The Death of Christian Britain*.

120. A. Laing, *R. D. Laing*, pp. 224–5, 228–9.

121. For example, his 'steaming drunk' appearance in 1974 at a Christian community near Kilmarnock; his 'inebriated' appearance on an Irish television chat show in 1982; and his arrest in 1984 for throwing a bottle of wine through the window of the Bhagwan Shree Rajneesh Centre in Hampstead (A. Laing, *R. D. Laing*, pp. 178–9, 210, 215–16).

122. Clare, *In the Psychiatrist's Chair*, pp. 201, 211–13.

123. Mullan. *Mad to be Normal*, p. 210.

124. Clay, *R. D. Laing*, p. 244.

125. Beveridge and Turnbull, *Eclipse of Scottish Culture*, p. 111.
126. On Scottish counterculturalists as 'justified sinners, strewing psychic chaos, inspiring a thunderous mixed-up scene', see Tom McGrath, cited in R. Birrell and A. Finlay, *Justified Sinners: an Archaeology of Scottish Counter-culture (1960–2000)* (Edinburgh, 2002), n.p. On post-countercultural critical theory, see M. Gardiner, *From Trocchi to Trainspotting: Scottish Critical Theory since 1960* (Edinburgh, 2006).
127. C. G. Brown, 'Religion', in L. Abrams, E. Gordon, D. Simonton and E. Yeo (eds), *Gender in Scottish History since 1700* (Edinburgh, 2006), p. 102.
128. Stanley, *Auto/biographical I*, p. 62.

Chapter 8

Culture in the Everyday: Art and Society

Angela Bartie

> For the last two years I have asked our devolved government to focus on deliver-
> ing better health care, improving schools, creating the infrastructure required
> to secure jobs, and tackling crime. But focusing on these priorities should not
> de-prioritise culture. Culture cuts across all of these, in fact all portfolios of gov-
> ernment, and it can make a difference to our success in each. Perhaps because it
> is part of so many aspects of our everyday lives it is difficult for a bureaucracy to
> cope with. Maybe it hasn't received the attention it should have. That will now
> change.[1]

On St Andrew's Day 2003, Jack McConnell, then First Minister of Scotland,
announced that the cornerstone of national cultural policy in Scotland was
to be the establishment and implementation of 'cultural rights', in order
that 'arts for all can be a reality'. Speaking at the Royal Scottish Academy of
Music and Drama in Glasgow, McConnell asserted: 'Culture and creativity
are woven into every part of our national life, and there is so much good
that government can do, by making those connections and having an eye to
the bigger picture.' McConnell quoted from the United Nations Declaration
of Human Rights – that 'Everyone has the right to freely participate in the
cultural life of the community, to enjoy the arts and to share its scientific
advancements and its benefits' – before he announced that the Scottish
Executive was about to conduct a review of Scotland's cultural sector. This
was to 'take as its starting point the premise that each person in Scotland has
cultural rights. That each person has rights of access to cultural activity.'[2]
This review, titled the Cultural Commission, published its final report in
June 2005. In it, plans were announced to create 'cultural entitlements' for
every citizen, increase investment in the arts, and establish a new 'cultural
development agency' called Creative Scotland (which would replace the
Scottish Arts Council and Scottish Screen). Its central tenet was a desire to
place culture at the heart of society and, in doing so, nurture creativity, drive
economic development, increase confidence, strengthen civil society, and,
overall, bring about a measure of national renewal and revival.[3]

This chapter approaches the study of culture in the everyday by considering the debates and discourses that occurred over the course of the twentieth

century about what place culture *should* have in the everyday lives of people in Scotland. The rhetoric of Jack McConnell and the Cultural Commission was not new. Throughout the twentieth century there were a number of attempts to make 'culture' an integral part of people's daily lives. However, the ideals often fell far short in practice. A fundamental and often over-looked reason for this was the inherent problem of defining what is meant by culture. It is a slippery term, and one that changes and shifts perpetually – and, more importantly, in response to very complex broader changes in society. In discussing 'culture' in relation to everyday life in twentieth-century Scotland, this chapter will explore how the very definitions of the term were constantly in flux. As twentieth-century cultural theorist Raymond Williams argued, some words (like culture) are difficult to define because they involve ideas and values.[4]

This chapter will map the increasingly central place culture was given in the public discourse, and will go on to explore some of the attempts that were made to make culture a part of the everyday life of people in Scotland. It will use examples of these attempts – specific events (with particular atten-tion paid to the Edinburgh International Festival, the Festival Fringe, the People's Festival and the Craigmillar Festival) and expressions of changing policy (for example, the 1965 Government White Paper *A Policy for the Arts: The First Steps*) – to illustrate the shifts in how culture was conceived in rela-tion to the 'ordinary' people of Scotland. Indeed, the festivals offer a fantas-tic opportunity to trace the various roles, meanings and functions ascribed to culture during the latter half of the twentieth-century. As we shall see, the International Festival displays the restorative and spiritual power of the arts and shows how one particular local council saw its role; the Fringe, by con-trast, represents the challenge made to the prescribed function of culture and the experimental aspect of the arts, while the People's Festivals symbolise the attempt to reclaim culture for the wider population; and the Craigmillar Festivals show the rise in community arts and the use of culture as a means of tackling social and economic problems. These examples will be used as a means of exploring culture as a site of contest and struggle, and demonstrate the importance of examining the interaction between the arts and society in twentieth-century Scotland.

TACKLING 'CULTURE' IN TWENTIETH-CENTURY SCOTLAND

In 1996, the study of popular culture in Scotland was described as being 'in its infancy' with 'massive gaps' in our understanding of various aspects of culture in Scotland.[5] In many ways, the whole arena of cultural history in twentieth-century Scotland is still underexplored and many massive gaps remain. For too long, too much emphasis has been placed on the quantitative study of culture – a desire to ascertain the place of culture in terms of the popularity of specific cultural forms (like cinema-going or football match attendance) and the growth of a 'mass culture' – along-side an almost obsessive need to identify and examine specifically *Scottish* cultural forms.

Historians have approached culture in Scotland in a number of different ways. One approach considered various cultural forms – such as language, leisure, customs and sport – and the levels of involvement in them in relation to social class. This study was underpinned by the idea that a distinctive Scottish identity in culture had been 'Anglicised', with Scotland 'essentially powerless and peripheral' in 'the slipstream of an overwhelming international capitalist civilization that takes its lead in popular culture from America (with secondary British input) and in high culture from an eclectic mix of London, Paris, Frankfurt, Rome, New York and California.'[6] The idea of homogenisation in Scottish culture has been expanded upon, with one study noting that the provision of mass education, the development of mass leisure pursuits, and the affordability of new cultural forms had led to the emergence of an almost 'homogenous national working-class experience'.[7] On the other hand, the continuation of a distinct popular culture in Scotland – at least until the 1960s – and the creation of an 'intellectual dialectic', whereby a Scottish Renaissance flourished but had a 'complex and unsatisfactory' relationship with both politics and popular culture, has been expounded.[8]

The relationship between identity and culture, particularly in relation to Scottish nationalism, has been repeatedly considered by historians. Of course, this is understandable since culture is so important in terms of how we imagine ourselves as a nation. From the 1960s, political philosopher Tom Nairn criticised Scottish parochialism and promoted a positive Scottish nationalism based on more solid foundations than what he called the constituents of the 'Great Scottish Dream' – such as tartanry, militarism, Robert Burns and Sir Walter Scott. His influential argument, echoed more recently by David McCrone, was that the 'partial suppression of Scottish nationhood' as a result of the Union Treaty of 1707 resulted in the creation of a 'dream-nationhood to take the place of the real one', in order to ease the strain of having a Scottish society without the framework of a 'Scottish nation'.[9] To Nairn, this has had a deep-seated influence: 'A very great part of modern Scottish culture, and almost all of Scottish nationalism, has been poisoned at the root by this obsessive need.'[10] These arguments impacted significantly on both the development of a new brand of Scottish nationalism and on the development of cultural enquiry in Scotland.

From the late 1970s, there was much discussion on the relationship between identity and culture in Scotland. During the early 1990s, attempts were made to explore and define Scotland in terms of its character, institutions and the myths that represented Scotland (as well as ascertain how relevant they still were). One conference, held in September 2006, asked participants to consider whether there was such a thing as a 'Scottish art' and, if so, what its characteristics were? 'Does Scottishness necessarily connote the marginal, the twee, the old-fashioned, or are Scotland's putative national traits more timeless and cosmopolitan – or is the notion nowadays so endlessly elastic a "brand" as to render it ultimately meaningless?'[11] This repeated search for a specifically Scottish national cultural identity has been described as the 'hunting of a Scottish snark', leaving a need to tackle the myth that Scotland was ever a single and fixed national or cultural entity. In short, there are as many Scotlands as there are Scots.[12] This has only become more complex since devolution in 1997.

Culture both evokes and disrupts the everyday. As one commentator remarks, 'cyclical arts festivals transform places from being everyday settings into temporary environments that contribute to the production, processing and consumption of culture, concentrated in time and place.'[13] In such a context, this chapter will reflect the constant reconstruction of culture in twentieth-century Scotland in relation to changing social, economic and political contexts, and notably in the middle decades of the century. This was a period of lively debate about the role of culture in society, especially in England. T. S. Eliot, for instance, opposed the post-war emphasis on government support for the spread of culture, believed that democracy and mass education were incompatible with cultural values, and supported the notion of a 'graded society' and of different levels of culture.[14] This put him firmly in opposition to contemporaries like J. B. Priestley, who was attracted to the idea of a 'nationalized culture' brought about by greater equality in a reconstructed Britain: 'the soul demands the arts as the body demands exercise . . . In the [new] Britain we want to build, then, there will be plenty of art of every kind.'[15]

In the late 1950s and early 1960s, debate continued, particularly in light of the rising influence of the media, the increasingly 'affluent society', the development of new approaches to the arts, and the growing visibility of 'youth' as a distinct social category. Of particular interest was the continuing hierarchy between 'high' and 'popular' (or 'mass') culture, which had become pertinent as television – and particularly commercial television – vastly increased in scope and popularity. This growing realisation of the importance of 'culture' as a key social issue developed from the mid-1950s, and was evidenced in part by the appearance of such writers as Raymond Williams, Richard Hoggart and Stuart Hall, who together helped to develop the new interdisciplinary field of cultural studies – from Hoggart's defence of the values of 'traditional' working-class culture from the threat of a new mass (commercial) culture, to Williams' approach to 'culture' 'as the study of relationships between elements in a whole way of life'.[16] What is evident is that the relationship and interaction, real or perceived, between 'culture' and the 'people' continues to provoke debate about the fundamental concept of culture and its place in society. The relationship between culture and everyday life is even more contentious.[17]

CULTURE IN PRACTICE

In Victorian and Edwardian Scotland, leisure has been characterised as the site of a struggle for control between 'respectable' and 'rough' culture 'in which the elites engaged to convert plebians from the pernicious hedonism of drink and urban low life, and create new loyalties – to God, employer, municipality and nation.' After the Second World War, leisure became a less crucial site of struggle for control – the state continued to promote rational recreation by adopting and institutionalising previously 'rough' forms of culture (in locations like the cinema, dance hall, music hall and football stadium).[18] Certainly, in the early years of the twentieth century, the music hall and, latterly, variety theatre were popular forms of entertainment in Scotland, with variety reaching its highpoint at the outbreak of the Second World War (at which point Glasgow alone had eighteen music halls). A 'mainstream popular theatre tradition', it left a legacy in terms of both its comedic representations of Scotland and Scots (and particularly the kind of wry, earthy humour associated with Glaswegians) and its connections to 'the people' as a working-class cultural form (although recent research has shown its popularity with middle-class audiences).[19] During the first half of the twentieth century, Scotland's industrialised central belt has been posited as 'a centre of left culture' in which cultural politics were increasingly influential, and with Glasgow the site of a 'socialist counter-culture'.[20] Left-wing groups that promoted a range of cultural forms, including sports, Sunday schools, Clarion groups, choirs and drama clubs, were particularly evident during the 1920s and 1930s. During the inter-war period, cinema began to take precedence, holding a 'peculiar importance' for Scots; there were significantly more cinema seats per head of population in Scotland than anywhere else in Britain.[21] However, while variety theatre began to decline, other forms of theatre blossomed.

From about 1890, church drama groups had been popular and by the 1920s and 1930s were part of congregational life in many suburban churches. Amateur drama in Scotland had had a 'boom period' of activity, with church groups making up a large proportion of the amateur groups in existence.[22] Indeed, the inter-war period was one of unprecedented interest in the theatre, with repertory theatres established in Perth (1935), Dundee (1939), Rutherglen (1939), Glasgow (1943) and Pitlochry (1951). Perth & Kinross County Council, in a 'quite unprecedented move', had formed a Committee of Management to run the Perth Repertory Theatre Company. This idea of 'civic theatre' was gaining popularity as, for the first time in Scottish history, theatre was seen as having a function that 'served the common good' in social and economic terms, as well as being a 'useful tool in the growing industry of tourism'.[23] The Church of Scotland had even set up a Kirk Drama Federation which ran competitions and co-ordinated drama groups across Scotland. Scullion points to the immense success of amateur theatre organisations like the British Drama League and the Scottish Community Drama Association during the inter-war period, both of which 'promoted a quintessentially bourgeois ethos of improvement through culture' and helped to popularise the 'fashionable and increasingly influential' idea that 'drama is good for you'.[24] Socialist individuals and organisations also believed this, and during the war and post-war years there was a rise in the number of left-wing theatre groups; this will be returned to later in this chapter.

It was out of the experience of the Second World War that culture in terms of the arts became a state concern. Cultural historian and critic Robert Hewison has argued that an unexpected outcome of the war was that 'people had realised spontaneously that culture was one of the things for which they were fighting', a realisation that was backed by Government support for the arts.[25] The Council for the Encouragement of Music and Art (CEMA) was created during the war (in January 1940) by an organisation financed from America, the Pilgrim Trust, which was dedicated to supporting cultural activity. Just three months after its creation, the British Government awarded it a grant of £50,000, apparently in recognition of the value of such an organisation.[26] Until this point, there had been little direct state involvement in the arts in Britain.[27] Just over six years later, in August 1946, CEMA became the Arts Council of Great Britain, a body subsidised by the British Government with the aim of providing 'State support for the arts, without State control'.[28] This commitment to the arts was consolidated with the Local Government Act of 1948, which gave municipal authorities the power to raise a six-penny rate 'purely for the support of the arts', and taken together, these developments were expressions of the Labour Government's commitment to the idea of the 'Welfare State', their belief that welfare included provision for the 'imaginative and intellectual side of life'.[29] In the years following the Second World War, there was a fairly widespread feeling that the arts should be made available to all, and part of the Arts Council's remit was to make the arts 'accessible to the people throughout the country'.[30] This was a time of idealism, with the war having been won by Britain and her allies, the Welfare State in its infancy and the idea of social reform in the air, bringing with it a hope of a more egalitarian society in post-war Britain. This was clearly reflected in the field of cultural provision.[31]

An interesting development in post-war Scotland was the way that the Church of Scotland began to engage with the arts and to conceive drama as a 'weapon of enlightenment'.[32] In 1946, the Church of Scotland officially welcomed the arts by opening its own theatre in Edinburgh, the Gateway Theatre in Leith Walk, and the following year closely allied itself with the new Edinburgh Festival of Music and Drama, inaugurated in August 1947. Indeed, each year the Festival officially opened with a ceremony in the 'Mother Kirk of Presbyterianism', St Giles' Cathedral in Edinburgh.[33] The churches had become increasingly concerned about popular faith and the role of religion and traditional Christian morality in people's lives

during the midst of war, and in the immediate post-war years the Church of
Scotland began to experiment with new ways to relay the Christian message
to Scotland's population – this included using the arts as one of the Church's
answers 'to the problem of our changing world'.[34] The kirk's new openness
to the arts reflected a widespread ecclesiastical surge in interest in the arts
that had developed during the war years. In 1946, the Christian newspaper
British Weekly announced a revolution in the theatre and referred to a movement that had been growing, spearheaded by the British Drama League,
which claimed that the art of theatre could be a factor in the cultural and educational progress of the population; the article concluded that the churches
'are at last alive to this weapon of enlightenment'.[35]

During this post-war period, the Arts Council essentially acted as a force
for 'cultural conservatism' and, although it was apparently funding arts to
make them accessible to all, it gave most money to the most expensive arts.
One writer has pointed out that the Arts Council 'defined its aims in the
Charter as increasing accessibility to and understanding of the fine arts exclu-
sively, thus excluding more popular and community forms of culture.'[36] The
BBC, through the medium of television and radio, continued to act for the
preservation of certain social and cultural standards and one contemporary
commented that the BBC 'has done more than any other body to buttress
the most conservative institutions in the country, to create and perpetuate
reverence for the orders, the privileges and the mysteries of a conservative
society.'[37] In all, the period 1947 to 1955 has been described as 'deeply old-
fashioned' and an altogether 'cosy and parochial era' during which the effect
of the Cold War, combined with Britain's economic difficulties and a drive
towards conservatism in politics, culture and social values, was a 'culture
of conformity'.[38] One commentator lamented the 'deadness' of the cultural
scene, while another contemporary commented in April 1956 that the 1950s
would be seen to have been a right-wing orthodoxy.[39]

Yet it was precisely this conservative and hierarchical social context that
provoked cultural protest, just as it was the strict conception and function
of culture composed by the Edinburgh Festival Society that allowed cultural
challenge to develop in Edinburgh. The Edinburgh Festival, founded in
1947, was committed to presenting the 'highest and purest ideals of art in its
many and varied forms' and actively continued this theme of what has been
referred to as 'bourgeois high culture'.[40] The programme was predominantly
made up of arts of the 'highest standard', which generally meant opera, especially since Glyndebourne had been instrumental in the creation and organisation of the venture, classical music concerts, ballet and drama, usually
reproductions of the classics.[41] In its inaugural year, these included the
Louis Jouvet Company, Vienna Philharmonic, London Old Vic Company
and Orchestra des Concerts Colonne. The BBC Scottish Orchestra was
part of the programme, and other 'Scottish' items were concerts of traditional Gaelic and lowland songs, piping and highland dancing on the Castle

Esplanade, and a pipe band championship. The first object of the Edinburgh Festival Society Limited, officially created in November 1946 to organise and administer the official Festival, had been to 'promote and encourage the arts, especially opera, plays, dramas, ballets and music'.[42] The Society consisted of municipal council members, with the Lord Provost of Edinburgh Corporation as Chairman, as well as practitioners and patrons of the arts in Scotland, and was financed by the Corporation, the Arts Council of Great Britain and private donations. By January 1952, a submission had even been made on behalf of the Edinburgh Festival Society for the Nobel Peace Prize, on the basis that it was 'a constructive effort on behalf of European civilisation'.[43] The Festival, the submission noted, demonstrated that it was a venture with Matthew Arnold's conception of the role of culture at its heart. The second Lord Provost to act as Chairman of the Festival, Sir Andrew Murray, developed a theory of the arts in which he promoted the Festival to the position of '*interpreter*' of the arts.[44]

It quickly became clear that a policy of presenting the music and art of the 'grand masters' meant that there would be no room for those who wished to *create* new culture, rather than interpret existing culture. There was a fundamental conflict emerging between the two views of culture dominant in the public arena during the post-war period: one of these derives from Matthew Arnold's definition of culture as the remedy to social anarchy, while the other sees culture as the 'common expression of a people, where values emerge from below and are not imposed from above'.[45] These conflicts were played out from the 1940s to the 1960s in the context of Edinburgh during Festival time each August and September, and this is what makes the event so important to understanding the history of culture and its uses in post-war Britain, and to demonstrating the gap that exists between discourse and practice.

At that very first Festival in 1947, eight theatre groups had turned up 'uninvited and unheralded', organised performance spaces for themselves, and put on their own shows outside the programme of the 'official' Festival. Of those first eight groups, six were from within Scotland: the Christine Orr Players (an amateur theatre company from Edinburgh) presented *Macbeth*, Edinburgh People's Theatre performed Robert Ardrey's *Thunder Rock*, the Edinburgh District Scottish Community Drama Association presented James Bridie's *The Anatomist*, Strindberg's *Easter* performed by Edinburgh College of Art Theatre Group, a production of *Everyman* sponsored by The Carnegie Trust, and the Glasgow Unity Theatre, which presented Maxim Gorky's *The Lower Depths* and Robert MacLellan's *The Laird o'Torwatletie*. The remaining two groups were from England: the Lanchester Marionette Theatre, which put on puppet plays in an Edinburgh cinema, and the Pilgrim Players from the Mercury Theatre in London, presenting Eliot's *The Family Reunion* and *Murder in the Cathedral* at the Gateway Theatre.[46] The key Scottish group was Glasgow Unity, a branch of the Britain-wide Unity theatre movement which was essentially a federation of amateur theatre groups committed to 'people's drama'.[47] Unity sought to present theatre that had a strong sense of social commitment and would attract working-class audiences to an activity that remained a predominantly middle-class pursuit. Expressing dismay at the 'high prices to be charged for both material and spiritual accommodation' at the forthcoming Festival, the lack of Scottish material on the programme, and the snub to the lively interest in theatre in Scotland, Unity had publicly challenged the organisers of the Edinburgh Festival to include culture that was both resonant with and affordable for people in Scotland. Firmly rebutted, Glasgow Unity had 'in the face of official and establishment opposition' proposed a season at an Edinburgh theatre during the three weeks of the official Festival – and thus arguably initiated the 'Fringe'.[48]

In 1946, a monthly magazine called *Scots Theatre* had been launched which emphasised both the political and social significance of theatre groups in Glasgow, and promoted Unity as 'the most vital native cultural influence in Scotland. Its actors, playwrights and technicians have been drawn from the ranks of ordinary working people, whose background and everyday life is identical with the masses who form its audience.'[49] In many ways, Unity championed a theatre that could empower people. Its most famous production, *The Gorbals Story*, a play about housing shortages in Glasgow, premiered in 1946 and toured round Scotland in cities, large towns and a number of mining communities in Fife, Ayrshire and Lanarkshire. As Scullion points out, the tour 'widened public awareness of the issue of housing and encouraged audiences from across the whole of Scotland to engage with and seek solutions for a problem of particular concern within the urban centres'. Glasgow Unity thus challenged the failure of Scots drama 'to come to terms with the urban, lowland experience of most of the nation'. Some commentators pointed to James Bridie (who had formed the Citizens' Theatre) and playwright James Barrie as factors, arguing that they were too focused on middle-class and, even, London's west end audiences. One critic wrote in 1946: 'In the new Scottish theatre there are two divisions: primarily middle-class repertoire and writers whose art is seen in Perth, the Glasgow Citizens' Theatre and elsewhere: and the tougher working-class dramas and performances to be seen in Glasgow Unity Theatre.'[50] Robert Mitchell, Unity's Director, commented in 1946: 'What we are trying to create is a native theatre, something which is essentially reflecting the ordinary lives of the ordinary people in Scotland.'[51]

Five years later, in 1951 (the same year that Glasgow Unity officially disbanded), the Edinburgh Labour Festival Committee (ELFC) was established 'to initiate action designed to bring the Edinburgh Festival closer to the people, to serve the cause of international understanding and goodwill', echoing the professed aims of the official Festival.[52] Martin Milligan, Communist Party member and one of the key organisers of the 1951 People's Festival, had noted that the Festival 'has a "Keep Out" notice posted for the working people of the city in which it takes place. This takes the form first, of high prices, and second, of a ludicrously cultivated air of "snootiness".'[53] Made up of representatives of the Communist Party, Edinburgh Trades Union Council, the Miners' Union and the Labour Party, as well as cultural groups, community organisations and independent art groups, the purpose of the Committee was to present a 'People's Festival'. This week-long event, held in August 1951, was committed to attracting working-class families and did so by maintaining affordable ticket prices and conveying a spirit of co-operation and inclusion.[54] The programme included Glasgow Unity Theatre performing Joe Corrie's *In Time of Strife*, a Theatre Workshop production of Ewan MacColl's *Uranium 235*, performances by Barrhead Co-operative Junior Choir, and various lectures (the speakers included Tom Driberg, Helen Cruickshank and Hugh MacDiarmid), all 'designed to show how all forms of cultural activity, at their best, depend on ordinary working people'.[55]

The Labour governments of 1945 to 1951 were concerned with the enrichment of the country's cultural life and with bringing culture within the reach of the people, but most of what they actually achieved related to 'elite' cultural activities.[56] The key motive of the People's Festival organisers (one of whom was Hamish Henderson, poet, cultural and political activist, singer-songwriter and folklorist) was to counter this notion of elite culture with something that originated from the people themselves, and this was why folksong culture was central to its inception and development.[57] In fact, the legendary People's Festival Ceilidhs, which included singers like Jimmy MacBeath, Flora McNeil and Jeannie Robertson, are recognised as the start-ing point of the subsequent folksong revival in Scotland, and their influence on the Britain-wide folksong revival is widely acknowledged.[58]

The People's Festival of 1951 was also significant to the broader con-temporary debate on the role of culture. It had opened with a one-day conference, attended by over 170 people, and described in the Communist newspaper *Daily Worker* as 'the first general conference of the Labour move-ment in this country to discuss the crisis of culture'.[59] This conference, titled 'Towards a People's Culture', unanimously passed a resolution 'recognising that working people have pressing cultural as well as material needs and that in this field there exist a number of urgent problems', and thus it called for working-class and cultural organisations around the country to establish committees similar to the ELFC as a matter of urgency.[60] In the two years after the first People's Festival, the National Cultural Committee of the Communist Party (founded in 1947) had become more active in relation to the role of culture in British society, holding a National Cultural Conference on Britain's Cultural Heritage in May 1952. During the war, socialists had begun to realise that the struggle to change society had to be 'waged' on cultural, as well as political and economic, grounds: 'The weapon to be used was an independent and assertive brand of socialist culture which fostered creativity, a communitarian spirit and a new socialist way of life.'[61]

The People's Festivals had appeared at a time when the 'official' Festival was beginning to attract criticism for being 'stuffy', with one newspaper critic suggesting an alternative festival programme with dance bands instead of orchestras, and clowns, acrobats, jugglers and strongmen instead of cellists. In 1951, the *Daily Worker* had proclaimed that the People's Festival was aiming at the 'ordinary man'; 'What is more,' it went on, 'it is hitting the target.'[62] By September 1953, it was reported that Ian Hunter, Artistic Director of the Edinburgh Festival from 1950 to 1955, had suggested that more needed to be done to interest 'the man on the street'. His ideas were: to revive the century-dead Grassmarket Fair and bring in folk dancers from Scotland and Norway as well as tribal dancers from Africa to dance on the street; publicise the famous musicians and artists so the 'man-in-the-street' will recognise them and know why they are famous (in the spirit of Eliot, Hunter was suggesting a *communication* of culture to 'the masses' here); decorate Princes Street; and finally, erect a 'big top' and invite a world-class circus.[63] This draws on a trend that was popular and even encouraged by the government during the Second World War as a means of providing entertainment for the wider population. Since the 1930s, but particularly during the Second World War, the circus had been heavily marketed as a 'unifying and democratic institution'.[64] However, Hunter was not suggesting that a circus would be part of the official Festival proceedings, nor be funded by it; rather he made a plea for a 'corporation of private enterprise' to shoulder the responsibility.[65] This is significant since during the war it was believed that 'good' culture should be supported by government subsidy while popular culture should be left to the 'dictates and uncertainties of commercial viability'.[66]

While the idea of having a circus didn't go anywhere, by the end of the 1953 Festival it was clear that the Fringe had mounted an effective challenge to the role assigned to culture by the Festival Society. Scottish actor Duncan Macrae, who had appeared in official Festival productions, led a skirmish on behalf of the Fringe in which he announced 'Let's have the best for the lowbrows, too.' He made it clear that he approved of the Festival Society but felt they had failed to recognise all of the opportunities open to them, in particular attracting ordinary people. He declared that the Fringe was for the people who could not afford the big shows, and argued that a Fringe show encouraged the beginnings of cultural discernment; without this, he reasoned the ordinary people of Scotland would not be able to appreciate the quality of official Festival productions.[67]

In many ways, Unity's season in Edinburgh in 1947 and the Edinburgh People's Festivals of 1951 to 1954 symbolised the attempt to reclaim culture for the wider population. Yet the 'brand' of culture promoted by Unity, the People's Festival organisers and the Communist Party was, in some ways, just as mediated as the 'elite' culture of the Edinburgh Festivals that it sought to challenge. There was a hierarchy within left-wing culture too.

Angus Calder has noted the tendency of the labour movement to assimilate the term 'worker's culture' with 'high culture' to a 'canon of suitably serious left wing art' (for example, industrial and political songs, and the plays of Joe Corrie).[68] Much of this stems from a long tradition of worker improvement schemes and activities, for example the Workers' Educational Association and the myriad cultural activities on offer in urban centres. In part, too, it was a response to a perceived corruption of 'authentic' working-class cultural forms, particularly as a result of 'Americanisation', and in fact the first conference of the Communist Party had been titled *The American Threat to British Culture* (held in London in April 1951). Indeed, Dan Knox has pointed out that cultural forms that deal with the everyday lives of 'the folk are inherently a part of "folk culture"' and thus 'are imagined to retain a degree of authenticity beyond that of apparently more contrived performances'.[69]

This is an area that is ripe for further research. In 1978, John Hill pointed out the inherent problem of Unity's attempts to create a drama that reflected the lives of 'the ordinary people of Scotland', placing it in the historical context of the repeated 'call of artistic movements for fidelity to "real" life': that 'realism is both inherently democratic and unstable – once it defines itself as an adequate correspondence to reality, it at the same time opens itself to challenge for failing in exactly that.'[70] Dan Knox has drawn on the notion of 'staged authenticity' to consider the ways in which Scottish song traditions (particularly the Doric dialect and culture of north-eastern Scotland) 'have moved from being everyday, unremarkable practice to public spectacle and tourist performance.'[71] Examining Unity and the People's Festivals can tell us much about changing concepts of culture and the effects of economic, political and social contexts on these – but were the people involved in these getting their messages across to the very people that they sought to reach and claimed to speak on behalf of? How did audiences receive these ideas, and did the cultures being presented resonate with their everyday lives?

The People's Festivals did help to give the Fringe a more visible identity, particularly in terms of presenting culture that was creative, contemporary, and represented some measure of protest against the kind of 'elite' culture presented by the official Festival. The concept of cultural protest gained wide currency in the late 1950s when the 'New Left' took shape, a development that reinvigorated the left in Britain after Communist Party support of the Soviet invasion of Hungary had sparked a crisis. It has been argued that the New Left were pivotal in creating 'cultural Marxism', a movement that fused cultural and political protest and sought to redefine the 'social struggle' in the light of social change.[72] The growing influence and impact of more contemporary art and its creators was to become more keenly felt in Edinburgh – as it was across the western world – by the 1960s, when it became clear that a young radical avant-garde was mounting a challenge to traditional barriers in 'culture' and between the different art forms.

In many ways a response to these challenges, the Labour Government published its White Paper, *A Policy for the Arts: the First Steps*, in 1965. This was the first major reappraisal of the role of culture in society since the Arts Council of Great Britain had been set up in 1946. This was mainly the work of Jennie Lee, Britain's first Minister for the Arts, appointed by the Labour Government in 1964. In the run-up to its publication there had been a noticeable shift in thinking about funding of the arts and to reflect that, between 1960 and 1964, the Arts Council's funding more than doubled.[73] Responsibility for arts expenditure was transferred from the Treasury to the Department of Education and Science, and a 'Housing the Arts' fund set up to allow the Arts Council to subsidise the buildings the arts were housed in. The White Paper symbolised the renewed commitment of the state to the patronage of the arts, but tried to diversify and widen the scope of those commitments made during the war and immediate post-war period. One crucial difference was that funding would be more widely disseminated (hitherto most money had gone into London's national companies) and local authorities would be encouraged 'to support not only libraries and museums but art, music, and drama in their schools; to aid amateur groups; to run local arts centres even in the smallest towns'.[74]

Apparently in response to these announcements, Edinburgh Corporation announced their plans for 'a complete cultural and conference centre unique in Scotland and probably Britain', while a Scottish Education Department circular sent out to local authorities in June 1965 asked for their support (financial and otherwise) in the creation and provision of arts centres in local communities.[75] At the beginning of 1964, Edinburgh Corporation announced its intention of running the Lyceum (which it had recently pur-chased) as a civic theatre 'owned by and administered on behalf of the citizens of Edinburgh', and on 29 May 1965, a body called Edinburgh Civic Theatre Trust Ltd assumed responsibility for the administration of the theatre from the Corporation.[76] This venture was part of a burgeoning Britain-wide civic theatre movement in which civic authorities had begun to place significance on and provide funding for theatre in their locales. This movement led to the proliferation of arts centres from the late 1960s onwards.

The White Paper also offered artists support 'in the years before they have become established', which demonstrated a shift from the Arts Council's earlier policy of funding a narrow range of more established artists and companies.[77] Furthermore, while the Arts Council had previously been guilty of supporting what was traditionally termed 'high' culture, the White Paper aimed to widen its scope:

> It is partly a question of bridging the gap between what have come to be called the 'higher' forms of entertainment and the traditional sources – the brass band, the amateur concert party, the entertainer, the music hall and the pop group – and to challenge the fact that a gap exists. In the world of jazz the process has already happened; highbrow and lowbrow have met.[78]

Figure 8.1   *Anna Kesselaar performing at the International Drama Conference of the Edinburgh Festival, 1963, being whisked along the gallery naked on a trolley in the McEwen Hall. www.scran.ac.uk.*

Challenges to the hierarchy of culture had been growing throughout the 1950s and were seen most obviously during the 1960s, a time described as one of 'cultural revolution'.

One example of this occurred in September 1963, during a drama conference organised for the Edinburgh Festival. As part of a theatrical 'happening', arguably the first to take place in Britain, a female art model was wheeled nude on a television trolley across the gallery, or balcony, of the hall.[79] The happening also included a number of events occurring simultaneously, including the actress Carroll Baker clambering over seats as if hypnotised, excerpts of the week's discussions being played back on a tape, and strangers at the windows overhead shouting out 'Me; Can you see me!'[80] The theory of the 'happening' had been developed during the 1950s in the United States; one of the contributors to the Edinburgh happening, Allan Kaprow, had coined the term in New York in 1959. Essentially, a happening was a pseudo-theatrical event intended to shake the audience's sense of reality and make them realise that the world is an uncertain place where anything can happen.[81] A key feature was the 'determination by those in the arts to blur the line between art and reality' and, indeed, happenings became an integral part of the counterculture movements of the late 1960s:

> The generation of the sixties had new ways of using culture. Deploying everyday ideas, objects and experiences as creative sources and materials indicates a rejection of Matthew Arnold's formulation of culture as an uplifting model of the best. The popular culture of the sixties saw a re-evaluation of transformative notions that drew on [. . .] an engagement with art as a model for everyday life.[82]

The Edinburgh happening helped to raise awareness of the challenge to traditional definitions of culture and concepts of the arts being presented by a vanguard of young, radical artists, while the Festivals became 'a forum for experimental and neo-conceptual art, much of it centred upon a confluence of drama, performance and the visual arts'.[83] These were important precursors to the political, experimental theatre of the late 1960s to early 1970s, and illustrate the kind of theatrical devices utilised by The Situationists, who protested against 'the society of the spectacle' – they saw society as overly consumer based and the majority of its citizens passive masses, reducing art to 'merely a part of consumerism'. Thus, they called on people to replace spectacle by constructing situations 'in which "everyone must search for what they love, for what attracts them," applying their imaginations to "the transformation of reality", thus making everyday life "passionate, rational, dramatic"'.[84]

UNDERSTANDING CULTURE IN THE EVERYDAY

Within the 1965 White Paper, the British Government had announced its commitment to experimental and participatory culture and to widening access to culture, a sentiment repeated by Jack McConnell in 2003: 'Culture should be for the many not the few. And the few must not be the only ones to experience or create the most brilliant productions or the most outstanding works of art.' Like the White Paper, the rhetoric of this major review of cultural provision emphasised a 'bottom up' rather than 'top down' approach – a 'citizen-first approach'.[85] However, the resulting draft Culture (Scotland) Bill, released in December 2006, markedly diverged from these initial ideals and the confusion over what was meant by 'cultural entitlements', and how exactly citizens go about accessing their 'rights' to culture, resulted in some strong criticism and debate. Criticising the move to increasing bureaucracy and centralisation inherent in the Bill, one critic noted that it presented 'an unimaginative, top-down model of cultural provision, placing delivery onto existing bureaucratic structures with little new money, and in the case of local authorities with no legislative authority attached. Above all, nothing – absolutely nothing – should be allowed to generate from below.'[86] It is highly significant that one of the key reasons for the failure of the most recent version, the Creative Scotland Bill, was confusion over its definition of 'culture'.[87]

In 1994, cultural theorist Paul Willis noted that 'the many strands of the community arts movement continue to carry the torch' of the early ideals of cultural policy in Britain, in that they 'share the continuing concern to democratize the arts and make them more a part of common experience'.[88] From the early 1970s it became more common for culture to be used as a device to tackle various social problems and concerns, as well as a potent means of social and economic regeneration. In fact, in 1965, another festival had been established in Edinburgh, the Craigmillar Festival of Drama, Music and the Arts on the initiative of a local woman, Helen Crummy, who aimed to use the arts to 'knit together' different groups and associations in the area and 'encourage people to take a more active part in drama in its broadest sense, and music'.[89] This was chiefly concerned with people living in Craigmillar, one of Edinburgh's outlying housing estates which, like many dormitory schemes of the 1960s, lacked amenities or any real community centres. The Craigmillar Festivals illustrate the rise in community arts and the use of culture as a means of tackling social and economic problems. As *The Scotsman* newspaper reported in 1971, 'In the Festival city of Edinburgh, a small local festival society have added a new dimension to culture – concern. Today the society publish their first report on a unique experiment that could have valuable lessons for problem areas throughout Britain.'

It has now become common for cultural activity to be utilised as a means of empowering individuals, groups and communities, as well as regenerating areas. When Glasgow was made the European City of Culture (ECOC) in 1990, the accompanying souvenir book pointed out the longer-term benefits: 'strengthening infrastructure, extending access, elevating popular and political attitudes to a level where people can see clearly what culture means to the city and imagine practical possibilities for the future'.[90] Nonetheless, when Gerry Mooney considered Glasgow ECOC 1990 from the vantage point of 2004, he pointed to the continuation of many of the social and economic problems that had plagued Glasgow and the social polarisation that was exacerbated by the event. Overall, by asking who it had actually benefited, he brought into question the advantages of using culture as a key element in the urban regeneration programmes of deindustrialised cities.[91] Many critics have argued that Glasgow ECOC was nothing to do with culture and all to do with property development and business relocation, and that this was demonstrated by Glasgow District Council's use of the advertising agency, Saatchi and Saatchi.[92] This was a strong feature of the 1980s: 'The shift that began in the seventies from an emphasis on the production of things to the production of images and ideas, where information in itself became a precious commodity, made culture as important an item of consumption as any other.'[93] The immediate and longer-term impacts and legacies of such community and social cultural activities and initiatives, the contexts in which they develop, and the debates that surround them are potentially fruitful areas of investigation for cultural historians – and ones that have been remarkably underresearched in a Scottish context.

Paul Willis has argued for the need to engage more fully with what he calls 'living common culture'. He noted that 'art' and its associated institutions, practices and terms have no real connection with the lives of most young people, and that, because it is generally identified and located within institutions and galleries, it is often given a heightened and special sense separate to ordinary, everyday life. This approach, he argued, neglects the 'vibrant symbolic life and symbolic creativity in everyday life, everyday activity and expression'. Arguing that 'arts' exclude and 'culture' includes, Willis called for recognition of the 'extraordinary, symbolic creativity of the multitude of ways in which young people use, humanize, decorate and invest with meanings their common and immediate life spaces and social practices' (for example, personal styles and choice of clothes, selective and active use of music and TV, and dance). In short, seeing that we live in a world of consumerism and cultural commodities, Willis argued against the base 'mass culture' theory, the basic 'production, reproduction, reception' model, and argued that the study of cultural consumerism exposes an active social process rooted in everyday life, whereby viewers, listeners and readers 'do their own symbolic work on a text and create their own relationships to technical means of reproduction and transfer'. Put another way, 'what goes on in everyday contexts of viewing and reading cannot simply be deduced from the messages themselves'.[94] Ultimately, 'Interpretation, symbolic action and creativity are *part* of consumption.'[95] This is a particularly important point in today's 'knowledge economy' – as the 'creative industries' continue to expand and heavier demands are made on the arts by politicians, artists take on an increasingly important role as manufacturers of meaning.[96]

Culture remains a potent site of struggle, shown by the strong (and often hostile) reaction to the draft Culture (Scotland) Bill in 2006. In many ways, by trying to shape culture, cultural policy provokes struggle and tension. It is not easy to define culture and, as Cairns Craig has pointed out, the 'apparent lack of a coherent tradition, the lack of a coherent national culture, far from impeding development, have been a major stimuli to creativity'.[97] Furthermore, culture must always be considered within a wider context and the meanings placed within teased out and examined. As Adrienne Scullion has noted, 'ideas, understandings, and manifestations of national, political, economic, and social identities lie at the contested heart of culture, cultural provision, and cultural analysis in Scotland.'[98] The gap between public discourses and everyday practice must also be tackled. This chapter has shown how culture has been raised as a standard, a rallying call – as something to be accessed, disseminated, created, defended, challenged or contested. One starting point, then, for examining culture in our everyday lives has to be the examination of the changing roles and definitions of culture espoused over the course of the twentieth century alongside the ways in which the place of culture in the everyday lives of the people of Scotland was conceived, presented and contested.

Notes

1. J. McConnell (First Minister of Scotland, 2001–7), St Andrew's Day speech given at the Royal Scottish Academy of Music and Drama, Glasgow, 30 November 2003. www.scotland.gov.uk/News/News-Extras/176
2. This review was initially headed by Frank McAveety, then Minister for Tourism, Culture and Sport, and completed by his successor, Culture Minister Patricia Ferguson. McConnell, St Andrew's Day Speech.
3. *'Our Next Major Enterprise . . .' Final Report of the Cultural Commission: June 2005* www.scotland.gov.uk/Publications/2005/09/01729/17314; 'Curtain Raised on Arts Shake-up' BBC News www.newsvote.bbc.co.uk
4. R. Williams, *Keywords: A Vocabulary of Culture and Society* (London, 1988), p. 17.
5. C. G. Brown, 'Popular culture and the continuing struggle for rational recreation', in T. M. Devine and R. J. Finlay (eds), *Scotland in the 20th Century* (Edinburgh, 1996), p. 211.
6. T. C. Smout, 'Patterns of culture', in A. Dickson and J. H. Treble, *People and Society in Scotland, Volume III, 1914–1990* (Edinburgh, 1992), p. 264.
7. W. W. Knox, *Industrial Nation: Work, Culture and Society in Scotland, 1800– Present* (Edinburgh, 1999), p. 202.
8. C. Harvie, *No Gods and Precious Few Heroes: Twentieth-Century Scotland*. 3rd edn (Edinburgh, 2000), p. 117.
9. See T. Nairn, 'Festival of the dead', in O. Dudley Edwards and G. Richardson, *Edinburgh* (Edinburgh, 1983) and, more recently, D. McCrone, *Understanding Scotland: The Sociology of a Nation* (London, 2001).
10. Nairn, 'Festival of the dead', in Dudley Edwards and Richardson, *Edinburgh*, pp. 275–6.
11. 'Writing Scottish Art: Historical Reflections in Contemporary Overviews'. Conference held at Visual Research Centre, Dundee Contemporary Arts (DCA), 8 September 2006.
12. McCrone, *Understanding Scotland*, p. 145; 'Writing Scottish Art' Conference, 2006.
13. S. Waterman, 'Carnivals for elites? The cultural politics of arts festivals', *Progress in Human Geography* vol. 22 issue 1 (1998), pp. 54.
14. Eliot won the Nobel Prize for Literature in 1948. T. S. Eliot, *Notes towards the Definition of Culture* (London, 1948), pp. 36–8, 42–8.
15. In 1946, Priestley had published his views on wartime diffusion of the arts in *The Arts Under Socialism*. N. Hayes, 'More than "Music-While-You-Eat"? Factory and hostel concerts, "good culture" and the workers', in N. Hayes and J. Hill (eds), *'Millions Like Us'? British Culture in the Second World War* (Liverpool, 1999), pp. 209–10.
16. Eliot wrote that 'culture is not merely the sum of several activities, but a *way*

of life.' Eliot, *Notes towards,* p. 41. To Williams, that was one of Eliot's key achievements and contributions: his adoption of the meaning of culture as 'a whole way of life' and, following on from that, the consideration of what is meant by the 'levels' of culture within that meaning. The other key contribution Williams identified was Eliot's efforts to distinguish between the terms 'elite' and 'class'. R. Williams, *Culture and Society, 1780–1950* (London, 1961), pp. 16, 229; Williams, *The Long Revolution* (London, 1961). See also R. Hoggart, *The Uses of Literacy: Aspects of Working-Class Life with Special References to Publications and Entertainments* (London, 1957; new edn 1992).

17. See, for example, D. Inglis, *Culture and Everyday Life* (London, 2005), p. 89.

18. Brown, 'Popular culture', in Devine and Finlay (eds), *Scotland in the 20th Century,* pp. 210–12.

19. See P. Maloney, *Scotland and the Music Hall, 1850–1914* (Manchester, 2003), pp. 39–40.

20. A. Scullion, 'Glasgow Unity Theatre: the necessary contradictions of Scottish political theatre', in *Twentieth Century British History* vol. 13, no. 3 (2002), p. 219.

21. T. Griffiths, 'The consumption of cinema: the economics of a mass entertainment industry', unpublished paper presented to the Scottish Economic and Social History Society conference, 2006. I am grateful to Trevor for allowing me to quote this paper.

22. See, for example, C. G. Brown, *Religion and Society in Twentieth Century Britain* (Harlow, 2006).

23. D. Campbell, *Playing for Scotland* (Edinburgh, 1996), p. 120.

24. Scullion, 'Glasgow Unity Theatre', p. 221.

25. Hewison, *In Anger,* p. 6.

26. D. Shellard, *British Theatre Since the War* (London, 1999), p. 6.

27. C. Gray, *The Politics of the Arts in Britain* (Basingstoke, 2000), p. 35.

28. Shellard, *British Theatre,* p. 6; see A. Sinclair, *Arts and Cultures: The History of the 50 Years of the Arts Council of Great Britain* (London, 1995).

29. A. Marwick, *The Penguin Social History of Britain: British Society Since 1945* (London, 1996), pp. 58, 75.

30. B. Conekin, *The Autobiography of a Nation: The 1951 Festival of Britain* (Manchester, 2003), p. 119.

31. D. Dworkin, *Cultural Marxism in Postwar Britain: History, the New Left, and the Origins of Cultural Studies* (London, 1997), pp. 15–16.

32. *British Weekly: A Journal of Social and Christian Progress,* 7 November 1946.

33. These attempts by the kirk to engage with the arts were to prove significant in the 1960s when, against the context of decreasing religiosity and increasing secularisation, representatives of the kirk made efforts to maintain contact with Scottish people, particularly youth, through the arts and media.

34. *The Scotsman,* 25 August 1947.

35. *British Weekly Journal,* 7 November 1946.

36. J. Weingartner, *The Arts as a Weapon of War: Britain and the Shaping of National Morale in the Second World War* (London, 2006), p. 166.

37. Marwick, *Penguin Social History*, p. 95; Hewison, *In Anger*, p. 171.

38. C. G. Brown, *The Death of Christian Britain: Understanding Secularisation* (London, 2001), p. 6; Marwick, *Penguin Social History*, p. 83; Hewison, *In Anger*, p. 24.

39. K. Allsop, *The Angry Decade: A Survey of the Cultural Revolt of the Nineteen-Fifties* (London, 1964), p. 21; Hewison, *In Anger*, p. 60.

40. Edinburgh City Council Archives (ECCA) Early Festival Papers. EIFMD Programme 1947; Weingartner, *Arts as a Weapon of War*, p. 163.

41. In fact, it was decided in the earliest planning stages that the artistic standard to be presented was to be 'superlative'. ECCA Early Festival Papers. EIFMD Report, summer 1945.

42. ECCA Early Festival Papers. Memorandum and Articles of Association of the Edinburgh Festival Society Limited, 22 November 1946.

43. Edinburgh Central Library (ECL), Edinburgh Room, qYML38E [C27270]. Submission on Behalf of the Edinburgh Festival Society for the Nobel Peace Prize (January 1952).

44. ECL, Edinburgh Room, qYML38E [C27270]. Nobel Peace Prize.

45. Hewison, *Culture and Consensus*, pp. 33–4.

46. The reasons these groups chose to appear in Edinburgh at the same time as the Festival are unclear, yet it seems realistic to suggest that the potential of having the attention of the world's press, critics and audiences would have been a strong incentive. *Everyman* was performed in Dunfermline, a Fife town around 20 miles north-west of Edinburgh, thus demonstrating the fluid location of the Fringe. Moffat, *Fringe*, pp. 15–16.

47. Founded in 1936, out of the earlier Workers' Theatre Movement, the popularity of Unity peaked in May 1947, when its national society could boast a membership of over 10,000, as well as over 3,000,000 affiliates and fifty branches in towns and cities throughout Britain. C. Chambers, *The Story of Unity Theatre* (London, 1989), p. 280.

48. Scullion, 'Glasgow Unity Theatre', pp. 103–5, 244.

49. *Scots Theatre*, 1 September 1946, cited in Scullion, 'Glasgow Unity Theatre', p. 238.

50. The writer on Unity was Joseph MacLeod. Hill, 'Glasgow Unity', pp. 28, 30.

51. Scullion, 'Glasgow Unity Theatre', pp. 240–3.

52. The Gallacher Memorial Library (hereafter GML). Final Draft Constitution of the Edinburgh Labour Festival Committee.

53. H. Henderson, *The Edinburgh People's Festival, 1951–54* www.edinburghpeoplesfestival.org.uk/background/hamish.html; GML: M. Milligan, 'Edinburgh People's Festival', in *Communist Review* (March 1952), p. 86.

54. Frontline, *Time for a People's Festival* www.redflag.org.uk/frontline/five/05Festival.html

55. Henderson, *People's Festival*.

56. J. Hill, '"When work is over": labour, leisure and culture in wartime Britain', in Hayes and Hill, *Millions Like Us?*, p. 257.

57. Hamish Henderson Obituary: http://thescotsman.scotsman.com/obituaries.cfm?id_272292002

226 *Angela Bartie*

58. See E. J. Cowan (ed.), *The People's Past: Scottish Folk. Scottish History* (Edinburgh, 1980) and A. Munro, *The Democratic Muse: Folk Music Revival in Scotland* (Aberdeen, 1996).
59. *Daily Worker*, 31 August 1951.
60. In Scotland, the People's Festival organisers were also keen to defend as well as develop 'Scottish culture'. GML Milligan, 'EPF', pp. 87–8.
61. Hill, 'When work is over', in Hayes and Hill, *Millions Like Us?*, p. 239.
62. *Daily Worker*, 31 August 1951.
63. *Scottish Daily Express*, 8 September 1953.
64. S. Dawson, 'Selling the Circus: Nationalism and Circus Fans in Britain, 1921–1945', Paper given at Pacific Coast Conference on British Studies, University of California (Berkeley), USA (March 2004).
65. Indeed these ideas were first aired by Hunter as part of a plea at an Edinburgh luncheon of the Sales Managers Association. *Express*, 8 September 1953.
66. Hayes and Hill, *Millions Like Us?*, p. 29.
67. *Scottish Daily Express*, 9 September 1953.
68. A. Calder, 'Conference paper: workers' culture/popular culture – defining our terms', *Scottish Labour History Society Journal*, 26 (1991), pp. 64–77, p. 71.
69. D. Knox, 'Spectacular tradition: performance and Scottish folk song', *Annals of Tourism Research*, 35: 1 (2008), pp. 242–56.
70. J. Hill, 'Glasgow Unity Theatre: the search for a "Scottish People's Theatre"', *New Edinburgh Review* no. 40 (1978), p. 28.
71. This notion was conceived by Dean MacCannell. Knox, 'Spectacular Tradition', p. 3.
72. Dworkin, *Cultural Marxism*, pp. 3, 79.
73. M. Donnelly, *Sixties Britain: Culture, Society and Politics* (London, 2005), p. 99.
74. P. Hollis, *Jennie Lee: A Life* (Oxford, 1997), p. 258.
75. National Archives of Scotland (NAS) CO1/5/883: Scottish Arts Council 1965–1973 Policy Files. Scottish Education Department Circular No. 589: *A Policy for the Arts*.
76. ECL, Edinburgh Room, YPN2605 L98, Lyceum. *Edinburgh Evening News and Dispatch*, 17 January 1964. ECCA Lord Provost's Committee: Edinburgh Civic Theatre Trust Ltd – Lyceum Theatre. Part 1 (1 February 1964–31, March 1966) Minutes of Meeting, 2 March 1965.
77. R. Hewison, *Too Much: Art and Society in the Sixties, 1960–75* (London, 1986), pp. 57–8.
78. *A Policy for the Arts: The First Steps*, paragraph 71, reproduced in H. Jenkins, *The Culture Gap: An Experience of Government and the Arts* (London, 1979), Appendix 1.
79. Both she and the main conference organiser, publisher John Calder, were arrested. The young model, Anna Kesselaar, was charged with acting in a 'shameless and indecent manner' and Calder with 'having been art and part [i.e. complicit] in this offence'. These arrests came one week after the Conference had ended, by which time various figures had publicly condemned the incident. For a detailed analysis of the moral and cultural impact of this event, see A. Bartie,

'Festival City: the Arts, Culture and Moral Conflict in Edinburgh, 1947–1967'. PhD thesis, University of Dundee, 2007.

80. C. Marowitz, 'Edinburgh happenings', in J.-J. Lebel et al., *New Writers IV: Plays and Happenings* (London, 1967), p. 59.

81. J. Green, *All Dressed Up: The Sixties and the Counterculture* (London, 1999), p. 132.

82. B. Levin, *The Pendulum Years: Britain and the Sixties* (London, 1970), p. 308; B. Curtis, 'A highly mobile and plastic environ', in C. Stephens and K. Stout, *Art & the 60s: This Was Tomorrow* (London, 2004), p. 52.

83. T. Normand, '55° North 3° West: a panorama from Scotland', in *Remapping British Art and Architecture*, p. 25. I am grateful to Tom Normand for sending me a draft of this chapter.

84. *International Situationist* 1 (1958), cited in A. Marwick, *The Sixties: Cultural Revolution in Britain, France, Italy and the United States, c. 1958–c. 1974* (Oxford, 1998), p. 32.

85. McConnell, St Andrew's Day speech.

86. *Variant: Cross Currents in Culture* no. 29, summer 2007, p. 27.

87. This failed to pass through Parliament in June 2008. See www.scottish.parliament.uk/s3/bills/07-CreativeScotland/index.htm

88. P. Willis, 'Symbolic creativity', in J. Storey (ed.), *Cultural Theory and Popular Culture: A Reader* (London, 1994), p. 526.

89. For more on the Craigmillar Festivals, see H. Crummy, *People in Partnership: The Report of the Craigmillar Festival Society, 1973/4*.

90. *Glasgow 1990 The Book: The Authorised Tour of the Cultural Capital of Europe* (Glasgow, 1990), p. 7.

91. G. Mooney, 'Cultural policy as urban transformation? Critical reflections on Glasgow, European city of culture 1990', *Local Economy* vol. 19, no. 4 (2004), pp. 327–40.

92. Coveney, *The Citz*, pp. 14–19.

93. Hewison, *Culture*, p. 220.

94. D. Inglis, *Culture and Everyday Life* (London, 2005), p. 89.

95. Willis, 'Symbolic creativity', in Storey (ed.), *Cultural Theory*, pp. 523–9.

96. See R. Hewison, *Towards 2010: New Times, New Challenges for the Arts* (Arts Council England, 2000).

97. Cited in R. Wishart, 'The arts, culture and identity', in M. Linklater and R. Denniston, *Anatomy of Scotland: How Scotland Works* (Edinburgh, 1992) p. 153.

98. Scullion, 'Glasgow Unity Theatre', p. 221.

Chapter 9

Sickness and Health

John Stewart

INTRODUCTION

The everyday experience of sickness and health in Scotland changed enormously during the twentieth century. These changes embraced everyone irrespective of age, social class or gender – albeit to differing degrees and at different times. The century witnessed a huge rise in life expectancy and an equally significant decline in a very sensitive indicator of social health, infant mortality. In part this was due to the virtual elimination of some major infectious diseases, although these have been replaced by what are sometimes called diseases of affluence such as cancer and heart disease. One consequence of the rise in life expectancy is that conditions associated with old age require much more medical attention now than at the beginning of the twentieth century.

Medical science and practice have likewise been transformed. In the early twenty-first century we are accustomed to receiving antibiotics should we contract, say, a debilitating and chronic condition such as bronchitis; and invasive surgery for a range of ailments and including organ transplant. None of this was possible one hundred years ago. Doctors and medical scientists now comprehend, moreover, the human body's requirements and functioning in ways inconceivable at the beginning of the twentieth century. People are thus not only living longer, they can be treated for illnesses which in the past might not necessarily have been life-threatening but which may nonetheless have severely impaired quality of life.

Changes in health and healthcare have embraced the mental as well as the physical.[1] Attitudes towards the treatment and care of the mentally ill altered considerably for several, inter-related, reasons. Around the turn of the century asylums began to be seen as more to do with therapy and cure and less to do with confinement, although the associated shift away from institutionalisation took, in practice, a long time to realise. Overcrowding was a serious issue which persisted into the 1960s. A patient at Gartnavel Royal Hospital in Glasgow described the 'torture' of communal sleeping accommodation and the 'daily contact with insanity and noise'.[2] Nonetheless patients more and more admitted themselves voluntarily rather than through certification, a trend culminating in so-called 'informal' admission from the 1960s.

The emphasis on therapy was further heightened after 1945 with the advent of new, powerful drugs. Other developments in the care of the mentally ill included the growth in out-patients clinics, the first of which was set up in Glasgow in 1910. In the late 1940s, meanwhile, the Dingleton Hospital in Melrose instituted a highly innovative 'open door' policy which was crucial in eroding the practice of confining patients in locked wards. Hospitals were to become therapeutic communities, a notion later developed into that of care in the community.

All these changes have both been caused by and contributed to increased medical specialisation, witnessed by the proliferation of healthcare professions. The way in which healthcare is delivered too has changed fundamentally. The National Health Service (NHS), whatever its actual or imagined shortcomings, provides a service which is universal, comprehensive, free at the point of delivery, and funded out of general taxation – principles established in the 1940s and still more or less present today.

Unfortunately, this is not the whole story. Scientific advances and free healthcare have combined to raise expectations. This is problematic in that, ultimately, there is no upper limit to what might be spent. Scientific medicine itself has been more closely scrutinised, especially since the 1960s. Unfulfilled expectations and the questioning of scientific medicine have resulted in, inter alia, an increasing interest in 'alternative' medicine from chiropractice to acupuncture, notwithstanding the lack of evidence for many of its claims. Focusing more particularly on Scotland, the country historically has better healthcare provision and, scientific advance notwithstanding, a poor health record, especially when seen against comparable societies.

The remainder of this chapter discusses these issues further. First, we introduce the idea of Scottish 'distinctiveness'. Second, we examine the impact of medical science. Third, we describe changes in healthcare delivery. Fourth, we focus on particular themes – urban and rural society; and the experiences of a particularly vulnerable group, the young.

SCOTTISH DISTINCTIVENESS?

During the crisis of the 1930s, the nutritionist John Boyd Orr suggested how to better the health of the Scottish people. In particular, housing had to improve and adequate quantities of good-quality food be provided. This would allow families of the future to 'live in decency' and to raise their children to 'attain their full inherited capacity for health and physical fitness'. Scots would thus become 'a race as vigorous as the Scandinavians', with the result that, for instance, Glasgow's infant mortality rate – which was then around one hundred deaths of infants under one year per thousand live births – would fall to that of Oslo's, then running at below thirty.[3]

A few years later, Scotland's former Chief Medical Officer, James Mackintosh, contributed to the debate over post-war reconstruction. He had no doubt of the need for improved health, recent progress notwithstanding. In 1938 – the healthiest year in Scottish history thus far – the general and tuberculosis death rates and the infant mortality rate were at record lows. Nonetheless, Scotland's health history remained a 'bleak record'. Mackintosh noted that while, for instance, Scottish infant mortality had certainly declined, this compared 'unfavourably with other socially competent countries' such as England. Mackintosh too raised the issue of urban living and its health consequences. The proportion of the population living in overcrowded circumstances was over 40 per cent in Coatbridge and Clydebank, 29 per cent in Glasgow, and 17 per cent in Edinburgh. This compared with 7.4 per cent in Liverpool and 2.1 per cent in Bristol. Looking to the post-war future, Mackintosh suggested that Scotland's problems were not 'just a replica, on a smaller scale' of England's. They were 'different in kind and in degree' and would thus not be best resolved by direction from London.[4]

This sense of distinctiveness was nothing new. The public components of healthcare provision had historically been administered within Scotland itself, the Union of 1707 notwithstanding. In at least partial fulfilment of Mackintosh's wish, this was further recognised by the 1947 National Health Service (Scotland) Act. The Scottish system, while in most respects identical with that elsewhere in the United Kingdom, was nonetheless the responsibility of the Secretary of State for Scotland and allowed for the retention of some particularly Scottish features – for example, a greater emphasis on hospital medicine.[5] The need for, and desirability of, a separate NHS was argued on a range of grounds. Introducing the Bill's Second Reading, the Scottish Secretary specifically alluded to his country's distinctive history, legal system, local government, and geography and population structure.[6] Such points were reiterated to political devolution and beyond. After New Labour's 1997 election victory, an official document noted the necessity of health policies appropriate to Scotland's 'distinctive needs'. The latter had 'long been reflected' in the Scottish health service and the forthcoming Parliament would continue to build on this foundation.[7] The Scottish Government's present healthcare responsibilities thus derive from a long historical process.[8]

A distinctive administrative profile is matched by a distinctive, unflattering profile in health outcomes. A 1971 report pointed to Scotland's 'historic record of achievement' in advancing medical science alongside 'a disturbingly unfavourable position when certain international health statistics are compared'.[9] A 2003 study surveying historic patterns of European mortality rates revealed that while there had been improvements in Scotland, as elsewhere, nonetheless for those in the age group fifteen to seventy-four years 'Scotland has had the highest mortality rates for men in Western Europe since 1978 and for women since 1958'.[10] In 2008, the Scottish Government noted that while taken as a whole the country's health was improving, 'the fact is that some (health) inequalities are widening'. These derived from various sources, including personal lifestyle issues such as smoking as well as broader socio-cultural and environmental factors. There thus remained 'many challenges to overcome to tackle the country's poor health record'.[11]

MEDICINE AND SOCIETY

Improvements in Scottish health pre-dated the twentieth century. In the latter part of the nineteenth century this was largely due to the public health movement which, at least in major urban areas, brought the supply of clean water accompanied by the sanitary disposal of waste. One of the movement's most famous achievements was the Loch Katrine reservoir which, from mid-century, supplied Glasgow's water. Consequently, by the end of the nineteenth century the major epidemic, water-borne diseases had been virtually eliminated.[12] The impact of all this on people's daily lives and health is difficult to overemphasise.

Concerns about the impact of environment on health continued into the twentieth century. However, from around the beginning of the century ailments such as cancer and heart disease came to the fore. In turn, there was an increasing emphasis on clinical medicine and its relationship to the individual patient, a shift further engendered by unprecedented advances in medical science and technology. In 1929, a celebratory history of Edinburgh Royal Infirmary observed that the hospital's 'remarkable expansion' since moving to its new site in 1879 was 'the visible, material expression of the development of the science and practice of medicine and surgery during the past fifty years'.[13]

The pace of medical scientific advance increased as the century wore on, especially after 1945, and these advances, combined with earlier public health measures, appear to have had very positive outcomes, as we can see from Table 9.1. Particularly notable here is the infant mortality rate. The

Table 9.1   *Life expectancy and infant mortality, Scotland 1860–2000.*

	Female life expectancy at birth	Male life expectancy at birth	Infant mortality rate
1860	44	40	127
1900	48	45	128
1950	69	64	39
2000	79	73	6

Source: These data are derived from B. R. Mitchell, *British Historical Statistics* (Cambridge, 1988), Chapter 1, Table 13; Lindsay Paterson et al., *Living in Scotland: Social and Economic Change since 1980* (Edinburgh, 2004), Table 2.8, Supplementary Table A2.2; and the General Register Office for Scotland website, http://www.gro-scotland. gov.uk/statistics/publications-and-data/life-expectancy/index.html – accessed 11 August 2008. The infant mortality rate is the number of child deaths under one year of age per thousand live births. See Table 2.8 for the full annual IMR data for Scotland.

death of a young child, all too common only a hundred years ago, is now a rare event.

Qualifications are, however, necessary. First, the century undoubtedly saw impressive health gains. But we have seen that Scotland historically has lagged behind other nations in crucial health indicators. Within Scotland itself, health inequalities have persisted throughout the century. While there are other causes, health inequalities are strongly related to social class. At the end of the century, men in the most deprived social circumstances were, for example, around three times as likely to suffer from lung and related cancers as those from the least deprived.[14] The everyday experience of sickness and health has depended, and still depends, on factors such as social class and place of residence and the lifestyles associated with these.

Second, advances in medical and pharmaceutical science have led to rising – and possibly unrealisable – popular expectations. Such attitudes are almost certainly heightened when healthcare services are part of a broader social contract, such as the post-war welfare state, in which citizens' rights can be invoked. At a mid-1960s conference on 'The Patient's Point of View' a Health Visitor remarked that while people were undoubtedly grateful for healthcare received, 'they now had a greater sense of entitlement to service and were more inclined to express their opinions' than previously.[15] A few years later, an official publication stressed the need to 'ensure that the old and mentally ill are not forgotten in the light of dramatic advances in medicine symbolised in the popular imagination by the development of transplant surgery'.[16] The clear implication here is that certain services might be pushed to one side as the public came to expect instant solutions to, in this particular case, heart disease. Such rising expectations lead to both constant upward pressures on expenditure and to frustrations and disappointments for patients and their families.

Third, the effects of the undoubted advances, in scientific terms, of medicine, medical techniques and pharmaceuticals are contested. It has been argued that improved mortality and morbidity rates over recent centuries owe less to medical intervention and more to improvements in living standards and in the socio-economic environment generally. So, for instance, the decline of tuberculosis (TB) after 1945 derives from better nutrition and housing conditions under the Welfare State and rather less from the increased availability and efficacy of antibiotics.[17]

The corollary of this is that poor socio-economic conditions lead to poor health. There can be little doubt that Scotland's experience of industrialisation and urbanisation was harsh, with dire health consequences. This was especially highlighted during the troubled inter-war period. It was with this era's deprivations in mind that Mackintosh claimed that the 'worst evils of the industrial revolution' found the Scots even worse prepared than their southern neighbours and that one consequence was that 'slums grew up with incredible speed'.[18] The economy changed fundamentally in the latter part of the twentieth century. As one historian puts it, 'Silicon Glen produces very different medical problems from the now redundant coal mines'. Health problems suffered by the modern workforce are thus much less likely to be diseases such as pneumoconiosis and other lung diseases such as silicosis and asbestosis, all largely caused by working conditions in the coal and construction industries, and much more likely to be 'those of repetitive strain injury or psychological stress in its many forms'.[19] Nonetheless, it is clear that the nature, intensity and consequences of industrialisation and its aftermath have had profound implications – both physical and psychological – for health and sickness experiences.

Fourth, concerns over personal behaviour and responsibility have, historically, also impacted on health analyses. Edinburgh's Medical Officer of Health (MOH) noted in the mid-1960s that, following the elimination of sickness and death from 'infectious and deficiency diseases', the principal causes of death for the young and middle-aged were 'accidents, cancer, suicide and heart disease'. All of these, he somewhat optimistically claimed, were preventable with 'self-knowledge' and he urged an education programme to prevent the 'horrible catastrophes caused by these largely self-inflicted diseases'.[20]

Smoking is a long standing concern. A mid-1970s report noted that Scots had higher rates of lung cancer, cardiovascular disease and bronchitis than other parts of the United Kingdom.[21] Tobacco consumption remains an important contributor to Scotland's poor record in lung and heart disease and an activity highly differentiated by social class.[22] The relationship between the Scots and alcohol too has long troubled commentators. Early in the century the physical condition of Edinburgh schoolchildren was investigated. The published report claimed that while poverty and housing went some way to explaining the survey's gloomy findings, much of the 'degradation of the people and the suffering of the children' was 'plainly and irrefutably attributable to an excessive indulgence in strong drink' by the parents.[23] In the late 1970s, the Chief Medical Officer stressed the ongoing need to tackle the causes of death and illness 'determined mainly by such personal habits as cigarette smoking, the excessive consumption of alcohol, injudicious diet and inadequate exercise'.[24] The present Scottish Government website, meanwhile, notes the doubling of alcohol consumption in the UK since 1950; the economic cost of alcohol misuse; and the hospitalisation of over 40,000 people annually as a result of alcohol abuse.[25]

Sexual conduct has likewise engendered debate about the relationship between health and personal behaviour, with moral questions becoming entangled with more obviously public health concerns. The medical understanding and treatment of sexually transmitted diseases undoubtedly improved dramatically over the century, although it is likely that at least prior to the First World War much went undetected due to, inter alia, social stigma and lack of resources. This was clearly not to the benefit either of the individuals concerned or the broader society. By the end of the century, although some conditions remained stubbornly persistent, the incidence of gonorrhoea and syphilis had declined dramatically. The availability of antibiotics was one obvious reason for this but the impact of HIV/AIDS was also important in alerting both individuals and public authorities to the need to address sexual health issues. The leading historian in this field, though, sees even in the post-war era concerns for sexual health as fundamentally structured 'as much by moral anxieties over the erosion of community and family values, as by the medical dimensions of the problem'. This he partly attributes to the long-standing influence of religion on Scottish civil and political life, thereby creating a rather different approach to the issue than in other, comparable, nations – a further instance of Scottish 'distinctiveness'.[26]

The determinants of health are thus complex, embracing the state of medical knowledge, socio-economic circumstances, personal behaviour and even social attitudes. We now examine in more detail a further contributory factor, the level and nature of healthcare provision.

TWENTIETH-CENTURY HEALTHCARE SERVICES

Historically, healthcare has been the remit of a range of bodies. Central government departments – whether part of the Scottish Office or the devolved administration – have been responsible for creating health policy and ensuring its implementation. At a lower official level, services such as the removal of noxious wastes have been carried out, since the nineteenth century, by local authorities under statutory regulation. Local authorities also had, for much of the twentieth century, responsibility for health functions such as the school meals and medical services. Workplace health has been the responsibility of, in varying combinations, employers, employees and official bodies – for example, the medical centres introduced in the Glasgow docks after nationalisation.[27] Charitable bodies have also played a role in healthcare provision and presently we shall encounter one important instance of this, voluntary hospitals. Less obviously, much healthcare has been carried out in the home. This has a significant impact on both cared-for and carers, the latter usually being female family members. All these sorts of provision together form a 'mixed economy of healthcare'. We focus, however, on two key institutions – hospitals and general practice.

Hospitals – public

In the first half of the twentieth century, there were two principal types of hospital – public and voluntary. The former, funded primarily through various forms of local taxation, were run by a range of statutory bodies. At the beginning of the century, the most notable of these was the Scottish Poor

Law. Although there were exceptions, public hospitals generally attracted poorer quality and fewer staff than voluntary hospitals.

By the beginning of the century, Poor Law hospital services were probably improving, at least in certain urban areas.[28] Nonetheless this was generally a service for those whose illness, age or economic status precluded admittance to voluntary hospitals. As an inspector remarked of Stirling Combination Poorhouse's medical facilities in 1913, the patients' appearance and average age 'indicated that here, as in poorhouse sick wards generally, infirmities associated with senility and chronic maladies were preponderant'.[29] Chronic conditions were those which were disabling over a long period but not immediately life-threatening and were generally rejected by voluntary hospitals. Care of the elderly, many of whom of course suffered chronic conditions, also largely devolved to public hospitals.

Such problems were not confined to large urban centres. A 1924 report observed that in many smaller institutions medical care fell 'short of the standard reached in respect of precisely similar cases, not only in the city infirmaries, but also in the hospital wards attached to the city Poorhouses'. Chronic or elderly patients might go many months 'without any re-examination or any attentative [sic] revision of their circumstances'.[30] These patients were, essentially, being 'dumped' in public sector institutions with little hope of remedial care – 'bed-blocking' (the practice whereby the elderly remain in hospital care for lack of a residential care place elsewhere) is thus nothing new. Those cared for in Poor Law institutions generally had nowhere else to go and were prepared, however unwillingly, to accept the social stigma attached to these services in the public mind. Such misgivings were not alleviated by practices such as those engaged in by Leith Parish Council, which in 1905 agreed that pauper cadavers unclaimed by relatives could be taken to Edinburgh University 'for use in the training of students in anatomy and surgery'.[31]

An enquiry into Poor Law medical services provides further insights into early twentieth-century conditions. One witness was Dr Laura Sandeman, Resident Medical Officer of Dundee's East Poorhouse and thereby responsible for a 320-bed hospital, the sick in the poorhouse itself and pauper lunatics. She had two other doctors working alongside her, but clearly this was an extremely onerous post simply in terms of patient numbers. Dr Sandeman had, moreover, to deal with all types of cases, medical and surgical. Asked whether she had an 'operating room and everything else as completely equipped as it would be in an infirmary' – that is, in a prestigious voluntary hospital – she replied: 'Most emphatically no. We have no theatre . . . If we have an operation, we . . . use a side room for it. I try to keep a side room which we can clear out at any time for an operation.'[32] From the patients' perspective all this suggests stretched resources, human and physical, and personal discomfort.

A further sense of patients' experience early in the century comes from two of Glasgow's fever hospitals. The first, Ruchill, was the subject of an official enquiry into overcrowding. In 1907, it had been overwhelmed by fever outbreaks resulting in, for example, a fifteen-bed ward containing '51 patients, both adults and children, suffering from cerebro-spinal fever, and 30 of them unconscious'. The overcrowding was such that nurses, of whom there were in any case not enough, could not adequately perform their duties. Patients, including very young children, had been left unclean and unattended for hours and 'the doctors were sometimes unable to tend them on that account'.[33] This was clearly a fragile system which, at times of pressure, was prone to breakdown, to everyone's detriment.

Ruchill's sister hospital, Belvidere, was described in a 1914 report. This noted, with a degree of pride, that the hospital's most modern acute wards were around 18 metres long and 7 metres wide, and contained eleven beds. While relatively generous by contemporary standards, at least for public hospitals, such lack of privacy would now be seen as highly intrusive. Dealing with infectious disease was a considerable problem. The report noted Glasgow's policy of hospitalising not only those with conditions such as smallpox. In the first half of the 1890s, for instance, around 69 per cent of scarlet fever cases were treated in hospital. By the late 1900s, this had risen to over 90 per cent.[34] This alerts us to the increasing acceptance of hospitalisation by both professionals and public. Problems notwithstanding, some hospitals at least were now seen as places where cure could be brought about rather than simply as places to die.

The evident strains on the public sector were partially addressed by the Local Government (Scotland) Act 1929. This allowed the transfer of Poor Law hospitals to the larger local authorities with the aim of encouraging co-operation, not least with the voluntary sector; the more systematic provision of medical services; a move away from the disparities of provision of the Poor Law system; and the elimination of the stigma associated with Poor Law provision. All this proved problematic and by 1936 only five Poor Law hospitals had become municipal general hospitals.[35]

A partial exception to this gloomy picture was Aberdeen. Here, under dynamic local leadership, municipalisation of hospital services pre-dated the 1929 Act and integration with the voluntary sector was relatively well-advanced.[36] But as an independent report further confirmed, outside the four major cities Scotland's public hospitals overwhelmingly catered for the chronic sick, infectious disease and maternity cases, while the ongoing 'stigma of the Poor Law' was hampering the development of public hospitals.[37] By the late 1930s, there was a broad consensus that satisfactory organisation of, and delivery by, public sector hospitals had not been achieved.

Hospitals – voluntary

Voluntary hospitals were funded from a variety of sources, notably charitable donations and subscriptions from individuals and groups. They ranged considerably in size and function and were unevenly distributed across the country. The most famous were the great infirmaries, prominent among which were the teaching hospitals associated with university medical faculties. Teaching hospitals in particular attracted the services of leading clinicians who gave their time and expertise without charge. Voluntary hospitals prioritised acute medicine at the expense of the chronic sick.

Poor Law authorities, generally unable to provide facilities for acute or specialist cases, often made donations to voluntary hospitals and similar charitable bodies. This was a form of insurance which might allow Poor Law patients access to otherwise unavailable services. So in 1900, Cathcart Parish Council donated seven guineas to Glasgow Victoria Infirmary, five guineas to Glasgow Royal Infirmary, three guineas to the Glasgow Samaritan Hospital, two guineas each to the Glasgow Eye Infirmary and the West of Scotland Sea-Side Homes, and one guinea to the St Andrew's Ambulance Association.[38]

A further, important, function of voluntary hospitals was their out-patients departments which frequently provided primary care for the neediest in society. At Edinburgh Royal Infirmary in the 1930s out-patients might, after a long wait, gain access to the dressing-rooms. As the hospital's historian remarks, every morning these were busy with 'the application of dressings to wounds and ulcers'. Dressing was carried out by nurses and student doctors 'guided by notes on the patients' cards indicating what of an imposing range of lotions was to be used, for this was before the era of antibiotics'.[39]

Originally, many voluntary hospitals had provided in-patient care free of charge to the needy, although some form of recommendation – a letter of support from a subscriber, for example – was generally required. By the 1930s, however, financial pressures were bringing the issue of payment to the fore and arguments were being made that those with sufficient means should pay for in-patient services. The Royal Alexandra Infirmary in Paisley was one example of an institution feeling the strain, largely due to the 'spiralling costs of medical technology and the expanding range of health care'. One measure of this was that by the early 1930s the number of in-patients had doubled when compared to the immediate post-war years. Although the number of beds remained the same, the 'average period of bed occupancy had fallen dramatically'.[40] From the patient's perspective, more and better treatment was increasingly the norm. But voluntary hospitals, while becoming more efficient, were also the victims of their own success and of advances in scientific medicine.

For the patient, the type of hospital care available thus depended on a complex combination of factors, including the nature of the illness; age; local Poor Law authority donations to voluntary services; the presence or otherwise of a voluntary hospital; and degree of access to financial support. The last point raises a further important issue about everyday perceptions of voluntary hospitals.

In 1920, Edinburgh Royal Infirmary held a fundraising parade during which donations were sought from spectators. Among those parading were 'Friendly Societies with gaily-coloured banners, representatives of the trades with their craft emblems, butchers, bakers, brass-finishers, coopers'.[41] Groups of individuals – the Friendly Societies noted here; trade unions; and places of employment (sometimes a combination of employers and employees) – subscribed collectively to particular institutions on the understanding that this would give their members right of immediate and automatic access to that hospital's services. A sense of ownership was thus engendered, a very different attitude to the stigma attached to Poor Law institutions. The Anchor Mills in Paisley subscribed to the Royal Alexandra Infirmary and as one of the owners remarked, the 'firm's contributions had always been regarded as payment for benefits received by the workers, and not as charitable subscriptions'.[42] Hospital contributory schemes attracted large memberships, with estimates suggesting that by the late 1930s some half million Scots belonged.[43]

A sense of ownership could lead to attempts to influence hospital policy. Paisley's mill workers flexed their muscles in the 1920s, objecting to charges imposed on the X-ray service. Although the hospital put up a cogent case for such charges, they were dropped in 1929.[44] More generally, Scottish schemes were more hostile than their English counterparts to any form of financial assessment for patients. They promoted instead what was effectively an 'open-door' policy for voluntary hospitals.[45] For this and other reasons, and again in contrast to England, Scottish voluntary hospitals did not usually attempt to recover costs directly from patients. Whatever this policy's social merits, it did little to alleviate financial pressures. The increasing strains inherent in voluntary hospital provision remained unresolved at the outbreak of the Second World War.

Hospitals – Second World War and the NHS

With the coming of war, hospitals throughout Britain came under the control of the regionally organised Emergency Medical Service which brought about the co-ordination of all hospital activities. The war also saw various surveys of Scottish hospital provision. An official committee reported in 1943 that even in the four major cities, but especially elsewhere, there was 'a clamant need for increased general hospital accommodation'. The challenge for voluntary hospitals was how to provide 'access by *all* classes in the community to the greater concentrations of medical skill and resources available in these hospitals as nowhere else' (emphasis in the original). The voluntary sector's present situation notably contrasted with that of public hospitals where, in effect, a means test operated (an unintended consequence of the 1929 Act). As a result of the 'chronic shortage of beds', the Secretary of State had, since the outbreak of war, dramatically expanded their number by a number of means. These included the building of seven new hospitals with, notably, units for specialisms such as neuro-surgery. Qualification conditions for admission to these had been eased so as to relieve the pressure on voluntary hospital waiting lists.[46]

This report, reflecting a widespread perception, assumed that the post-war hospital system would continue to be run by voluntary bodies and local authorities. However, the post-war Labour Government effectively 'nationalised' all hospitals. Scottish institutions were now organised into five Regional Hospital Boards under the direction of the Secretary of State. Scotland's particularities remained and subsequently played themselves out in a range of ways.[47]

It was, for instance, a bonus for the Scots that their service was led by the Scottish Secretary and not by the Minister of Health, not least because the former was always a Cabinet member whereas the latter was not. This gave the Scottish Secretary bargaining power over resources. Even before the introduction of the advantageous Barnett Formula in the 1970s, Scotland received a disproportionately high level of health service funding. Partly as a result of this advantage, Scotland was better off in respect of hospital doctors per head of the population. The Royal Commission on the NHS reported in 1979 that the UK average was 6.45 hospital doctors per 1,000 population, with the Scots coming out best with a figure of 9.19.[48]

Huge changes took place in the organisation and control of hospital services under the NHS. From the patient's point of view, access was now a right of citizenship and so not determined by the complex range of factors identified earlier. However, the NHS could not resolve all healthcare problems overnight. It was not until the Scottish Hospital Plan of the 1960s, for example, that any new hospitals were built. Many patients thus continued to be accommodated in buildings which had served as municipal and voluntary hospitals and which were often inadequate for the ever-growing demands of modern medicine.

Moreover, problems of access to hospital care were present before the NHS and have not entirely disappeared. In 1970, a paediatrician told a conference that Inverness District Hospital served a population of around 200,000 people. Of these, fewer than 20 per cent lived within 10 miles of the hospital, with over 40 per cent more than 50 miles away. Some 50,000 lived on islands. Communication links were therefore 'few and long', public transport infrequent and expensive. While small peripheral hospitals were doing a good job, nonetheless patients had to be brought to Inverness for specialist care. Citing the specific example of Caithness, the speaker pointed out how the 'difficulty of getting the acutely ill baby or child to the central hospital often frustrated efforts to lower (infant and child) mortality in these areas'. Not least among these difficulties, he continued, was that the weather 'was often a serious handicap to the acutely ill when journeys exceeded 100 miles'.[49] Coming up to the present, a recent initiative stressed the need for the development of small, community hospitals to meet the 'vast majority of the needs of the whole local population'.[50] This is both recognition of access problems and a shift away from the emphasis on large hospitals characteristic of the Hospital Plan era.

General practice

At the beginning of the twentieth century, individuals might seek access to a General Practitioner (GP) – the front line of primary medical care – in a number of ways, depending on circumstances. First, those who could afford to do so would simply pay for consultation and treatment. Second, groups of individuals – for example, Friendly Societies – might pool resources to establish a contractual relationship with individual practitioners. Third, those with entitlement could consult a Poor Law doctor at no charge. Fourth, voluntary hospital out-patients departments offered primary care for the neediest in society. From the patient's perspective, the quality of the doctor/patient encounter might vary significantly depending on which path was taken. Furthermore, for a wide range of illnesses and conditions there was not much a GP could do, advances in medical science notwithstanding. Drug therapies had not yet caught up with ever-increasing scientific precision in identifying disease and understanding its causes. Also, many people, and especially women, went without primary care for economic reasons.

Change came with the 1911 National Insurance Act which required wage-earners, employers and the state to contribute to a fund which could be drawn on by workers at times of ill-health. Sickness benefit was paid, albeit of a limited amount and for a limited period. Contributors could also seek consultations with participating GPs. However, the scheme had limitations. The cost of prescriptions and treatment still had to be met by the patient, directly or indirectly. The scheme was not, moreover, administered directly by the state but by so-called Approved Societies. These might be, for instance, Friendly Societies or commercial insurance companies. Some Approved Societies offered services beyond the most basic, albeit at additional cost, others did not. Once again, there were wide variations in patient experience. Those outside the scheme – for example children, and married women not in employment – generally had to resort to other sources of primary care.[51]

As with hospitals, the NHS dramatically improved access. All citizens had the right to GP services at no direct financial cost. Initially, prescriptions, dentures and spectacles were also available without charge, although this was modified fairly early on. Nonetheless, primary healthcare since 1948 effected a huge change in patient experience. And just as Scotland has been well-served with hospital doctors, so too with GPs. With the NHS settlement, as one commentator notes, Scotland retained an existing advantage over England. It had relatively more doctors, which meant fewer patients on individual GP lists – on average 2,000 compared to 2,400 in England and Wales.

This led to less pressure on Scottish GPs, and perhaps in consequence 'there were relatively few complaints from patients'.[52] Scotland's advantageous position compared to England continues, with recent research revealing that English GPs had a higher workload than those in Scotland and that this persisted post-devolution.[53]

This does not mean that GPs were evenly distributed throughout Scotland; that they all behaved in the same way; or that their services were as highly valued as those of hospital doctors. On this last point, a report noted that Scotland's 'powerful hospital system' had tended to erode the 'opportunities and capabilities' of general practice. The most 'striking developments' under the NHS had been in the hospital service. In 1968, for instance, hospital expenditure constituted 62 per cent of total health expenditure compared with 55 per cent twenty years earlier. The proportion of health service personnel in hospitals, meanwhile, had risen from 40 per cent at the start of the NHS to the present 54 per cent.[54] This is not simply an arcane policy issue. From the patients' viewpoint it suggests that hospital services have been given priority over other forms of healthcare, including primary care. It is noticeable, for example, that the percentage of women giving birth in Scottish hospitals rose from 56 to 79 per cent in the first decade of the new health service, the comparable figures for England being from 45 to 64 per cent.[55] Overall, at least when compared with England, expenditure and doctor/patient ratios consistently favour Scotland and this sits uneasily with the country's poor health outcomes.

THEMES IN SICKNESS AND HEALTH

We now turn to our first theme in the everyday experience of sickness and health in twentieth-century Scotland.

Rural society

Just prior to the First World War an enquiry was held into health services in the Highlands and Islands. The evidence it gathered gives revealing insights into health and sickness experiences. A Rona fisherman told of how the island's inhabitants had access only to the Portree doctor on Skye. The latter had to 'come in a boat, and in the winter-time he cannot come'. A wait of as long as a fortnight might sometimes occur 'and the patient will be suffering pain all the time. It is quite possible that the patient may die without seeing a doctor at all'. The District MOH for Lewis, meanwhile, attested to the island's poor and insanitary housing and the consequent impossibility of isolating TB patients. All too frequently, moreover, 'the patient spits on the floor, and the floor of churches and meeting houses, scattering tubercle bacilli all round'. Little else could be expected, he concluded, 'than a wide prevalence of the disease'.[56]

One outcome of the enquiry was a uniquely Scottish phenomenon, the Highlands and Islands Medical Service (HIMS), which expanded primary care within the region using, effectively, government subsidies. The service is sometimes seen as a prototype of the NHS. While something of an exaggeration, HIMS was, nonetheless, an acknowledgement that the region's healthcare had to be dealt with in a particular way.[57] We have also seen that a separate Scottish NHS was defended on topographical and geographical grounds and that difficulties persisted in remote areas. A report of the mid-1990s observed that the 'intensity of the problems of remoteness varies significantly'. Some isolated districts were, through the presence of community hospitals in small towns, reasonably well served. Nonetheless, and especially on remote islands, people might live a considerable distance from a GP. Echoing earlier analyses, it was noted that bad weather 'exacerbates these problems', especially where air or ferry travel was required.[58] The difficulty in providing medical services to distant communities continues to be used as a justification for Scotland's disproportionately high share of public expenditure allocated under the Barnett Formula.[59]

Of course, not all of rural Scotland is located in the Highlands and Islands. As its historian remarks, prior to the setting up of the Peel Hospital in Galashiels in 1939 'there was no General District Hospital provision in the Scottish Borders'. Those requiring specialist treatment had to travel to Edinburgh or, for those located in the region's most easterly or southerly parts, to Newcastle or Carlisle. As he further comments, the 'inconvenience and expense of such an arrangement must have placed a considerable burden on patients and their families'.[60]

An enquiry conducted during the First World War noted of a Lanarkshire mining village that the four outside privy middens generated 'conditions of filth . . . such as could not be described in decent language' and remarked further of this and similar areas that 'the Public Health Acts might as well not exist'. More positively, it also noted changing rural attitudes to 'sanitary provision'. The present generation of farm-workers – implicitly in contrast to its predecessors – was 'far from indifferent either to the minimum essentials for decent cottage life or to the dangers of the indiscriminate dissemination of domestic filth'. But there was more to it than individual sensibilities and health precautions. There was now much evidence that insanitary conditions on farms had resulted, through the supply of contaminated milk, in disease in urban areas.[61]

Urban milk supply continued to be an issue, although problems were gradually eradicated. In 1945, Aberdeen experienced an outbreak of dysentery. The source was traced to one dairy where, it transpired, the staff were victims of the disease and had contaminated the milk during bottling.[62] The reliance of urban areas on the countryside for milk thus reinforced the symbiotic relationship between town and country, one aspect of which was greater social concern for rural health standards. Further regulation was introduced after 1945 and pasteurisation of milk was made compulsory with effect from 1983.[63]

Urban society

What, though, of the urban areas themselves? Rapid industrialisation and the attendant urbanisation – by 1914 over 40 per cent of the Scottish population lived in towns of over 20,000 people and Glasgow's population had reached one million – generated considerable problems. In the 1930s, Lewis Grassic Gibbon claimed that over 150,000 Glaswegians dwelt 'in such conditions as the most bitterly pressed primitive in Tierra del Fuego never visioned'. They lived five or six to one room, the latter 'part of some great sloven tenement' whose windows were 'grimed with the unceasing wash and drift of coal-dust' and whose stairs were 'narrow and befouled and steep, [with an] evening breath like that which might issue from the mouth of a lung-diseased beast'. These unfortunates 'eat and sleep and copulate and conceive and crawl into childhood in those waste jungles of stench and disease and hopelessness'.[64] For Grassic Gibbon, diseased individuals were part of a broader social sickness.

As such remarks attest, housing was a particular concern, not least because crowded and insanitary conditions encouraged the spread of disease. Although the issue had been addressed since the late nineteenth century, problems persisted. In his 1949 report, Glasgow's MOH noted that while the number of houses provided by the Corporation was the highest on record, this was 'still woefully short of what is required'. This point was amply illustrated by the observation in the same report that the number of new cases of pulmonary TB recorded was the highest since 1910.[65] As Sir Alexander Macgregor, a previous and highly influential Glasgow MOH, had recently remarked, Glasgow's housing problems were 'peculiarly difficult both in kind and in magnitude'.[66]

One consequence of such concerns was 'Glasgow's X-Ray Campaign Against Tuberculosis' of 1957. The campaign report noted that Glasgow had a 'varied record in tuberculosis' but, by 1956, its position had deteriorated so that it 'has now become the worst city of comparable size in Britain'. In that year the notification rate in Glasgow was 160, compared to 130 in England's worst-affected city, Liverpool. The report further noted how everyday health was largely determined by everyday living experiences. Overcrowding, for instance, remained a serious problem because of the way in which disease spread. In Glasgow, 48 per cent of all dwellings consisted of one or two rooms, compared to Birmingham's 2 per cent.[67]

In Edinburgh, meanwhile, an event took place in 1926 which illustrates the depth of concern over TB. A man was compulsorily detained in hospital, for the first time in Edinburgh and probably only the second in Scotland. This individual had previously been hospitalised but had discharged himself

Figure 9.1   *Patients on the carriages for spines and hips, Mearnskirk Hospital for children, 1930 (image courtesy of the Royal College of Physicians and Surgeons of Glasgow).*

voluntarily. His detention was deemed necessary because of 'the infectious nature' of his 'tuberculous lung condition' combined with his domestic circumstances. He was part of a large family living in 'unsatisfactory home conditions' and in an environment conducive to the rapid spread of the disease. After 1945, the city instituted a mass radiography programme which identified 'numerous cases' of individuals unaware of their condition and in fact symptom-free. A few years later, Edinburgh took advantage of a scheme, initiated by the Scottish Secretary, whereby TB sufferers were sent to Swiss and Danish clinics for treatment and recuperation. Tuberculosis rates continued to rise in Edinburgh until 1954, the general trend thereafter being a steady decline.[68]

Other diseases too posed problems. Aberdeen reported ten cases of infective jaundice in 1950. The majority of these were fish-workers or those associated with the trade, a reminder of the relationship between occupation and health.[69] The city also famously experienced an outbreak of typhoid in the early 1960s. Over 500 cases were identified with, at the onset, some 35,000 people potentially at risk. The source of the disease was contaminated corned beef sold in a supermarket. As was pointed out at the time, such outbreaks were by that point extremely rare. But the outbreak highlighted the expanding role of health education, a process which engages with everyday life in a range of ways. So, for instance, Aberdeen health visitors stressed 'the importance of personal hygiene' when meeting with groups and individuals. On a practical level, paper towels were installed in all schools and attempts were made to 'enlist the help of school teachers in improving the hygiene of pupils'.[70]

Aberdeen in the 1960s saw itself as particularly progressive in areas such as health education. In a thoughtful passage, the MOH's 1962 report noted the '(a)ltering pattern of disease'. Infectious diseases and those 'associated with dirt and destitution' had been virtually eradicated. But this meant that local health authorities would now be faced with other conditions, for example alcoholism, road accidents, and age-related conditions such as coronary thrombosis and rheumatism. It was also possible that 'financial prosperity' – the rise in standards during the long period of post-war growth – might lead to 'excessive drinking and excessive smoking'. Key to the health department's functions would thus be 'the promotion of physical and emotional health', this in turn emphasising the role of the health visitor and health education.[71] A few years later, the city was congratulating itself on achieving the lowest infant mortality rate for Scottish cities with a ratio which 'approaches the figures of Swedish towns'. Health education was expanding qualitatively and quantitatively with research taking place on, for instance and revealingly, 'the smoking habits of about a thousand children'.[72]

Nonetheless, broader environmental problems continued to have health implications. Macgregor noted in the late 1940s the 'still formidable' figures for air pollution, one obvious manifestation being heavy fogs such as that of over three days' duration in Glasgow in 1929. This had coincided with both a frost and an influenza outbreak. Consequently, the city's death rate rose to a highpoint of 50.3 per thousand of the population, compared to an annual rate of 15.3.[73] Smoke pollution had been a concern from the late nineteenth century, as recognised by, for example, the 1897 Public Health (Scotland) Act.[74] It was, though, more systematically addressed after 1945 with smoke from domestic fires now identified as a major issue. The 1956 Clean Air Act was the key breakthrough. It allowed local authorities to establish smoke-free zones, Scotland's first being in the Sighthill district of Edinburgh.[75] A 1975 report remarked that the Act had engendered a 'great improvement . . . in most urban areas'. Nonetheless, more had to be done, especially given the pollution levels occurring in winter-time. 'Undesirable' levels of sulphur oxide had prevailed on more than five days in the Glasgow conurbation, Edinburgh, Dundee and Aberdeen.[76]

By the 1980s, this form of health hazard was virtually eradicated. Coatbridge, formerly one of its most polluted areas, became Scotland's first 'smoke free' town in 1969.[77] Clearly not all environmental issues had been resolved by 2000. The present Scottish Government argues that pollution 'to land, air and water can have serious health and environmental implications', hence the ongoing imposition of various 'regulations and strategies'.[78] But it is undeniable that the dense fogs produced by industrial and domestic coal use are now a thing of the past and that this is one undoubted improvement in the last century's everyday health experience.

The young in sickness and in health

We now focus on the sickness and health experiences of the young, a particularly vulnerable group. One early health intervention was the 1908 Education (Scotland) Act, which introduced both school meals and school medical inspection. Ill-nourished children, it was argued, could neither fully benefit from compulsory education nor be wholly efficient members of society in adulthood, able to contribute to the nation's economic and military requirements. As early as the 1880s, the Dundee School Board had (illegally) been providing over 8,000 free meals and another 24,000 at a halfpenny each. The passing of the 1908 Act attests to the poor nutrition and health of many children at this time.[79]

Nutritional and dietary problems nonetheless persisted. In the 1930s, John Boyd Orr experimented with the provision of milk to children in Scotland's largest urban areas. The results were a 'marked improvement' in health and in growth rates, especially for those from the poorest families. This was followed up by a wide-ranging survey which, Boyd Orr later claimed, showed that at least one-third of the population could not afford certain foodstuffs necessary for health maintenance. One consequence of these investigations was that local authorities were empowered to provide their pupils with cheap or free milk.[80] Alexander Macgregor noted in 1938 that some 100,000 Glasgow children in state-aided schools received one-third of a pint of milk daily, overall some 4,000 gallons.[81] All this in turn reflected a long-standing belief that milk was important to child growth; and, much more problematically, the increasing realisation that the urban Scot's diet was nutritionally inadequate. Surveys of inter-war Aberdeen and Peterhead revealed a 'very low fat intake' and 'dangerously low levels of calcium' intake, such data leading one historian to conclude that there was 'sub-clinical and even overt malnutrition in Scotland'.[82]

There can be little doubt that the provision of milk to schoolchildren, which lasted well into the post-war era, had a positive health effect. The Second World War itself was important for child health because of the experience of evacuation. Children in urban areas at risk from bombing were sent to safer, usually rural, locations. Many evacuees, although by no means all, came from deprived inner-city locations and their condition was the subject of much comment. *The Glasgow Herald*, for instance, noted in September 1939 that of some three and a half thousand children evacuated from Glasgow to Dumfriesshire, around one-third could not, after medical examination, be admitted to school because of vermin or disease.[83] Children from a 'very poor Roman Catholic school in a large Scottish city' relocated to Aberdeenshire had similar problems. Half had 'dirty heads', around one-third had impetigo, and one-fifth was incontinent in bed.[84] Such data reveal that for many pre-war children the daily experience of health, even when not threatened by major diseases, was at the very least uncomfortable and even debilitating. The conditions revealed by evacuation informed debates about post-war reconstruction.[85]

And for children there were, before drug therapies became available, very real threats from diseases such as diphtheria, poliomyelitis and rickets. The last of these was a deficiency disease and thus largely attributable to poor or insufficient diet. Ralph Glasser recalled of his inter-war Gorbals childhood that:

> Rickets was common. Many children had bone and joint deformities, bow legs, knock knees, limbs of unequal length. Some clanked along with a leg enclosed in iron struts from ankle to knee, or thumped the ground with an iron frame attached to the sole of a boot, a device to make a short or bowed leg function as though it were of equal length with the other. These were everyday sights.[86]

The post-war rise in living standards and creation of the Welfare State were crucial in the eradication of rickets.

The elimination of diphtheria and polio came by other means. In Edinburgh, over 350 diphtheria cases were notified in 1945, with thirteen fatalities. In the same year, though, over 11,000 schoolchildren were immunised against the disease.[87] Two years later, in common with other parts of central Scotland, the city experienced a serious polio outbreak. Just over 150 cases were notified, of which over three-quarters were children or young people, an age group which also suffered over a third of the nineteen deaths.[88] By the early 1970s, however, the capital's health authority was reporting that the 'control of killing and crippling infectious disease by immunisation in childhood is one of the significant medical achievements of the present century'. There had been no cases of diphtheria since the mid-1950s and none of polio since the early 1960s. Morbidity from other infectious diseases which particularly affected children, such as whooping cough and measles, had also sharply declined.[89]

If considerable advances were made in some areas of child health, others proved more intractable. A 1913 report noted that examination of various groups of Aberdeen children had shown that 'the percentages of bad teeth everywhere are enormous', with some revealing nearly half the children having five or more problem teeth. Tooth decay was not just a bad thing in itself, for '(s)eptic conditions of the mouth are among the commonest causes of bad health'. Alarmingly, the report argued that the idea that children consumed too many sweets was 'peculiarly inept'. Sugar was as essential a food as meat or bread, 'a physiological fact that might be inferred from the very strength of the appetite for sugar'.[90] The immediate pre-war era was nonetheless important. While attempts had been made in Dunfermline and Dundee to run school dental services, it was in 1913 that School Boards were formally enabled to undertake such work. In Leith, for example, a clinic was set up that year and in the first few months of its operation some 318 children were treated. Reflecting both the dentistry of the time and the scale of the problem, these children experienced between them over a thousand extractions but only 115 fillings.[91]

Such efforts notwithstanding, later commentators have continued to lament children's dental health. The Aberdeen MOH noted in 1966 that around two-thirds of children needed dental care; that this proportion was consistent; and that it was so 'simply because too many parents do nothing about their children's dental condition'.[92] This was despite a national dental health campaign the previous year which had complemented that under-taken in individual urban centres. Edinburgh, for instance, had set up its 'Mr Happy Smile' campaign in the early 1960s. The eponymous hero 'dressed in his outsize papier maché head, visited schools distributing tubes of tooth-paste, apples and other fruits and good dental advice'.[93] Even so, the city's MOH remarked a few years later that of 30,000 children recently examined, over three-quarters were found to need treatment, the efforts of the school dental service and NHS dentists notwithstanding. He found it 'most frustrat-ing' that, despite the high level of children experiencing dental decay, the 'strange' policy of allowing the provision of water 'grossly deficient in fluo-ride' persisted.[94] It is thus unsurprising to find the Scottish Home and Health Department remarking in the late 1970s that the country's dental health 'is internationally among the worst recorded'.[95] Child dental health remains a concern for the Scottish Government at the start of the twenty-first century. Discussing the vexed question of children's diets, it notes that consumption of nutritionally poor foods by the young, and the ensuing dietary imbal-ances, contributes not only to long-term problems such as diabetes but also to more immediate concerns such as 'poor dental health'.[96]

CONCLUSION

In many ways the everyday Scottish health experience has been, in the course of the twentieth century, one of continuous improvement. Life expectancy has increased and diseases once major contributors to high levels of morbid-ity and mortality have all but disappeared. Death in early childhood, the cause of so much anguish only one hundred years ago, has likewise become extremely rare. All this has come about through a combination of improved social conditions, advances in medical science, and the quality and quantity of healthcare provision – although historians continue to debate in what proportions.

However, some problems have persisted, albeit at a reduced level – for example, children's grim dental health record. Meanwhile, other ailments have come to the fore. We have noted Scotland's poor heart disease record and here we need to recognise the role of personal behaviour in matters such as tobacco consumption while also acknowledging that such activities are strongly related to social class. The broader context here is a society which retains significant social and health inequalities. Scotland's poor health

record is especially highlighted when set against that of comparable countries. At least until the economic crash of 2008, some Scots expressed the
desire to emulate the social successes of Scandinavian countries. As we have
seen in respect of health, this is nothing new and was based on the (generally
correct) perception of those nations' historically better health outcomes.
Scotland's aspirations in this respect have unfortunately not, as yet, been
realised.

Notes

1. This and the following paragraph are based on Drummond Hunter, 'Mental
   health', in Gordon McLachlan (ed.), *Improving the Common Weal: Aspects of
   Scottish Health Services, 1900–1948* (Edinburgh, 1987); and Jonathan Andrews,
   'The patient population', in Jonathan Andrews and Iain Smith (eds), *'Let There Be
   Light Again': A History of Gartnavel Royal Hospital from Its Beginnings to the Present
   Day* (Glasgow, 1993).
2. Cited in Andrews, 'The patient population', p. 114.
3. Sir John Boyd Orr, 'Scotland as it might be', in Alexander Maclehose, *The
   Scotland of Our Sons* (London, 1937), pp. 87, 84, 85, and Ch. VI passim.
4. James M. Mackintosh, *The Health of Scotland* (Edinburgh, 1943), pp. 7–8, 18,
   22.
5. John Stewart, 'The National Health Service in Scotland, 1947–1974: Scottish or
   British?', *Historical Research* vol. 76 (2003); and, idem, 'Hospitals, regions and
   central authority: issues in Scottish hospital planning, 1947 to 1974', in Margaret
   Pelling and Scott Mandelbrote (eds), *The Practice of Reform in Health, Medicine,
   and Science, 1500–2000* (Aldershot, 2005).
6. Parliamentary Debates, 5th Series, vol. 431, col. 995ff.
7. The Scottish Office: Department of Health, *Designed to Care: Renewing the
   National Health Service in Scotland* (Edinburgh, 1997), p. 1.
8. John Stewart, *Taking Stock: Scottish Social Welfare after Devolution* (Bristol, 2004),
   Ch. 5.
9. SHHD, *Doctors in an Integrated Health Service* (Edinburgh, 1971), p. 4.
10. Suzanne Cannegieter et al., *Understanding the Health of Scotland's Population in
    an International Context: Part II – Comparative Mortality Analysis* (London, 2003),
    p. 6.
11. www.scoltand.gov.uk/Topics/Health/Inequalites, accessed 9 May 2008.
12. T. C. Smout, *A Century of the Scottish People, 1830–1950* (London, 1986),
    pp. 43–44, 119.
13. A. Logan Turner, *The Royal Infirmary of Edinburgh: Bicentenary Year, 1729–1929*
    (Edinburgh, 1929), pp. 54–5.
14. Paterson et al., *Living in Scotland*, Table 2.9.
15. Scottish Hospital Centre, *Centrepiece: Collected Conference Reports, 1966*
    (Edinburgh, 1967), p. 36.
16. SHHD, *Health Services in Scotland: Report for 1969, Cmnd.4392* (Edinburgh, 1970),
    p. 1.

17. This is the 'McKeown Thesis' – see Bernard Harris, 'Public health, nutrition, and the decline of mortality: the McKeown thesis revisited', *Social History of Medicine* vol. 17, no. 3 (2004).

18. Mackintosh, *The Health of Scotland*, pp. 7–8.

19. Helen Dingwall, *A History of Scottish Medicine* (Edinburgh, 2003), p. 154.

20. City of Edinburgh, *Annual Report of the Health and Social Services Department for the Year 1967* (Edinburgh, 1968), p. x.

21. SHHD, *Health Services in Scotland: Report for 1975*, Cmnd.6506 (Edinburgh, 1976), p. 3.

22. Paterson et al., *Living in Scotland*, pp. 22–4, Table A8.5.

23. City of Edinburgh Charity Organisation Society, *Report on the Physical Condition of Fourteen Hundred School Children in the City* (London, 1906), p. 1.

24. SHHD, *Health Services in Scotland: Report for 1979*, Cmnd.7941 (Edinburgh, 1980), p. 3.

25. www.scotland.gov.uk/Topics/Health/health/Alcohol, accessed 11 August 2008.

26. Roger Davidson, *Dangerous Liaisons: A Social History of Venereal Disease in Twentieth Century Scotland* (Amsterdam, 2000), p. 323. The preceding part of this paragraph also draws heavily on this work.

27. Ronnie Johnston and Arthur McIvor, 'Marginalising the body at work? Employers' occupational health strategies and occupational medicine in Scotland, c. 1930–1974', *Social History of Medicine* vol. 21, no. 1 (2008), p. 131.

28. John Stewart, 'The provision and control of medical relief: urban central Scotland in the late nineteenth century', in Mark Freeman et al. (eds), *Medicine, Law, and Public Policy in Scotland, 1850–1980* (Dundee, forthcoming).

29. Stirling Council Archives, Hill and Robb, Solicitors, Deposit, PD 84 Box 3, Minutes of a Meeting of the House Committee, 23 October 1913.

30. Cited in Ian Levitt, *Poverty and Welfare in Scotland, 1890–1948* (Edinburgh, 1988), p. 157.

31. Edinburgh City Archives, SL 21/2/10, Minutes of Leith Parish Council, 9 January 1905.

32. British Parliamentary Papers (hereafter BPP), 1904, vol. XXXIII, Report of the Departmental Committee on Poor Law Medical Relief in Scotland: Volume 2: Minutes of Evidence, Qs.1632–1738.

33. Ian Levitt (ed.), *Government and Social Conditions in Scotland, 1845–1919* (Edinburgh, 1988), p. 150ff.

34. City of Glasgow, *Municipal Glasgow: Its Evolution and Enterprises* (Glasgow, 1914), pp. 216–17, 215.

35. Jacqueline Jenkinson, *Scotland's Health, 1919–1948* (Bern, 2002), p. 110ff.

36. Martin Gorsky, '"Threshold of a new era": the development of an integrated hospital system in Northeast Scotland, 1900–39', *Social History of Medicine* vol. 17, no. 2 (2004).

37. Political and Economic Planning, *Report on the British Health Services* (London, 1937), pp. 258, 251.

38. Mitchell Library, Glasgow, D-HEW 3/2/2, Minutes of Cathcart Parish Council, 3 April 1900.

..

39. E. F. Catford, *The Royal Infirmary of Edinburgh, 1929–1979* (Edinburgh, 1984), p. 17.

40. Derek A. Dow, *Paisley Hospitals: The Royal Alexandra Infirmary and Allied Institutions, 1786–1986* (Glasgow, 1988), pp. 38, 43.

41. Catford, *The Royal Infirmary of Edinburgh*, p. 10.

42. Dow, *Paisley Hospitals*, p. 33.

43. Martin Gorsky et al., *Mutualism and Health Care: British Hospital Contributory Schemes in the Twentieth Century* (Manchester, 2006), p. 72.

44. Dow, *Paisley Hospitals*, p. 41.

45. Gorsky et al., *Mutualism and Health Care*, pp. 136–7.

46. BPP, 1942–3, vol. IV, *Report of the Committee on Post-War Hospital Problems in Scotland*, Cmd.6472 (Edinburgh, 1943), pp. 4, 6, 17, 18, 30–1.

47. The following paragraph draws on Stewart, 'The National Health Service in Scotland'; idem, 'Hospitals, regions and central authority'; and idem, *Taking Stock*.

48. *Report of the Royal Commission on the National Health Service*, Cmnd.7615 (London, 1979), Table 3.2.

49. Scottish Hospital Centre, *Centrepiece: Collected Conference Reports, 1970* (Scottish Hospital Centre, 1971), sections 3.3–3.4.

50. http://www.scotland.gov.uk/Topics/Health/NHS-Scotland/community-hospitals, accessed 15 October 2008.

51. On National Insurance, see Bentley B. Gilbert, *The Evolution of National Insurance in Great Britain* (London, 1973).

52. James Hogarth, 'General practice', in Gordon McLachlan (ed.), *Improving the Common Weal: Aspects of Scottish Health Services, 1900–1984* (Edinburgh, 1987), p. 189.

53. Jennifer Dixon et al., 'Is the English NHS underfunded?', *British Medical Journal* 318 (1999), pp. 522–6; and Arturo Alvarez-Rosete et al., 'Effect of diverging policy across the NHS', *British Medical Journal* 331 (2005), pp. 946–50.

54. SHHD, *Doctors in an Integrated Health Service* (Edinburgh, 1971), p. 10.

55. Webster, *The Health Services since the War, Vol. II*, p. 21.

56. BPP, 1912–13, vol. XLII, Report of the Highlands and Islands Medical Service Committee, vol. 1, pp. 7, 9.

57. On the HIMS, see Jenkinson, *Scotland's Health*, Ch. 2.

58. Scottish Health Service Advisory Council, *Health Care Services in Remote and Island Areas in Scotland* (Edinburgh, 1995), p. 9.

59. Stewart, *Taking Stock*.

60. Trevor Austin, *The Story of Peel Hospital, Galashiels* (Bordersprint, 1996), p. 33.

61. *Report of the Royal Commission on the Housing of the Industrial Population of Scotland, Rural and Urban*, Cd.8731 (Edinburgh: HMSO, 1917), pp. 159, 166.

62. City of Aberdeen, *Report by the MOH for the Years 1940–1945* (Aberdeen, 1947), pp. 3–7.

63. Scott Wilson, 'The Public Health Services', in McLachlan (ed.), *Improving the Common Weal*, pp. 292–94.

64. Lewis Grassic Gibbon, 'Glasgow', in Lewis Grassic Gibbon and Hugh MacDiarmid, *Scottish Scene: or, an Intelligent Man's Guide to Albyn* (London, 1934), p. 137.
65. *Report of the MOH, City of Glasgow, 1949* (Glasgow, 1950), p. 9.
66. Archives of the Royal College of Physicians and Surgeons of Glasgow (hereafter RCPSG) 86/4/18, reprint of Sir Alexander Macgregor, 'Glasgow's Housing Problems', *Town and Country Planning*, 1945, p. 1.
67. City of Glasgow, *Glasgow's X-Ray Campaign Against Tuberculosis, 11th March – 12th April, 1957* (Glasgow, 1957), pp. 6, 7.
68. H. P. Tait, *A Doctor and Two Policemen: the History of Edinburgh Health Department, 1862–1974* (Edinburgh, 1974), pp. 62–5, 67.
69. City of Aberdeen, *Report by the MOH for the Year 1950* (Aberdeen, 1952), p. 24.
70. City of Aberdeen, *Report by the MOH for the Year 1964* (Aberdeen, 1965), pp. 4–17.
71. City of Aberdeen, *Report by the MOH for the Year 1962* (Aberdeen, 1963), pp. 2–3.
72. City of Aberdeen, *Report by the MOH for the Year 1966* (Aberdeen, 1967), pp. viii–ix.
73. RCPSG 86/4/19, Sir Alexander Macgregor, typescript 'Smoke and the Public Health', July 1947.
74. Scott Wilson, 'The public health services', in McLachlan (ed.), *Improving the Common Weal*, pp. 289–91.
75. Tait, *A Doctor and Two Policemen*, pp. 182–3.
76. SHHD, *Health Services in Scotland: Report for 1975, Cmnd.6506* (Edinburgh, 1976), p. 7.
77. Wilson, 'The public health services', p. 291.
78. www.scotland.gove.uk/Topics/Environment/Pollution, accessed 24 September 2008.
79. John Stewart, '"This Injurious Measure": Scotland and the 1906 Education (Provision of Meals) Act', *Scottish Historical Review* LXXVIII, 1 (1999).
80. Lord Boyd Orr, *As I Recall* (London, 1966), pp. 114, 116.
81. RCPSG 86/4/14, reprint of Sir Alexander Macgregor, 'Pasteurisation of Milk Supply', *Scottish Milk Trade Journal*, June 1938, p. 2.
82. D. J. Oddy, 'The paradox of diet and health: England and Scotland in the nineteenth and twentieth centuries', in Alexander Fenton (ed.), *Order and Disorder: the Health Implications of Eating and Drinking in the Nineteenth and Twentieth Centuries* (East Linton, 2000), pp. 57–8. On milk see, in the same volume, John Burnett, 'Glasgow Corporation and the food of the poor, 1918–24: a context for John Boyd Orr'.
83. *The Glasgow Herald*, 21 September 1939, p. 8.
84. Anon, 'Our evacuees: a social study by a Billeting Officer', *Aberdeen University Review* XXVII (1939–40), pp. 237–8.
85. John Stewart and John Welshman, 'The evacuation of children in wartime Scotland: culture, behaviour and poverty', *Journal of Scottish Historical Studies* vol. 26, nos 1 and 2 (2006).

86. Ralph Glasser, *Growing Up in the Gorbals* (London, 1986), p. 2.
87. City and Royal Burgh of Edinburgh, *Annual Report of the Public Health Department for the Year 1945* (Edinburgh, 1946), pp. 16, 4.
88. City and Royal Burgh of Edinburgh, *Annual Report of the Public Health Department for the Year 1947* (Edinburgh, 1948), pp. 8, 25.
89. City of Edinburgh, *Annual Report of the Health Department for the Year 1972* (Edinburgh, 1973), p. 6.
90. W. Leslie Mackenzie, *First Report of the Medical Inspection of School Children in Scotland* (London, 1913), pp. 84, 83, 85.
91. Tait, *A Doctor and Two Policemen*, p. 109.
92. City of Aberdeen, *Report of the MOH for the Year 1966* (Aberdeen, 1967), p. 107.
93. Tait, *A Doctor and Two Policemen*, p. 117.
94. City of Edinburgh, *Annual Report of the Health Department for the Year 1972* (Edinburgh, 1973), p. 7.
95. SHHD, *Health Services in Scotland: Report for 1978*, Cmnd.7607 (Edinburgh: HMSO, 1979), p. 5.
96. www.scotland.gov.uk/Publications/2008/09/12090355/8, accessed 15 October 2008.

Chapter 10

Passing Time: Cultures of Death and Mourning

E. W. McFarland

Rites of passage are our milestones in life.[1] Although the modern customs and ceremonies surrounding childbirth, coming of age or marriage may not always be recognised as such by society, they represent a diverse set of culturally prescribed rituals, typically accompanying changes in social or sexual status. According to the classic anthropological texts, they also have a strong functional component, typically affirming community solidarity, especially at times of transition and crisis.[2] As such, these practices offer an expressive vantage point on everyday life experiences and cultural values during periods of fundamental social and economic change.

The focus of this chapter is on death in twentieth-century Scotland. It considers the shifting framework of social behaviours, activities and settings, which have come to mark this final major turning point in the life cycle. Like other major life crises, the ways in which we handle death are bound up with a broad range of ideas and beliefs concerning, for example, the community, gender relations and the family.[3] Death is similarly eloquent on the relationship between the individual and the collective and between the private and public spheres. Yet, for a person this is hardly an 'everyday' event – on the contrary, it reveals an inevitable truth and strips away the routines of daily behaviour. Indeed, death is the ultimate rite of passage: it is universal and unavoidable; it undermines our sense of security, and it brings our efforts to create a meaningful personal and social identity to a very definite conclusion.[4] Death also differs from other rites of passage in that the dead person occupies a ritual status not as an 'actor', but an 'object', with funeral and mourning customs also directed at supporting the bereaved during a critical period of adjustment. Accompanying an event which entails fundamental questions of human existence, death customs have tended to be inherently conservative. Compared with childbirth and marriage rituals in Scotland, which were subject to significant renegotiation during the later twentieth century, and which came to draw more heavily on a secular framework of meaning and practice, Scottish funerals were slow to abandon a formal religious dimension, a feature which symbolically raises death from a natural to a 'spiritual' event, however tenuous the deceased's actual church connection.

Therefore, it is hardly surprising that the modern funeral in Scotland retained an outwardly familiar format, usually involving a combination of memorial service, committal ceremony and social gathering, which would have been recognisable to Scots at the beginning of the twentieth century. Yet the appearance of continuity is deceptive here. In fact, the century's closing decades witnessed a revolution in the cultural practices and behavioural codes associated with death and mourning. Although regional variations were evident, including a persistent gap between rural and urban experience, this was a concentrated process in which the 1970s stands out as a particular watershed. Once highly standardised and shaped by tightly prescribed protocols rooted in religious observance and social obligation, the funeral in Scotland began to emerge as a more diverse, consumer-driven 'performance', intended as a meaningful celebration of the life of the deceased. In addition, growing demands for personalised rituals were underpinned by the development of a highly sophisticated death management system, characterised by striking commercial, professional and technical development in the undertaking profession.

Commentators have identified a number of overarching and interlinked processes which have combined to shape the contemporary organisation of death and dying throughout western Europe and North America.[5] Some of them are incremental, bound up with long-term demographic patterns. Falling death rates, it is argued, have reduced our exposure to the physical reality of death in the family in the space of two or three generations. Equally significant is the process of rationalisation, gathering speed as modernity has advanced and reaching its highest level in the late twentieth century. Its effects have been witnessed in a variety of ways: the changing physical location of death; the medicalisation of the dying process; and the bureaucratisation and professionalisation of 'disposal'. The century's two world wars have also been credited with accelerating these processes in a dramatic fashion. In addition, the evolution of modern 'deathways' or death cultures has responded to the impact of rapid cultural change, particularly during the 1990s. Of considerable influence here has been the role of secularisation, evidenced in the waning influence of religious conventions in both the public and private realms. As well as encouraging the customisation and search for alternative meanings in funeral practices noted above, these processes have tended to diminish the role of the sacred in terms of the general experience of death, further shifting the symbolic boundaries which separate the dead from the living.

The specific Scottish experience of these developments has been largely ignored by scholars. Ethnographic material on Scottish customs and folklore certainly does exist, chiefly focusing on the nineteenth and early twentieth centuries, but there has been little systematic attempt to integrate this with broader areas of historical writing, tracing, for example, the impact of demographic pressures or the movement of ideas.[6] Nevertheless, modern Scotland offers a fascinating laboratory for the study of death cultures. Not only does death take place in a unique legal context, but the medicalisation of death which is such an important part of modern experience has also been shaped

by distinctive patterns of health provision, especially since 1945.[7] Specific
religious and cultural inheritances have also historically encouraged an emotional landscape in which, as some commentators suggest, reticence in the
face of bereavement has been positively valued.[8] Against this background, a
major task for the chapter is clearly to consider the continuing salience of a
'Scottish way of death' during the twentieth century.

Here, the subsequent discussion will draw significantly on oral history.
Although much of the century is already beyond the reach of this approach,
its techniques do prove useful not only reconstructing but also in interpreting the nature, meanings and significance of death customs from the 1950s
onwards.[9] Oral testimony is employed from two professions – funeral directors and nurses – who have been located in the front line of changes in the
social and cultural management of late twentieth-century death. Fieldwork
for the chapter involved interviews with funeral directors working in eight
firms, drawn from members of the National Society of Independent Funeral
Directors. Personal recommendation was also used. While two had started
up in business during the 1980s and early 1990s, the remainder were second-
or third-generation concerns, the earliest dating from 1907. In these cases the
personal experiences of respondents stretched back to the 1950s and 1960s.
In three cases interviews were conducted with contributions from other col-
leagues or family members engaged in the business – in two cases these were
women funeral directors. Interviews were also conducted with a sample of
five nurses, their backgrounds ranging from hospice care to district nursing
and acute hospital nursing. These were selected by personal recommendation and 'snowballing'. Their experience covered from the 1960s to the
present. Interviews with both groups took place in urban and rural contexts
in four key geographical regions: Glasgow and West of Scotland; Dumfries
and South-West Scotland; Edinburgh and Lothians; Highland Region.[10]
This is supplemented by documentary analysis, concentrating, for example,
on mortality patterns, the institutionalisation of death and the development
of funeral business networks. The first task, however, is to establish the basic
contours and changing social distribution of death in Scotland.

PATTERNS OF MORTALITY

While much contemporary writing stresses death's 'hidden' status in
modern society, it is actually through state agencies and the public realm
that death has been made formally 'visible' for most of the late nineteenth
and twentieth centuries. As Prior suggests, the emergence of attempts to
register and measure national rates of mortality represented a form of demographic bio-politics, driven by concerns to control and predict the fate of
populations.[11] The momentum of rationalisation continued to increase with
even finer instruments of measurement, such as crude death rates, infant
death rates and occupational mortality rates. In Scotland, the key legislation

underpinning this new social organisation of death was the 1854 Registration Act. Transferring the responsibility for registration from church to state, this Act placed a statutory obligation on individuals to register vital events and provided for the appointment of registrars in every parish. Since then, Scotland has enjoyed statistical indices of mortality in abundance.

At first sight the picture emerging from the official statistics seems one of unqualified improvement, keeping in pace with the advance of modernity. Against a background of rising living standards and improved medical and public health technologies, the crude death rate in Scotland (deaths per 1,000 of population) fell from 17.1 in 1905 to 11.7 in 2000. After a period of relative stability, this decline accelerated, so that by 2005 the lowest annual total of deaths was recorded in Scotland since civil registration began.[12] A dramatic decline in deaths from infections and epidemic diseases, and associated improvements in patterns of infant mortality, both undoubtedly played their part here: the crude rate of infant deaths during the century, for example, dropped from 116.2 per 1,000 live births in 1905 to 5.2 in 2001.[13] Above all, in common with most other western societies, death has now become increasingly associated with old age. About 60 per cent of deaths in Scotland in the early twenty-first century were of people aged 75 and over, compared with only 12.8 per cent a century before. Meanwhile, life expectancy for Scots has risen from 69.1 years for males and 75.4 years for females born around 1981 to 74.3 years and 79.4 years respectively for those born around 2004.

Yet, other trends are less positive, especially when set in a wider comparative context. Despite a century of falling mortality, Scottish men and women still have almost the lowest expectation of life at birth in western Europe.[14] Even within Scotland death is far from the great leveller that it is commonly represented. A total of eight Scottish council areas – most of them in west central Scotland – have a standardised mortality rate that is more than 10 per cent higher than the Scottish average.[15] The worst, Glasgow City, is 24 per cent higher than the Scottish average, which is itself around 16 per cent higher than the UK average. Above all, it is degenerative diseases which have become the most significant causes of death. By 2005, cancer in all its forms was responsible for 27 per cent of total deaths in Scotland, while ischemic heart disease accounted for 19 per cent. Since the 1980s, however, alcohol-related deaths have also been rising, particularly among the 45–59 age group. These continued to register an increase of 72 per cent between 1995 and 2005, while drug-related deaths also rose by 60 per cent during the same period, with 90 per cent of cases being of persons under forty-five.[16]

CHANGE BY UPHEAVAL?

Bureaucracy can measure and predict but not tame death. Nor can the scientific language of mortality statistics convey the private and public meanings of death and loss during a century of change. These meanings have been shaped by the ways in which the extended demographic transition has gradually post-poned death and stripped it of its everyday familiarity. However, illustrating the often paradoxical nature of society's engagement with death, the twentieth century also experienced a dramatic acquaintance with loss on a mass scale through the medium of modern warfare. This recurring external pressure also contributed to the continuing evolution of Scottish death culture.

It is precisely the background of falling mortality rates which made the losses of the First World War so agonising. The conflict, as Cannadine argues, had huge consequences for attitudes to death, encouraging a new 'cult of the dead'.[17] This emphasised shared, wordless grief for the military dead in a way that reduced the significance of 'ordinary' civilian death and challenged the elaborate mourning rituals which had traditionally accompanied it. Similarly, drawing on Australian experience, Jalland views the war as a watershed in the emotional history of death and grieving, ushering in a new model of stoicism and 'suppressed private grief', which supplanted established forms of Christian consolation.[18]

Some aspects of the Scottish war experience already stand out in sharp relief. For young Scots males, death now indeed became an everyday event, with the First World War killing around 10 per cent of those aged between sixteen and fifty.[19] Recent estimates place the total of Scottish dead above the generally accepted figure of 100,000, with most of the famous Scottish regiments, as front-line infantry units, suffering spectacular casualties.[20] Dying far from home, the absence of a deathbed, an accessible grave or even in some cases a body, at once undermined the rites which had traditionally surrounded death and mourning in Scotland. Ostentatious funeral display and intricate mourning etiquette had persisted for longer here during the Victorian and Edwardian period, despite being forsaken by the upper middle classes in the southern metropolis from the 1880s onwards.[21] While carefully choreographed funeral processions and graveside attendance under-lined the social worth of the deceased, these were also the product of an older collective impulse to care for the corpse on its last journey and support the bereaved by a display of communal solidarity.

The emotional dislocation which resulted in the absence of familiar conventions found voice in the poignant litany of *in memoriam* notices. The wife of Private William Irvine of Kilmarnock, who died of wounds at Gallipoli, reflected:

> Had I but seen him at the last,
> And watched his dying breath,
> Or heard the last sigh of his heart,
> My heart, I think, would not have held,
> Such bitterness and grief.
> But God had ordered other wise,
> And now he rests in peace.[22]

Scotland's response to this, like many other combatant nations, was to evolve new public rituals of mourning and commemoration. These found their most tangible expression in the construction of the National War Memorial at Edinburgh Castle, opened in 1928 to serve as a lament for the dead, 'in form and colour'.[23] This communal symbol of grief was soon given individual meaning as a site of pilgrimage, with simple lithographic prints of the memorial also hanging in many Scottish homes, where a family member was among the fallen.

Yet, if there is a resonance here with the broader western experience of public acts of commemoration, the relationship between soldiers' deaths and the changing cultures of civilian death in Scotland is more ambiguous. In particular, the extent of simplification in funeral rituals which followed in the aftermath of the First World War needs further systematic investigation. Certainly, the Scottish funeral industry does not seem to have been curtailed by any such demands, with the number of undertaking firms in Glasgow, for example, expanding by 30 per cent between 1918 and 1928.[24] Indeed, even the great influenza epidemic of 1919 could not dent the desire to maintain the familiar observances surrounding the decorous disposal of the dead. As one third-generation funeral director recalled, the pauper's pit burial was still one of the worst affronts to 'decency' in death, quite unmitigated by the recent experience of the mass disposal of military casualties. This was a prospect his grandfather was determined to avoid for his clients, even though the epidemic had wiped out entire families:

> One of the local solicitors . . . went to the workshop, and that's all they were doing was making coffins, and he said to my grandfather, 'Willie, you'll not get paid for some of these', and he says, 'I know, but we have buried the rest of the family so we have got to bury these'.[25]

The extent to which the experience of death in war rendered open grieving socially unacceptable and led to a new 'death denial', as in Australia, is also obscured in the Scottish case by a much older culture of emotional restraint. Writing in 1858, Dean Ramsay linked this to the salience of religious belief in traditional Scottish society:

> In connection with the awful subject of death . . . it has often been remarked that the older generation of Scottish people used to view the circumstances belonging to the decease of their nearest and dearest friends with a coolness which does not at first sight seem consistent with their deep and sincere religious impressions . . . It seems to me that this plainness of speech arose in part from the *sincerity* of their belief in all the circumstances of another condition of being.[26]

Nor does the First World War appear to have fundamentally undermined the salience of popular religious sensibilities in smoothing the final rite of passage. New forms of warfare had clearly challenged the Christian ideal of the 'good death', but some denominations were better placed than others to respond. The Roman Catholic Church, for example, possessed a clear set of rituals to deal with death, including sudden death. This meant Catholics did not require the notion of an 'immediate reward' for sacrifice on the battlefield, which came to dominate popular religious sentiment. In contrast, the First World War prompted a crisis of confidence among the mainstream Protestant denominations in Scotland over the ability of existing theology to address the challenge of mass bereavement.[27] Faced with grieving congregations, some churchmen were now increasingly forced to sanction the practice of prayers for the dead and even the doctrine of Purgatory. Also eloquent on the continuing search for spiritual consolation in the inter-war years were the war memorials which began to populate the civic landscape. Rather than sculpted military figures or allegorical forms, it was the cross, the symbol of sacrifice and resurrection, which constituted by far the largest single category of commemorative monument.[28]

The impact of the Second World War on Scottish death culture is even more difficult to specify, not least because the Scottish experience of this conflict is itself an underdeveloped field. Again, the war has been identified as a landmark in discouraging expressive mourning and promoting abbreviated death rituals.[29] For Scotland, the collective impact of military deaths was mitigated by a more random casualty pattern than in the First World War, so that mass mourning rituals were not repeated. Modern war did, however, further reduce the distance between the home front and the fighting front. The Clydebank air raid in 1941, for example, resulted in the highest density of damage suffered by any British town or city, illustrating the vulnerability of Scotland's tightly packed urban and industrial centres.[30] Yet, as death then became an unpredictable but insistent presence, the shortages and dislocations caused by war imposed restrictions on normal funeral practice. The use of horse transport for funerals was finally curtailed when the German occupation of the Low Countries blocked the supply of the black Friesian horses on which the trade had traditionally relied.[31] By the end of the war, the traditionally ornate Scottish coffin was also disappearing. This had changed little from the Victorian period, being hand-made of pine boards, covered in black, mauve or white cloth, and surmounted by a hand-painted name plate. In its place came a manufactured polished version, finished in 'English Elm or Oak', which would dominate the trade completely by the 1950s.[32]

Perhaps even more significant than the direct effects of war on death practices and attitudes was its indirect impact, through the fundamental forces for change that it unleashed. Most important was the new attitude towards the use of power by the national state, particularly in the areas of medical services, housing and town planning. The NHS hospital increasingly became the most likely place of occurrence for death – by 1956 two-fifths of all deaths in Britain occurred in this clinical location.[33] During the 1950s, modern council housing design and the dispersal of established communities

Figure 10.1 *The old 'Scottish way of death': funeral hearse in Edinburgh in the early twentieth century. www.scran.ac.uk.*

to new towns and peripheral estates were already imposing their own constraints on the funeral day. Families became less willing to accommodate the body prior to burial and lacked the traditional networks which had provided collective support.[34] Key elements of the 'modern' British funeral were now in place: removal from the hospital mortuary; shelter in the 'chapel of rest' and conveyance by the motorised hearse. A growing destination was the municipal crematorium, itself promoted under a post-war 'national plan' for crematoria to expand local authority provision in areas of proven need.[35]

Nevertheless, the depth of any cultural shift underpinning the Scottish experience of these developments is open to debate. At the core of death rituals remained the desire to restore dignity and identity to the deceased, while managing the emotions of the bereaved through a display of social solidarity. These codes of behaviour were structured by a shared understanding of 'decency' in the public and private treatment of the dead, which would have been familiar to nineteenth-century Scots. Not surprisingly, practices surrounding death, burial and commemoration that were designed to provide comfort, familiarity and reassurance proved inherently enduring. Moreover, formal church adherence and personal religious belief, which gave meaning to traditional observances, retained considerable strength in Scotland after the Second World War. Indeed, the ten years following the end of the war saw a striking increase in church connections, with the number of presbyterian communicants reaching an all-time peak by 1956.[36]

Against this background, Geoffrey Gorer's classic study of bereavement across Great Britain gives a fascinating snapshot of Scottish death culture in the early 1960s, following decades of social change.[37] He suggested that the British were no longer guided by social ritual on death and mourning, instead encouraging 'maladaptive' patterns of public denial, which divorced death from its natural emotion, which is grief. In Scotland, however, he found that the formal ritual of mourning had been more completely maintained.[38] Exposure to the physical fact of death, for example, was still widespread, with attendance at the death bed more common than in any other area of mainland Britain. The same was true of the practice of 'paying one's respects' – as viewing the body was termed – while burial continued to be strongly preferred to cremation in the proportion of two to one. Traditional public signs of mourning had also held their ground. The abandonment of distinctive mourning clothes had been a major change in British custom over the previous fifty years, but Scotland had one of the lowest proportions of those who rejected the practice: 43 per cent of Scottish men in the survey, for example, reported wearing a black armband or tie for weeks after the funeral, while 35 per cent of women continued to wear 'major mourning apparel'.[39] Abstention from social and leisure activities was reported by over a third of Gorer's Scottish sample, a custom which had practically disappeared in England. Grave visiting was more common, while stylised forms of condolence in the form of mourning cards were also more likely to be employed than elsewhere in Britain. One explanation, he believed, was Scotland's religious culture and the persistence of closer links between ministers and parishioners. Indeed, the Church of Scotland was one of only three 'communities' in his study whose members had shared protocols of mourning behaviour available to them, which were followed by a sizeable section of the group: these governed, for example, the structure of the funeral day, the length of the subsequent mourning period, and appropriate forms of behaviour towards the bereaved. The other communities similarly identified with prescribed mourning styles were Irish Catholics and Orthodox Jews, the latter exhibiting the most detailed 'cultural rules'.[40] In such company, the 'Scottish way of death' seemed a notable historical survival, still resisting the tendency of the post-war reconstruction to level out regional distinctiveness. Its fate in the later part of the twentieth century is the subject of the remainder of the discussion.

WHERE WE DIE

In the professional experience of the nurses and funeral directors interviewed in this study, changes to death culture and practices in Scotland had occurred very quickly. Innovations in the post-war period had accelerated during the 1960s, with the process of change picking up speed from the 1970s onwards. One unifying theme underlying these changes was a sharpening of the physical and symbolic boundaries between the living and the dead, with most Scots becoming increasingly sheltered from actually viewing the process of dying. Besides the impact of demographic change in identifying 'normal' death with old age, two more immediate sources of change identified were the intensified medicalisation of dying, coupled with further organisational and professional development in the funeral business. Both of these features appear bound up with a broader current of rationalisation, which has produced a greater degree of control and observation of the body in modern societies.[41] Indeed, further indicative of the fragmenting effects of this process were the separate worlds inhabited by the two sets of 'death professionals' – nurses and funeral directors – with a strict division of labour surrounding the preparation and disposal of the dead, which meant decreasing knowledge of each other's specialist role.

Less tangible, but equally profound, were the effects of another vital cultural process, that of secularisation. A range of factors undermined institutional religion in modern Scotland, including not only industrial decline and shifting settlement patterns, but also the liberalisation of culture and expanding recreational opportunities. Here scholars have particularly identified a 'moral turn' in the early 1960s, undermining the protocols of individual religious identity and halting the churches' cycle of renewal in Great Britain.[42] Unlike the sacraments of baptism and marriage, this process has taken some time to begin reshaping the Scottish way of death, as the cohort of Scots dying from the 1960s onwards had been socialised in an older culture of religious belief and observance, but its impact on funeral practice was reported by respondents to have become more visible during the last decade of the century. As will become evident, however, these tendencies do not constitute a simple progression to modernity. They are in themselves complex and ambiguous, while the recent tendency of 'modern' Scottish death culture to borrow traditional symbolism further qualifies the nature of change in the late twentieth-century experience.

Turning firstly to the advance of medicalisation, in Philippe Ariès' grim and sweeping thesis on the forbidden and pathologised nature of twentieth-century death, the role of the hospital as a controlling environment is assigned a privileged position. In this location, he suggests, where most now died alone, death had become a technical phenomenon rather than the occasion of a ritual ceremony: 'All these little silent deaths have replaced the great dramatic act of death, and no one any longer has the strength or patience to wait over a period of weeks for a moment which has lost part of its meaning.'[43] Given Ariès' tendency to generalise across cultures, it is important to consider how far the Scottish case fits this model of relentless rationalisation.

The basic contours of institutional change are fairly clear. The shift to hospital-based death which had already become established nationally in the post-war decades certainly gathered further momentum in Scotland from the 1960s onwards. Here a historically higher level of healthcare funding

Table 10.1 *Deaths in Scotland by place of occurrence, 1963–2003.*

Year	Home (% of total deaths)	NHS hospital (%)	Non-NHS hospital (%)	Other homes (%)
1963	46.1	49.5	1.7	2.3
1973	38.0	57.4	1.6	3.0
1983	34.5	61.2	1.4	2.8
1993	26.1	62.7	8.7	2.3
2003	23.1	60.1	14.3	2.0

Source: Table compiled from statistics on place of occurrence of death 1963–2003 provided by Registrar General's Office, Scotland.

than the rest of the Britain and a larger 'acute' general hospital sector combined with more general acceptance of the NHS settlement ensured that the displacement of the home as the site of death was particularly in evidence.[44] Indeed, the fall in deaths at home, outlined in Table 10.1, was even more rapid than in England and Wales.[45]

Despite changing patterns in the location of death, the NHS in the first decades of its existence, as Clark suggests, had offered little operational or strategic leadership on the care of the dying.[46] It was striking that those nurses interviewed who had qualified in the 1950s and 1960s had not been trained in handling death and bereavement, both experiences which appeared antithetical to the values of curative, technocratic medicine which had reached its peak of prestige in Scotland during these decades.[47] Instead, mechanisms of informal socialisation had developed, alongside a series of professional conventions and routines for managing death in a clinical setting.[48]

The first of these conventions was the importance of 'discretion' and 'privacy' – for example, screening the dying from other patients in a busy ward. One nursing auxiliary recalled practice in an acute medical ward in the 1970s, where on average there were two or three deaths a week:

> Well it was business as usual, is that a terrible thing to say? Life goes on, and you had to be discreet . . . and some of the patients would say, 'Oh, what's happened to the wee lady', but they knew, they actually knew, and we just said, 'Well, unfortunately, she passed away, you know.'[49]

The attendance of family members at the death bed was already in decline by this point – indeed the lack of engagement with patients' families was commented on by those accustomed to the more personal relationships encouraged in district nursing practice.[50] However, where staff ratios permitted, the hospital patient was not left alone, the dying process being closely monitored by staff. As the auxiliary went on to comment:

> That was one of the things, I think was kind of standard, but sometimes during the night when you knew the patient was dying, sometimes they would just sleep

away. There was always somebody there or thereabout checking on them, but sometimes if they were still alive at one point and during the night or even during the day, we would make them very comfortable.[51]

Following the formal declaration of death, the next stage was the initial cleansing and preparation of the corpse. Traditionally carried out by women in the family or the local community, the 'Last Offices' were now undertaken by female health professionals.[52] On their completion, the body could be viewed by the family behind a screen and later wheeled by porters to the hospital mortuary in a galvanised 'coffin'. One former orthopedic nurse described the intimacy of her part in these procedures:

> . . . the nursing staff then go in and wash the body and in those days [1960s] we had to pack all the orifices and they would have a shroud. They would be washed and dressed, orifices packed, eye lids closed, false teeth put back in, replaced and just the mouth would be closed to the best of our ability – sometimes that didn't work. And presented very peacefully, laid out on the bed and covered with a sheet.[53]

Yet, while ostensibly hygienic and practical in intent, some nurses practising in the 1960s and 1970s recalled enveloping the 'Last Offices' with a traditional Christian outlook: 'You get a sort of sense of peace. There is a sort of calm comes over you and you say well, there but for the grace of God go I, and that's how I feel about it . . . I always talked to them and I thought well, they are still human beings.'[54]

Perhaps medicine's historic replacement of the church as 'manager of death' during this period is best viewed against this background as a fluid and uneven process, with death spoken of in a range of 'languages', from the technical to the spiritual, sometimes simultaneously. However, even if such personal initiatives of emotional investment could soften rigours of 'acceptable' death in an institutional setting, this was not enough to prevent rising levels of dissatisfaction with terminal care provision in Britain from the 1960s onwards. This was prompted partly by earlier nationwide surveys, which had presented a distressing indictment of the social conditions of dying, not only in institutional settings, but also in unsupported home environments.[55] Also influential were emerging professional agendas, encouraged by new research into the dying patient's own experiences, which sought to invest dying with secular concepts of 'dignity' and 'meaning'. These promoted both an active approach to the palliative care of the dying and a growing appreciation of the need for a 'holistic' solution to address psychological as well as physical distress.

It was in this context that the modern hospice movement in Britain developed. Its emphasis was on non-hierarchical, multi-disciplinary treatment teams, viewing the patient *and* family as the unit of care, rather than the patient alone, as in conventional hospital-based medicine. Significantly, as Clark suggests, these initiatives also drew on earlier religious ideas of 'care

and solicitude, coupled with charitable endeavour', which challenged the
claims of scientific rationality and orthodox medical management of death.[56]
The movement made substantial progress in Scotland, where a number of its
most influential enthusiasts were motivated by a strong Christian commitment.[57] The first hospice had been opened at Clydebank as early as 1950 by
an Irish order, The Sisters of Charity, but modern provision developed in
two main phases. The initial take-off from 1981 onwards resulted in thirteen
new hospices or extensions, followed by a second wave of expansion in the
1990s, fuelled by matching funding from the Scottish Office, which produced
a further ten new foundations or extensions. Indeed, the rise from 1.4 to 14.3
per cent in the proportion of deaths in non-NHS hospitals between 1983
and 2003 (see Table 10.1) is largely explained by these initiatives, although
significantly home care also became an increasing feature of provision during
the 1990s.[58] Nursing in this new 'humanising' environment was particularly
rewarding for some respondents, restating the personal dimension of their
profession. As one former Marie Curie worker commented:

> Contact with people, just contact with people and sometimes they would spill
> out their problems and there again it was a kind of privilege if they felt they could
> talk to you. I mean you weren't going to solve their problems, but it was a leaning
> post.[59]

The personal connection between nurse and patient was often extended
beyond death. Some respondents commented that whereas the 'Last Offices'
became less widely practised in the hospital setting from the late 1980s, these
functions continued to be performed by specialist nurses in hospices or in
home care.[60] As one funeral director reflected, it seemed as if a pattern of
cyclical change in the site of dying and the handling of death was beginning to
assert itself, with a return to the home as the ideal site of the 'good death'.[61]
However, while the hospice movement may have extended good practice in
palliative care and nurse education to a wider audience, other commentators have suggested more pessimistically that it is becoming a victim of its
own success, facing the pressures of bureaucratisation and professionalisation implicit in managing a complex funding environment and delivering
externally driven standards of care.[62]

THE BUSINESS OF DEATH

Complementing the process of medicalisation, the evolution of the funeral
business in Scotland during the twentieth century can be interpreted as the
development of a sophisticated system for the disposal of the dead. The application of rational business principles to Scottish undertaking was already
well established in the Victorian era, with Scotland well in advance of the
rest of Britain in terms of trade associations and price cartels.[63] However, in
the next century – and again particularly from the 1970s onwards – the trade

was fundamentally reshaped by a new set of organisational, professional and technical changes, which affected its internal structure and operation.[64]

Funeral directing is a service industry, with all the usual characteristics of that sector.[65] Susceptible to variable levels of short-term demand, yet with high fixed overheads, the business during the late twentieth century became an increasingly resource-intensive operation, requiring a range of specialist staff and equipment.[66] These factors encouraged the concentration of ownership through a pattern of mergers and acquisitions, with larger firms achieving cost savings by managing funeral operations on a centralised basis. Indeed, during 1970 to 1994, this upsurge became the industry's most significant characteristic. By 1986, for example, the Co-operative Wholesale Society, which had entered the sector in the 1920s, was conducting 52 per cent of funerals in Glasgow and 32.8 per cent of all funerals in Scotland.[67] These multi-branch operations also began to adopt 'Fordist' production methods, establishing specialist functions and departments. Symptomatic of task fragmentation was the emergence during the 1980s and 1990s of the 'funeral arranger' – usually female – who became responsible for initial interaction with the bereaved family, while the funeral director – usually male – remained responsible for the actual conduct of the funeral.[68]

Yet, the full unfolding of the process of rationalisation faced resilient cultural barriers. As enquiries into the funeral business in the 1970s and 1980s demonstrated, the market for funerals remained essentially local, with price competition limited. In addition, the funeral was a 'distress purchase', with the patina of personal attention and 'reputation' still vital in gaining custom. These factors helped sustain and even expand the numbers of smaller independent enterprises from the 1990s onwards, especially in smaller towns and rural areas beyond the west central belt.[69] As an undertaker in a small town in central Scotland explained:

> the new generation coming up are more aware of ownership, I think because we have a Tesco and a Co-op these days and the small corner shop is disappearing very fast, people are looking towards that personal touch as far as the undertaker is concerned.[70]

Organisational change in the funeral business was also paralleled by the emergence of a more complex role for the undertaker as 'custodian of the dead'. The rise of 'expert knowledge' at the expense of the informal collective control over death and disposal, formerly exercised by the family and the community, has been a prominent theme in the twentieth-century history of death. In the Scottish case, this again appears to have gathered speed in the last three decades of the century, assisted by the twin processes of specialisation and professionalisation.

It was not until the 1950s that Scottish undertakers began to use the 'funeral director' designation, originally employed in the USA in the late nineteenth century; the first listing under the 'Funeral Director' heading in the *Glasgow Post Office Directory*, for example, was in 1950. The subsequent growth in the popularity of this nomenclature was indicative of the way that undertaking had developed from being a sideline of other trades to become a 'compassionate profession' in its own right. The shift in occupational description also underlined the increasing range of services offered to the bereaved – ranging from care of the body to arrangement of the headstone – which required increasing co-ordination. A Perthshire respondent explained:

> We are not even called undertakers now, we are called funeral directors, you know, even the word has changed over the number of years – now there are no undertakers, they are all funeral directors . . . An undertaker undertakes all the wishes of the family, where a director is someone who will put numerous things in place, and because obviously we specialise in funerals these days, that's why we're called funeral directors, whereas, the undertaker was joiner-undertaker, so that's how I believe things have changed now. There are very, very few joiner-undertakers now.[71]

Initially, the pattern of change across Scotland was uneven. The undertaking business in the south-west and the Highlands, both with lower population densities than the urban belt, proved most resistant to specialisation and professionalisation, but even here, respondents suggested, the pace of change seemed to have quickened during the 1980s. Both processes drew strength from a complex and highly controlled institutional and bureaucratic environment, governing the business of 'disposal'. This included a growing medico-legal system of documentation and stricter health and safety demands, operating at a national and even supra-national level. These considerations became even more important from the 1990s onwards, given the rise in drug-related deaths. As a Renfrewshire respondent confirmed:

> Regulations now are changing things . . . and, you know, we have got to be able to concentrate solely on these changes and all the demands of bereaved families and I don't know how anyone can actually do it – jump from a hammer and nail bag to become an undertaker . . . Health and safety is a big issue now, lifting especially, taking care of yourself and obviously your colleagues, regarding so many diseases today: Hepatitis, HIV . . . Where the old joiner used to get stuck in, no gloves, no protective clothing, these days are past.[72]

Allied to the changing legislative context was rapid technological development in the preparation of the body and in moving and handling techniques. Embalming was perhaps the most prominent example of scientific innovation, although again the spread of this practice appears to have been slow to develop across Scotland, partly reflecting a shorter time period between death and burial and cremation compared with England: traditionally, this had been around three days in the former case, as opposed to up to ten days or two weeks in the latter.[73] Taken together, these developments encouraged

an increasing emphasis on professional education, although practical training on the job is still felt to be important by funeral directors in developing
one's own 'style'.[74] At the same time, respondents noted that the profession
had also become more diverse from the late 1970s, attracting retired policemen and civil servants, for example, who were well placed to cope with
paperwork demands.[75] While still overwhelmingly male, more women also
began to enter the business, especially from the mid-1990s, in some cases
resulting in a gendered division of labour, as they worked largely with female
clients.[76]

The cumulative impact of these internal developments helped reshape
the daily working environment of the funeral director in the closing decades
of the twentieth century. This was reinforced by the changing use made
by families of professional funeral services at the point of bereavement, a
feature which in turn reflected the switch in the location of death from the
home to the institutional setting. Rather than laying out bodies at home, the
undertaker by the 1970s had become more accustomed to removing bodies
from the hospital mortuary, and by the 1980s and 1990s from the nursing
home. The proprietor of an independent family firm in Ayrshire, reflecting
on his experience over the last twenty years of the century, suggested that
this had placed his initial dealings with the family at a distance:

> Prior to that [referring to the 1980s] you would receive a phone call from 'the
> family' to say 'my mother has passed away, can you come up to this address and
> do what's necessary' . . . You asked for a white sheet, a pillowcase, you laid the
> body out tidily on the bed and you came away and then you came back the next
> morning with the coffin; you coffined the body, you set it up on trestles in the
> bedroom, and then come the day of the funeral, when the minister was arriving,
> you screwed the lid down, took the body away for burial or cremation. The point
> is that now you are not getting a phone call from the family. Most often, you are
> getting a phone call from the staff at a nursing home to say that 'Mrs So and So
> has passed away' . . . So you go to the nursing home, you haven't met the family;
> you've been out in the middle of the night, they've gone back home and you go
> alone and arrange the funeral next day.[77]

Increasingly, the destination following 'removal' was the funeral parlour. In
contrast to the stigma of the public mortuary, the provision of these commercial facilities was framed by a vocabulary structured around 'convenience', 'hygiene' and 'dignity', with funeral directors increasingly taking over
elements of the 'Last Offices'.[78] Clearly, the privatisation of family life had
left little space for the corpse, which as a result passed into the more complete custody of the funeral director. As a Greenock respondent explained:

> People have got kids running around the house and maybe don't want their kids
> seeing the coffin and things like that – oh I've seen four coffins in the house. I think
> it's modern not to go home, or people think it's 'modern' not to go home.[79]

Significantly, the practice of 'viewing' the body similarly almost ceased in some areas.[80] Where this persisted, embalming and other presentational techniques ensured that the deceased appeared suitably sanitised and indeed 'lifelike'. As one woman funeral director commented:

> It's up to ourselves to change the way they look and how the family remember them when they were alive. They are in a coffin – that's obviously something that can frighten people is a coffin – but nowadays there are so many colourful frillings and things like that which make things a lot nicer than they used to be done.[81]

This example from a small, modern funeral firm illustrates with some clarity that the business of the modern funeral director has now become that of an intermediary between the bereaved and the means of disposal, balancing demands of efficiency with the requirement to provide a caring, personal service. The overall effect, however, has been further to insulate modern Scots from the realities of dying and the dead.

CONSUMERS OF GRIEF

The funeral day has been described as a 'complex social drama' where elements of performance and ritual have traditionally been prescribed by social and religious convention.[82] The description of a funeral from the 1950s and 1960s from one undertaker from a long-established family firm in the south-west is worth quoting at length. The scenes have a timeless quality that would have been appreciated by earlier generations:

> We would go into the house and bring the coffin downstairs to the front room and it would be placed in the front room with the lid screwed down. Family and friends would then gather at the house for the service at the arranged time. The minister would come to the house and he would take the service in the house, quite often if there wasn't enough room in the house people stood outside. At the end of the service we would bring the coffin out of the house and into the hearse and then people would follow us up to the graveyard, whereupon we would, the interment would take place. But it was fairly short services – fifteen minutes in the house at the very most, because there wasn't any singing – it was normally just a reading from the Bible and prayers.
>   . . . at the churchyard the coffin would be carried by ourselves from the hearse to the grave and we would wait for people to gather round. Then we would pull the cords – there are eight cords on a coffin in Scotland – and we would call the numbers out . . . These people with the cords, would come forward and they would be lowering the coffin, but we actually have webs below the coffin and we would actually support the coffin and lower it with their help. The coffin is then lowered into the grave and we step back and the family members throw the cords in. They then step back and the Minister then does the committal part of the service . . . Then shovels full of soil are placed on to the top of the coffin at

different points, one at the head, one at the middle and one at the feet and then we would bow and step back and that's actually the official end of the service.[83]

However, the pressures which had already begun to transform the nature of the funeral director's work and business from the 1970s onwards would also combine with broader cultural shifts to influence the contours of their main 'product'. Again slowest to take off in the south-west and the Highlands, these changes would become more general across Scotland by the end of the century. While relatively minor in themselves, they threatened in combination to undermine the distinctiveness of the Scottish funeral. In some areas, for example, the weight of bureaucracy, particularly surrounding cremations, tended progressively to lengthen the time elapsing between death and the funeral.[84] The unique Scottish practice of offering the family cords was also targeted by health and safety legislation, which attempted to limit numbers around the grave.[85] In compensation, the figure of the lone piper did begin to appear at funerals during the late 1990s, but, unlike weddings in Scotland, the trappings of 'tartanry' did not extend to the final rite of passage to any great extent until the new century.[86]

Even more instrumental in changing the nature of the funeral day was the growing popularity of cremation over burial. All of the funeral directors interviewed noted that the balance began to shift from the late 1970s onwards so that the ratio at the end of the century stood at around two-thirds (cremation) to one-third (burial), although in some urban areas in the west of Scotland cremations accounted for 90 per cent of business. Various triggers have been suggested for this movement, such as the pressures on local authority burial land and the improvement of alternative disposal facilities, including an increasing input from large private funeral corporations.[87] Attitudinal change was also important. The Vatican Council's lifting of the prohibition on cremation in 1965, for example, formally cleared the path for Roman Catholic cremations, though some local clergy in Scotland remained resistant and uptake appeared slow to develop in scale until the 1980s.[88] Tenacious popular beliefs among Protestants regarding the necessity of bodily integrity for resurrection fell into more rapid abeyance, eclipsed by the desire to sanitise death through a final 'cleansing process'. Cremation indeed represented the highest stage of efficient, mechanised disposal, reducing the funeral involvement for undertakers to three hours, compared with six hours for a burial.[89] The highly controlled regulatory environment for death was also strongly evident here. European Community directives regarding environmental pollution, for example, meant that bodies could only be cremated wearing natural fibres.[90] Meanwhile, the location of facilities at a carefully prescribed distance from dwellings further underlined the physical boundary between the living and the dead.

The choice available between cremation and burial was symptomatic of a broader pattern of 'customisation' in the organisation of the funeral day.

This in turn reflected the impact of fundamental cultural change on death rituals. As Strange suggests, culture provides the resources through which we make sense of our emotional responses to death and loss – a feature which makes it often difficult to separate individual from culturally required mourning.[91] However, it can be argued that the balance between the individual and the collective contexts of mourning shifted in the last three decades of the twentieth century. This was a feature of most western countries, particularly northern European ones, and for Elias reflected a more general shift in social 'habitus' in which the 'I-identity' of individuals assumed a stronger emotive charge than the traditional 'We-identity'.[92]

Most significantly, the declining dominance of religious protocols for handling death left a vacuum in which individuals were required to shape their own rituals or invest existing ones with new meanings. In the Scottish case, we can trace here the effects of the rupture in formal church adherence, which began in the Protestant denominations in the 1960s and extended to Roman Catholicism in the 1970s. Yet, whereas baptisms declined sharply, with a 67 per cent fall in the Church of Scotland between 1961 and 1990, the impact on funerals was slower to develop, keeping pace with generational change. As the national church with a mission to serve the whole territory of Scotland, the Church of Scotland is empowered by its Declaratory Acts to conduct funeral services for those in its local parishes who request them. However, while older Scots, born in the first three decades of the century, may have chosen a traditional religious funeral as the last public expression of their Christian conviction, families had now come increasingly to view this as the 'default option' for their deceased relatives. As one Edinburgh undertaker of over twenty years' experience explained, '. . . sometimes almost as a panic measure people say, "we better go to the church". It's what they remember from a long time ago and it's the way they think they ought to turn.'[93]

In the face of falling popular allegiance, church ministers were also forced to adopt a more flexible and accommodating attitude to the needs of the 'unkirked'.[94] Despite these efforts, all of the funeral directors interviewed reported an increase in humanist funerals, especially from the mid-1990s. Indeed, the Humanist Society of Scotland reported a tenfold increase in these ceremonies since it began keeping records in 1998, with over 1,800 performed in the course of 2005 alone.[95] The Christian monopoly of death rites has also been challenged by Scotland's emergence as an increasingly multi-ethnic society, although the age structure of its minority communities and the frequent practice of repatriating bodies for burial has limited the rise of 'alternative religious funerals' for the present.[96]

Even where a Christian religious funeral was retained in the late twentieth century, families were anxious to individualise the format of the service – although the traditional Roman Catholic funeral mass left less space for these initiatives.[97] As another funeral director from a long-established family firm reflected:

I think people are looking for a much more personal tribute to the family member that they have lost. They want it to reflect the person's life and beliefs . . . Traditionally you went to the parish minister and they really took control and they told you this is how things will be done . . . It's what the family wants, not what the minister wants, but what the family want for that person.[98]

However, in avoiding prescription and attempting to exercise 'choice', families discovered that new secular codes were required to replace the shared understandings that would have formerly shaped socially acceptable mourning.[99] Funeral directors now found themselves increasingly slipping into a delicate, informal guidance role:

when folk are very emotional, they start to think emotional things that mum or dad would love and sometimes it gets totally out of control [. . .] But as long as you have a solution that is practical then it gets you off the hook. Sometimes you've not and you've got to do as they ask, and it's not the best.[100]

A further powerful source of new mourning repertoires during the 1990s was the media – one Ayrshire cremation, for example, featured the theme of *Casualty* as an *introit* for the coffin.[101] As another respondent explained, national TV coverage raised general expectations of the undertaker's role:

There have been so many programmes on TV regarding undertakers . . . the general public are actually getting more insight. Families are actually becoming more demanding in a way. People always want more of the undertaker because of these programmes on TV. They obviously see that they can have horse-drawn hearses; they can have floral tributes saying, 'mum, dad, whatever' on them; they can have a large reception after the funeral. Everything has got to be done differently from when you were invited back to the scullery in the family home.[102]

Yet as consumer choice made the funeral day in Scotland an increasingly diverse experience, some unifying themes remained evident. In the first place, the active participation of families in the arrangement of the funeral was carried on into the conduct of the actual event. This is well illustrated by the process of changing gender roles on the funeral day. Whereas women in Scotland had traditionally been excluded from the cemetery and were expected to prepare the funeral meal in the home, they became progressively more involved at all levels of the proceedings. This had begun with simple graveside attendance, dated by most respondents as beginning in the 1960s or 1970s, but was extended during subsequent decades to include the taking of cords at the grave and the delivery of eulogies.[103] Again, the process was subject to geographical variation, with the various Presbyterian communities of the Highlands and Islands being the most resistant to active female participation.

Secondly, as the sacred realm surrounding death began to retreat, the funeral was increasingly viewed as a celebration of the life of the deceased rather than a formal committal of remains. This left little space for social mourning obligations, such as the wearing of dark clothes, which once bestowed public recognition of loss and grief.[104] Instead the 'performance' element of the funeral day was enhanced. The shift was aided partly by technical innovations, such as modern sound systems and CDs, but also featured the borrowing of funeral symbolism of the past.[105] Some funeral directors, for example, adopted more elaborate dress and accessories during the 1990s, including top hats and silver canes, while their older dramaturgical role as 'master of ceremonies' was also revived in some areas through the reintroduction of traditional practices such as 'paging', where the undertaker solemnly precedes the hearse on foot.[106] Yet, the reinvention of mourning as a public ritualised activity took place within definite boundaries. The ability of the funeral earlier in the twentieth century to claim the streets and halt routine activity as a mark of respect, was now firmly curtailed by modern traffic management systems.[107]As an Ayrshire funeral director who had begun the paging practice in the mid-1990s explained, this dignified practice had originally been intended as a statement of the 'worth' of the deceased, but it now also performed the simple expedient of ensuring that the modern driver gives way to the funeral cortège.[108]

CONCLUSION

Death practices in twentieth-century Scotland faced decades of exposure to broader structural and cultural change, which accelerated and intensified from the 1970s onwards. Above all, it was the cumulative impact of processes of rationalisation and secularisation which came to determine where Scots died, how they were disposed of, and who mourned them. Amid greater diversification of practice, it became increasingly difficult to specify a distinctively 'Scottish' experience of death in the family and community setting. Most notably, the new personalised rituals of funeral observance left little space for the collective codes of reticence and stoicism which traditionally shaped Scottish mourning custom. Indeed, there was widespread agreement among interviewees from both nursing and undertaking that grief in Scotland had become more expressive towards the end of the century. One funeral director who entered the business in the 1950s reflected on how this pattern had cut across gender identities:

> it's become far more natural for people to express their grief . . . now as many men as women show emotion and become very distressed and yes it has changed. You can see that quite a lot actually. There is far more emotion shown at funerals than there used to be by both sexes, but woman do cope with it better actually, even though they are emotionally upset. You can have a man who just can't cope at times; most women do cope unless it's very sad circumstances like a baby or a child . . . but there is far more emotion.[109]

This new openness was attributed by some respondents to the loosening cultural grip of Presbyterianism, with its emphasis on individual self-control.[110] However, while Roman Catholics were thought to cope better with death due to their retention of a traditional ritual framework, it was less clear to one Renfrewshire funeral director how this situation would survive the pressures of further secularisation:

> Now, if you've not got the faith then you have nothing to cling onto . . . but I find Catholics have got that. Now, I think thirty years down the line, they won't because there are not so many of them at Church and not as many of them accepting the faith as is. So I think it will probably change again.[111]

The characteristic 'hidden' or 'taboo' status which death had once possessed in Scottish society was also felt to have weakened. As an experienced funeral director from the south-west commented:

> I think far more people are involved in the whole process from younger people to older people. I think you know in years gone by it wasn't talked about when granny was ill, but that was it, but now young people realise exactly what is happening and are involved more. We have a lot more children coming to funerals now than was the case in the past. You didn't get very many children attending, but now there are more, not every funeral, but quite a few.[112]

There are other indicators of the rising visibility of death in modern Scotland. Personal loss is no longer a prerequisite of grieving. Scots have become enthusiastic participants in the mass mourning which has swept Britain periodically from the late 1980s, following incidents such as the 1988 Lockerbie disaster and the 1996 Dunblane school shooting.[113] Individual sites of violent and untimely death are also liable to be transformed by floral tributes into wayside 'shrines', sometimes interpreted as a new medium for communicating an older collective solidarity with the bereaved.[114] On a more practical level, regular charity events on behalf of local hospices cannot conceal that it is the provision of support for the terminally ill which lies at the heart of their activities.

And yet 'death' in these contexts remains to a large degree abstract, given that our exposure to its physical realities has become increasingly limited. Even the 'funeral pre-paid planning' schemes, which grew in popularity during the late 1990s, offer 'death delayed' in the shape of an inflation-proof funeral that will cost your family no more, 'in even twenty or thirty years time'.[115] Moreover, while sensitive medical intervention and compassionate funeral care may have soothed some of our apprehensions of mortality, they have been less successful in checking a new cultural terror which has gained ground towards the end of the twentieth century – that of 'social death', of ostracism from family and friends in care homes, or even their own home. The fear of being trapped in a body that refuses to die is the underside of the cumulative improvements in healthcare and the changing distribution of biological death that have been a hallmark of the century, in Scotland as in other developed societies.[116] It is this gradual withdrawal from social existence prior to clinical extinction which provides a last ironic counterpoint to human attempts at dominion over death.

Notes

1. The research for this chapter was supported by a grant from the Wellcome Trust. Thanks are due to Dr Hilary Young for her excellent assistance with fieldwork. I am also very grateful to Ronnie Johnston for his comments on the piece.
2. A. Van Gennep, *The Rites of Passage* (Chicago, 1960); R. Hertz, *Death and the Right Hand* (Glencoe, 1960).
3. J. Strange, *Death, Grief and Poverty in Britain, 1870–1914* (Cambridge, 2005), p. 14. See also L. Prior, *The Social Organisation of Death* (London, 1989).
4. See A. Giddens, *Modernity and Self-Identity* (Cambridge, 1991); P. Mellor, 'Death in high modernity: the contemporary presence and absence of death', in D. Clark (ed.), *The Sociology of Death* (Oxford, 1993); C. Shilling, *The Body and Social Theory* (London, 2003).
5. P. Ariès, *Western Attitudes towards Death: From the Middle Ages to the Present* (Baltimore, 1974), and *The Hour of Our Death* (Harmondsworth, 1981). Note also M. Vovelle, 'On Death', *Ideologies and Mentalities* (Cambridge, 1990); P. Chaunu, *La Mort au Paris* (Paris, 1978). For British examples, see G. R. Richardson, *Death, Dissection and the Destitute* (Harmondsworth, 1987); S. M. Barnard, *To Prove I'm Not Forgot: Living and Dying in the Victorian City* (Manchester, 1990); M. Wheeler, *Death, Heaven and the Victorians* (Cambridge, 1994); E. Schor, *Bearing the Dead: The British Culture of Mourning from the Enlightenment to Victoria* (Princeton, 1994); P. Jalland, *Death in the Victorian Family* (Oxford, 1996).
6. M. Bennett, *Scottish Customs from the Cradle to the Grave* (Edinburgh, 1992); A. Gordon, *Death is for the Living* (Edinburgh, 1984).
7. The dimension of registration, for example, has been highlighted in the current Wellcome-funded 'Scottish Way of Birth and Death' project. For the NHS background, see J. Stewart, 'The National Health Service in Scotland: Scottish or British', *Historical Research* vol. 76, no. 193 (August 2003); D. McCrae and W. Morrice, *The National Health Service in Scotland. Origins and Ideals* (East Linton, 2002).
8. R. Finlay, *Modern Scotland 1914–2000* (London, 2003), p. 119.
9. See R. Perks and A. Thomson (eds), *The Oral History Reader* (London, 1998); J. Bornat (ed.), *Oral History, Health and Welfare* (London, 2000).
10. Respondents were interviewed employing a dedicated semi-structured questionnaire probing changes and continuities in their roles and experiences.
11. Prior, *Social Organisation*, p. 9.
12. The total number of deaths that year numbered 55,747. All statistics taken from *Scotland's Population (2006): The Registrar General's Annual Reviews of*

Demographic Trends (2007). See also C. E. V. Leser, 'Births and deaths', in A. K. Cairncross (ed.), *The Scottish Economy: A Statistical Account of Scottish Life by Members of Glasgow University* (Cambridge, 1954), pp. 21–5.

13. In 1905, 96 per cent of deaths from whooping cough and 93 per cent of deaths from measles involved children under five: *Scotland's Population (2006).*

14. For both sexes, the expectation of life is about four years lower than the countries with the highest expectation of life: *Scotland's Population (2006).*

15. Standardised Mortality Rates (SMRs) are calculated to compensate for the fact that men and women have different death rates and that these rates also vary by age.

16. General Registrar for Scotland's Office, *Drug-Related Deaths in Scotland 2002:* http://www.gro-scotland.gov.uk/statistics/publications

17. D. Cannadine, 'War and death, grief and mourning in modern Britain', in J. Whaley (ed.), *Mirrors of Mortality: Studies in the History of Death* (London, 1981), p. 230.

18. P. Jalland, *Changing Ways of Death in Twentieth Century Australia* (Sydney, 2006).

19. T. C. Smout, *A Century of the Scottish People, 1830–1950* (London, 1986), p. 267.

20. T. Royle, *The Flowers of the Forest. Scotland and the First World War* (Edinburgh, 2006), p. 284.

21. E. McFarland, 'Researching, death, mourning and commemoration in Scotland', *Journal of Scottish Historical Studies* vol. 24, no. 1 (2004), p. 41.

22. *Kilmarnock Standard,* 10 July 1915.

23. Sir Lawrence Weaver, *The Scottish National War Memorial* (London, 1927).

24. Mitchell Library, Glasgow, *Glasgow Post Office Directories 1918–39.* One funeral director interviewed also commented on the dense distribution of undertaking firms in the Old Town of Edinburgh during the 1920s, when his grandfather had set up in business: Scottish Oral History Centre Archive (SOHCA), University of Strathclyde, Death in Scotland Project (SOHCA, DSP), Interview FD 7.

25. SOHCA, SOHCA, DSP, Interview FD 5.

26. *Reminiscences of Scottish Life and Character* (Edinburgh, 1909), pp. 75–7.

27. J. L. Macleod, '"Greater love hath no man than this": Scotland's conflicting religious responses to death in the Great War', *Scottish Historical Review,* vol. LXXXI, 1, no. 211 (2002), pp. 70–96. These practices were strongly resisted by some sections of Protestant opinion: see *Life & Work,* February 1966, for opposition to 'Popish practices' at the graveside in a Highland parish as late as the 1930s.

28. The UK National War Memorials Inventory records 283 of these Great War crosses in Scotland, almost 40 per cent of all free-standing memorials: http://www.ukniwm.org.uk For a comparative perspective, see T. Kselman, 'The de-Christianisation of death in modern France', in H. McLeod and W. Ustorf (eds), *The Decline of Christendom in Western Europe 1750–2000* (Cambridge, 2003), pp 145–62.

29. See G. Howarth, 'Professionalising the funeral industry 1700–1960', in P. C. Jupp and G. Howarth (eds), *The Changing Face of Death,* pp. 126–7.

30. Finlay, *Modern Scotland*, p. 86.

31. Howarth, 'Professionalising the funeral industry', p. 131 According to one Edinburgh respondent, the horse-drawn hearse had already been dying out in his grandfather's time in the late 1930s: SOHCA, DSP, Interview FD 6.

32. SOHCA, DSP, Interview FD 5. Black denoted a deceased male, mauve a female and white a child.

33. *Peace at the Last. A Survey of Terminal Care in the United Kingdom*, A Report to the Calouste Gulbenkian Foundation 1960 (London, 1960), p. 15.

34. P. C. Jupp and T. Walter, 'The healthy society: 1918–98', in P. C. Jupp and G. Gittings (eds), *Death in England. An Illustrated History* (Manchester, 1999), p. 262.

35. Jupp and Walter, 'Healthy society', pp. 264–6.

36. C. Brown, *Religion and Society in Scotland since 1707* (Edinburgh, 1997), p. 162.

37. G. Gorer, *Death, Grief and Mourning in Contemporary Britain* (London, 1965).

38. Gorer, *Death, Grief and Mourning*, p. 41.

39. Gorer, *Death, Grief and Mourning*, pp. 51, 76, 143.

40. Gorer, *Death, Grief and Mourning*, p. 63.

41. N. Elias, *The Loneliness of the Dying* (Oxford, 1985).

42. C. Brown, *The Death of Christian Britain* (London, 2001), p. 2.

43. Ariès, *Hour of Our Death*, pp. 87–9.

44. For the Scottish NHS background, see D. Carter, 'Scotland's acute hospital services', in K. Wood and D Carter (eds), *Scotland's Health and Health Services* (London, 2003). McCrae suggests that in 1948 Scotland had a hospital bed complement 15 per cent greater than in England and Wales, *National Health Service*, p. 244.

45. For comparative data on England and Wales, see D. Field and I. Johnson, 'Volunteers in the British hospice movement', in Clark, *Sociology of Death*, pp. 198–217.

46. D. Clark, 'Cradled to the grave? Terminal care in the United Kingdom, 1948–67', *Mortality* vol. 4, no. 3 (1999), p. 226.

47. SOHCA, DSP, Interviews N 1, 2 and 3.

48. SOHCA, DSP, Interviews N 1, 2 and 3.

49. SOHCA, DSP, Interview N 1; and see Interview N 5.

50. SOHCA, DSP, Interview N 2.

51. SOHCA, DSP, Interview N 1.

52. For traditional practices, see SOHCA, DSP, Interview FD 2.

53. SOHCA, DSP, Interview N 2.

54. SOHCA, DSP, Interview N 2.

55. *Peace at the Last* (Gulbenkian Report); Joint National Cancer Survey Committee of the Marie Curie and the Queen's Institute of District Nursing, *Report on a National Survey Concerning Patients with Cancer Nursed at Home* (London, 1952).

56. Clark, 'Cradled to the grave?', pp. 242–3.

57. D. Clark, N. Small, M. Wright, M. Winslow and N. Hughes, *A Little Bit of Heaven for the Few. An Oral History of the Modern Hospice Movement in the United Kingdom* (Lancaster, 2005), p. 33.

58. Compiled from 'Timeline of Hospice Development', The Hospice History Programme, Lancaster University: http://www.hospice-history.org.uk/timelinemain.htm

59. SOHCA, DSP, Interview N 1; and see Interview N 5.

60. SOHCA, DSP, Interviews FD 5 and 6.

61. SOHCA, DSP, Interview N 2.

62. SOHCA, DSP, Interview N 4: the respondent suggested that while training for nurses in preparing patients and their families for the dying process, it did not equip nurses in handling their own responses to death. For more negative developments in the hospice movement, see N. James and D. Field, 'The routinization of the hospice: charisma and bureaucratisation', *Social Science and Medicine* 34 (1992), pp. 1363–75.

63. McFarland, 'Researching death, mourning and commemoration', pp. 20–44.

64. See, for example, The Price Commission, *Funeral Charges* Report no. 22 (HMSO, 1977). For a fuller discussion, see E. W. McFarland, 'Working with death: an oral history of funeral directing in late twentieth-century Scotland', *Oral History* vol. 36, no. 11 (2008), pp 58–69.

65. B. Parsons, 'Change and development in the British funeral industry during the 20th century, with special reference to the period 1960–1994', PhD thesis, University of Westminster, 1997, p. 99.

66. The funeral directors interviewed in this survey emphasised this element of their work: their firms averaged two to three funerals per week, but frequently had five per week, or none.

67. The Monopolies and Mergers Commission, *Cooperative Wholesale Society Limited and the House of Fraser PLC. A report on the acquisition by the CWS of the Scottish Funerals Business of the House of Fraser PLC* (London, 1987), p. 4.

68. SOHCA, DSP, Interview FD 3.

69. Price Commission, *Funeral Charges*, para 8:7; Parsons, 'Change and development in the British funeral industry', p. 158.

70. SOHCA, DSP, Interviews FD 3 and FD 4.

71. SOHCA, DSP, Interview FD 3.

72. SOHCA, DSP, Interview FD 4.

73. Embalming seems to have got underway in Britain during the 1950s. A National Association of Funeral Directors survey in 1967 revealed, however, that while 52 per cent of bodies were embalmed on average, this dropped to 12 per cent in Scotland: Parsons, 'Change and development in the British funeral industry', p. 96.

74. SOHCA, DSP, Interview FD 3.

75. SOHCA, DSP, Interview FD 5.

76. SOHCA, DSP, Interview FD 4.

77. SOHCA, DSP, Interview FD 1.

78. For background, see Howarth, 'Professionalising the funeral industry', pp. 130–1.

79. SOHCA, DSP, Interview FD 4.

80. SOHCA, DSP, Interviews FD 2 and FD 4.

81. SOHCA, DSP, Interview FD 3.

82. D. L. Steinberg and A. Kear (eds), *Mourning Diana: Nation, Culture and the Performance of Grief* (London, 1999), pp. 3–4.

83. SOHCA, DSP, Interview FD 5. See also Interview FD 2 for Highland variations.

84. SOHCA, DSP, Interview FD 6. Respondents suggested that average time lapse has shifted from 2–3 days to 4–5. But for variations in local practice, see SOHCA, DSP, Interview FD 1.

85. SOHCA, DSP, Interview 5.

86. Following the precedent of military and state funerals, funeral pipers are now becoming increasingly available for hire both north and south of the border. Laments are played outside the crematorium or at the graveside, or can be incorporated during the service: http://www.scotiapipers.co.uk/funeral.htm

87. See P. C. Jupp, *From Dust to Ashes. Cremation and the British Way of Death* (London, 2006). Unfortunately, the study does not cover Scotland.

88. SOHCA, DSP, Interview FD 5.

89. SOHCA, DSP, Interview FD 3.

90. SOHCA, DSP, Interview FD 5.

91. Strange, *Death, Grief and Poverty*, p. 15.

92. N. Elias, *The Society of Individuals* (Oxford, 1991).

93. SOHCA, DSP, Interview FD 6.

94. SOHCA, DSP, Interview FD 5. See *Life & Work*, July and October 1970 for early debates over services for 'unbelievers'.

95. *Humanist Living*, Spring 2006.

96. See Interview FD 3. For plans to establish a Muslim cemetery near Glasgow, see *Glasgow Herald*, 23 August 2007.

97. SOHCA, DSP, Interview FD 4.

98. SOHCA, DSP, Interview FD 3. The same respondent noted that consumer choice had equally extended to the disposal of cremated remains. Besides the traditional 'garden of remembrance' these could now be placed in casket plots in conventional cemeteries or scattered at a location with sentimental associations of the deceased. They could even be made into fireworks or jewellery.

99. C. Wouters, 'The quest for new rituals in dying and mourning: changes in the we-I balance', *Body and Society* vol. 8, no. 1 (2002), pp. 1–27.

100. SOHCA, DSP, Interview FD 4; see also Parsons, 'Change and development in the British funeral industry', p. 265.

101. SOHCA, DSP, Interview FD 1.

102. SOHCA, DSP, Interview FD 3.

103. SOHCA, DSP, Interviews FD 2 and 6. Formerly, a unique Scottish custom was to cut the tassels from the coffin cord and bring these back for female relatives. In time, they would be buried themselves with these keepsakes – in some cases elderly women were buried who had collected five or six.

104. SOHCA, DSP, Interview FD 2.

105. See J. Dollimore, *Death, Desire and Loss in Western Culture* (London, 2001), p. 21.

106. SOHCA, DSP, Interview FD 1.
107. SOHCA, DSP, Interview FD 5.
108. SOHCA, DSP, Interview FD 1.
109. SOHCA, DSP, Interview FD 6.
110. SOHCA, DSP, Interview N 1.
111. SOHCA, DSP, Interview FD 4.
112. SOHCA, DSP, Interview FD 5.
113. S. Greenhalgh, 'The ambiguous politics of Diana's floral revolution', in Steinberg and Kear (eds), *Mourning Diana*, pp. 40–59.
114. G. Monger, 'Modern wayside shrines – floral tributes – in response to Tony Walters', *Folklore* vol. 107 (1997), p. 106.
115. SOHCA, DSP, Interviews FD 2 and FD 6. For examples, see http://www.co-operativefuneralcare.co.uk
116. Indeed, it is women, who have benefited most from the expansion of human life expectancy, who are precisely those most likely to suffer social death in its prolonged form: M. Mulkay, 'Social death in Britain', in Clark, *Sociology of Death*, pp. 31–49.

Further Reading

INTRODUCTION: CONCEIVING THE EVERYDAY IN THE TWENTIETH CENTURY

For an introduction to the theory of everyday life a good start is Ben Highmore, *Everyday Life and Cultural Theory: an Introduction* (London, 2002) and his edited collection, *The Everyday Life Reader* (London, 2002). More challenging is M. De Certeau, *The Practice of Everyday Life* (Berkeley, 1984). On the recording of the everyday by Mass-Observation, see N. Hubble, *Mass-Observation and Everyday Life: Culture, History, Theory* (Basingstoke, 2006) and the various publications based on the material collected by Mass Observation, notably C. Madge and T. H. Harrisson, *Mass Observation* (London, 1937); H. Jennings and C. Madge, *May the Twelfth: Mass-Observation Day Surveys* (London, 1937); *The Pub and the People: A Worktown Study* (London, 1943). A full list of their publications can be found at http://www.massobs.org.uk/menu_publications. htm

CHAPTER 2: FROM SCULLERY TO CONSERVATORY: EVERYDAY LIFE IN THE SCOTTISH HOME

Secondary literature on the Scottish home is limited in contrast with the extensive coverage of housing and the urban environment in the twentieth century. For the latter the best surveys are R. Rodger (ed.), *Scottish Housing in the Twentieth Century* (Leicester, 1989), and John Butt, 'Working-class housing in the Scottish cities 1900–1950', in G. Gordon and B. Dick (eds), *Scottish Urban History* (Aberdeen, 1983). For a detailed survey of one of Scotland's largest housebuilders, see M. Glendinning and D. Watters (eds), *Home Builders: McTaggart and Mickel and the Scottish Housebuilding Industry* (Edinburgh, 1999). On new towns in general, see David Cowling, *An Essay for Today: the Scottish New Towns 1947–1997* (Edinburgh, 1997) and on high rises Pearl Jephcott, *Homes in High Flats* (Edinburgh, 1971) based on a survey of several high-rise housing developments in Glasgow. Social housing is covered in Tom Begg, *50 Special Years: a Study in Scottish Housing* (London, 1987). There is as yet no study of Scottish suburbia. The recent volumes of *Scottish Life and Society: a Compendium of Scottish Ethnology* on *The Individual and Community Life* (Edinburgh, 2005), *Scotland's Domestic Life* (2006) and

Scotland's Buildings (2003) contain material on various aspects of Scottish housing and community life.

This chapter was heavily influenced by writing on home in the English context, particularly Judy Giles, *The Parlour and the Suburb: Domestic Identities, Class, Femininity and Modernity* (Oxford, 2004) and her *Women, Identity and Private Life in Britain, 1900–1950* (Basingstoke, 2004). Readers might also want to consult G. Allan and G. Crow (eds), *Home and Family: Creating the Domestic Sphere* (Basingstoke, 1989); T. Chapman and J. Hockey, *Ideal Homes? Social Change and Domestic life* (London, 1990) and D. S. Ryan, *The Ideal Home through the Twentieth Century* (London, 1997).

Primary sources are more helpful in ascertaining how Scots turned their houses into homes. For a collection of documents on Glasgow spanning the century and ranging from oral histories to social surveys, see *Housing in 20th Century Glasgow: Documents 1914 to the 1990s* (Glasgow, 1996). Primary sources on the new towns are held in the relevant council archives, and generally contain New Town Corporation minutes, plans and newspaper cuttings. Experiences of high-rise housing were collected by the Economic and Social Research Unit at Glasgow University in the 1960s; the research materials are held in Glasgow University Archives. Finally, the history of the suburb in history is best approached via the business records of the house builders McTaggart and Mickel, held in the Royal Commission on Ancient and Historic Monuments in Scotland. This archive also holds numerous other sources documenting the built environment in twentieth-century Scotland.

CHAPTER 3: CHANGING INTIMACY: SEEKING AND FORMING COUPLE RELATIONSHIPS

For a general background on family life in modern Scottish history, see E. Gordon, 'The family', in L. Abrams, E. Gordon, D. Simonton and E. J. Yeo (eds), *Gender in Scottish History Since 1700* (Edinburgh, 2006), pp. 235–68, and from a demographic perspective, M. Anderson, 'Population and family life', in A. Dickson and J. H. Treble (eds), *People and Society in Scotland, vol. 3* (Edinburgh, 1992), pp. 12–47 and his 'Why was Scottish nuptiality depressed for so long?', in I. Devos, and L. Kennedy (eds), *Marriage and the Rural Economy: Western Europe Since 1400* (Turnhout, 1999). On gender relations in the post-industrial Scottish family, see D. Wight, *Workers not Wasters: Masculine Respectability, Consumption and Employment in Central Scotland* (Edinburgh, 1993). For studies of family, friendship and sexual relationships in modern society, see A. Giddens, *The Transformation of Intimacy* (Cambridge, 1992) and L. Jamieson, *Intimacy: Personal Relationships in Modern Societies* (Cambridge, 1998). More generally on social trends in the British context the *British Social Attitudes* reports contain revealing material on relationship issues (see endnotes to Chapter 3 for details). There is still very little published research on same-sex relationships. On the state's attitude, see R. Davidson, '"The Sexual State": sexuality and Scottish governance, 1950–1980', *Journal of the History of Sexuality* 13 (2004), pp. 500–21. Oral histories conducted by Ourstory Scotland http://www.ourstoryscotland.org.uk/ and the Remember When project http://livingmemory.org.uk/rememberwhen/ are beginning to document the lives of the lesbian, gay, bisexual and transgender communities in Scotland since the Second World War.

CHAPTER 4: THE REALITIES AND NARRATIVES OF PAID WORK: THE SCOTTISH WORKPLACE

W. Knox, *Industrial Nation: Work, Culture and Society in Scotland, 1800–Present* (Edinburgh, 1999) provides a good overview of the changing nature and meaning of work in the twentieth century, while A. McIvor, *A History of Work in Britain, 1880–1950* (Basingstoke, 2001) provides useful background. For the most comprehensive recent survey of working lives in Scotland (and a stimulating collection of essays), see M. A. Mulhern, J. Beech and E. Thompson (eds), *The Working Life of the Scots, vol. 7 of Scottish Life and Society: A Compendium of Scottish Ethnology* (Edinburgh, 2008). For gender relations and the experience of women at work, see E. Gordon and E. Breitenbach (eds), *The World is Ill-Divided* (Edinburgh, 1990). For a stimulating study of the work culture of managers, see A. Perchard, *The Mine Management Professions in the Twentieth Century Scottish Coal Mining Industry* (Lampeter, 2007). For studies of occupational health and safety, see R. Johnston and A. McIvor, *Lethal Work* (East Linton, 2000), A. McIvor and R. Johnston, *Miners' Lung* (Aldershot, 2007) and C. Woolfson, J. Foster and M. Beck, *Paying for the Piper* (London, 1996). The journal *Scottish Labour History* has consistently published articles on various aspects of the history of work in Scotland. The numerous oral history-based works by Ian MacDougall also merit attention, for example *Voices from Work and Home* (Edinburgh, 2000).

For primary sources, there are many collections of oral testimonies that explore experiences and perceptions of work. Among the largest are the Scottish Working People's History Trust (mostly collected by Ian MacDougall), the Scottish Oral History Centre Archive (University of Strathclyde), the Scottish and Celtic Studies Archive (University of Edinburgh) and the Manpower Services Commission oral history projects undertaken in the 1980s (such as the Stirling Women's Oral History Collection, housed at the Smith Museum, Stirling). Glasgow Museums holds a substantial archive of oral interview material, including the *Glasgow 2000 Lives* interviews and the Springburn oral history project. There are also substantial collections of oral interviews of Scots stored in the ESDS (Qualidata) Archive, Essex and in the British Library Sound Archive, London (including the impressive *Oil Industry Lives* interviews conducted by Hugo Manson). R. Perks and A. Thomson (eds), *The Oral History Reader* (London, 2nd edn 2006) remains the most useful and comprehensive guide to oral history methodology and theory.

Other primary source material can be found in a wide collection of archives, including the Scottish Trade Union Congress Archive (Glasgow Caledonian University), the Business Archives (University of Glasgow) and in the Government Publications sections of most large public libraries (for the ten-yearly census, Factory Inspectors' Reports and other government enquiries and reports relating to the workplace).

CHAPTER 5: BEING A MAN: EVERYDAY MASCULINITIES

There is, as yet, no single text on the history of Scottish masculinity. The best introduction to the development of Scottish gender history is Lynn Abrams, Eleanor Gordon, Deborah Simonton and Eileen Janes Yeo (eds), *Gender in Scottish History since 1700* (Edinburgh, 2006). For more on theories of masculinities, see Robert Connell, *Masculinities* (Cambridge, 1995) and Lynne Segal, *Slow Motion: Changing Masculinities, Changing Men* (Palgrave, 2006). For a selection of writings on men ranging from chapters on boys' comics to the post-1945 'company man', see Michael Roper and John Tosh, *Manful Assertions: Masculinities in Britain since 1800* (London, 1991).

Eleanor Gordon and Gwyneth Nair's *Public Lives: Women, Family and Society in Victorian Britain* (London, 2003), along with John Tosh, *A Man's Place: Masculinity and the Middle-Class Home in Victorian England* (London, 1999), have been useful when writing this chapter as there is very little written on twentieth-century middle-class men and masculinity. On working-class men, industrial toil and unemployment, see Daniel Wight, *Workers Not Wasters, Masculine Respectability, Consumption and Unemployment in Central Scotland: A Community Study* (Edinburgh, 1993) and Arthur McIvor and Ronnie Johnston, 'Dangerous work, hard men and broken bodies: masculinity in the Clydeside heavy industries, c. 1930–1970s', *Labour History Review* vol. 69, no. 2 (2004).

Primary sources are integral to understanding the history of men and masculinity. Historians of masculinity use several types of primary sources. For an official report on male youth, see C. Cameron, *Disinherited Youth: A Report on the 18+ Age Group Enquiry prepared for the Trustees of the Carnegie United Kingdom Trust* (Edinburgh, 1943). Oral histories have formed the basis of evidence of this chapter. For an introduction to oral history and a discussion on the gender dynamics at work in an interview, see Alistair Thomson and Rob Perks, *The Oral History Reader* (London, 2006) and Hilary Young, 'Hard man, new man: re/composing masculinities in Glasgow, c. 1950–2000', also in *Oral History* vol. 35, no. 1 (Spring 2007). Oral history collections are held in archives and museums across Scotland. The Scottish Oral History Centre

Archive based at the University of Strathclyde holds several collections which pertain to men and masculinity such as occupational health and the Stirling Women's Oral History Archive. The forthcoming West of Scotland Regional Framework for Local History and Archaeology details collections of oral history held in local archives.

Depictions of Scottish men's changing working, familial and leisure relationships feature extensively in historical and contemporary literature, such as Edward Gaitens, *Growing Up and Other Stories* (Edinburgh, 1942), Andrew O'Hagan, *Our Fathers* (London, 1999) and William McIlvanney, *Docherty* (London, 1975). Films such as *Small Faces* (d. Gillies MacKinnon 1995) and *Trainspotting* (d. Danny Boyle 1995) depict representations of Scottish male youth culture in the late 1960s and 1990s. Autobiographical accounts are good sources of descriptions of men's youth, working conditions and family life. See Ralph Glasser, *Growing Up in the Gorbals* (London, 1986).

CHAPTER 6: SPECTACLE, RESTRAINT AND THE SABBATH WARS: THE 'EVERYDAY' SCOTTISH SUNDAY

Among recent work, the starting point is Clive Field's study of '"The secularised Sabbath" revisited: opinion polls as sources for Sunday observance in contemporary Britain', *Contemporary British History* vol. 15 (2001), pp. 1–20. Leading figures in presbyterian sabbatarianism are discussed in Fraser Macdonald, 'Scenes of ecclesiastical theatre in the Free Church of Scotland 1981–2000', *Northern Scotland* vol. 20 (2000), pp. 125–48. A wider review of religious attitudes in Scotland is to be obtained in C. Field, ' "The haemorrhage of faith"? Opinion polls as sources for religious practices, beliefs and attitudes in Scotland since the 1970s', *Journal of Contemporary Religion* vol. 16 (2001), pp. 157–75. General surveys of the place of religion in Scottish life in the century are to be found in C. G. Brown, *Religion and Society in Scotland since 1707* (Edinburgh, 1997) and idem, *Religion and Society in Twentieth-century Britain* (Harlow, 2006).

CHAPTER 7: AFTER 'THE RELIGION OF MY FATHERS': THE QUEST FOR COMPOSURE IN THE 'POST-PRESBYTERIAN' SELF

Primary and secondary sources on the lives of Semple, Govan and Laing are identified in footnotes. For introductions to critical biographical method, see the essays by Kadar, 'Coming to terms: life writing – from genre to critical practice', in M. Kadar (ed.), *Essays on Life Writing: from Genre to Critical Practice* (Toronto, 1992) and Ruth Finnegan, 'Storying the self', in H. Mackay (ed.), *Consumption and Everyday Life* (London, 1992). On achieving 'composure' in self-identity, see Chapter 1 in P. Summerfield, *Reconstructing Women's Wartime Lives. Discourse and Subjectivity in Oral Histories of the*

Second World War (Manchester, 1998). On Christian 'discursive bereavement' and the gendering of modern religious identities, see C. G. Brown, *The Death of Christian Britain: Understanding Secularization 1800–2000* (London, 2001). For a history and ethnography of 'new age' religion with special reference to Scotland, see S. Sutcliffe, *Children of the New Age: a History of Spiritual Practices* (London, 2003). For descriptions of 'post-presbyterian' diversity and dissent, see R. Birrell and A. Finlay, *Justified Sinners: an archaeology of Scottish counter-culture (1960–2000)* and S. Sutcliffe, 'Unfinished business: devolving Scotland/devolving religion', in S. Coleman and P. Collins (eds), *Religion, Identity and Change: Perspectives on Global Transformations* (Aldershot, 2004).

CHAPTER 8: CULTURE IN THE EVERYDAY: ART AND SOCIETY

There are a number of secondary texts that cover aspects of culture in twentieth-century Scotland, but as yet there are no survey texts available for the whole period. Books that have chapters or sections on Scottish culture in the twentieth century include T. M. Devine and R. J. Finlay (eds), *Scotland in the 20th Century* (Edinburgh, 1996), A. Dickson and J. H. Treble, *People and Society in Scotland, Volume III, 1914–1990* (Edinburgh, 1992), C. Harvie, *No Gods and Precious Few Heroes: Twentieth-Century Scotland*, 3rd edn (Edinburgh, 2000) and W. W. Knox, *Industrial Nation: Work, Culture and Society in Scotland, 1800–Present* (Edinburgh, 1999). There are a number of secondary texts available on theatre, folksong and the music hall, and for each of these aspects of culture readers might begin with (respectively): D. Campbell, *Playing for Scotland* (Edinburgh, 1996); E. J. Cowan (ed.), *The People's Past: Scottish Folk. Scottish History* (Edinburgh, 1980); and P. Maloney, *Scotland and the Music Hall, 1850–1914* (Manchester, 2003). While this area of Scottish history is in many ways still in its infancy, a number of research projects and doctoral theses are currently in progress; for example, *Pantomime in Scotland: 'Your other national theatre'* (University of Glasgow).

This chapter drew heavily on studies covering Britain as a whole which, although often heavily focused on England, gave a strong contextual basis for broad patterns and shifts in culture in the twentieth century: N. Hayes and J. Hill (eds), *'Millions Like Us'? British Culture in the Second World War* (Liverpool, 1999); R. Hewison, *Too Much: Art and Society in the Sixties, 1960–1975* (London, 1986); M. Donnelly, *Sixties Britain: Culture, Society and Politics* (London, 2005). The chapter was also strongly influenced by theories on the place and role of culture in society – here, readers should consult Raymond Williams, particularly *Culture and Society 1780–1950* (Middlesex, 1958) and *Keywords: A Vocabulary of Culture and Society* (London, 1988) and, on culture in the everyday, D. Inglis, *Culture and Everyday Life* (London, 2005). Finally, an important issue dealt with throughout the chapter was that of state cultural policy. Readers might want to begin with A. Sinclair, *Arts and Cultures: The History of the 50 Years of the Arts Council of Great Britain* (London, 1995) and, for an empirical and reflective study on Glasgow in 1990, G. Mooney, 'Cultural policy as urban transformation? Critical reflections on Glasgow, European city of culture 1990', *Local Economy* vol. 19, no. 4 (2004).

To understand culture in Scottish society in the twentieth century, an approach that uses primary and secondary sources alongside one another is necessary. This chapter was heavily based on the records of cultural events and venues like the Edinburgh Festival, the Edinburgh People's Festival, and the Traverse, Lyceum and Gateway Theatres. Both the National Library of Scotland and Edinburgh City Council Archives hold records of the Edinburgh Festival Society Limited, which include programmes, minutes of meetings and (in the Council Archives) original correspondence; the Council Archives also hold materials on the Lyceum Theatre (when it was owned as a civic theatre). Material relating to the People's Festival can be found in the Gallacher Memorial Library (Glasgow Caledonian University); the Traverse in the National Library of Scotland (although permission is required); and the Gateway in the Scottish Theatre Archive.

CHAPTER 9: SICKNESS AND HEALTH

Surprisingly, given the country's dismal health record, the history of sickness and health and of the health services in Scotland have been, until recently, relatively neglected by historians. Now rather dated, there is nonetheless still much useful material in G. McLachlan (ed.), *Improving the Common Weal: Aspects of Scottish Health Services, 1900–1948* (Edinburgh, 1987). The decades immediately preceding the creation of the National Health Service are comprehensively dealt with in J. Jenkinson, *Scotland's Health, 1919–1948* (Bern, 2002) and M. McCrae, *The National Health Service in Scotland: Origins and Ideals, 1900–1950* (East Linton, 2003). The twentieth century is usefully put into longer historical context in H. Dingwall, *A History of Scottish Medicine* (Edinburgh, 2003) and also in D. Hamilton, *The Healers: A History of Medicine in Scotland* (Edinburgh, 1981). For post-Second World War Scotland in a British context, see C. Webster, *The National Health Service: A Political History* (Oxford, 2nd edn, 2002), a text which ranges more broadly than its title might suggest. Works which deal with a number of the issues raised in this chapter, again in the wider British context, include A. Hardy, *Health and Medicine in Britain since 1860* (Basingstoke, 2001) and V. Berridge, *Health and Society in Britain since 1939* (Cambridge, 1999).

There are a range of primary sources which illuminate at least parts of the health and sickness experience in twentieth-century Scotland. Many hospitals, for example, have had their own histories published. Although such works are frequently celebratory and thus need to be read with caution, nonetheless they can provide valuable insights into institutions and the lives of staff and patients. Until the 1970s, when the post was abolished, the reports of Medical Officers of Health contained important material on the health situation in their localities. These reports are often easily available in local libraries and archives. Local libraries and archives may also hold, at least down to the creation of the National Health Service, materials from local authority committees and bodies charged with providing various forms of healthcare – for example, the Poor Law. There was, over the course of the twentieth century, a significant number of official enquiries into various aspects of healthcare and social welfare provision. The findings of these enquiries, and the evidence given to them, can be found in British Parliamentary Papers. The records of the government bodies which administered the health services – for example, the Scottish Home and Health Department – can be located in the National Archives of Scotland. Archives which provide insights into health and healthcare from a professional point of view include those of the Royal College of Physicians and Surgeons of Glasgow. What is much harder to access, however, are individual patient records as these are generally closed for a hundred years.

CHAPTER 10: PASSING TIME: CULTURES OF DEATH AND MOURNING

Scholarship on the historical aspects of death has blossomed since the 1970s. For a short overview of the literature which has resulted, see P. Jupp and C. Gittings, *Death in England: An Illustrated History* (Manchester, 2002). One obvious starting point for further reading is Philippe Ariès' short but magisterial survey, *The Hour of Our Death* (Harmondsworth, 1981), which traces western attitudes to death from the middle ages to the late twentieth century. Equally controversial is David Cannadine's seminal essay, 'War and death, grief and mourning in modern Britain', in J. Whaley (ed.), *Mirrors of Mortality: Studies in the History of Death* (London, 1981). Pat Jalland has also produced a highly engaging and sophisticated body of work, which includes *Changing Ways of Death in Twentieth Century Australia* (Sydney, 2006). Unfortunately, Scotland has been less well served by the revolution in death studies. However, a number of classic ethnographic studies have been undertaken, particularly of the Highlands and Islands, including F. G. Vallee's 'Burial and mourning customs in a Hebridean community', *Journal of the Royal Anthropological Society of Great Britain and Ireland*, 1955, pp. 119–30. Useful and accessible collections of Scottish customs and folklore more generally also include M. Bennett's *Scottish Customs from the Cradle to the Grave* (Edinburgh, 1992). However, there is also a developing journal literature, covering specific aspects of death, mourning and commemoration in modern Scotland. Recent examples include: J. L. Macleod, ' "Greater love hath no man than this": Scotland's conflicting religious responses to death in the Great War,' *Scottish Historical Review* vol. LXXXI, 1, no. 211 (2002), pp. 70–96; and E. W. McFarland, 'Working with death: An oral history of funeral directing in late twentieth-century Scotland', *Oral History* vol. 36, 1 (2008), pp. 58–69.

Notes on the Contributors

Lynn Abrams is Professor of Gender History at the University of Glasgow. She is the author of *The Making of Modern Woman: Europe 1789–1918* (Longman, 2002) and *Myth and Materiality in a Woman's World: Shetland 1800–2000* (Manchester, 2005). She also co-edited and contributed to *Gender in Scottish History Since 1700* (Edinburgh, 2005). Her current research focuses on the social practices of masculinity in Scotland and on theories of oral history.

Angela Bartie's research interests centre on social and cultural change in post-war Britain, particularly during the 1960s. Currently a Research Fellow at the Scottish Oral History Centre, she has published in the anthology *New World Coming: the Sixties and the Globalisation of Ideas* and in the *Journal of Oral History*. She is currently working on her first book, *The Edinburgh Festivals: Culture, the Arts and Social Change in Post-war Britain*, and writing an article on the moral panic over youth gangs in sixties Glasgow.

Callum Brown is Professor of Religious and Cultural History at the University of Dundee. He is the author of eight books, including *Religion and Society in Scotland since 1707* (1997), *Up-helly-aa* (1998), *The Death of Christian Britain* (2001, 2nd edn 2009), *Postmodernism for Historians* (2005) and *Religion and Society in Twentieth-century Britain* (2006), and co-editor of *Secularisation in the Christian World* (2010). He is a past editor of *Journal of Scottish Historical Studies*.

Linda Fleming undertook doctoral studies at the University of Glasgow. Her PhD (2005) looked at the influence of gender in the process of immigrant acculturation to Scottish society for Glasgow's Jewish community. She is now employed as a post doctoral researcher within the Scottish Centre for the Book at Edinburgh Napier University. Her current work on the AHRC funded project, *Scottish Readers Remember*, examines the place of the printed word within everyday life for twentieth century Scots.

Lynn Jamieson is Professor of Sociology at the University of Edinburgh. She is the author (with C. Toynbee) of *Country Bairns* (Edinburgh, 1992) and of *Intimacy: Personal Relationships in Modern Societies* (Cambridge, 1998). Her research interests include the study of families, households and all personal relationships, the life course, identity and the study of sexual offences in Scotland. Her current research under the umbrella of the Centre for Research on Families and Relationships (CRFR) www.crfr.ac.uk includes a study of people living alone.

E.W. McFarland is Professor of History at Glasgow Caledonian University. Her publications include, *Protestants First: Orangeism in Nineteenth Century Scotland* (1990); *Ireland and Scotland in the Age of Revolution* (1994); *Scotland and the Great War* (1999) and *John Ferguson 1836–1906: Irish Issues in Scottish Politics* (2004). Her current research examines disabled Great War veterans in Ireland and Scotland.

Arthur McIvor is Professor of Social History and Director of the Scottish Oral History Centre at the University of Strathclyde. He is the author of *A History of Work in Britain, 1880–1950* (Palgrave, 2001) and (with R. Johnston) *Miners' Lung* (Ashgate, 2007). He is currently working on the history of occupational health in Scotland and an oral history of the Reserved Occupations, 1939–45.

John Stewart is Professor of Health History at Glasgow Caledonian University and Director of the Centre for the Social History of Health and Healthcare. The latter is a research collaboration between historians at Glasgow Caledonian and Strathclyde Universities and is funded by the Wellcome Trust under its Enhancement Award scheme. His research interests are the history of the post-war European welfare states; health and welfare policy in twentieth-century Britain and Scotland; and the history of child psychiatry. His recent publications include 'The scientific claims of British child guidance, 1918–1945', *British Journal for the History of Science* (2009).

Steven Sutcliffe is Lecturer in Religion and Society in the Religious Studies Subject Area of the School of Divinity, University of Edinburgh. His main interests are the modern history and ethnography of 'new age' religion in Europe, and theories of 'religion'. He is the author of *Children of the New Age: A History of Spiritual Practices* (Routledge, 2003) and editor of *Religion: Empirical Studies* (Ashgate, 2004).

Hilary Young is a post-doctoral reseacher at the Open University. Her research is focused on twentieth-century British social and cultural history with a particular interest in oral history and life writing. Her publications include 'Scotland and "The Coalition for Justice Not War" march, Glasgow 15 February 2003' with Angela Bartie and Neil Rafeek in *Oral History* Autumn 2004; and 'Hard man, new man: re/composing masculinities in Glasgow, c. 1950–2000', in *Oral History* Spring 2007. She is currently working on a study of gender and reading during the 1940s and 1950s as well as an oral history of the Open University.

Index

Broughty Ferry, 156
Buddhism, 24, 185, 187, 196–7
Bunter, Billy, 133
Burns, Robert, 208
Burnside, John, 11
buses, 42

Caddy, Eileen, 193
Caddy, Peter, 189, 193–4
Caithness, 239
Calder, Angus, 217
Calder, John, 226–7n79
Caledonian MacBrayne ferries, 173
Callanish, 165
Calton (Glasgow), 12, 54
Calvinism, 189, 198, 200n19
Cambusnethan, 139–40
cancer, 31–2, 131, 228, 233
capital punishment, 45
capitalism, 4, 174
car *see* motor car
Carlyle, Thomas, 182–3
carnival, 5, 15
Carpenter, Edward, 187
Castlemilk, 56, 70,
Casualty (TV series), 272
Catholicism *see* Roman Catholicism
censuses, 8, 185
Central Statistical Office, 10–11
Certeau, Michel de, 4–5, 173
Chambers Street Museum, 162–3
childcare, 52
children, 23, 82–3, 96, 157–8, 163,
    246–8
Chinese, 24, 185
Christians, 24, 103, 173–4, 195, 211–12,
    266; *see also* religion *and also by*
    church
Church of Scotland, 22, 24–5, 153, 155,
    161, 165, 167–70, 172, 185, 189, 272
    and drama, 210–11
churchgoing, 157–9, 167
cinema, 13, 15, 88, 91–2, 137, 207–8,
    210
    admissions, 37–8
    and Sunday closing, 172
Citizens' Theatre, 214

Clare, Anthony, 196–7
class struggle, 4, 111
clerical work, 105–6
clothes, 160–1
Clydebank, 57, 68, 70, 230, 266
    air raid, 260
coal industry, 26, 105, 117–18, 161, 242
    and miners' strike (1984), 132
Coatbridge, 230, 245
cohabitation, 22–3, 91–96
Cohen, Anthony, 12
Cohen, Stanley, 6, 9, 14
Colinton, 91
Communist Party, 104, 109, 214,
    216–17
composure, 183–99
computers, 106
condoms *see* birth control
Congregational Church, 153, 189
conscientious objectors, 132, 186
Conservative Party, 35
conservatories, 48, 71
construction industry, 26–7, 35–6, 70
consumption, 2, 36–41
contraceptives *see* birth control
cooperativism, 188, 267
coronation, 8
Corrothie, Harry, 153, 175
Council for the Encouragement of
    Music and Art, 211
council houses, 35–6, 54, 58
Court of Session, 156
Covenanters, 187
Cowcaddens, 60
Cowie, 160
Craig, Cairns, 222
Craigmillar Festival, 207, 221
Crampsey, Bob, 159
Cranston, Sir Robert, 67
Creative Scotland, 206, 220
cremation, 262, 271
Crewe, 164
crime, 43–5
croft houses, 34, 58
crofting, 12
Crummy, Helen, 221
culture, 206–23